HIKING NORTH CAROLINA'S
MOUNTAINS-TO-SEA TRAIL

Allen de Hart

Hiking North Carolina's Mountains-to-Sea Trail

The University of North Carolina Press

Chapel Hill and London

Designed by Heidi Perov
Set in Garamond MT and MetaPlus
by Keystone Typesetting, Inc.

All photographs, unless otherwise credited, are
by the author. Trail markings on topographical maps
also by author. Inset maps by Mike Cinoman.

Manufactured in the United States of America

The paper in this book meets the guidelines for
permanence and durability of the Committee on
Production Guidelines for Book Longevity of the
Council on Library Resources.

Library of Congress Cataloging-in-Publication Data
De Hart, Allen.
Hiking North Carolina's Mountains-to-Sea Trail / Allen de Hart.
    p.   cm.
Includes index.
ISBN 0-8078-4887-5 (pbk.: alk. paper)
 1. Hiking—North Carolina—Mountains-to-Sea Trail—
Guidebooks. 2. Mountains-to-Sea Trail (N.C.)—Guidebooks.
I. Title.
GV 199.42.N662 M682   2000
917.56—dc21   00-062864

04   03   02   01   00   5   4   3   2   1

De # 2000

5.19.03
SC

CONTENTS

ACKNOWLEDGMENTS

The subject of this book has become possible through the efforts of the dreamers, planners, organizers, and trail-oriented enthusiasts of North Carolina within the past twenty-five years. Some were volunteer leaders and workers involved in local trail projects. Others were staff members of state and national government departments. Together and separately they saw the potential for a trail from the Appalachian Mountains to the Atlantic Ocean. I knew most of these leaders from their beginnings; the majority of them are still living in the state. Dedicated to their work and leadership, this book makes an effort to inspire others to continue the dream of development of a major cross-state trail, the Mountains-to-Sea Trail. In addition, I hope to encourage others to experience the adventure of walking across the state from the high-elevation Appalachian Trail to the highest sand-dune trail on the nation's East Coast.

To acknowledge everyone who has played a part in bringing the Mountains-to-Sea Trail into reality would take another book. Some of those special leaders are described elsewhere in this book, but here I wish to acknowledge some of the leaders who have been an inspirational influence for me. One is Bob Buckner, a former staff member of the N.C. Department of Environment and Natural Resources. He researched and completed a project on the trails in North Carolina in 1972. Other staff members in the past quarter of a century have been Kay Scott, Bill Flournoy, Alan Eakes, and Jim Hallsey. The latter two are still employed in the Division of Parks and Recreation. In the past ten years there have been John Shaffner, Dwayne Stutzman, Beth Timson, and Tom Potter, all trails specialists. Also, Susan Currie, followed by Darrell McBane, for state trails coordinator. Others in state government have been some of the directors of the Division of Parks and Recreation, James Stevens, William (Wes) Davis, and Phil McKnelly. Secretaries of the Department of Environment and Natural Resources, Joe Grimsley, Thomas Rhodes, Bill Cobey, Jonathan Howes, and Wayne McDevitt. From the beginning, Governor Jim Hunt has given his support to both the concept and the trail's development. On the federal government level, I wish to acknowledge Gary Everhart, Harry Baker, and Will Orr of the Blue Ridge Parkway, and Melinda Waldrep, George Olsen, and John Ramey of the U.S. Forest Service. Some of the state senators who have been an inspiration to me have been Marc Basnight, Howard Lee, and McNeil Smith.

Another inspiring group of leaders I wish to acknowledge are citizen volunteers, many of them leaders in the North Carolina Trails Association. They include the late Louise Chatfield, first president of the North Carolina Trails Committee, Doris Hammett, Don and Kathy Chatfield, Willie Taylor, Bill Sims, Larkin Kirkman, L. P. McElroy, Mary Joan Pugh, David Drexel, the late Hazel Monroe, Frank McNutt, and Suzanne Riley.

Yet another group of volunteers who were highly dedicated to my efforts to hike, measure, and describe every trail in the state gave extra time and effort. Many hiked with me on the Mountains-to-Sea Trail's completed sections, sections under construction, and sections in the planning stages. Among this group are Robert Ballance, Ray Benedicktus, Kevin Bighannitti, Jeremy Bond, Chris Bracknell, Jeff Brewer, Cathy Carter, Travis Combest, John Culbertson, Trevor Flanery, Greg Frederick, Todd Gregory, Geoff Haas, David Hicks, Steven Hughes, Steve King, Jason Mason, John Matthews, Glenn McLeroy, Dennis Parrish, Reggie Ponder, Tyler Ruey, Scott Smith, Steve Strader, Martin Sweat, and Travis Winn. Special acknowledgment goes to some of the Carolina Mountain Club's leaders—Bob Johnson, Dick Johnson, Sherman Stambaugh, John Hillyer, Jorge Munoz, Walt Weber, and the late Arch Nichols. I am indebted to a number of families who provided Alan Householder and me a place to stay or camp at their homes in 1997 when we hiked across the state. Among them are Drs. Frank and Doris Hammett and Mr. and Mrs. Kenneth Ayala (Waynesboro); Mr. and Mrs. R. M. Collins (Pilot Mountain); Mr. and Mrs. Don Chatfield and Mr. and Mrs. Tobe Sherrill (Greensboro); Mr. and Mrs. Dean Coleman (Graham); Mr. and Mrs. Steve Strader (Wilson); and Mr. and Mrs. Norman Chadwick (Harkers Island).

Black Dome Mountain Sports and Earthsports Design of Asheville are thanked for hiking gear given to Alan Householder. Thanks also to Susan Clark, who assisted him for shuttle, and Andrew Wenezel, who hiked with him on the most difficult sections of the trail that crossed the Catawba River and the Linville River.

I especially appreciate the support given by Alan Householder, when he hiked the Mountains-to-Sea Trail with me. A hiking companion for nearly twenty years, Alan has assisted me in exploring and measuring other trails in North Carolina.

HIKING NORTH CAROLINA'S
MOUNTAINS-TO-SEA TRAIL

INTRODUCTION

The Mountains-to-Sea Trail brings us together on a path to learning, enjoying, and preserving the natural heritage of the Tar Heel state. This living outdoor laboratory that spans the border of our state offers us a venue to focus on stewardship and to chart a course for the natural trust we hold for future generations.—WAYNE MCDEVITT, Secretary, North Carolina Department of Environment and Natural Resources, 1997

North Carolina's Mountains-to-Sea Trail (MST) follows a corridor that traverses thirty-seven counties, from the state boundary with Tennessee at Clingmans Dome in Great Smoky Mountains National Park, east to the sands of Jockey's Ridge State Park at the Atlantic Ocean. The distance along the main route is 938 miles. Using alternate routes such as one through the spectacular Davidson River valley and the Pink Beds in the Mills River Valley of Pisgah National Forest, and one through the city of Goldsboro, the total distance is 981 miles. The 33.0 miles for the three ferry routes—Minnesott Beach, Cedar Island, and Ocracoke Island—are included in the total distances. Because there are numerous short spur trails to scenic mountain peaks, waterfalls, wildlife observation stands, historic sites, and campsites, you can expect to cover more than 1,000 miles on your adventurous through-hike of the state.

In planning your journey you will notice that most of the mileage in the mountain sections is, or will be, for hiking only. Through the central part of the state and about half of the coastal part, the MST predominately follows official bicycle routes on back roads. These routes, designated by the N.C. Department of Transportation, can also be used by pedestrians for hiking until a foot trail is completed. Currently there are five scattered sections in the central and coastal areas for hiking only. They are 7.5 miles through Hanging Rock State Park near Danbury, nearly 20 miles of hiking trails bordering Lake Brandt and Lake Townsend at the north edge of Greensboro, 26 miles bordering Falls Lake north of Raleigh, 8.7 miles through Goldsboro, and 21 miles in Croatan National Forest east of Havelock. Additionally, there are a few sections for hiking only among the 81 miles that include Cape Hatteras National Seashore and Jockey's Ridge State Park.

The Mountains-to-Sea Trail is a state trail under the guidance and supervision of the Division of Parks and Recreation, which is part of the N.C. Department of Environment and Natural Resources. Planning, construction, and maintenance of the MST is traditionally the work of trail task forces, environmental groups, clubs, college/university teams, Boy Scouts, and allied organizations. Almost always nonprofit, these groups receive financial assistance from state Adopt-a-Trail grants, federal government grants, commercial and nonprofit organizations, and shared funding from some projects in federal parks and forests. Three, and formerly four, state trails specialists and one state trails coordinator assist and counsel the trail building organizations. This joint arrangement whereby federal, state, and local governments work with nonprofit citizens groups has resulted in 434.6 miles of officially designated sections of the Mountains-to-Sea Trail. (The Division of Parks and Recreation has also officially designated 592 miles of river trails, 8.5 miles of greenways, and 188 miles of state park trails since the North Carolina General Assembly ratified the North Carolina Trails System Act in 1973.) All of the existing MST sections are on public property. The hard work ahead is to purchase or provide easements on private lands to finish constructing the trail. In early 1997 a nonprofit citizens organization, Friends of the Mountains-to-Sea Trail, was chartered to promote, support, and provide guidance for the future of the trail. (See Chapter 16 on the history of the Mountains-to-Sea Trail.)

At the time the Friends of the Mountains-to-Sea Trail was being formed, Alan Householder and I became the first hikers to completely follow the proposed corridor route. Our journey took nearly two months, from April 18 to June 12, 1997. Past experience indicated that we could have completed the trail nearly three weeks earlier if we had used bicycles on the highway bicycle routes. On our exciting and challenging adventure we connected all the completed trails, trails under construction, and proposed trails with convenient state bicycle routes. Within the past twenty years I had hiked all of the foot trails at different times in preparation for the editions of *North Carolina Hiking Trails*. This book, *Hiking North Carolina's Mountains-to-Sea Trail*, is a merging of the earlier research, the knowledge that Householder and I gained in our joint hiking effort, and our subsequent, but separate, research and re-hiking of sections of the trail that have changed.

Today's Mountains-to-Sea Trail provides a diverse travel experience, following both old and new trails, particularly in Pisgah National Forest and within the corridor of the Blue Ridge Parkway, and state-designated and undesignated bicycle routes on back roads. To assist you in understanding this diversity I have included topographical and other maps covering the entire corridor. In addition, a development chart in Appendix 1 indicates the areas for hiking only and for combined hiking and bicycling, the status of work and completion of trail projects, and where the N.C. Division of Parks and Recreation has approved the trail's development with official designations.

In crossing the state west to east you will pass through fifteen mountain counties: Swain, Jackson, Haywood, Transylvania, Henderson, Buncombe, Yancey, McDowell, Burke, Avery, Caldwell, Watagua, Ashe, Alleghany, and Wilkes, in that order. In the central area of the state, the MST traverses Surry, Stokes, Forsyth, Guilford, Alamance, Orange, Durham, Granville, Wake, Franklin, and Nash Counties. Coastal counties are Wilson, Johnston, Wayne, Greene, Lenoir, Jones, Craven, Pamlico, Carteret, Hyde, and Dare.

Located throughout these counties are diverse natural and cultural sites, farms, churches, schools, residences, commercial buildings, towns, and cities. At times you will witness where and how people live and work. In the mountainous counties most of your hiking will be in the forests, but when you leave Stone Mountain State Park for the foothills, agricultural and grazing lands will become prominent. Extensive forests will appear again only around the lakes of Greensboro and Raleigh, and in the pocosins of Croatan National Forest, east of Havelock. The last deep forest will be Buxton Woods near Hatteras Lighthouse.

You are likely to see apple orchards in Haywood, Transylvania, Buncombe, Henderson, and Wilkes Counties, grapes and figs in Dare County, and workers harvesting blueberries and peanuts in Craven County. Soybeans are common in almost all the counties except in the mountains and the most coastal areas. Cornfields are seen along all of the trail except in Hyde and Dare Counties. Tobacco fields are also common in all counties from the foothills to the coast, with the exception of Pamlico, Hyde, and Dare Counties. Grains, such as wheat and oats, grow near sections of trail in the central counties but rarely in some of the mountain counties and are even less likely along the Outer Banks. Livestock can be seen in all counties, but poultry houses and hog farms are not commonplace in Jackson, McDowell, Avery, Watagua, Ashe, Alleghany, Durham, Lenoir, Jones, Carteret, Hyde, and Dare Counties.

Along the way some of the small towns that you pass through, from west to east, are Cherokee, Oteen, Dobson, Ararat, Pilot Mountain, Danbury, Walnut Cove, Stokesdale, Summerfield, Ossipee, Altamahaw, Butner, Wake Forest, Youngsville, Black Creek, Eureka, La Grange, Dover, Reelsboro, Araphoe, Minnesott, Bettie, Otway, Williston, Davis, Stacy, Cedar Island, Ocracoke, Hatteras, Buxton, Avon, Salvo, Waves, Rodanthe, and Whalebone. Larger towns or cities that are near to the trail are Asheville, Greensboro, Raleigh,

Wilson (Goldsboro has 8.7 miles of trails that have been designated for the MST), Kinston, Havelock, and Nags Head. New Bern is the only city through which the trail directly passes.

You will cross thousands of small streams and creeks, but among the major rivers are the Oconaluftee, French Broad, North Fork of the Catawba and the Linville (which in 2000 required wading, but there are plans for footbridges), Fisher, Haw, East Fork of the Eno, South Fork of the Little, Flat, and Neuse (five or seven times for the latter). The longest bridge that you will cross is the Oregon Inlet Bridge in the north part of Cape Hatteras National Seashore. The second longest is the Neuse River bridge at New Bern. Although you will pass through a number of swampy areas, the largest is Cedar Island National Wildlife Refuge. Sections of the highway have been elevated, but you will notice water in channels by the road shoulders and in the marsh vegetation. A few highway bridges rise above the swamps and bays. From them are superb views to the horizon of the marshlands and bays. Waterfowl are prominent. The most prominent inland lakes will be seen in Stokes, Guilford, and Wake Counties.

The Mountains-to-Sea Trail exposes the traveler to North Carolina natural areas as it passes through three major national parks: Great Smoky Mountains National Park (visited by 9,564,030 people in 1998, a record annual number and more than any other national park in the nation), the Blue Ridge Parkway (which the MST frequently crisscrosses for at least 233 miles), and Cape Hatteras National Seashore (with famous lighthouses, the longest beach trail in the world, and the nearby Pea Island National Wildlife Refuge, home to millions of waterfowl).

You will also pass through three of the state's national forests—the mountainous Nantahala and Pisgah forests and the coastal Croatan—a combined total of 1,189,344 acres teeming with wildflowers and wildlife. In addition, the trail passes through or nearby seven state parks. Starting in the west you will encounter Mount Mitchell State Park, whose namesake peak stands at elevation 6,684 feet (the highest peak east of the Mississippi River); Stone Mountain State Park, a major attraction to rock climbers, with its Big Sandy Creek plunging 200 feet along a granite slope; Pilot Mountain State Park, whose majestic pinnacle rises 1,400 feet from a pastoral countryside; Hanging Rock State Park's towering 400-foot cliffs and scenic waterfalls; Falls Lake, near the capital city of Raleigh, where a wide variety of recreational options welcome the visitor, including fishing in a 12,000-acre lake; Cliffs of the Neuse, a remarkable revelation of geological formations where wildflowers that usually grow in the mountains can be admired; and Jockey's Ridge, the eastern terminus of the trail and the highest sand dune on the nation's East Coast.

How to Use This Book

The directions and conditions of the sections of Mountains-to-Sea Trail described in this guidebook have been carefully measured and checked. Alan Householder and I have hiked many of the sections more than once, sometimes in opposite directions. We have examined dozens of maps with the goal of providing accurate yet simple descriptions. Proper use of this guidebook and the maps will provide you with an easy to follow and successful journey. Watch for new editions of this guidebook in the future; changes in trail routing and blazing, new construction, and opening of new sections will be continuous. The following paragraphs explain each subtitled part of the trail section descriptions that form the bulk of this guide.

SECTION NAME AND NUMBER: The trail sections are numbered beginning with Clingmans Dome in the west and ending with Jockey's Ridge State Park in the east. I have broken down the journey into thirty-eight sections because either I hiked that many miles between food and lodging sources, or the geographical emphasis was logical, or there were convenient parking areas for pick-up and shuttle arrangements. You may wish to plan your journey with more or fewer miles in the sections. You could also check out the road routes in advance to determine if you prefer to hike or bicycle on the back roads after leaving Stone Mountain State Park.

COUNTIES: The Mountains-to-Sea Trail passes through 37 of the state's 100 counties. For your own sense of place and to inform you of what sheriff office to call in an emergency, the counties each section passes through are listed first. A brief account of each county's origin, its namesake, the major highways that pass through it, and other highlights are provided.

LENGTH AND DIFFICULTY: Mileage is listed to one-tenth mile and was measured either by an official measuring wheel (walking), by bicycle odometer, or by motor vehicle, where possible. (Appendix 2 lists mileage for each section as well as cumulative mileage.) I describe the route's difficulty in terms of an average adult: *strenuous* (requiring extra energy and endurance for a steep single or multiple climbs), *moderate* (requiring average exertion and with less steep grades), and *easy* (involving gentle grades or flat lands). A more athletic individual probably will need to alter these difficulty ratings, as will children, who may need to classify strenuous as *exceptionally strenuous*. Where a change in elevation is indicated, read the trail description in advance to determine if you will be descending or ascending.

USGS TOPO MAPS AND OTHER MAPS: The topographic maps for each section are listed because I have dotted the MST route on the topo maps for the national and state parks, forests, and preserves, primarily in the mountain sections and a few central and coastal ones. Larger dots indicate connections with other trails (or some roads). Open dots signify alternate MST routes. Highway/road maps are used for most sections east of the mountains because the back roads there do not need as much detail and are easy to follow. Some of my dots may not be as accurate on the altitude lines as I would have wished, but research is continuing.

If you want to examine full USGS topo maps, I recommend that you purchase them from a local outfitter store, where you can examine the maps carefully. If you know exactly what you want, you can contact the following government center, pay in advance, and receive maps in the mail in two to three weeks: Branch of Distribution, USGS, Box 25286 Federal Center, Denver, CO 80225 (telephone: 303-236-5900). A free catalog available from the same place lists map dealers in the state as well as map depository libraries (at most of the major universities in the state). You should not need to carry full topo maps: the maps provided here, at the back of the book, should be sufficient. These are placed in order of chapter and section, and are identified by headings that correspond with the sequence (e.g., "Chapter 1, Section 1, Clingmans Dome GSMNP to BRP"). Of course, you are advised to pack a state highway map. For a detailed state map, I recommend the *North Carolina Atlas and Gazetteer*, usually found in newsstands and bookstores.

FEATURES OR EMPHASIS: As with all trails, there is usually something special about the scenery, terrain, plants and animals, historic sites, rivers, streams, lakes, and business or residential areas that you pass by. I have listed some of the major features and left some surprises for you.

TRAILS FOLLOWED, TRAIL CONNECTIONS: Particularly in the mountain region, you will be following some trails that were constructed and named before they became part of the MST route. I list intersections with trails that may be a convenience and diversion for you to explore, or which will take you to a campsite or water source. Some of the topo maps give the names of these trails, but in the national forests you will probably see trail numbers rather than names. If you would like to have a map with the names, you may purchase a "district map" (for a particular ranger district) from the Nantahala, Pisgah, or Croatan National Forests.

The trails followed or connected are also described in detail in *North Carolina Hiking Trails*, 3rd edition. Remember that there is only one Mountains-to-Sea Trail with the word *trail* in it. It is the hiking trail that you will follow for about 425 miles (nearly half of your journey), in scattered sections. It is a state trail under the jurisdiction of the N.C. Division of Parks and Recreation, but only certain sections have been designated. (See the development chart in Appendix 1.) There is another Mountains-to-Sea title, but it has the words *bicycle highway* or *bicycle route* in its title. Mountains-to-Sea Bicycle Route #2 (MSBR #2[A]) consists of sixteen sections, each with about 45 miles, from Murphy to Manteo. It is one of nine major state bicycle highways that crisscross the state and three connector routes in the state's mountain area for a total of more than 3,000 miles. All of these are under the jurisdiction of the N.C. Department of Transportation. Every few miles on all the bicycle routes there are small metal signs with a white background and green oval in the center. Inside the oval are a white bicycle symbol and the route's number.

You will first make contact with the MSBR #2(A) (Section 3, Sliding Rock) in Balsam Gap (South) at milepost 443.1 of the Blue Ridge Parkway, south of Waynesville. It is here that MSBR #2(A) (Section 2, Nikwasi) comes up the mountain from Cullowhee and then follows the Blue Ridge Parkway to north of Linville, where it leaves the parkway and heads east on NC-181. Southeast of Winding Stair Knob, the MST crosses NC-181 and MSBR #2(A) (Section 5, Brown Mountain Lights). It is illegal for you to ride a bicycle off the highways onto a foot trail such as the MST. You will not cross the MSBR #2(A) (now Section 11, New Tryon) again until you cross NC-98 on the Falls Lake Trail (MST) north of Raleigh. You meet MSBR #2(A) again on Six Forks Road, but leave it to continue on the Falls Lake Trail. You will get to know the MSBR #2(A) better when you join it at a junction of Thomson Mill Road and Purnell Road (Purnell community), where you turn right (east) and jointly follow the same road routes for about 42 miles. At the intersection of Whitney Road and Lamm Road (northwest of Wilson), you leave MSBR #2(A) (Section 12, Green Gold) and turn right on Ocracoke Option Bicycle Route #7(F) (Section 1, Bright Leaf). Except for through the Croatan National Forest, you will follow that bicycle route all the way to Cedar Island (Section 4, Roads End), where it ends and you take a ferry to Ocracoke Island. This will be described beginning with Section 30.

You will also be on North Line Trace Bicycle Route #4(G) after you leave Stone Mountain State Park on your way to Hanging Rock State Park, but this is described in Section 19. For information or free maps on bicycling North Carolina's highways, call the Division of Bicycle and Pedestrian Transportation in Raleigh (telephone: 919-733-2804), or write to P.O. Box 25201, Raleigh, NC 27611.

WEST AND EAST TRAILHEADS: The Mountains-to-Sea Trail is considered a west-to-east or east-to-west route, even though in the mountains the trail travels north and south at different times. Its route is north from Buxton to Nags Head at the Atlantic Ocean. For simplicity, I have described the passage across the state beginning in the west and always going east. The descriptions and maps should give you sufficient information to choose the opposite if you wish. If you are walking or bicycling on the N.C. Department of Transportation bicycle routes (#2A, #4G, and #7F) you will notice that the green bicycle signs are arranged for both directions. The same is true for the white-dot blazes in the national parks and forests, and on the state properties. Until the section of MST is designated, you will not see the MST blazes (see below) in the Great Smoky Mountains National Park, on shoulders of the Blue Ridge Parkway, or on federal or state roads/highways. MST blazes may not be visible in Cape Hatteras National Seashore because of wind and sand damage. One advantage you have here is that when you cannot find the trails in the woods or marshlands of the wildlife refuge or at lighthouses as described and mapped in this book, you have the beach of the Atlantic Ocean and highway NC-12 to guide you.

CAMPING, LODGING, AND PROVISIONS: Veteran hikers usually say that any hike is a success if you stay dry and warm, have food to eat, know where you are going, have proper gear, and have a safe place to sleep. On the MST you will not find the convenient campsites and shelters that are available on the Appalachian Trail. You will need to plan to stay in motels, bed and breakfast places, or in a farm barn or shed (with permission, of course). Otherwise, there will be places to camp almost anywhere in the national forests, as long as you honor the prescribed or recommended distances from streams and roads. Such is not the case in federal, state, or local parklands. For example, in Great Smoky Mountains National Park you will be able to choose among one Appalachian Trail shelter on the main ridge, a half dozen campsites along Deep Creek, and one campground on US-441 west of Cherokee. Except for in the campground, you will need a permit. You are advised to examine your maps to determine the boundary lines between the Blue Ridge Parkway and the national forests. Do not camp on the Blue Ridge Parkway property (except at its campgrounds). You can leave the property and camp in the national forests without permits. If you are biking, you will need the N.C. Division of Bicycle and Pedestrian Transportation bicycle route maps and a listing of recommended campgrounds. I have listed additional campgrounds.

In this section and throughout this book there will be information that will help you to find safe and legal places to sleep. This listing will also provide information on food sources, services, and supplies.

INFORMATION AND SECURITY: This listing provides a telephone number for the trail task force leader (usually a nongovernment volunteer) who is responsible for either maintaining the section of trail or knowing who does, or for the state trails specialist (employed by the Division of Parks and Recreation), or for both. In addition, there may be names, addresses, and telephone numbers of federal, state, or local forests and parks, visitor centers, commercial establishments, and chambers of commerce. Usually last on the list is the county sheriff's office, with an address and telephone number. If there is an emergency, call 911. If you have a cordless telephone and have access to keeping it charged, it could be a wise decision for you to take it on the trip, particularly while on the highways. Do not carry firearms.

DESCRIPTION: This is the description of the section of trail. In addition to describing terrain, geology, plant and animal life, scenic features, campsites, and history, it lists the accumulative distance of the trail. It may also describe connecting trails and their distances. It may indicate if the trail is for hiking only or if it is appropriate for multiple uses. I have offered additional, in-depth descriptions or stories in boxed text—usually a cameo of a historic, famous, or unique person or place that will provide intrigue and recognize a special quality of life on or near the trail.

You may find some errors in names on road signs. When counties changed from using route and box numbers to road names and house numbers for mailing addressees, some road names were changed. Furthermore, a few counties are still in transition with this process and names were not available at the time of publication of this guide.

DIVERSIONS: For a few sections of the MST I have listed activities unrelated to the trail. These diversions from the trail routes can be a side trip for cultural arts programs, athletic events, festivals, or tours of museums within cities or towns. An example is an extra summer night stay in Cherokee to see the outdoor drama *Unto These Hills*.

CAMPSIDE STORIES: Do you remember some of those tales told around the campfire when you attended a summer camp or went on an organized hiking trip? Perhaps they were stories about famous and noble people, inspirational tales accompanying spiritual songs, ghost tales, historic narratives, and mythical accounts told by Scout leaders or camp managers. I remember some of them, especially the ones that scared me and my two younger brothers and that gave us nightmares. Furthermore, we had a grandfather who could dramatically spellbind us. We always knew that somewhere, usually at the end of the tale, his large frame and powerful voice would give us chill bumps and pounding hearts. One of his most frightening stories was "Rawheads and Bloody Bones." It was not the story content so much that terrified us as the way he mastered our imaginations. He would tell stories of about ten minutes each in serial fashion, creating an imaginary chapter each night we visited. Sometimes he would ask us to tell how we thought the story should end. Alison Laurie, who teaches children's literature at Cornell University, states that scary stories enable children to develop the courage to find a solution that gives them a sense of bravery and identity.

Some of the stories I remember from childhood and more recently may be briefly recounted at the end of a section. Other stories, true or mythical, may be related to an incident that took place on or near the MST. All of us have had experiences that were exciting, or perhaps even dangerous and fearful, or others that were associated with pleasure and happiness. If you have not been keeping a diary of your trail and travel adventures, perhaps hiking the Mountains-to-Sea Trail is the time to begin. It could be a story to tell your children and their children.

Signs and Blazes

The Mountains-to-Sea Trail blaze is a three-inch-diameter white dot. You may see other trails marked by vertical two-inch by six-inch bars in the national forests. Among these, color may vary, but the white bars are for the Appalachian Trail (AT), although side trails to springs or campsites along the AT are often blazed blue. You will pass through areas where you may not see any blazes, for the Mountains-to-Sea Trail or otherwise.

On the Department of Transportation bicycle trails, you will instead see a green and white sign with a bicycle logo and the trail number (such as #4, #2, and #7, for routes followed by the MST). From the town of Danbury to Greensboro, you will be on state roads or back roads without any blazes or bicycle route signs. Here, carefully follow the instructions in this guidebook and the dotted line on the enclosed maps. After following the trails in Greensboro, you will again be on back roads without blazes or trail signs, but in Alamance County you will follow a numbered county bicycle route for parts of the cross-county passage. (This county bicycle route makes a loop through Alamance County, and on the southern part of the trail it makes a junction with the state's Mountains-to-Sea Bicycle Route #2[A].) After leaving Alamance County, you will again be on back roads without trail blazes or bicycle signs until you arrive at Falls Lake State Recreation Area and Falls Lake Trail. Once on this trail, you will see the familiar white blaze of the Mountains-to-Sea Trail.

Health and Safety

For a successful hike across the state, it is essential that you carefully complete your planning before you start. The most important planning goal is to make the trip healthy and safe. Because you will be on back roads and highways for at least half of the journey, extra caution must be taken to ensure that you are not injured or killed in a traffic accident. If you are bicycling, you must have safe equipment, clothes that avoid entanglement with the bicycle, helmet, proper eye protection, and excellent rear-view mirrors. Regardless of the size of your backpack and kind of clothing you wear, be sure that nothing on your body could be hit by or entangle with a motor vehicle. Bicycle stores can provide you with a safety checklist. One basic rule is that it is better to get off the road if you detect an irate automobile or truck driver following you too close. Given the increase in "road rage," it is wiser to push your bicycle up a hill rather than to cause backed-up highway traffic. Be exceptionally careful at narrow highway bridges. Always ride on the right side of the road. If you are an inexperienced bicyclist, I recommend you ride with experienced off-road bicyclists for a period of time before you begin the long journey. A recommended reference book is Sloane's *Complete Book on Bicycling*.

It is risky and dangerous on any road, but some statistics show that hiking or biking is safer than driving or riding in a motor vehicle. To a great extent you are safer as a hiker on the shoulder of the road than the bicyclist on the pavement. Where possible, always walk on the left shoulder of the highway, facing traffic: you can see the traffic ahead, even the face of the driver. One suggestion is that you carry a high walking staff with a small pennant or flag at the top. This can bring attention to you and give the driver a visual message that you are on a special mission. T-shirts or clothing that illustrates an athletic image is also suggested.

You will find that on back roads, almost all drivers will respond in kind if you wave or lift your hand in a greeting. (Alan Householder and I received about 95 percent friendly responses.) You will also probably notice that if the drivers are not facing oncoming traffic, they will move away from you even if you are on the shoulder and five feet from the pavement. I strongly recommend that you avoid bicycling or hiking after dark.

Your chance of hitch-hiking a ride is more favorable if you appear clean and collegiate to avoid the image of a drifter or vagrant. Of course, your own safety when hitch-hiking is a concern if you are picked up by a stranger. And though you have road rights as a pedestrian, do not walk on the pavement unless you are absolutely sure that there is not any traffic, including a vehicle that may be passing another vehicle behind you. If you must cross the road, as you may frequently have to do, use your common sense as you would when crossing roads in other situations. Another precaution is to forego wearing headphones. Although it might seem like a good idea to listen to your favorite music, to prevent boredom on a long stretch of road, this can also prevent you from hearing a vehicle or other potential dangers. You may think these suggestions and reminders are simplistic, but all of us who have walked these roads . have observed that safety precautions cannot be overemphasized.

Safety precautions are also essential on the trails through the woods. Be alert to slippery areas, loose rocks, fallen or falling trees and limbs, cliffs, flimsy footbridges, flooded rivers (particularly the Catawba and the Linville), creeks and streams, rock slides, and storms. I also recommended that you not hike alone. In the event you had an accident, became sick, or there was an emergency, others could call for help.

You probably already have a list of essential first aid items, but as a reminder, here is a list that is frequently published by wilderness guides: water purifier, antibiotics, disinfectant ointment, assorted band-aids, prescription pills for severe pain, simple painkiller, calamine lotion, gauze pads, adhesive tape, tweezers, biodegradable soap, moleskin, sunburn ointment, insect repellent, medicine for an upset stomach, and your personal medical prescriptions. A safety package could include waterproof matches, maps, compass, emergency food (preferably freeze-dried), a whistle, pocketknife (preferably Swiss), flashlight (preferably one with krypton bulbs), and a windproof and waterproof jacket with a head cover. Among recommended books on medication is *Medicine for the Outdoors* by Auerbach, and for health and safety use McDougall's *Practical Outdoor Survival*.

A major danger in cold weather is hypothermia, a lowering of body heat. It can be fatal, and some fatalities have occurred from cold and wet exposure in the summertime. If you are subjected to wet clothing and the wind chill is high, the first defense is to remove yourself from wind, rain, or snow: get dry and avoid exhaustion. Know the symptoms: there can be uncontrollable shivering, vague, incoherent speech, frequent stumbling, and drowsiness. The victim may become unaware of all of these. In mild cases treatment can be to place the victim in a dry place wearing dry clothes and in a dry sleeping bag. Warm drinks are helpful (but do not use alcohol or sedatives). If the impairment is serious and the victim is semiconscious, try to keep the person awake, warm the head and face, and provide person-to-person warmth; but if possible, quickly evacuate to an emergency hospital.

The Mountains-to-Sea Trail has a number of unfinished sections. To prevent becoming lost you should carry maps. The ones in this guidebook should be adequate, or you may wish to have more detailed topo maps. Be aware that old topo maps would not have the MST route noted. Therefore, be alert at all times for the white-dot blazes. Where there are not any blazes, check on other options listed in this book. If you are lost, remember a basic suggestion from "safety-first" rules and regulations: walk downstream along a creek or stream and follow it out to a road or civilization. If this is not possible, you need to stay where you are, signal your distress with the universal signal of three of anything. Examples are shouts, whistles, light flashes, or smoke signals. Do not panic, stay warm and protected, conserve your drinking water and food, and if possible climb a tree to provide orientation of your location. If you have a global positioning system (GPS) with you, you can probably locate yourself. Also, if you have a cellular telephone, you may wish to call 911 for rescue assistance.

Weather is a constant concern among long-distance hikers and even sometimes for a short day trip. If you are carrying a small radio, keep informed. If you hike in the wintertime, you could become dangerously disoriented in a white-out along the high ridges of the Blue Ridge Mountains. Seek shelter or set up camp early if you have warning of snow, sleet, or ice. Bicycling or walking on the sections of roads and highways could also be risky in snowy and icy weather. Because most hikers are on the MST in springtime or in autumn, the weather risk factor is low for hypothermia or for being disoriented. Other hazards are lightning, flooding, and heat exhaustion. As precaution against lightning strikes, it is wise to stay off of sharp prominent peaks during approaching or actual storms. Also, avoid standing under a tree, or in the mouth of a cave, or near seams or crevices on rocks. One suggestion is to squat down and insulate yourself from the ground with a space blanket or anything waterproof. If you have a backpack with metal parts, remove it from your body.

In reading this guidebook, you will notice that a few sections of the MST require that you wade across rivers, such as the Catawba, Linville, Harper, and Lost Cove. (There are plans for a footbridge over the Catawba River.) You are advised to stay informed about rivers that may be flooded. The descriptions here offer options if you approach a flooded area. If the rivers or streams are safe enough to wade (usually no higher than your knees), take precautions to unfasten your backpack bellyband, and have a dependable pole or staff to provide balance. Either keep on your hiking boots or use a lighter spare pair, and always face or be prepared to face upstream.

A continuous need on the trail is pure drinking water. The descriptions in this guidebook indicate sources of water, but most sources will need to be purified. Be sure you have a dependable water purifier with you every day. You will see many clear streams (including such rivers as the Catawba) that appear to be clear and safe for drinking. Do not take the risk. The microscopic protozoan Giardia can be lurking, and it can make you painfully sick for weeks, enough for an immediate need to abort your trip. Known as the cause of "backpackers' disease," Giardia can be carried in both humans and wildlife. If you do not have a water purifier, properly boiling (some trails specialists recommend one to three minutes) the water remains an option. For health reasons, camp at least 100 feet away from streams and water sources, and bury human waste 300 feet away.

Other health and safety guidelines include packing out all trash, avoiding hiking at night, and watching for poisonous snakes (but do not kill them). Stop and use moleskin when you first notice blisters developing on your feet. Be cautious with any type of knife, and unless you have a license for hunting in a hunting area, do not carry a firearm. Firearms are prohibited in national, state, and local parks, but they are allowed at specific seasons in national forests and in national and state game lands. National, state, and local recreation parks forbid the use of alcohol.

In each section of this guidebook I have listed the telephone number and address of the county sheriff, for use if you have an emergency or if a crime needs to be reported. If you wish to report violations of hunting and fishing laws, call 800-662-7137. To purchase licenses to hunt or fish, call the N.C. Wildlife Resources Commission (telephone: 888-248-6834).

Cross-State Equipment

Equipment needs vary a little by region. While you are in the mountains you will need the same kind of equipment you would take on the Appalachian Trail, but you may be able to carry a lighter load in both the central and coastal areas, depending on the type of campground facilities or motels you plan to use. If you will be setting up a tent in sandy areas, longer tent pegs may be needed. If you plan to bicycle parts of the MST, additional equipment will be involved, as well as some shuttle arrangements. State bicycle routes have suggested campgrounds. (Call 919-733-2804 for "N.C. Bicycling Highways Campground Directory.")

On our cross-state journey in 1997, Alan Householder and I chose the least expensive method. We ate cold food or cooked (usually at dinner) instead of eating at restaurants, and we camped instead of staying in motels. Our individual cost was about $800, not including the costs of using single or double vehicle shuttles between campgrounds or unexpected costs for equipment. A hiking and biking combination could have reduced our trip from two months to about one month and one week, and at less cost. In one of my earlier cross-state arrangements I hiked one month and took eight days for bicycling with a cost of about $600. I believe it will take a few years with a number of cross-state hikers for a dependable average of costs to be known.

To estimate your expenses, I recommended that you make a list of what you already have in the way of hiking gear, such as backpack, tent, sleeping bag, space blanket, roll-up mattress, first-aid equipment, cooking equipment, hiking boots, and clothing. Determine the cost for whatever equipment you do not have and for food. Estimate the number of nights you will be staying at motels (probably between $45 to $65 per room, depending on season) or campgrounds ($12 to $16 per site, depending on season) (see options in the descriptions ahead). There will be a number of nights that you will not be near a campground and will be sleeping off the trail without charge in the national forests. Some who have hiked or biked part of the journey inquired at country stores and farmhouses for space to set up a tent under a tree. They reported favorable results. Your inquiry may be more likely honored if your host trusts your story of crossing the state, and if you describe an acceptable purpose or mission. You can call or write the Friends of the Mountains-to-Sea Trail, 3585 US-401 South, Louisburg, NC 27549 (919-496-4771) for an ID card that may support your purpose.

Rules and Regulations

You will pass through national parks and forests and state parks where there are rules and regulations; these are sometimes called forest or park ethics. Individual parks in cities or towns, also described here, also have rules of usage. I provide the addresses, telephone numbers, or both, of all parks, forests, and preserves through which the Mountains-to-Sea Trail passes. Users of these natural areas can assist in protection and preservation by being good stewards.

Here are some of the important regulations that apply in Great Smoky Mountains National Park. Maximum size of a camping party is eight. Only one consecutive night at a shelter and three persons at a campsite are permitted. Campers must stay in designated sites of the itinerary. Damage to plant or animal life is prohibited. Carry out all food and trash. Bury all solid human waste at least 300 feet from campsite. Do not wash dishes or bathe with soap in a stream. Use only wood that is dead and on the ground. Practice minimum impact on campsites. No pets, bicycles, firearms, or hunting or feeding of wildlife allowed.

Here are the rules and regulations to be followed within the boundaries of the Blue Ridge Parkway. If you are driving a motor vehicle, the enforced speed limit is 45 miles per hour. All plants and animals are protected by law. Plants cannot be picked or removed, and animals cannot be harassed, harmed, or killed. No natural feature can be defaced. Pets must be kept on a leash; they are not allowed in parkway public buildings. Swimming is not permitted within the parkway boundaries. No hunting or trapping is allowed, but fishing is allowed if you have a valid state permit. No firearms are allowed. Camping is permitted only in designated campgrounds. Fires are allowed only at designated picnic areas and campgrounds.

The following rules and regulations apply in all national forests. Pack out all trash. Bury all human waste and toilet paper at least 300 feet from any water. Never bathe or wash anything in a creek. Scatter wash water well away from a stream and use biodegradable soap. For fires, use existing fire rings and make sure the fire is dead out before leaving. Use only dead and downed wood for fires. Leave no-trace campsites. If you are riding a horse, stay on designated horse trails. Forest trails are for hikers only, unless signed and designated for bicycles, horses, or off-road vehicles.

The state parks also have rules and regulations. The removal of any plant, animal, artifact, or mineral is prohibited. All state parks are wildlife preserves, and hunting or trapping is unlawful. Do not feed or frighten wildlife. Fishing and boating regulations in the parks are under the supervision of the N.C. Wildlife Resources Commission. Do not litter. Firearms and fireworks are prohibited. Possession or use of alcohol and illegal drugs are prohibited. Pets must be on a leash no longer than 6 feet. Camping and fires are permitted at designated places only. Rock climbing is permitted by registration only and at designated sites only.

Preferable Seasons to Hike

If you wish to experience the resurrection of springtime with its wildflowers, songbirds, cool weather, and fewer biting insects, I recommended you consider beginning your hike at Clingmans Dome in the Smokies about the middle of April and ending at Jockey's Ridge State Park about the middle of June. In early springtime you have better views before heavy foliage appears in the forest. Another advantage is less climbing of long, steep mountain trails in the heat. This period also showcases agricultural plantings throughout the central and coastal areas.

One potential advantage of hiking, instead, from east to west in the springtime is to escape some of the coastal mosquitoes and reach the mountains when the weather is warmer. The other preferred season is autumn when the forest leaf colors are at their peak; begin in the first week of October in the high elevations and end in late November at the coast. If you plan to bicycle sections of the central part of the state, the best plan could be to finish earlier in November. Although wintertime provides scenic views not available in other seasons, the snow and ice create hazards. Also, wading of rivers and creeks becomes more dangerous during icy conditions. Farmlands appear exceptionally bleak. Remember that summertime heat can make for an uncomfortable journey, and the biting insects may assault you in dense swarms throughout swampy coastal areas.

The Trails of the Future

Assisting in the construction of trails and their management in public and private natural areas are dedicated task forces and organizations. To be informed of the current and planned activities of the Friends of the Mountains-to-Sea Trail, you may call 919-496-4771 or write to 3585 US-401 South, Louisburg, NC 27549. For e-mail, use ADH4771@aol.com. To talk with a N.C. Division of Parks and Recreation trails coordinator, call 919-846-9991, or write to 12700 Bayleaf Church Road, Raleigh, NC 27614. State trails specialists are as follows: Mountain Region, DENR, 59 Woodfin Street, Asheville, NC 28802 (telephone: 828-251-6208); Piedmont Region (address and telephone number the same as trails coordinator, above); Coastal Region, Cliffs of the Neuse State Park, 345-B Park Entrance Road, Seven Springs, NC 28578 (telephone: 910-778-9488).

ONE

GREAT SMOKY MOUNTAINS
NATIONAL PARK

In 1999 Great Smoky Mountains National Park encompassed 520,004 acres, of which 276,239 acres were in North Carolina (the remainder is in Tennessee). Geologists estimate that the original peaks of these mountains were about 15,000 feet in elevation when they were formed 250 million years ago.

Authorized by Congress in 1926 and dedicated in 1940 by President Franklin D. Roosevelt, the park would not have been possible without the financial help from thousands of citizens, state and federal allocations, and a $5 million gift from John D. Rockefeller Jr. Nearly 85 percent of the original acreage belonged to eighteen timber companies. It took fourteen years of negotiations and some litigation to purchase more than 6,000 separate tracts. But what an extraordinary gift Americans gave themselves. Nearly 10 million visitors access the park annually. In addition to the recreational activities and the protective management of the preserve, the national park offers educational programs and summer camps to more than 8,000 school-age children, and rangers conduct numerous tours and hikes for all age groups from May 31 to usually the third week in August.

The park's natural diversity has never been completely researched. That changed in 1999 when the National Park Service (NPS) established a long-term, perhaps up to 15 years, All Taxa Biodiversity Inventory. The NPS claims the effort will attract international attention and will be the "most ambitious undertaking in the history of natural science." Scientists believe only 25 percent of the potential 100,000 biological species of the park have been catalogued. Currently known are more than 130 species of trees, 21 of which are world champions in size. Other species include 205 mosses, 1,400 flowering plants, 2,000 fungi, 200 birds (one of which is the peregrine falcon, recently returned after the species virtually vanished more than fifty years ago), 65 mammals, 38 reptiles, and 58 fish. There are more than 600 miles of streams for fishing.

Although you will hike less than 30 miles of the park's approximately 900-

mile trail system while on the MST route, this will be an excellent example of the kind and type of trails in the park. The MST route follows nine trails in the park, one of which is a short section of the Appalachian Trail from Clingmans Dome to an access of the Mount Collins shelter. The group of trails was officially designated as part of the Mountains-to-Sea Trail in September 2000.

SECTION 1. Clingmans Dome, Great Smoky Mountains National Park to Blue Ridge Parkway (MP 469.1)

SWAIN COUNTY: The county, which encompasses 544 square miles, received its name in honor of David L. Swain (1801–68). Swain, who was appointed governor by the General Assembly for 1833, was president of the University of North Carolina at Chapel Hill from 1836 to his death in 1868. In 1871 the county was formed from parts of Jackson and Macon Counties. In the middle of the county is part of Fontana Lake and the Tuckasegee and Oconaluftee Rivers, and in the south is the Nantahala National Forest, which receives downstream flow from the Nantahala and Little Tennessee Rivers. To the west and north is Great Smoky Mountains National Park (GSMNP), and in the north and east is the Cherokee Indian Qualla Boundary. To the northeast is the southwestern terminus of the Blue Ridge Parkway.

Bryson City, the county seat, was first incorporated as Charleston in 1827 but changed to Bryson City in 1889 to honor Captain Thaddeus D. Bryson (1829–90), who had been a leader in the town's development. Main east-west highways are NC-74 and US-19, and running north-south is US-441.

LENGTH AND DIFFICULTY: 27.4 miles (main route), 28.7 miles (alternate route); strenuous (change in elevation: 4,593 feet)

USGS TOPO MAPS: Clingmans Dome, Smokemont

FEATURES OR EMPHASIS: Spectacular panoramic views of Tennessee and North Carolina from Clingmans Dome Observation Tower, exceptional autumn leaf colors, hemlock forest, Deep Creek, Kephart Campsite, Mingus Mill, Oconaluftee Visitor Center, Mountain Farm Museum.

TRAILS FOLLOWED: Appalachian Trail, Fork Ridge Trail, Deep Creek Trail, Martin's Gap Trail, Sunkota Ridge Trail, Thomas Divide Trail, Newton Bald Trail, Mingus Creek Trail, Oconaluftee River Trail

TRAIL CONNECTIONS: Pole Road Creek Trail, Indian Creek Trail, Deeplow Gap Trail

WEST TRAILHEAD: Vehicular access in GSMNP is on Clingmans Dome Road, 7 miles from Newfound Gap Road, 18 miles west of Cherokee or 16 miles east

Observation tower at Clingmans
Dome in the Great Smoky Mountains
National Park (Courtesy of GSMNP)

of Gatlinburg on US-441. (Clingmans Dome Road is closed in winter. Foot trail access on the Appalachian Trail is 7.5 miles south from Newfound Gap parking area.) Park at the Forney Ridge parking area and hike 0.5 miles on a paved access trail to the Appalachian Trail and Clingmans Dome (elevation 6,643 feet), the highest point in the Smokies and on the 2,157-mile Appalachian Trail. An observation tower provides descriptive information for panoramic views of the Smokies.

EAST TRAILHEAD: Either at the Smokemont Campground (3.7 miles west on Newfound Gap Road [US-441] from the Blue Ridge Parkway), at the Oconaluftee Visitor Center (0.7 miles west on US-441 from the Blue Ridge Parkway), or at the end of the Blue Ridge Parkway, all west of Cherokee.

CAMPING, LODGING, AND PROVISIONS: Self-assigned permits or reservations for numbered backcountry campsites in the Deep Creek Valley area are available at the Oconaluftee Visitor Center. Walk behind the Visitor Center to an office-type room to fill out a free camping permit. You should also purchase a map ($1), which will list where to camp and indicate availability of campsites. Remember that you must have the permit on your person during the time of camping. Your group cannot consist of more than eight people, and the maximum stay at one campsite is three nights (only one night at a shelter). No pets are allowed. Take sufficient rope to tie your food 10 feet above the ground and 4 feet away from trees to prevent access by black bears. For information in advance, call 423-436-1297 (9 A.M. to 4 P.M.); for reservations, call 423-436-1231 (8 A.M. to 6 P.M.). If you stay at Smokemont Campground, which operates year-round, note that a fee is charged; you can call reservation information at 800-365-2267 or risk finding a space among the 140 campsites on arrival.

The nearest motels and restaurants are at Chief Saunooke Village, 1.4 miles south (0.7 miles from Blue Ridge Parkway) on US-441 from the Oconaluftee Visitor Center, at the junction of Acquoni Road and US-441. Here are Little Princess Restaurant, Dairy Queen, Best Western Inn and Restaurant (telephone: 828-497-2020), Econo Lodge (telephone: 828-497-2226), and Budgetel Inns (telephone: 828-497-2102). If you wish to walk farther or you have vehicular transportation, there are more motels, restaurants, laundry, and grocery stores 0.8 miles farther south. Another 0.7 miles brings you to the Museum of the Cherokee Indian (9 A.M. to 8 P.M.), Mountainside Theatre, and Oconaluftee Indian Village.

INFORMATION AND SECURITY: Trail Maintenance: GSMNP staff (telephone: 828-497-1902), Mountain Region State Trails Specialist (telephone: 828-251-6452). Great Smoky Mountains National Park: Main Headquarters, 107 Park Headquarters Road, Gatlinburg, TN 37738 (telephone: 865-436-1200); District Ranger Office, Box 4, Park Circle, Cherokee, NC 28719 (telephone: 828-497-1902); Oconaluftee Visitor Center is open daily from 9 A.M. to 5 P.M. except Christmas Day (telephone: 828-497-1900). Cherokee Chamber of Commerce: Main Street (P.O. Box 460), Cherokee, NC 28719 (telephone: 828-497-9195 or 800-438-1601). Swain County Sheriff's Office: P.O. Box 1398, Bryson City, NC 28713 (telephone: 828-488-2197). Cherokee Police (telephone: 828-497-4131).

DESCRIPTION: Begin your journey on the Mountains-to-Sea Trail route by walking north on the Appalachian Trail (AT) from Clingmans Dome. At 1.0 mile reach Old Buzzards Roost in a spruce/fir forest. A spring is on the right. Descend. Reach Collins Gap at 2.0 miles among the shrubby moosewood, ferns, and mosses. Ascend to Mount Collins summit (elevation 6,188 feet; named for Robert Collins in 1858 or 1859) at 3.0 miles. At 3.2 miles the Sugarland Mountain Trail from Tennessee will come in from the left. (You can descend on this trail for 0.5 miles to the Mount Collins shelter, which has twelve bunk beds. A permit from the GSMNP is required for overnight camping; telephone 423-436-1231 for information and reservations, daily, twenty-four hours.)

Thomas L. Clingman and Arnold Guyot

Clingmans Dome (elevation 6,643 feet) is the Great Smoky Mountains' highest peak and the third highest peak east of the Mississippi River. The Cherokee Indians called it Ku-wa-hi, meaning "mulberry place." The dome, then known as Smoky Dome, was first surveyed in 1858 by a local guide, Robert Collins, and a geologist and mountain climber named Thomas L. Clingman (1812–97). About two years later geographer Arnold Guyot, who, like Clingman, measured the mountains with mercurial barometers, named the peak in Clingman's honor. Clingman, who was also a congressman and senator from North Carolina and a Civil War general, died poor and homeless. During the period 1856 to 1860 Guyot climbed and measured most of the peaks in the state's Appalachian chain and produced topographic maps. Mount Guyot (elevation 6,621 feet), farther north and the second highest peak in the Smokies, is named in Guyot's honor.

At 3.5 miles a spur trail from the right leads 125 feet to Clingmans Dome Road. (The AT continues ahead for 4.0 miles to Newfound Gap and a parking area.) Turn right on the spur trail, cross Clingmans Dome Road to the small parking area and the northwest trailhead of the Fork Ridge Trail. (To the right, on the road, it is 3.5 miles to the Forney Ridge parking area near Clingmans Dome, and to the left it is 3.5 miles to Newfound Gap Road.) Follow the Fork Ridge Trail and descend 2,800 feet in elevation for the next 5.1 miles. There are scenic views along the way. At 3.6 miles pass a spring surrounded by the flowering herbs golden Alexander and white snakeroot. Enter a virgin hemlock forest at 5.6 miles and descend on switchbacks. Galax patches, a mountain laurel and azalea arbor, and views of Bearpen Ridge, to the right (south), are at 7.1 miles. At 8.6 miles you will cross Deep Creek (the footbridge may have washed away from floods). This is the end of the Fork Ridge Trail, the juncture with the Deep Creek Trail (this is a multiple use trail for hikers and equestrians), and the location of the Poke Patch backcountry campsite #53. Turn right, downstream along Deep Creek.

Ascend left of a precipice at 9.6 miles. At 10.8 miles pass banks of Fraser's sedge. Pass Nettle Creek backcountry campsite #54 at 11.2 miles; Pole Road backcountry campsite #55 at 12 miles; Burnt Spruce backcountry campsite #56 at 12.3 miles; and Bryson Place backcountry campsite #57 at 12.8 miles. (See "Camping, Lodging, and Provisions" above for necessary campsite permit.) There are equestrian campsites at all of the above numbered sites except #53 and #54. Hike beside the cascading stream in a forest

Horace S. Kephart

Horace Kephart (1862–1931), often referred to as a principal founder of the Great Smoky Mountains National Park and "Dean of American Campers," had his last long-term campground near the junction of Martins Gap Trail and Deep Creek Trail. Kephart was devoted to the protection of the Smokies and said the area was "an Eden still unpeopled and unspoiled." He was killed in an automobile accident near Bryson City on April 2, 1931. Northwest of here is Kephart Prong and Kephart Shelter. Northwest of the shelter is Kephart Mountain (elevation 6,400 feet), named in his honor October 3, 1928. The mountain has a vertical cliff measuring nearly 500 feet and another 1,000-foot nearly vertical drop. An authority on mountain lore, Kephart was the author of Our Southern Highlanders *(1913 and 1922),* Camping and Woodcraft *(1916), and* The Camper's Manual *(1916 and 1923).*

of tall hardwoods and hemlocks. The Pole Road Creek Trail comes in on the right at 12.1 miles in a scenic creek area; continue downstream. Along this part of the trail you may see evidence of wild hogs and deer. At 12.8 miles reach Bryson Place backcountry campsite #57 and a junction with Martins Gap Trail, where the MST turns left.

To the right, about 200 feet off the trail, if you cross a small steam, is a plaque on a millstone honoring Horace Kephart. (Deep Creek Trail continues downstream 3.9 miles to Deep Creek Campground, where there are 108 campsites for tents and RVs [no hook-ups or showers], flush toilets, water, and a large picnic area. It is 3.0 miles farther into Bryson City where there are motels, restaurants, shopping centers, commercial campgrounds, and a hospital.)

Ascend on Martins Gap Trail, a moderately graded old road with excellent scenery for hikers and equestrians. At 14.3 miles arrive at Martins Gap (elevation 3,430 feet) and a junction with the Sunkota Ridge Trail. Turn left. (Indian Creek Trail goes ahead 3.9 miles to juncture with Deep Creek Trail.) Ascend gradually on the east slope of the ridge among hardwoods, a particularly colorful area in autumn. You may notice that wild hogs have been wallowing in the springs. The Thomas Divide Trail crosses at 19.1 miles; turn right.

At 19.5 miles leave the Thomas Divide Trail, turn left, and begin walking the Newton Bald Trail to Newton Bald backcountry campsite #52 at 19.7 miles. Water is available at 50 yards to the right, on a steep slope. At 20.2 miles arrive at Newton Bald Ridge (elevation 5,142 feet). To the right is the Mingus Creek Trail. (At this juncture the main MST route follows

William H. Thomas

A twelve-year-old white boy known to the Cherokee as Will Usadi, Little Will, was adopted by Cherokee peace chief Yonaguska as his son in 1817. Little Will, who as a child had already shown great interest in the history of the Cherokee, began his Indian trading career in the year of his adoption, managing a post on Soco Creek. William Holland Thomas (1805–89) became the preserver of what are known today as the Qualla Boundary Cherokee (those Cherokee who escaped the death march, the Trail of Tears, to Oklahoma Territory by the U.S. Army in 1838).

Because the Cherokee were not considered citizens, Thomas, as an American citizen, purchased land and held it in trust until the Cherokee could legally own it. Later Thomas became an official U.S. Indian Agent for the Cherokee Nation and represented them in legal and financial matters. During the Civil War Thomas was promoted to a colonel and created the Thomas Legion of the Confederate Army, in which the majority of about 400 soldiers were Cherokee.

Thomas is commemorated on three state highway historical markers: one on US-19 at Soco Gap, another on US-19 northeast of Bryson City, and another at US-19A at US-441, east of Whittier. The latter is inscribed as follows: "White Chief and agent of N.C. Cherokee. Secured reservation for them. Confederate colonel. State senator. Home, 'Stekoih Fields,' stood ¼ mi. S." Thomas Divide and the Thomas Divide Trail in Great Smoky Mountains National Park are named for him. At milepost 463.9 on the Blue Ridge Parkway is a view of Thomas Divide and the Oconaluftee River valley.

Mingus Creek Trail for 5.8 miles to the Mingus Mill parking area at Newfound Gap Road [US-441], a descent of 3,090 feet in elevation. The alternate MST route follows the Newton Bald Trail to Smokemont Campground and the shoulder of Newfound Gap Road for 7.1 miles to the Mingus Mill parking area.)

Descend on the Mingus Creek Trail along a dry ridge, but skirting from side to side, in an oak forest with scattered pines, rhododendron, and mountain laurel. After 0.7 miles the descent is more rapid with six switchbacks. At 23.2 miles arrive at a gap. (To the right it is 6.0 miles to Deeplow Gap Trail.) Turn left and descend on a foot trail of switchbacks to the headwaters of Madcap Branch at 23.8 miles. Continue among groves of rhododendron and large hardwoods to a confluence with Mingus Creek at 24.7 miles. Keep right on an old road and arrive at the Mingus Mill parking area at 26.0 miles. Mingus Mill, a heritage, water-powered grist mill, is open from 9 A.M. to 5 P.M. daily, usually from mid-April to the end of October.

(If you are following the alternate MST route, continue on the Newton Bald Trail for the next 4.7 miles in a descent of 2,900 feet. Cross a small stream and pass a tall hemlock grove at 22.6 miles. At 24.4 miles turn left on a horse trail, and left again after 0.2 miles. At 24.8 miles arrive at Newfound Gap Road [US-441] and turn right. [The GSMNP has a regulation that prohibits hitchhiking.] Reach a parking area at 24.9 miles, opposite the entrance to Smokemont Campground [telephone: 800-365-2267]. Facilities at the campground include 140 campsites [no hook-ups and no showers], sewage disposal, flush toilets, tables, and grills. It is open all year, but is not fully operational from November to April. This is black bear country and food storage regulations are enforced. From the campground continue southeast on Newfound Gap Road for 2.4 miles to the Mingus Mill parking area, right, to reconnect with the MST main route.)

From the Mingus Mill parking area continue south for 0.5 miles on US-441 to the Oconaluftee Visitor Center (telephone: 828-497-1900). Turn left at the entrance driveway. The center is open daily from 9 A.M. to 5 P.M., except on Christmas Day. Adjoining the center is a self-registration facility for hiking and camping trips. Because there is not a parking area ahead at the junction of US-441 and the Blue Ridge Parkway, you may wish to make the center, at 27.9 miles, the end of this section. Otherwise continue on the walkway behind and to the right of the center to pass the Mountain Farm Museum. (The museum represents a pioneer farm of about 1900 with farm equipment and animals.) Follow the 1.3-mile Oconaluftee River Trail, which goes through a wide and scenic meadow. At 0.8 miles it passes under the Blue Ridge Parkway bridge. If you are continuing to hike the Parkway, ascend an embankment at the bridge. (If you are continuing on the trail, it will end at a parking space near the river after 0.5 miles. It is 0.2 miles downstream to the Chief Saunooke Village, on the left [see "Camping, Lodging, and Provisions" above]. In another 1.5-miles you will find yourself in the town of Cherokee [*E-gwan-ul-ti*, meaning "by the river"]).

DIVERSIONS: In Cherokee you can see Kermit Hunter's outdoor drama "Unto These Hills," about Cherokee history, from the second week in June through the third week in August. Also worthwhile are the Museum of the Cherokee Indian (telephone: 828-497-3481) and Oconaluftee Indian Village (telephone: 828-497-2315).

CAMPSIDE STORIES: In 1817 the U.S. government broke some of its treaties with the Cherokee Indians. A new treaty provided for marching the Cherokee to Oklahoma Territory. The day came in May 1838 when U.S. Army General Winfield Scott, chief officer in charge of the removal, sent 7,000 troops into the mountains of North Carolina, north Georgia, and east Tennessee. At first the Cherokee were rounded up like cattle and placed in stockades. During the final march of an estimated 15,000 or more people, termed the "Trail of Tears," at least 4,000 died on the way.

Among the Cherokee was Tsali (Charlie) and his family, who lived in the Oconaluftee Valley. While being marched to a stockade, Tsali's wife was prodded with a bayonet by a soldier. As a result, Tsali spoke in Cherokee to his sons and others about an escape. Tsali feigned a broken ankle, and a soldier came to investigate. In a struggle and melee that followed, the soldier was accidentally shot and killed. The other soldiers in the group fled and the Indians escaped.

Colonel Stanhope Foster was ordered to find Tsali and the others who had escaped. William Thomas, a white U.S. citizen who had been adopted as a child by Chief Yonaguska, agreed to find Tsali. Thomas located him and his family in a cave on the west side of Thomas Ridge in the Smoky Mountains. The U.S. Army terms were that if Tsali and his sons were executed, all other escapees, about a thousand, would be allowed to stay. It has been written that Tsali begged, "If I must die, let it be by my own people." Three Cherokee men were ordered to be the firing squad. Three of the accused were shot on November 23, 1838, and Tsali, his oldest son, and a son-in-law were executed two days later.

On a state highway historical marker in Bryson City is the following inscription: "Tsali Cherokee Brave, surrendered to Gen'l Scott to be shot near here, 1838, that remnant of tribe might remain in N.C."

For nearly 150 years stories have passed from one generation to the next about seeing the ghost of Tsali appear in the evening mists and moonlight shadows at Echota, Oconaluftee, and elsewhere in the Great Smoky Mountains and Cherokee area. One story originated with Union soldiers during the Civil War when they reported Tsali's silhouette on the mountain ridge tops. Other stories about his legendary life have been printed, including one by the Associated Press that appeared in North Carolina newspapers on August 3, 1940.

TWO

BLUE RIDGE PARKWAY
(WEST AND SOUTH AREA)

Linking the Great Smoky Mountains National Park of Tennessee and North Carolina with Shenandoah National Park of Virginia is the 469.1-mile Blue Ridge Parkway, of which 252.2 miles are in North Carolina. During the construction of the Parkway, Senator Harry F. Byrd of Virginia prophetically said in 1936 that "this road will be the greatest scenic road in the world and will attract millions of tourists." A report from the Parkway headquarters indicates more than 21 million visitors came to the Blue Ridge Parkway in 1998; the all-time high was 25.6 million visitors in 1988.

A number of historians have credited Senator Byrd with the original idea of the Parkway when he suggested a southern extension of the Skyline Drive to President Franklin D. Roosevelt in August 1933. Theodore E. Straus of Maryland, who was a member of the Public Works Administration, claimed to have been the real originator, and Fred L. Weede, a leader in the routing of the Parkway near Asheville, agrees that Straus was "the father of the idea." Senator Byrd described how President Roosevelt asked that he and Secretary Harold L. Ickes "get together for the right-of-way." It was not a simple matter. Immediately a congressional controversy erupted over whether the route would include Tennessee. Because the owners of Grandfather Mountain initially would not approve the route of the Parkway over their property, the last-completed 6.5 miles were not dedicated until September 11, 1987.

The Blue Ridge Parkway almost did not happen. After North Carolina congressman Robert Lee Doughton introduced the bill April 24, 1936, many others opposed it. Jesse P. Wolcott of Michigan argued that it was "the most ridiculous undertaking that has ever been presented to Congress . . . a colossal steal." The bill barely passed in the House (145 for, 131 against, and 147 abstaining). The Senate, more supportive, easily passed the bill. Regardless of who deserves the credit for the idea and the legislative success, we can focus our attention today on the scenic roadway's preservation and use as a priceless gift to our nation.

We can benefit from the Blue Ridge Parkway's eternal scenic value, its biological and social heritage, and its unprecedented recreational options. In addition to its more than 250 scenic parking overlooks, there are twenty-four special locations that include a visitor center, exhibits, camping, lodging, and restaurants. Of the five Parkway campgrounds in North Carolina, the Mountains-to-Sea Trail passes close to three: Mount Pisgah (milepost 408), Julian Price Park (milepost 297.1), and Doughton Park (milepost 241.1). The campgrounds are open May 1 through October. For information on all facilities call 828-271-4779. Please note that no other camping is allowed on the Parkway. (To modify this restriction, the Friends of the Mountains-to-Sea Trail has requested that small backcountry spaces be set aside at appropriate intervals for through-hikers only until commercial campgrounds or motels are available. Please contact the Parkway office for an update on this request.) Meanwhile, hikers have options to choose "no trace camping" sites wherever there are adjoining national forests. Some Parkway guidelines are as follows: do not feed any wildlife, do not harm or harvest any plant life, if driving do not exceed 45 miles per hour, do not leave a vehicle parked overnight on roadsides or overlooks unless you inform a park ranger, do not swim in any streams or lakes, and keep all domestic pets on a leash. Weapons and hunting are forbidden. For emergencies, call 800-727-5928, and for general information, call 828-298-0398.

Bicyclists use the Parkway, and about 130 miles of the road (from Balsam Gap [south] to a turn-off connection to NC-181 north of Linville) is part of the Mountains-to-Sea Bicycle Route #2. Working mile-by-mile, volunteer task force groups are now in the process of creating a hiking route, the Mountains-to-Sea Trail, within the Parkway's boundary. It will parallel the Parkway for 233.4 miles and frequently crosses the Parkway's ribbon of asphalt. In addition, the MST will weave and undulate through sections of the Nantahala and Pisgah National Forests that adjoin the Parkway. As a result the hiking distance may be closer to 310 miles when completed.

SECTION 2. Great Smoky Mountains National Park and Blue Ridge Parkway (MP 469.1) to Soco Gap (US-19 and Blue Ridge Parkway MP 455.7)

SWAIN AND JACKSON COUNTIES: (See Swain County discussion in Section 1.) Jackson County's name honors Andrew Jackson (1767–1845), seventh president of the United States. The 499-square-mile county, formed in 1851 from parts of Macon and Haywood Counties, shares a southern border with South Carolina and Georgia. The north-centrally located county seat is

Sylva, first settled in 1861, incorporated in 1889, and named for William D. Sylva, a Danish carpenter. Nearby is the town of Cullowhee, home of Western Carolina University (founded in 1899). In the county are large sections of Nantahala National Forest; Thorpe, Bear Creek, and Wolf Reservoirs; numerous waterfalls; Sapphire Lake; Whiteside Mountain; Panthertown Valley; and headwaters of the Chattooga River. Major east-west highway routes are US-64, US-74, and, in part, US-23 and 19; north-south routes are NC-107 and US-441.

LENGTH AND DIFFICULTY: 13.4 miles (plus), strenuous (change in elevation: 3,130 feet)

USGS TOPO MAPS: Smokemont, Bunches Bald, Sylva North

FEATURES OR EMPHASIS: Scenic overlooks to Thomas Divide, Jenkins Ridge, Bunches Bald, and Plott Balsams; Heintooga Spur; Cherokee Qualla Reservation

WEST TRAILHEAD: Junction of US-441 and southwest entrance (MP 469.1) of the Blue Ridge Parkway

EAST TRAILHEAD: Junction of US-19 and Blue Ridge Parkway (MP 455.7)

CAMPING, LODGING, AND PROVISIONS: See this item in Section 1. In addition, the following are in or near Soco Gap. On US-19 on the south side of the Parkway, it is 0.3 miles to Blue Ridge Motel, Soco Campground, a grocery store and gasoline station, and a restaurant (where you can catch rainbow trout in an adjoining pond and have the restaurant cooks prepare it for your dinner; telephone: 828-926-3635). The services are open from April 1 to November. Farther down the mountain on US-19 it is 12.0 miles to Cherokee. Down the mountain on the north side of the Parkway it is 6.0 miles to Maggie Valley, but the nearest motel and restaurant is 2.0 miles from Soco Gap. Lodging is at Abbey Inn, which offers scenic views of the valley and the Great Smoky Mountains (telephone: 800-545-5853). The restaurant is called Mountaineer Buffet. Nearby is Ed's Motel and Chalet Cottages (telephone: 828-926-1879). Farther down the mountain for 4.0 miles is Maggie Valley, where you can find a variety of craft shops, motels, restaurants, laundry, and at least two shopping centers: Eagle Shopping Center and Stallard Shopping Mall.

INFORMATION AND SECURITY: Trail Maintenance: Balsam Highlands Task Force (telephone: 828-456-3392). Cherokee Chamber of Commerce: US-19/441 Main Street (P.O. Box 460), Cherokee, NC 28719 (telephone: 828-497-9195, or 800-438-1601). Oconaluftee Visitor Center (telephone: 828-497-1900). Maggie Valley Chamber of Commerce: 2487 Soco Road (P.O. Box 87), NC 28751 (telephone: 828-926-1686 or 800-785-8259). Blue Ridge Parkway (telephone: 828-298-0398; for emergencies or accidents: 1-800-727-5928).

Swain County Sheriff's Office: P.O. Box 1398, Bryson City, NC 28713 (telephone: 828-488-2197). Jackson County Sheriff's Office: 330 Keener Street, Sylva, NC 28779 (telephone: 828-586-8901). Haywood County Sheriff's Office: Courthouse Annex, 215 North Main Street, Waynesville, NC 28786 (telephone: 828-452-6666).

DESCRIPTION: This section of the MST is in the planning, flagging, and blazing stage. The distance will be more than 13.4 miles, the current distance of the Parkway. Because of the presence of Rattlesnake Mountain, Big Witch, Bunches Bald, and Lickstone Ridge Tunnels, the trail will need special grading to avoid these areas. The final MST route may be partly within the Cherokee Qualla Reservation Boundary. (Call 828-251-6542 for an update.) Meanwhile, you could travel by vehicle on the Blue Ridge Parkway, ride a bicycle on the Parkway's right side, or walk carefully on the left shoulder of the road, facing traffic. (If you are using a vehicle or bicycle, I recommend that you visit the Balsam Mountain Campground [no hook-ups or showers] at the end of Heintooga Ridge Road, a paved 9-mile spur from milepost 458.2. Overlooks are along the way, and the campground has a picnic area, nature trails, and a waterfall at Flat Creek. The Heintooga Ridge Road spur is closed in the winter.)

If you are walking, begin from the Oconaluftee Visitor Center for Great Smoky Mountains National Park, or on the Parkway from the Oconaluftee River Trail at US-441 and cross the Oconaluftee River (elevation 2,020 feet) on the Parkway bridge. (There is a gate here for closing the Parkway in the winter.) On the way you will see a variety of plant species, including oaks, rosebay rhododendron, black locust, basswood, flame azalea, eastern hemlock, ferns, and serviceberry (also called Juneberry, shadbush, and sarvis; see Sarvis Gap ahead). Some of the bird species you would be likely to notice are tanager, warbler, vireo, and Carolina junco.

Pass over a road, ascend, and at 0.7 miles pass Oconaluftee River Overlook, on your left, and two other scenic overlooks—Raven Fork (elevation 2,400 feet) at 1.2 miles and Ballhoot Scar (elevation 2,550 feet) at 1.7 miles. At Ballhoot Scar Overlook are views of Raven Fork, whose horseshoe shape cut into the mountains has left a peak in the center. To the left of the view is Stony Mountain Ridge. (North of this overlook, outside the Parkway boundary, is the border of the 56,000-acre Cherokee Indian reservation, known by the Cherokee as the Qualla Boundary. The property continues on both sides, north and south of the Parkway, to near Docks Gap, a distance of nearly 10 miles.)

At 2.8 miles go through Sherrill Cove Tunnel, and at 3.4 miles is Rattlesnake Mountain Tunnel. Continue ascending and reach Thomas Divide

Overlook, on the left (milepost 464.5, elevation 3,735 feet) at 5.2 miles. From here is a view of the Oconaluftee River Valley, and beyond to the left is a high ridge, Thomas Divide, named for William Thomas (see Section 1, above). At 6.7 miles pass access, on the right, to Barnett Knob (elevation 4,665 feet). (A 0.5-mile hike up the access road to a lookout tower provides exceptional views of the Smokies, north and west, and of the Oconaluftee River valley to the west; to the east is a view of mile-high Bunches Bald, and south are views of Dobson Ridge and Rattlesnake Mountain toward Cherokee.)

Reach Big Witch Overlook (elevation 4,150 feet), on the left, at 7.2 miles. After 0.2 more miles to Big Witch Gap, you will come to an exit to Bunches Creek Road, on your left from the Parkway. (Big Witch [*Tskil-e-gwa* in Cherokee], the highly revered, last of the big eagle hunters, also developed a reputation as an herbal medicine doctor.) After crossing a bridge over the road, continue to ascend, go through Big Witch Tunnel at 7.9 miles, and cross the Parkway for views at Jenkins Ridge Overlook (milepost 460.8, elevation 4,445 feet) at 8.3 miles. Within the next 2.6 miles are two overlooks on the right, Bunches Bald (elevation 4,925 feet) and Lickstone Ridge (elevation 5,150 feet), as well as two tunnels named for the same features. The name Lickstone probably came from rocks on which early settlers placed salt for cattle they grazed on the high ridges.

At 10.9 miles arrive at Wolf Laurel Gap (milepost 458.2, elevation 5,100 feet), at the top of the Balsam Mountains range. To the left is Heintooga Spur Road (which immediately crosses Indian Road). (For the first 3.6 miles the spur road is within the Blue Ridge Parkway boundary, but the next 5.3 miles is in Great Smoky Mountains National Park. It takes you to Balsam Mountain Campground and picnic area [elevation 5,340 feet].) Pass Plott Balsam Overlook on the right (milepost 457.9, elevation 5,045 feet) at 11.2 miles and begin to descend. At milepost 457.6 is Sarvis Gap (also known as Docks Gap). Sarvis is a colloquial name for the serviceberry. The soft white or pale pink flowers of this small tree are harbingers of springtime in the mountains. Reach Jonathan Creek Overlook (milepost 456.2, elevation 4,460 feet), on your left, at 12.9 miles. At 13.4 miles in Soco Gap (milepost 455.7) there is an exit to, and a bridge over, US-19 (elevation 4,340 feet).

DIVERSIONS: The Maggie Valley Opry House in Maggie Valley is a venue for heritage bluegrass and folk music (May through October, telephone: 828-926-9336). Maggie Valley Stampin' Ground hosts regional and national clogging teams nightly, May through October (telephone: 828-926-1288).

CAMPSIDE STORIES: In the folklore and history of Native Americans and early European settlers in Appalachia, there are many stories about both good

Soco Gap

The plans to connect Great Smoky Mountains National Park and Shenandoah National Park with the Blue Ridge Parkway almost failed, and the southern terminus of the parkway would have been at Soco Gap. It took five years of negotiating between state and federal government officials and Cherokee leaders to agree on a right-of-way. In the original planning, North Carolina's senior engineer and claim adjuster for the parkway, R. Getty Browning, had an agreement with the Cherokee for the parkway to descend from Soco Gap and through Soco Valley to end in the town of Cherokee. But after Cherokee Chief Jarrett Blythe learned more about how the route would deny commercial access, he argued his case before a congressional hearing. One of the Cherokee representatives stated that his people did not wish to be reduced to showmen "for entertainment of the rubber-necked tourists."

The New York Times *reported on August 27, 1939, that plans for the "$35 million pleasure boulevard across 500 miles of mountain country in Virginia and North Carolina" had been foiled by the Cherokee who "refused to grant, trade, or sell a right-of-way." The issue ran its course through congressional hearings, the U.S. Department of Interior, the state Department of Transportation, and the Cherokee Indian Council. Near the end of the dilemma, three leaders—Browning, Blythe, and Clyde M. Blair, superintendent of the Cherokee Indian Agency—finally reached a compromise.*

The parkway would follow the current route through the Qualla Boundary for a connection to Great Smoky Mountain National Park north of the town of Cherokee, and a new U.S. highway (us-19, without federal expense) would be built to satisfy the wishes of the Cherokee through reservation property in Soco Valley. The Cherokees would be paid $30 an acre or $40,000, whichever was the larger, for the right-of-way.

and evil spirits haunting people or places. The story of Chief Whiteface, a Cherokee from the vicinity of Ellijay, Georgia, who with thousands of other Cherokee Indians were herded to Oklahoma Territory on the Trail of Tears in 1838–39, is one of these. On leaving, he placed a curse on the land where he had lived and anyone who settled on it. The first owners constructed a mineral springs health lodge. By the turn of the century there had been a number of mysterious deaths and murders on the property. Later the buildings were destroyed by fire, with the exception of one building, which was purchased and moved to Gainesville, Georgia. After years passed, another owner purchased the property to build a cultural and recreational center on former Chief Whiteface's property. In the process of moving the building from Gainesville, the new owner was killed by a flash of lightning.

Another story is about James MacLambert, a Scottish settler who laid claim to a part of Pine Tree Cove and Eaglenest Ridge. The area, southwest of Maggie Valley, was also claimed by the Cherokee Indians who lived along Jonathan Creek. After a Cherokee Indian was killed in an 1836 skirmish with MacLambert and his party of hunters, the Cherokees declared a jinx on all trespassing hunters.

After the Cherokees were removed from this area by the U.S. Army in 1838, MacLambert continued his hunting. In October 1840 he did not return from a hunting trip. A month later his brother Jacob found only a pair of hunting shoes belonging to his brother. Three years later Jacob and a hunting companion went on a hunting trip up the nearby waters of the North Fork of Campbell Creek. They were never seen or heard from again.

SECTION 3. Soco Gap (US-19 and Blue Ridge Parkway MP 455.7) to Balsam Gap (South) (US-23/74 and Blue Ridge Parkway MP 443.1)

JACKSON COUNTY: See Jackson County description in Section 2.

LENGTH AND DIFFICULTY: 12.6 miles (plus), strenuous (change in elevation: 2,450 feet)

USGS TOPO MAPS: Sylva North, Hazelwood

FEATURES AND EMPHASIS: Scenic overlook views of Hornbuckle Valley, Woolyback, Cranberry Ridge, Waterrock Knob, Fork Ridge, Woodfin Cascades

TRAIL CONNECTIONS: Waterrock Knob Trail

WEST TRAILHEAD: See East Trailhead of Section 2 above

EAST TRAILHEAD: Driving from Waynesville or the Parkway exit, go under the Parkway bridge and then 0.3 miles farther (descending because of a center road barrier) to a U-turn, left. Returning 0.2 miles, turn right across Southern Railway tracks at a "No Through Access" sign and Mountains-to-Sea Trail sign. If you are accessing the trailhead from the east end of the Parkway bridge over US-23/74, turn into the paved Parkway maintenance road, but immediately turn right and descend to a parking area on the right. Ahead and to your left near the Southern Railway tracks is the MST sign and white blaze on a telephone pole.

CAMPING, LODGING, AND PROVISIONS: See information in Section 2 for US-19 crossing. In addition, the following are on the north side of the Parkway on US-23/74 from Balsam Gap (South) to Waynesville. The nearest motel, 5.0 miles north on US-23/74, is Best Western Great Smokies Inn in Hazelwood (telephone: 828-497-2020). You can get there by turning right at exit 98, then turn left and go under the US-23/74 bridge; after 0.2 miles turn right to the Inn. (See Chapter 5 for information on other motels and provisions.)

INFORMATION AND SECURITY: Trail Maintenance: Balsam Highlands Task Force (telephone: 828-456-3392). Blue Ridge Parkway: 199 Hemphill Knob Road, Asheville, NC 28804 (telephone: 828-271-4779; for emergencies or accidents, call 800-727-5928). Haywood County Chamber of Commerce: 112 Walnut Street (P.O. Drawer 600), Waynesville, NC 28786 (telephone: 828-456-3021). Balsam Highlands Task Force: (telephone 828-456-3392). Jackson County Sheriff's Office: 330 Keener Street, Sylva, NC 28779 (telephone: 828-586-8901).

DESCRIPTION: The Mountains-to-Sea Trail in Section 3 is currently under construction. All of this section will be on the north side of the Parkway, except about 1.4 miles west from Balsam Gap, where it may take a route both on and off the Parkway because private property is close to the Parkway's south side. Note the location of the proposed MST route on the maps; it may be completed by the time this book is published. (Call 828-456-3392 for an update.) When finished it should be about the same distance as the Parkway. If you are walking or biking, the Parkway continues east from Soco Gap and gradually ascends. Pass Soco Gap Overlook (milepost 455.5), right, at 0.2 miles, and arrive at Fed Cove Overlook (milepost 455.1), right, at 0.6 miles. Across the Parkway is a boxed concrete spring. Reach Thunderstruck Ridge Overlook, right, at 1.3 miles. Below you is Cranberry Creek basin and to your west is Thunderstruck Ridge, most of which is within the Qualla Boundary of the Cherokee Indians. To the southwest is Blackrock Ridge, and to your right is Cranberry Ridge.

Arrive at Hornbuckle Valley Overlook (milepost 453.4, elevation 5,105 feet), right, at 2.3 miles. Both the valley below and Hornbuckle Creek are named for James Hornbuckle, a Cherokee Indian whose family lived here in the nineteenth century. To the right is Cranberry Ridge and to the immediate south is Green Mountain. At milepost 452.7 are patches of flame azaleas that are likely to be blooming in late May. Reach Woolyback Overlook (milepost 452.3, elevation 5,420 feet), right, at 3.4 miles. To the right is a ridge covered with rhododendron and mountain laurel. Only 0.2 miles ahead is Cranberry Ridge Overlook (elevation 5,475 feet). Here you are looking down the gorge of a stream that feeds Hornbuckle Creek. Beyond it, to the northwest, is Cranberry Ridge.

Continue to ascend. At 4.5 miles you have arrived at Waterrock Knob Overlook (milepost 451.2, elevation 5,820 feet). From this exceptional point on the Blue Ridge Parkway you can access the Waterrock Knob Trail, a 1.1-mile round-trip path to the summit of Waterrock Knob (elevation 6,292 feet). (When the MST is completed in this area the trail will connect with the Waterrock Knob Trail.) About halfway up the trail is a spring that, like the trail, is the highest of any on the entire Parkway. The refreshing fragrance on this peak comes from the fir and spruce trees growing there. Other plants you will see are gooseberry, bush honeysuckle, meadow parsnip, turtlehead, and mountain lettuce. The panoramic views are the most outstanding since leaving Clingmans Dome. The Plott Balsams are to the southwest and the Great Balsam Mountain range is to the southeast, both in Nantahala National Forest. To the north, across Maggie Valley, is the Cataloochee Divide and other ranges in the Smokies. Northeast, across the Pigeon River Valley, is Newfound Mountain, and more to the east is Pisgah National Forest. Directly and most immediately to the east is Browning Knob. Beyond it is Mount Lyn Lowry, a privately owned mountain with a lighted sixty-foot-high steel cross. A sign bears the inscription, "in loving memory of Lyn Lowry, a saint in heaven." Lieutenant General and Mrs. Sumter Lowry had the cross erected in 1964 to honor their daughter who died of leukemia at age fifteen.

From Waterrock Knob pass Yellow Face Overlook (milepost 450, elevation 5,588 feet) at 5.7 miles. There is a scenic view of Narrows Cove below and Yellow Face summit (elevation 6,032 feet), with its yellowish rock, in the Plott Balsams mountain range to the southwest. Fork Ridge Overlook (milepost 449, elevation 5,280 feet), at 6.7 miles, offers views into Scott Creek Valley between Fork Ridge and Cutoff Ridge. Behind you are rock faces of gneiss with granite veins. This type of rock is also visible at other places on the Parkway.

Continue to descend and pass Scott Creek Overlook, on the right at 7.2 miles, where you may take in western views of Fork Ridge, and Wesner Bald Overlook (milepost 448.1, elevation 4,912 feet), at 7.6 miles. At 9.0 miles, on the right, is Woodfin Cascades Overlook (milepost 446.7, elevation 4,535 feet). Woodfin Creek flows under the Parkway here. Woodfin Valley Overlook (milepost 446) is ahead at 9.7 miles. Jones Knob Overlook, right, is at milepost 445.2, and from here, if you look northwest, you may see Mount Lyn Lowry. The last overlook on this section is at 11.1 miles; the Orchards Overlook (milepost 444.6, elevation 3,810 feet) is the only overlook on the left. At 12.2 miles is an access road to the left to US-23/74. (It is 0.5 miles to US-23/74, where it is 5 miles left and down the mountain to Hazelwood and 7 miles to Waynesville. A right onto US-23/74 leads 12 miles down the mountain to Sylva.) Continue on the Parkway, which after 0.4 miles crosses US-23/74 and the Southern Railroad tracks. After a few yards turn right off the Parkway on an access drive to Parkway maintenance buildings, but then turn right and down to a parking space near the railroad tracks. Continue a few more yards on the narrow but paved road to a telephone pole, where there is a white dot, a Mountains-to-Sea Trail sign, and a sign saying "No

H. Getty Browning

A plaque at Waterrock Knob honors H. Getty Browning (1881–1966), the North Carolina Highway Commission's claim engineer and advisor for the Blue Ridge Parkway. Without Browning's energy, leadership, and political finesse, the parkway might not be here but in Tennessee, instead. After the parkway project was authorized in 1933, a decision had to be made on its name and its route (it was listed as "Park to Park Highway" or "Appalachian Park to Park Highway" on previous planning maps).

Governor Hill McAlister, the legislature, and citizens of Tennessee expected to have a fair share of the parkway on its route south of Virginia. Tennessee's plan would have the parkway turn west at Linville, cross into Tennessee north of Erwin, and end in Gatlinburg. As for prior history of a parkway plan, North Carolina had the advantage. As early as 1909, Joseph Hyde Pratt, head of the North Carolina Geological and Economic Survey, had proposed a recreational road (similar to the current parkway) called "The Crest of the Blue Ridge Highway." In his plans he wrote that "it will make the ride over this highway one never to be forgotten." His design would have the road end near Tullulah Falls and Cornelia in Georgia.

Both Asheville and Knoxville city governments campaigned for the parkway's proximity. Even mayors from out of state (from Charleston, South Carolina, and Saint Petersburg, Florida) crusaded for the through-Asheville plan. In Asheville the chief spokesman was Fred L. Weede, manager of the Asheville Chamber of Commerce. Browning worked diligently between Asheville, Raleigh, and Washington, D.C.

When Secretary of the Interior Harold Ickes called for the final meeting in Washington on September 18, 1934, Browning was there with North Carolina governor J. C. B. Ehringhaus and a well-trained delegation. Governor Hill McAlister of Tennessee was likewise represented. Browning's goal was that the parkway should take the most scenic route; he presented a colorful diorama of the projected location to prove his argument. On November 10, 1934, Secretary Ickes notified the governors that Browning's plan by Asheville had been approved.

Through Traffic." This is the trail entrance to MST Section 4, also maintained by the Balsam Highlands Task Force.

CAMPSIDE STORIES: North of Balsam Gap and Waynesville on US-23/74, and west on US-276 to the junction with US-19 west of Lake Junaluska, is one of seven official highway markers recognizing a man who for thirty-six years traveled 270,000 miles by horseback and on foot. There is another marker farther north on US-276 to I-40 at Cove Creek. Both markers honor his name and the ancient Indian path, Cataloochee Trail. Among his horses he favored the names of Jane and Little Fox. Sometimes he walked beside his horse at four miles an hour. Occasionally he had a wagon or carriage, but most of his seventy-two rides across the state were on horseback. He rode in other states, from Maine to Georgia, and over the Appalachian Mountains to the Ohio Valley.

The man was born in Handsworth, England, in 1745 and began his travels throughout the colonies in 1771. His first circuit rides in North Carolina were in 1780. He was about five feet and nine inches tall and weighed about 150 pounds, and he usually wore gray clothes and a broad-brimmed hat. A leader by nature, he was indefatigable and made friends for moral goodness wherever he went. On some of his journeys he was accompanied by Henry Hill, John Wesley Bond, or others. He slept on mountain tops, beside rivers and creeks, in sheds, barns, private homes, and chapels. A diary of his travels reveals his times of hunger, lack of maps, and the times of suffering from ice and snow, fevers and disease. He preached 16,425 sermons, presided over 224 conferences, and ordained at least 4,000 preachers. By now you probably know that this ecclesiastical statesman, "The Prophet of the Long Road," was American Methodism's Bishop Francis Asbury (1745–1816).

 **THREE**

NANTAHALA NATIONAL FOREST
(HIGHLANDS RANGER DISTRICT)

The Nantahala National Forest was established in 1920, and with 526,061 acres, it is the state's largest national forest. It has four districts: Cheoah (120,110 acres), with boundaries to the Smokies, the Tennessee state line, and the Fontana Lake area; Highlands (113,000 acres), bounded on the north by the Blue Ridge Parkway, on the south by the South Carolina and Georgia state lines, and on the west by the Watauga District; Tusquittee (158,348 acres), the westernmost district, bordering on Tennessee's Cherokee National Forest and Georgia's Chattahoochee National Forest; and Watauga (133,894 acres), which adjoins the west side of the Highlands District. *Nantahala* is a Cherokee word meaning "land of the noonday sun."

All of this immense forest, harboring tracts of evergreens and hardwoods, numerous waterfalls in deep gorges, mountain peaks, rubies and sapphires, rare orchids, and roaming bears, was home to the Cherokee Indian Nation before Europeans claimed it for themselves. By the nineteenth century the Cherokee's domain from Virginia to Alabama was being assimilated, as was their culture. The relationship between the Cherokee and the settlers was one of both allies and enemies. For example, the Cherokee, with their famed Chief Junaluska, joined the troops led by General Andrew Jackson to fight against the Creek Indians at the Battle of Horseshoe Bend in 1814. Chief Junaluska said later that "if I had known that Jackson [U.S. president, 1829–37] would drive us from our homes, I would have killed him that day at the Horseshoe." Although the Supreme Court ruled in favor of protecting the rights of Native Americans in Georgia, President Jackson and his successor, Martin Van Buren, supported the removal of approximately 15,000 Cherokees to an area now known as Oklahoma in the winter of 1838–39. The march is remembered as the "Trail of Tears" because of the many who perished on the way. An estimated 1,000 Cherokees fled to the rugged coves of the mountains. (See the story of Tsali, described in Chapter 1.)

There are 29,138 acres in three tracts of wilderness in the Nantahala forest, plus the 3,800 acres in the sanctuary of the Joyce Kilmer Memorial Forest. The latter is a spectacular grove of tulip trees, unlike any of its kind. Also within the national forest's acreage are the valuable 40,000 acres in Jackson County named the Roy Taylor Forest, in honor of a congressman who led the efforts for its purchase in 1981. A more recent purchase, in 1988, was the 6,295-acre Panthertown Valley tract. This national natural landmark, with its upland bogs, bare-rock mountainsides, rare botanical sites, waterfalls and sculptured rocks, and trail network, was made possible by congressional help and the wisdom of The Nature Conservancy.

For a number of years some environmentalists have been opposed to timber harvesting in the Nantahala and other national forests. A chance finding of a cluster of endangered Indiana bats in the summer of 1999 in Macon County supported their cause. On August 3, 1999, the U.S. Forest Service in North Carolina temporarily suspended timber cutting in Cherokee, Swain, Graham, and Macon Counties. John Ramey, forest supervisor, stated that more research was necessary before a permanent decision could be made, but Andrew George, executive director of the Southern Appalachian Biodiversity Project in Asheville, stated that commercial logging in public forests should end, both in the Nantahala and Pisgah National Forests. The Indiana bat is about two inches long and has a wingspan of one foot. It has been on the nation's endangered species list since 1967. On September 8, 1999, the U.S. Forest Service restored timber cutting in about half of the area, mainly in Macon and Graham Counties.

Commercial timber companies considered the suspension of logging another economic setback. Earlier in the year, on February 11, 1999, the U.S. government suspended construction of new logging roads, an issue that had been debated by Congress for a year. The moratorium affected thirty-nine places with a total of 173,000 acres in North Carolina. Nationwide it affected 33 million acres. It is estimated that the entire U.S. National Forest System has a total of 400,000 miles of roads.

SECTION 4. Balsam Gap (South) (Blue Ridge Parkway MP 443.1 and US-23/74) to Bear Pen Gap (Blue Ridge Parkway MP 427.6)

JACKSON COUNTY: See Jackson County discussion in Section 2.
LENGTH AND DIFFICULTY: 24.2 miles, strenuous (change in elevation: 2,245 feet)
USGS TOPO MAPS: Hazelwood, Tuckasegee, Sam Knob
FEATURES OR EMPHASIS: Wildlife, wildflowers, solitude, Richland Balsam Overlook

TRAIL CONNECTION: West Camp Gap Trail

WEST TRAILHEAD: There are two Balsam Gaps on the Blue Ridge Parkway. The southern one is here, and the northern one is in MST Section 9 at milepost 359.8. (Here is also a significant crossing of trails: the Mountains-to-Sea Trail [hiking] and the Mountains-to-Sea Bicycle Route #2 from Murphy to Manteo. To the southwest from here the bicycle route is on US-23/74, to US-64, on which it goes to Murphy, its western terminus. On its way east it follows the Blue Ridge Parkway for 119 miles, then joins NC-181 at Jonas Ridge. About 5 miles down the mountain on NC-181 it crosses the hiking MST. It crosses the MST again at the Falls Lake Trail in north Raleigh. Near Wake Forest the hiking MST joins the bicycle route and follows it to the edge of Wilson.)

To reach Balsam Gap (south), drive 8 miles south of Waynesville on US-23/74, or 12 miles north from Sylva. Turn east in the gap off the highway on the nearest driveway at the south side of the Parkway overpass. Cross the railroad, turn left, and park near the railroad in a grassy area. (See trailhead description in Section 3, above.)

EAST TRAILHEAD: Bear Pen Gap Overlook on the Blue Ridge Parkway (milepost 427.6)

CAMPING, LODGING, AND PROVISIONS: No-trace camping is allowed off of the Mountains-to-Sea Trail in the Nantahala National Forest. (Camping is prohibited within the Blue Ridge Parkway corridor except at specified campgrounds.) The nearest lodging is 5.0 miles down the mountain to Hazelwood on US-23/74. Turn off right at exit 98, turn left under a US-23/74 bridge, and after 0.2 miles turn right to Best Western Great Smokies Inn (telephone: 828-497-2020). The nearest restaurant is Clyde's: on exit 98 turn right to take US-23 Business, and at 0.1 miles turn left from an Exxon Gas and Groceries; Clyde's Restaurant is on the right (open Tuesday–Sunday 6 A.M. to 10 P.M., closed Monday; telephone: 828-456-9135). Ahead 0.4 miles is a shopping center with groceries, restaurants, and pharmacy. Downtown Waynesville, 2.0 miles ahead, has more motels and restaurants toward the US-23/74 expressway.

INFORMATION AND SECURITY: Trail Maintenance: Balsam Highlands Task Force (telephone: 828-456-3392). Blue Ridge Parkway: 119 Hemphill Knob Road, Asheville, NC 28803 (telephone: 828-271-4779; for emergencies or accidents call 800-727-5928). Haywood County Chamber of Commerce: 112 Walnut Street (P.O. Drawer 600), Waynesville, NC 28786 (telephone: 828-456-3021). Jackson County Sheriff's Office: 330 Keener Street, Sylva, NC 28779 (telephone: 828-586-8901).

DESCRIPTION: From the grassy/gravel area where you parked, walk on the narrow paved road to its exit at the railroad crossing. On a telephone pole are both a white dot blaze and a Mountains-to-Sea Trail sign. The MST entrance is beyond the telephone pole, among wild roses and a honey locust tree; it takes you into a forest with a dense understory. Cross a footbridge at 0.1 miles before two switchbacks. Cross a ridge and descend to a series of small stream crossings, all flowing north toward the Parkway. Pass near the Parkway boundary and right of an old home site foundation at 1.3 miles. At 1.4 miles cross Hood Road and a stream before ascending on seven switchbacks. (Water sources are scarce for the next 11 miles.) Cross Red Bank Road at 2.4 miles. (There is an access point here, left [north], to the Parkway; to the right is a rock overlook.) Cross Redbank Creek at 2.5 miles, then ascend eight switchbacks. Along the way, in dense vegetation, are logs bearing shelf fungi and rock tripe. After 3.1 miles is a refreshing view, to the left, of a Parkway overlook below and Waynesville in the valley.

Wildflowers are prominent throughout this section of the trail, and at 3.7 miles you can see Dutchman's pipe, a perennial vine with heart-shaped leaves. Cross a number of spur ridges to Grassy Bald, one of which is called Pinnacle Ridge, where unseen to the left is the Parkway's Pinnacle Ridge Tunnel. Arrive at a small clearing (elevation 4,920 feet) at 5.6 miles. Views of the Parkway are to the southwest, and peaks to the south are visible to the right. Wild quinine, a perennial not commonly seen in the high mountains, grows here. Among the wild animals in this area are black bear, deer, and raccoon. Birds include owl, wild turkey, Carolina towhee, and black-billed cuckoo.

Ascend four switchbacks and gradually climb through a yellow birch forest to a rocky area (elevation 5,400 feet) at 7.4 miles. Pass patches of fragrant trailing arbutus and pungent galax at 7.9 miles. At 8.2 miles approach a grassy ridge with a spur trail to the left for northeast views. For the next 1.1 miles are scattered flame azalea, bluebead lily, and wood sorrel among hardwoods and conifers. At 9.3 miles arrive at Licklog Gap (elevation 5,135 feet). The gap is named for boxes, hewed in logs by herders, in which salt was set for cattle grazing on the mountain pastureland. Ascend and reach a Parkway overlook (milepost 435.3) at 10 miles. (A spur trail runs left 145 feet to the south end of the overlook parking lot, from which Doubletop Mountain can be seen.) Continue among chestnut oaks, Indian snakeroot, and yellow birch to Old Bald Ridge at 11.2 miles. (The above segment of this section of the Mountains-to-Sea Trail was designated a state trail by the N.C. Division of Parks and Recreation in September 1992.) A spur trail on the left goes 0.1 miles to a curve in the Parkway at milepost 434.2.

*View of Great Balsam Mountain
range from Waterrock Knob*

On the MST turn right, follow an old road on Old Bald Ridge into Nantahala National Forest property (where hikers are allowed to camp), and descend. At 11.8 miles turn sharply left at an old road junction. After 0.2 miles leave the roadbed (watch for the trail's white-dot blaze) and hike along a grassy mountainside where there are blueberry patches, evergreens, and wildflowers. To the south and southwest are scenic views of the Tuckasegee River Valley and Great Balsam Mountains. At 12.3 miles turn left onto an old roadbed. Leave the footpath at 13 miles. Turn left on an old roadbed into an open forest with fern carpets. Descend among large chestnut oaks. At 13.5 miles turn sharply left. For the next 0.4 miles you will cross a number of streamlets and make right turns on two old roadbeds.

At 14.5 miles leave the old roadbed and enter a footpath through wildflowers and scattered elephant plant, elm, and rhododendron in a cove. Ascend four switchbacks. At 15.4 miles ascend two switchbacks. For the next 0.5 miles you will walk through a rocky, damp section of trail with a rough treadway in a botanical paradise. Exit the footpath to an old road at

16.1 miles. Take a left turn over a tank trap at 16.4 miles. (Here and else-where for the next 8.5 miles may be horse and bicycle traffic. You may hear all-terrain vehicles [ATVs] in the distance, usually to the right.) Pass some natural campsites along the way and notice deer tracks near the streams. Keep right at a road fork. Cross a small stream, the headwaters of Beechflat Creek at 16.7 miles, Chestnut Creek at 17.9 miles, and Bearwallow Creek at 19.3 miles. At 19.8 miles begin a descent on a series of switchbacks to a junction with a Nantahala National Forest road, on the right, at 20.3 miles. Cohosh (both black and blue) and other wildflowers such as baneberry, are on the trail for the next 0.4 miles. Deer, wild turkey, and squirrels are in the area. Cross Birch Ridge Creek at 21.1 miles and Piney Mountain Creek at 22 miles. (Here, to the left, is an abandoned road that ascends steeply to the Parkway.)

For the next 1.8 miles the trail is on a generally even contour with ten streamlets flowing right (southwest or west) to Piney Mountain Creek. At 23.4 miles the trail crosses other woods roads, but stay left and ascend steeply to a juncture with the West Camp Gap Trail, right and left, at 24.2 miles. (The last 13-mile segment of the MST in this area was designated a state trail in August 1994.) The Mountains-to-Sea Trail continues to the right along this part of the West Camp Gap Trail. To the left, it is 0.6 miles to the Bear Pen Gap Overlook on the Parkway at milepost 427.6 (elevation 5,560 feet). On the Parkway it is 7.7 miles back to Doubletop Overlook, if you are arranging a shuttle for this MST segment, and it is another 7.8 miles to Balsam Gap (South), where this section began.

CAMPSIDE STORIES: Stories about the legend of Bigfoot or Sasquatch have circu-lated for many centuries and in many parts of the world. When I was a boy I heard these stories on camping trips. When I saw black bear tracks I thought of reports about Sasquatch protecting Native American tribes. In July 1993 one of my large-footed hiking friends noticed a large shoe print in the mud alongside tracks made by ATVs south of West Camp Gap Trail. When he placed his size-17 foot in the depression, it appeared that the print was made by a size-20 shoe. This incident started a discussion on Sasquatch. (The average size of a Bigfoot's footprint is 16 inches long.)

Sasquatch, according to Native American stories, was a tall, hairy, apelike creature who roamed the forests barefooted, usually at night. To some tribes he (always referred to as masculine) was a protector, though others claimed that he kidnapped children. The trail tales of his sightings are not only told by residents of North American mountains and swamps. A similar creature has been seen elsewhere in the world. In Russia the beastlike Bigfoot is called Almas. In the high Himalayan Mountains, particularly in the nineteenth century, he was known as the Abominable Snowman or Yeti. A few zoologists have studied the possibility of existence of this crypto-being. Their questions relate to fossils of the Gigantopithecus, a giant primate from the Pleistocene Era found in China.

Seven years after we saw the large shoe print, one of my students on a group camping trip said that Bigfoot was a hoax, "just like flying saucers." Flying saucers? Had he seen a report by Yankelovich Partners for *Life Magazine* in *USA Today*, February 16, 2000? Forty-three percent of Americans believe flying saucers (UFOs—unidentified flying objects) are real; 49 percent believe the U.S. government is withholding information; and 6 percent stated they had personally seen a UFO. And where are the barefooted Bigfoots to be found? Jeff Harris of the *Raleigh News and Observer*, on February 29, 2000, had a caricatured crustacean remark that the best place to find a big foot is in a big shoe.

 **FOUR**

PISGAH NATIONAL FOREST
(PISGAH RANGER DISTRICT)

Pisgah National Forest has four ranger districts and encompasses a total of 495,979 acres. To get a general idea of the vastness of these high and scenic mountains, cliffs and caves, rivers and waterfalls, you can examine the large green borders on the official North Carolina Transportation Map (free on request at interstate highway visitor centers or by calling 919-733-7600; outside the state call 800-VISITNC). If you are using a topographic map you may notice not only the irregularities of the national forest's borders, but also the fragmentation and interspersed tracts of private property (commonly referred to as inholdings).

Adjoining Tennessee's Cherokee National Forest are the French Broad Ranger District (80,335 acres) north of I-40, and the Toecane Ranger District (76,640 acres) north and west of Boone. The largest and easternmost portion of the national forest is the Grandfather Ranger District with 186,735 acres. South of Asheville and reaching to the South Carolina border and adjoining the Nantahala National Forest to the west is the Pisgah Ranger District (156,103 acres), the most visited of any of the four districts.

The Pisgah Ranger District is home to the Cradle of Forestry in America, a 6,500-acre historic site. The birthplace of American scientific forestry, it receives approximately five million visitors annually. The MST passes through the Pisgah, Grandfather, and Toecane Districts, but weaves in and out as a result of its crossing or following the Blue Ridge Parkway. Sections 5, 6, and 7 of this book are in the Pisgah Ranger District (except the part of Section 5 from West Camp Gap to Haywood Gap at the Blue Ridge Parkway, which is 2.3 miles in the Highlands Ranger District of Nantahala National Forest).

More than 300 miles of the MST fall within the Pisgah District's network of trails. Some are multi-use trails, while others are only for hiking or for biking. There are miles of old roads for equestrians and sections set aside for ATV use. Other than the MST itself, the 30-mile Art Loeb hiking trail is the longest trail. There is also an alternate MST (AMST) that descends into the Davidson River

Valley to make a 43-mile loop with the MST. It is described in this section. The Pisgah Ranger District also has three wilderness areas with a total of 37,375 acres.

SECTION 5. Bear Pen Gap (Blue Ridge Parkway MP 427.6) to NC-215 (Blue Ridge Parkway MP 423.2)

JACKSON AND HAYWOOD COUNTIES: (See Section 2 for Jackson County discussion.) Haywood County, 544 square miles, borders Cocke County in Tennessee. A section of Great Smoky Mountains National Park and the Appalachian Trail fall into the western part of this county. In the south, east, and north are large sections of Pisgah National Forest, including Middle Prong Wilderness and Shining Rock Wilderness. The Blue Ridge Parkway follows a southern and eastern high mountain rim. The Pigeon River is the county's most publicized river for pollution problems.

Haywood County is named in honor of John Haywood (1755–1827), state treasurer from 1787 to 1827. In 1808 the county was formed from part of Buncombe County. Waynesville, the county seat, was settled at the turn of the nineteenth century and incorporated in 1810. Its name was presented by Colonel Robert Love (1760–1845), a prominent landholder, to honor General Anthony Wayne of the Revolutionary War, with whom he had served. The adjoining town of Hazelwood was incorporated into Waynesville in 1953. A nearby town and lake, Lake Junaluska, is well-known for its United Methodist Conference Center. The county's east-west highway arteries are I-40, US-19/23, US-23/74, and US-74, and the south-north routes are US-276, NC-215, and NC-209.

LENGTH AND DIFFICULTY: 8.5 miles, easy to moderate

USGS TOPO MAP: Sam Knob

FEATURES OR EMPHASIS: Blueberries, wildlife, wildflowers

TRAILS FOLLOWED: West Camp Gap Trail, Buckeye Gap Trail

TRAIL CONNECTIONS: Haywood Gap Trail

WEST TRAILHEAD: Bear Pen Gap Overlook (elevation 5,560 feet) on the Blue Ridge Parkway at milepost 427.6 miles. Enter the forest on the West Camp Gap Trail at the southeast corner of the overlook parking lot.

EAST TRAILHEAD: On NC-215, 0.5 miles west of the Blue Ridge Parkway at Beech Gap, milepost 423.2

CAMPING, LODGING, AND PROVISIONS: Self-chosen camping in grassy field at West Camp Gap in Nantahala National Forest, and into Pisgah National Forest 0.2 miles after Buckeye Gap at milepost 425.5 on the Parkway.

INFORMATION AND SECURITY: Trail Maintenance: Balsam Highlands Task Force (telephone: 828-456-3392). Blue Ridge Parkway: 199 Hemphill Knob Road, Asheville, NC 28803 (telephone: 828-271-4779; for emergencies and accidents, call 800-727-5928). Haywood County Chamber of Commerce: 112 Walnut Street (P.O. Drawer 600), Waynesville, NC 28786 (telephone: 828-456-3021). Jackson County Sheriff's Office: 330 Keener Street, Sylva, NC 28779 (telephone: 828-586-8901). Haywood County Sheriff's Office: Courthouse Annex, 215 North Main Street, Waynesville, NC 28786 (telephone: 828-452-6666).

DESCRIPTION: This section of the Mountains-to-Sea Trail is unique because it stays one mile high in elevation for the entire distance. It is also the only section where the MST passes from Nantahala National Forest to Pisgah National Forest across the Blue Ridge Parkway. From the parking lot descend on an old road. After 0.1 miles enter Nantahala National Forest. Cross a streamlet at 0.4 miles by a grove of yellow birches, and join with the Mountains-to-Sea Trail, right and left, at 0.6 miles. (The right access is described in Section 4 above, and the mileage count for this section begins here.) Continue ahead, following jointly with the West Camp Gap Trail for an ascent on an eroded dirt road (used by ATVs). After 0.6 miles arrive at a scenic open area, the end of West Camp Gap Trail, and take an abrupt left turn off from the old road, near a rock, for the MST. (To the right is an old road in a large grassy plateau, excellent for campsites. Deer, turkey, and songbirds frequent the area.)

From the rock, pass through goldenrods and asters and after 110 feet reenter the woods. You will begin to ascend the east side of Rough Butt Bald (elevation 5,925 feet) on switchbacks at 1.0 mile. Wildflowers are prominent, particularly in autumn. At 1.4 miles enter a berry field: blueberry, blackberry, strawberry, and gooseberry. On the airy slope are ferns, gentians, fly poison, songbirds, butterflies, and honeybees. Continue among red spruce, hardwoods, and rhododendron to Haywood Gap (elevation 5,225 feet) of the Blue Ridge Parkway (milepost 426.5) at 2.3 miles.

Cross the Parkway and enter a thick mint patch, where the Haywood Gap Trail enters from the left after 185 feet. (A descent of 0.2 miles on the Haywood Gap Trail and into Pisgah National Forest leads to a spring known as Sweetwater Spring. The 5.8-mile trail descends through the obscure and adventurous Middle Prong Wilderness to exit at Sunburst Recreation Area on NC-215.) Continuing on the MST, the pathway follows a handcrafted footpath through a beautiful forest of red spruce, birch, maple, rhododendron, and wood sorrel. There are rocks, moss beds, and springs along the way. Curve around Parker Knob and an unnamed knob. At 4.1 miles reach Buckeye Gap and cross the Buckeye Gap Trail (to the right is Buckeye Gap on the Parkway at milepost 425.5). Turn left on an old railroad grade. (Up the bank, right, it is 260 yards to Rough Butt Bald Overlook access, Parkway milepost 425.4.) Continue on the old railroad grade; from here to NC-215 you will be on Pisgah National Forest property, where camping is allowed.

Make a sharp right at 4.8 miles among red spruce, yellow birch, turtlehead, and ferns. At 5.1 miles cross Buckeye Creek, which cascades left. Go 75 yards to a sharp right turn off the Buckeye Gap Trail and up the bank. (The Buckeye Gap Trail continues on the old railroad grade, where you may see old railroad artifacts, before descending to juncture with the Haywood Gap Trail in the Middle Prong Wilderness.) Continuing on the MST, ascend to enter an open area of blueberry and blackberry patches. (You may see a spur trail, left, that ascends 0.2 miles to a campsite on Fork Ridge.) At 5.6 miles cross the headwaters of Buckeye Creek. Ferns, birches, and rhododendrons are prominent here. An old trail comes in from the right at 5.8 miles; keep left and descend easily. Leave the foot trail at 6.5 miles and follow an old railroad grade. At 6.7 miles are views of Beech Gap ahead, Mount Hardy to the right, and more blackberry patches on the trailside. After another 0.2 miles there are views to the left of large cliffs on Fork Ridge. Cross a ravine at 7.1 miles and follow to the right of an old railroad grade, but then rejoin it after 0.2 miles. Turn left sharply to follow another old railroad grade.

Arrive at the confluence of streams in a rocky streambed at 7.5 miles. Rock-hop and enter an area of rhododendron and fetterbush. Follow an old railroad grade to a grazing field. At 8.1 miles reenter the woods, pass a spring on the right, and follow an old road. Turn right off the old road, and within 0.1 miles rock-hop the cascading Bubbling Spring Branch. Pass a Middle Prong Wilderness sign. After 60 yards you will ascend to NC-215 at 8.5 miles. The MST continues across the road and up an embankment. (A parking area is 200 feet up the road on the right, and it is 0.5 miles farther to the Blue Ridge Parkway in Beech Gap. From here it is 4.4 miles back on the Parkway to Bearpen Gap Overlook parking area.) Section 5 of the Mountains-to-Sea Trail was designated a state trail in May 1987. Cross the road to continue.

CAMPSIDE STORIES: This section of trail is one of my favorites. I have been here many times, for designation ceremonies, camping, exploring, and berry-picking. Photographs show Jim Hallsey of the state Division of Parks and Recreation picking berries with us. Alan Householder, on hiking across the state, came through on this trail after I had hiked it. He was alone and one of those fierce high mountain storms found him. He wrote: "Huge thunderstorm hit me at Rough Butt Bald. Dry inside my tent, I felt as if my tent was being run through a car wash." I know the feeling. That storm was looking for me and found another Alan. Years earlier Darin Matthews and I were exploring Middle Prong at the base of Beartrap Ridge. When we stopped to rest, we saw an adult bear on a large rock watching us. We passed without incident. Two years later, in 1986, Cecil Parker was with me on the unmaintained Haywood Gap Trail near Beartrap Branch. We surprised two large bears near the stream and were also surprised when they did not run. We moved on but carefully observed them when they followed us for about 0.2 miles.

I thought of Israel ("Wid") Medford, Haywood County's legendary "master hunter of the Balsam Range," whose bear tales were first published (*In the Heart of the Alleghanies*) in the nineteenth century. Wid's stories were enriched by his accent and vocabulary. On one of his bear hunts with his brother El, Bill Massey, and Bill Allen, he described how he had to "brogue" (meaning climb) through a laurel thicket to reach an open forest where the dogs has roused a "bar."

"I seed the bar comin' on a dog trot under the trees. He war a master brute, four hundred and fifty pounds net. . . . I brought my old flint lock to my shoulder . . . and fired. The brute never stopped, but I knowed I'd hit him. . . . As he brashed by me I lent over him grabbin' the ha'r o' his neck with one hand and staubed him in the side with a knife with my other hand. . . . Hit lay dead by the branch staubed clean through the heart."

SECTION 6. Beech Gap, NC-215 (Blue Ridge Parkway MP 423.2) to Mount Pisgah Inn (Blue Ridge Parkway MP 408.6)

HAYWOOD AND TRANSYLVANIA COUNTIES: (See Section 5 for discussion of Haywood County.) Transylvania County, incorporated in 1861, received its name as a combination of Latin words for "across the woods." It was formed from parts of Jackson and Henderson Counties and is highly publicized as the "land of waterfalls." Nantahala National Forest is in the western corner of the county, and Pisgah National Forest has a large area in the northern part of the county. Brevard, the county's largest town, is the county seat. Incorporated in 1889, the town was named for Ephriam Brevard (1744–81), a Revolutionary War surgeon, teacher, and political leader. The town is home to Brevard College, founded in 1853 (and formerly called Rutherford College).

Transylvania County is bordered on the south by Oconee and Pickens

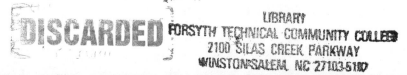

Counties, South Carolina, and on the north by the rim of mountains traversed by the Blue Ridge Parkway. The county is famous for its major waterfalls and scenic beauty. North Carolina's newest state park will be located in a combination of wild and spectacular gorges north of Lake Jocassee. The news media has suggested the new park be called "Gorgeous Gorges." Among the county's scenic and historical areas are The Cradle of Forestry in America, Looking Glass Rock, and the 400-foot Whitewater Falls. The county's major access roads are the east-west running US-64 and US-276 (that also partly serve a north-south route), and the north-south running NC-215, NC-280, and NC-281.

LENGTH AND DIFFICULTY: Mainline (MST) route (white blaze) 21.4 miles, strenuous; alternate (AMST) route (blue blaze) 37.8 miles, strenuous (change in elevation: 3,835 feet).

USGS TOPO MAPS: Sam Knob, Pisgah Forest, Shining Rock, Cruso

FEATURES OR EMPHASIS: Devil's Courthouse, Pilot Mountain, Davidson River, Pink Beds, Yellowstone Falls, botanical diversity

TRAILS FOLLOWED: Art Loeb Trail, Sycamore Cove Trail, Black Mountain Trail, Buck Spring Trail

TRAIL CONNECTIONS: Little Sam Knob Trail, Devil's Courthouse Spur Trail, Farlow Gap Trail, Butter Gap Trail, Cat Gap Loop Trail, North Slope Connector Trail, Grass Road Trail, Thrift Cove Trail, Pressley Cove Trail, Turkey Pen Gap Trail, Pink Beds Loop Trail, Graveyard Ridge Trail, Graveyard Trail

WEST TRAILHEAD: From Blue Ridge Parkway milepost 423.2, turn northwest on NC-215 and descend 0.5 miles to a parking area, on the left, and walk 200 feet to a trailhead on the right.

EAST TRAILHEAD: Pisgah Inn parking area at Blue Ridge Parkway milepost 408.6

CAMPING, LODGING, AND PROVISIONS: If you are taking the white-blazed mainline MST, be aware that there are not any campgrounds, shelters, or food services available on this route. Observe boundary lines to select no-trace camping outside the Blue Ridge Parkway in Pisgah National Forest. At the east trailhead is the fifty-two-room Pisgah Inn and Restaurant (telephone: 828-235-8228), which is usually open from April 1 to November 1. Its location provides outstanding views of the Mill River valley and Black Mountain beyond. The Mount Pisgah Campground is open from May 1 to November 1, but there are no hook-ups. A gasoline station and gift shop are also here.

If you are following sections of the AMST (blue blazes), you have three shelter options—two on the Art Loeb Trail and one on the Black Mountain Trail—as well as the Davidson River Campground. (Camping is not allowed at the Davidson River swinging bridge area.) The large seasonal campground has full service from April 1 through November, with hot showers and outdoor telephone, but no hook-ups. The campground (reduced service) is free from December through March. The telephone, in season, is 828-877-4910/862-5960. East on US-276 for 1.2 miles is a juncture of US-64 with NC-280. Here is a shopping center, motel, groceries, and restaurant. On US-64/276 south toward the town of Brevard at 2.2 miles is V&A Wash House Laundromat (corner of Osborne Road), which has hot showers for hikers all year (8 A.M. to 8 P.M. daily; 9 A.M. to 6 P.M. on Sunday; telephone: 828-884-9358).

INFORMATION AND SECURITY: Trail Maintenance: South Pisgah Task Force of the Carolina Mountain Club (telephone: 828-693-3979). Blue Ridge Parkway: 199 Hemphill Knob Road, Asheville, NC 28803 (telephone: 828-271-4779; for emergencies and accidents, call 800-727-5928). Pisgah National Forest: Pisgah District Ranger, 1001 Pisgah Highway, Pisgah Forest, NC 28768 (telephone: 828-877-3350). Brevard-Transylvania County Chamber of Commerce: 35 West Main Street (P.O. Box 589), Brevard, NC 28712 (telephone: 828-883-3700). Pisgah Task Force of Carolina Mountain Club: 156-A Campbell Drive, Pisgah Forest, NC 28768 (telephone: 828-693-3979). Haywood County Sheriff's Office: Courthouse Annex, 215 North Main Street, Waynesville, NC 28786 (telephone: 828-452-6666); Transylvania County Sheriff's Office: 201 East Morgan Street, Brevard, NC 28712 (telephone: 828-884-3168).

DESCRIPTION: This section has two options. One option is to follow the original 37.8-mile route (designated September 1985) east of the Blue Ridge Parkway. The other is a newly constructed route of 11.9 miles (designated in June 1996 and known as the Pisgah Ledges section) that travels mainly west of the Blue Ridge Parkway. The longer route is blue-blazed as an alternate trail (AMST), and the shorter route is the new white-blazed mainline trail (MST). Together they become the longest and most topographically diverse 43-mile-long loop in any of the state's national forests.

Begin from the road (NC-215) by ascending an embankment and entering a rhododendron thicket. At 0.5 miles cross a cascading stream in a grove of yellow birches, and after crossing over a ravine begin ascending on six switchbacks. Curve around a low knob to views of Devil's Courthouse at 1.0 mile. At 1.5 miles a short spur trail to the right provides views of Devil's Courthouse. Enter a dense and beautiful red spruce and balsam grove. At 2.0 miles juncture right with a 0.1-mile spur to the Devil's Courthouse Trail (over a Parkway tunnel), which after another 0.1 miles takes you to a spectacular and panoramic overlook. To the east are the valleys of the French Broad, Pigeon, and Tuckasegee Rivers. Some of the mountain peaks you can

Arthur J. Loeb

The 30-mile Art Loeb Trail has been called North Carolina's best example of a trail similar to the Appalachian Trail. Among the characteristics that give it this rating are the high mountain peaks, some of which are grassy balds and massive rock faces; fresh springs; evergreen forests and a wilderness area; wildflowers and wildlife; and trailside shelters. Its original blaze was the image of a hiker. Some hikers say the trail lost some of its uniqueness when the Mountains-to-Sea Trail began to surpass even the Appalachian Trail in distance through the state. But the Art Loeb Trail retains its charm and splendor, and its history. It was named to honor the late Arthur J. Loeb, a hiking enthusiast and dedicated leader of the Carolina Mountain Club.

In 1979 the trail was designated the Art Loeb National Recreation Trail. Some of Loeb's favorite spots on the trail were on grassy Black Balsam Knob (elevation 6,214 feet) and Tennent Mountain (elevation 6,046 feet). The latter was named in honor of Dr. G. S. Tennent, an early leader in the Carolina Mountain Club. Going west through the Shining Rock Wilderness, the trail originally ended at the summit of Cold Mountain (elevation 3,030 feet), a former hunting ground of the Cherokee Indians. Later the trail was rerouted to the Daniel Boone Boy Scouts Camp. The old 1.5-mile Cold Mountain Trail continues to be used to access the forested summit. In 1997 Charles Frazier published a best-selling novel, Cold Mountain, "a love story . . . that takes readers on a long . . . harrowing walk" from Raleigh to the mountains in 1864, near the end of the Civil War. Some of Frazier's ancestors lived (as other Inmans do today) at the base of the mountain, outside the national forest.

see are Pilot Mountain, Tanasee Bald, Herrin Knob, and Mount Hardy. To the west are Little Sam and Big Sam Knobs, and Devil's Courthouse. Inside this bare rock profile, according to Cherokee legends, is a huge cave where the Devil holds court over his demons. (The Devil's Courthouse Trail descends 0.3 miles to a parking area overlook on the Blue Ridge Parkway at milepost 422.4.)

Continue on the Mountains-to-Sea Trail and at 2.2 miles the Little Sam Knob Trail comes in from the left. Ahead, on the left, at 2.3 miles is a large rock outcropping. A climb will provide you with splendid views of Mount Hardy and Little Sam Knob. Curve around Chestnut Bald in patches of large, sweet blackberries (usually ripe the second week in August). Arrive at the Art Loeb Trail near Silvermine Bald at 3.2 miles.

Here the MST divides into two routes. The new and mainline route follows the Art Loeb Trail to the left. This route is described first. Described second

Footbridge over Yellowstone Prong of the East Fork of the Pigeon River

is the alternate blue-blazed MST, which turns right and then descends on the Art Loeb Trail for the next 18 miles, a descent of 3,835 feet in elevation. After another 14.2 miles over Black Mountain and across the Pink Beds it rejoins the mainline Mountains-to-Sea Trail.

Follow the white-blazed route on the Art Loeb Trail, left, for 1.2 miles to reach Forest Service Road (FR)-816 at 4.4 miles (off the Blue Ridge Parkway at milepost 420.2). (The Art Loeb Trail continues left [west], across the road, for 10.9 miles to the Daniel Boone Boy Scout Camp at the end of Little East Fork Road, off NC-215 and 13 miles north from its junction with the Blue Ridge Parkway.)

Continuing on the MST, after crossing FR-816, descend right through a grove of red spruce. The trail comes out into the open among grasses and ragwort with a view of Black Balsam Knob to the left. Cross a footbridge over cascades (the headwaters of Yellowstone Prong) at 4.8 miles. Ascend on the scenic east slope of Black Balsam Knob among thick grasses, blueberry bushes, and scattered rocks. Descend into a beech grove at 5.6 miles. At 5.9 miles cross the Graveyard Ridge Trail, an old railroad grade whose south trailhead is at Graveyard Fields at milepost 418.8 on the Blue Ridge Parkway; its north trailhead is at the junction of the Art Loeb Trail in Ivestor Gap.

Descend on the north side of Graveyard Ridge, join an old railroad bed at 7.1 miles, but after 50 yards leave it to enter a beech grove and conifers. A 0.2-mile spur trail to Yellowstone Falls takes off to the right at 7.8 miles. (The spur trail connects with a bridge over the river to Graveyard Fields Overlook on the Blue Ridge Parkway at milepost 418.8.) Continue on the MST through rhododendron in a descent to a rocky area, and cross a ravine at 8.6 miles. Curve around the east end of Graveyard Ridge, after switchbacks among cherry and other hardwoods, at 8.8 miles. Keep right from a side trail on the left. Cross the skillfully constructed footbridge over Yellowstone Prong of the East Fork of the Pigeon River at 9.3 miles. Upstream are cascades and waterfalls; underneath the bridge is a crystal clear pool. Ascend steps, pass a handcrafted wall placed to prevent erosion, and join with a spur trail at 9.6 miles.

(The spur goes right 150 yards to Looking Glass Rock Overlook, at 4,493 feet elevation, on the Blue Ridge Parkway at milepost 417. Here you will find an outstanding view of Looking Glass Rock [elevation 3,969 feet], a monolithic 400-foot-high granite knob. A traditional claim for its name is the glassy appearance it gives when ice coats the north side in wintertime. Also seen from here are John Rock and Cedar Rock Mountain to the right. Major valleys are the Davidson River to the right and Looking Glass Creek to the left.)

Continue left, gently descend to Bridges Camp Gap, cross an unmarked trail to the East Fork of the Pigeon River at 9.9 miles, and begin an ascent on a ridge. Descend to Tunnel Gap on the Blue Ridge Parkway at milepost 415.6, at 11.0 miles. Follow the west shoulder of the Blue Ridge Parkway for 0.1 miles to reenter the forest understory of rhododendron, mountain laurel, and galax on Chestnut Ridge. Descend, cross the Blue Ridge Parkway at 11.9 miles, ascend a knoll, and descend to cross the Blue Ridge Parkway in Bennett Gap at 12.4 miles. To the west side of the Parkway, ascend gradually along cliffs on Green Knob (elevation 5,056 feet), a habitat for wild turkey, at 13.2 miles. Return to the main ridgeline for a descent on switchbacks. Reach the Blue Ridge Parkway at Pigeon Gap at milepost 412.5 at 14.3 miles. Cross the Blue Ridge Parkway under a Carolina Power and Light Company power line, curve around a knob, and cross US-276 at 14.7 miles. (To the left it is 0.4 miles to the Blue Ridge Parkway overpass; to the right it is 1.6 miles to the south trailhead and parking area for the Buck Spring Trail, on the left.)

On the slope of the mountainside, at Wagon Road Ridge, enter a tunnel of mountain laurel and rhododendron, and cross a small headwater stream at 15.2 miles; cross another after 320 yards and a third at 15.8 miles. Descend on steps and come to a junction with the Buck Spring Trail, right and left, at 16.3 miles. (To the right it is 0.9 miles to the parking area on US-276, the south trailhead for the Buck Spring Trail.) Turn left and cross a scenic cascading stream in a gorge. After 290 yards on the Buck Spring Trail you will arrive at the alternate Mountains-to-Sea Trail (AMST) from the right.

Continue ahead on a gentle grade but with some rocky sections. En route you will see many species of wildflowers, such as trillium, bloodroot, and bellwort. In a forest of mainly hardwoods, there is an understory of flowering shrubs—azaleas, rosebay rhododendron, dogwood, and mountain laurel. There are at least a dozen small streams draining from the mountainside between spur ridges to your left. A few of the more scenic stream crossings are at 17.0, 17.9, 18.8, 19.9, and 20.3 miles. On the way you will curve left on a flat ridge with dense rhododendron. To the left is an excellent campsite at 18.2 miles. (On a few large trees along the way, usually to your right, are old and faint red blazes: a red vertical bar and dot at the top. Also, there are some triangular red metal blazes.)

Arrive at the first of eight switchbacks at 20.5 miles. Ascend to a grassy, old, level road. At 21.3 miles approach Pisgah Inn, ascend to the parking area, and follow right on the sidewalk to a trail signboard at the northeast corner of the parking lot at 21.4 miles. This is the end of this section.

If you choose to hike the blue-blazed alternate Mountains-to-Sea Trail (AMST), follow the Art Loeb Trail from its juncture near Silvermine Bald east (right) for the next 18 miles, a descent of 3,835 feet in elevation. Descend steeply among rock ledges to cross the Blue Ridge Parkway at 3.6 miles and enter into a hardwood forest. At 5.1 miles the blue-blazed Farlow Gap Trail joins from the left, and at 6.1 miles you will arrive at an A-frame shelter. (Water is 75 yards northwest of the shelter.) Ascend on switchbacks to Pilot Mountain (elevation 5,040 feet) for panoramic views at 6.8 miles. Descend on multiple switchbacks and reach Gloucester Road (FR-475) at 9.0 miles. (To the east, left, it is 6.7 miles to US-276.) At 12.4 miles you will come to a juncture with the Butter Gap Trail, left, and in 0.9 miles you will come to the Cedar Rock Trail, ahead. Continue right on the Art Loeb Trail.

Reach the Cedar Rock A-frame shelter near a stream and other campsites at 12.6 miles. Pass Cedar Rock Trail, left, at 14 miles, and Cat Gap Loop Trail, left (formerly Horse Cove Trail), at 15 miles. At 17.6 miles, on a north ridge of Stony Knob, you will come to a juncture with the North Slope Connector Trail. (This is a steep 1.1-mile yellow-blazed trail down the mountain that eventually meets with the 3.7-mile North Slope Loop Trail at Davidson River Campground.) Pass Neil Gap at 17.9 miles. Begin the final descent to the Davidson River at 20 miles. At the base of the ridge cross a footbridge

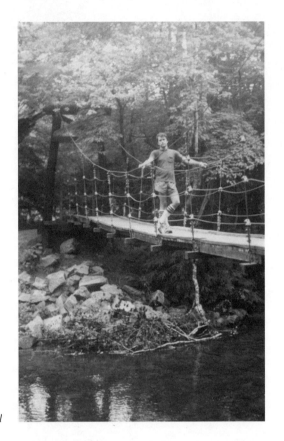

*Robert Ballance on the Davidson
River footbridge of the Art Loeb Trail*

over Joel Branch, then pass through a floodplain of tall poplars and oaks, and trailside patches of bee balm and coneflower. Cross the Davidson River swinging bridge at 21.2 miles, the east end of the Art Loeb Trail. To the right the alternate Mountains-to-Sea Trail continues to a crossing of US-276. To the left is an old road that runs 0.3 miles to a parking lot at the entrance road from US-276, right, and to Davidson River Campground, left, across the bridge. (Ahead, across the entrance road and 230 feet down a service road is a footpath, right, for a 0.3-mile walk to the Pisgah Ranger Station Visitor Center on US-276. There is an outdoor telephone at the ranger station.) The large seasonal campground (full service April 1 through November) has hot showers, outdoor telephone, but no hook-ups. The campground is free December–March. The telephone number, in season, is 828-877-4910/862-5960. (See "Camping, Lodging, and Provisions" for services at the intersection of US-276 and US-64.)

To continue on the alternate MST from the swinging bridge, turn right, cross a small stream, and turn sharply left at 50 yards to cross US-276 and join the Sycamore Trail. Follow it over a low area through tall poplars, hemlocks, beeches, and sycamores. Alder, spice bush, and ferns border the trail. After 0.6 miles the Sycamore Trail curves right and the alternate Mountains-to-Sea Trail goes ahead. Juncture with the Grassy Road Trail, right, and the Thrift Cove Trail (Road). (The Thrift Cove Trail [Road] goes left 0.2 miles to the Black Mountain Trail.) Walk up the Thrift Cove Trail [Road] 230 feet, turn left on a footpath, and descend. Cross several streams and juncture with the Black Mountain Trail at 22.2 miles. (It is 0.5 miles left to the Black Mountain Trail entrance at the parking area near the Pisgah Forest maintenance center.)

Turn right and follow the Black Mountain Trail for the next 6.6 miles, gaining 1,984 feet of elevation. At 24.8 miles cross Pressley Gap Road (formerly the Pressley Cove Trail). Then pass the juncture, right, with the Turkey Pen Gap Trail at 25.8 miles on the side of Black Mountain. Descend on five switchbacks. Arrive at Clawhammer Mountain (elevation 4,140 feet) at 26.7 miles for superb mountain views. Descend on ten switchbacks to the Buckhorn Gap Trail junction, right and left, and a forest road crossing at 27.7 miles. Ascend an embankment and at 27.9 miles arrive at Buckhorn Gap Shelter on the right, where you will find bunk beds and a nearby spring. Ascend to Rich Mountain, where, at 28.9 miles, the AMST leaves the Black Mountain Trail and turns right to follow a new trail down the northwest slopes of Soapstone Ridge toward the Pink Beds. (The Black Mountain Trail continues 0.8 miles left to juncture with the Club Gap Trail and Avery Creek Trail. The Club Gap Trail goes right to descend 0.8 miles to access US-276 near the historic Cradle of Forestry in America, and the Avery Creek Trail descends left 3.2 miles into a pristine cove of cascades, waterfalls, wildlife, and wildflowers.)

Continuing on the alternate Mountains-to-Sea Trail, descend on an old timber road, and at 29.5 miles arrive at a juncture with the North Trail, left. It is an access trail to the Cradle of Forestry. At 30.4 miles leave the old road in a curve, left, to descend on a ridge spur. Pass through a grassy open forest. At 31.4 miles come to the junction with the orange-blazed Pink Beds Loop Trail, which crosses from left to right. Turn left, go 75 yards, turn right off the Pink Beds Loop Trail, and go another 75 yards to cross a log footbridge over the South Fork of the Mills River. Pass through a beautiful fern glen, part of the area known as the Pink Beds, and cross the north side of the Pink Beds Loop Trail at 31.7 miles. The name of the Pink Beds most likely comes from the dense pink rosebay rhododendron and laurel common throughout this upland bog with an average altitude of 3,250 feet. Other sources may be the pink rock formerly quarried in the region, or the masses of wild pink

Carl A. Schenck

You can visit the Cradle of Forestry Discovery Center by taking either one of the junctions with the Pink Beds Loop Trail on the left: the first is a 1.6-mile walk and the second is 1.2 miles. Included among the historic buildings is the one that housed the Biltmore Forest School, which was founded by Carl A. Schenck, a German forester employed by George Vanderbilt to manage his vast forest empire. Schenck became known as the father of American forestry from his work here spanning the years 1897 to 1909. The school opened in 1898 and had 376 alumni when it closed in 1914. In 1968 the U.S. Congress passed the Cradle of Forestry in America Act, which established 6,400 acres commemorating a national historic site. The site includes a 1.0-mile interpretive loop featuring exhibits on forestry management practices and logging equipment, and a 0.9-mile national historic tour. The center is open from the first of May to the end of October, 10 A.M. to 6 P.M. daily. There is a fee. (For information call 828-877-3130.)

phlox and pink roses among the fern meadows. The Pink Beds extend more than 5 miles between the east slopes of Pisgah Ridge and the west slopes of Soapstone Ridge and Dividing Ridge. The headwaters of the South Fork of the Mills River converge here.

Continuing on the AMST, follow an old road through white pines, hemlocks, and oaks to Yellow Gap Road (FR-1206) at 32.2 miles. (A parking area is 200 feet left. To the left FR-1206 goes 1.3 miles to US-276.) Cross FR-1206 and at 32.5 miles pass right of some cascades. Ascend on switchbacks to meet with the Buck Spring Trail and the mainline Mountains-to-Sea Trail, right and left, at 32.9 miles in a hardwood forest of oaks, hickories, and maples. (The Buck Spring Trail goes left 1.1 miles to its south trailhead at US-276. On the way, after 290 yards, is the juncture, right, with the mainline Mountains-to-Sea Trail.)

Turn right and ascend if you are going northeast to Pisgah Inn on the Buck Spring Trail and Mountains-to-Sea Trail. (See description above of the Buck Spring Trail.) En route are many species of wildflowers, hardwood trees, rosebay rhododendron, azaleas, and blueberries. There are frequent coves and streams, some with cascades between the ridgelines. At 34.6 miles on a left curve around a ridge is an excellent flat campsite on the left. Make a left turn at the first of eight switchbacks at 36.9 miles. After the last switchback, at 37.5 miles, follow an old road to leave the national forest and enter the Blue Ridge Parkway boundary. Arrive at Pisgah Inn and ascend to the parking lot. Turn right and follow the sidewalk to a trail signboard at the northeast corner of the parking lot at 37.8 miles. This section of the

> **Pisgah Inn**
>
> *The one-mile-high Mount Pisgah Inn complex includes a modern fifty-two-room motel and a dining hall. It is open from May 1 through October. The area is part of the original 130,000-acre estate owned by the late George W. Vanderbilt. George Weston, who was Vanderbilt's farm superintendent, built and opened the first inn in 1920. In the 1940s it fell into disrepair but was reopened in 1952 by Leslie and Leda Kirschner of New York. The present-day inn was opened in 1967 and operates under a concession contract with the National Park Service. The complex also has a restaurant, service station, picnic area, and a large (140 sites) campground for RVs and tents (no hook-ups), drinking water, and flush toilets. For information about all facilities, call 828-235-8228 (usually open from April 1 to November 1).*

Mountains-to-Sea Trail is maintained by the South Pisgah Task Force of the Carolina Mountain Club.

CAMPSIDE STORIES: In this enormous area of multiple-trail complexes, I have met and talked to all types of users who have trail stories of their own. Some of these stories are about apparitions, ghost and "hant" tales, but some are very personal: stories of accidents, love, and humor.

One spring afternoon in 1987 I met a wedding entourage on the way down from Pilot Mountain, a peak on the Art Loeb Trail. In a conversation with the bride and groom, the bride told me that the peak was her choice because her husband had proposed to her on the mountain the year before. "We found more lady bugs there than anywhere in our travels. You know lady bugs are good luck charms," the bride said.

Meeting them reminded me of a story I had heard about another bride and groom of Pisgah, who should also have had some good luck charms. It seems some generations ago, as the story goes, Jim Stratton and Mary Robinson were young and courting. Jim lived on the other side of Big Bald Mountain and Mary lived to the east near Frying Pan Gap. They wished to marry but Mary's father would not agree and forbade her to ever see him again. Jim and Mary then met secretly. Both Jim and Old Man Robinson had liquor stills, and when Jim heard that Old Man Robinson had tipped off the revenuers, who were on their way to raid his still, he took action. In the attack Jim killed a revenuer.

During his escape Jim received the help of Peggy Higgins, a widow, who fetched a local preacher while he went to bring Mary for a wedding. Widow Higgins gave her wedding dress to Mary. Quickly afterward the couple slipped away into the darkness. It began to snow and by the next day the snow was waist deep. Old Man Robinson learned about the wedding and he and a posse searched well into springtime without finding them. Old-timers say that when the first snow falls in the winter, there is a silhouette on the north side of Mount Pisgah. The ghost of Mary is in a wedding dress and Jim is kneeling by her side.

FIVE

BLUE RIDGE PARKWAY
(CENTRAL AREA)

This chapter describes what I consider the central section of the Blue Ridge Parkway's MST route. This section lies between the Parkway's southwest entrance area (Chapter 2) and the Parkway's northernmost MST stretch. It includes 55.4 miles of the 92.8 miles of MST that fall within or near the boundaries of the Parkway and are maintained by the Carolina Mountain Club.

Thus far in your hiking of the MST you have seen vast forestlands on both sides of the Parkway. In the sections covered by chapters 5 and 8 you will notice an increase in new home construction near Parkway boundaries. Margaret Newbold, assistant director of the Conservation Trust for North Carolina, was quoted on this matter in an Associated Press release dated January 10, 1999. The Parkway's beautiful views are "highly threatened. . . . A lot of people want to live where they can look across a pasture and see the Parkway." All told, the Conservation Trust (the largest Parkway preservation organization), a number of other groups, and several state and federal government agencies have spent about $5 million to purchase adjoining property in an effort to preserve Parkway vistas. Of that amount $2 million was raised by the Blue Ridge Parkway Corridor Protection Project.

SECTION 7. Pisgah Inn (Blue Ridge Parkway MP 408.6) to Folk Art Center (Blue Ridge Parkway MP 382)

TRANSYLVANIA, HENDERSON, AND BUNCOMBE COUNTIES: (See Section 6 for discussion of Transylvania County.) Henderson County, with 382 square miles, was created in 1836 from part of Buncombe County. The county, and its county seat, Hendersonville, received their names in honor of Leonard Henderson (1773–1833), who was chief justice of the North Carolina Supreme Court. The town was laid out in 1840 and incorporated seven years later.

Henderson County is bordered on the south by Greenville County, South

Carolina. The French Broad River flows north through the county, on the north side of the Tennessee Valley Divide. In the south part of the county the Green River flows east of the divide to form Lake Summit, south of Flat Rock. The Blue Ridge Parkway weaves across the county's northwest border. Part of Pisgah National Forest and the North Mills River also lie in the county. Historic sites in the town of Flat Rock are the Carl Sandburg Home and the Flat Rock Playhouse. The county's main north-south highways are US-25, I-26, NC-280, and NC-191. East-west routes are US-64 and US-176.

Named for Colonel Edward Buncombe (1742–78) of the Revolutionary War, the 770-square-mile Buncombe County was formed in 1791 from parts of Burke and Rutherford Counties. Asheville, the largest city in the western part of the state, was incorporated as Buncombe's county seat in 1797. The city was named to honor Samuel Ashe, state governor from 1795 to 1798. Publicized as the "Land of the Sky," it is internationally known for its Biltmore Forest and Estate, Grove Park Inn, and Thomas Wolf Memorial. The city also is home to the University of North Carolina at Asheville, the Botanical Gardens of Asheville, and the Asheville Art Museum. South of Asheville and near the Blue Ridge Parkway are Lake Powhatan, Bent Creek Experimental Forest, and the North Carolina Arboretum. Other natural and historic attractions in the county are the Zebulon B. Vance Birthplace, the Folk Art Center, and Craggy Gardens along the Blue Ridge Parkway. In Montreat is the 4,500-acre Montreat Conference Center and Montreat-Anderson College, which include an expansive trail network. The Blue Ridge Parkway and the Mountains-to-Sea Trail that parallels it pass through the entire county, from the southwest to the northeast borders. The county's major highways are I-40, I-26, US-74, and US-70 for east-west travel; US-25, US-19/23, NC-151, NC-191, and NC-63 are the north-south routes.

LENGTH AND DIFFICULTY: 32.3 miles, moderate hiking north; strenuous hiking south (change in elevation: 3,611 feet).

USGS TOPO MAPS: Cruso, Dunsmore Mountain, Skyland, Asheville, Oteen

FEATURES OR EMPHASIS: Mount Pisgah, scenic views of Asheville area, North Carolina Arboretum, French Broad River, Blue Ridge Parkway Headquarters, Folk Art Center

TRAILS FOLLOWED: Buck Spring Trail, Shut-in Trail

TRAIL CONNECTIONS: Pilot Rock Trail, Laurel Mountain Trail, Mount Pisgah Trail, Bad Fork Trail, Sleepy Gap Trail

WEST TRAILHEAD: At the parking lot of Pisgah Inn, enter northeast at the trail signboard and follow the MST north, jointly with the Buck Spring Trail.

EAST TRAILHEAD: After entering the driveway to the Folk Art Center, keep left in the parking lot (toward the Parkway) and near the Arch Nichols memorial.

CAMPING, LODGING, AND PROVISIONS: Mount Pisgah Campground, off of trails in Pisgah National Forest, and Lake Powhatan Campground (accessible from the MST and from the Blue Ridge Parkway, milepost 393.6, on NC-191 west 0.4 miles to a left turn at sign). Lodging is available at Pisgah Inn (described above) and at Biltmore Square Mall. To reach the latter: when you come off the MST to the access road for the Parkway and NC-191, turn left, pass the entrance to the North Carolina Arboretum, and after 80 yards turn left on NC-191. It is 1.8 miles to Biltmore Square Mall and Comfort Suites (telephone: 800-622-4005 or 282-665-4000). A restaurant, Ryans, is nearby (open Sunday through Thursday 10:45 A.M. to 9:30 P.M., and to 10:30 P.M. on Friday and Saturday). At the large mall are department stores, grocery stores, restaurants, supplies, laundry, and more. Other lodging and shopping areas are described ahead for US-25, US-74, and US-70 interchanges.

INFORMATION AND SECURITY: Trail Maintenance: Pisgah Task Force of the Carolina Mountain Club (telephone: 828-693-3979). Asheville Area Chamber of Commerce: 151 Haywood Street (P.O. Box 1010), Asheville, NC 28802 (telephone: 828-258-6101). Pisgah Ranger District of Pisgah National Forest: 1001 Pisgah Highway, Pisgah Forest, NC 28768 (telephone: 828-877-3350). Blue Ridge Parkway: 119 Hemphill Knob Road, Asheville, NC 28803 (telephone: 828-271-4779; for emergencies and accidents, call 800-727-5928). Transylvania County Sheriff's Office: 201 East Morgan Street, Brevard, NC 28712 (telephone: 828-884-3168). Buncombe County Sheriff's Office: 393 Hendersonville Road, Asheville, NC 28803 (telephone: 828-277-3131). Henderson County Sheriff's Office: 107 Second Avenue West, Hendersonville, NC 28792 (telephone: 828-697-4596).

DESCRIPTION: Begin at the signboard at the northeast corner of the Pisgah Inn parking lot to follow the 1.1-mile continuation of the Buck Spring Trail. Near the start there is an unmaintained trail connection, right, to the Pilot Rock Trail in Pisgah National Forest. Pass right of a section of Pisgah Inn staff housing at 0.1 miles, and enter an area of galax and conifers. At 0.7 miles is a junction, right, with the orange-blazed Laurel Mountain Trail, which accesses a desirable campsite outside the Parkway boundary in Pisgah National Forest. At 1.0 mile you will come to the historic site of George Vanderbilt's Buck Spring Hunting Lodge and a view of Mount Pisgah. At Buck Spring Gap Overlook on the Parkway, the Buck Spring Trail ends and the Shut-in Trail begins. The Mountains-to-Sea Trail continues on the Shut-in Trail, a National Recreation trail (as is the Buck Spring Trail) and former property of the Biltmore Estate. The 18.5-mile Shut-in Trail oscillates between Blue Ridge Parkway boundaries and Pisgah National Forest boundaries. (Camping is not allowed on Parkway property.) Because the boundary lines are not

---

Shut-in Trail

In the 1890s George W. Vanderbilt had a horse trail carefully engineered from the Biltmore Estate, which included property on the north side of the French Broad River, to his Buck Spring Lodge, south but in view of Mount Pisgah. He called the winding route up the mountains (3,611 feet in elevation change) the Shut-in Trail, probably because the route was in a pristine forest with a dense understory of rhododendron and mountain laurel that shut out sunlight.

After Vanderbilt's death in 1914, the trail became abandoned; then the construction of the Blue Ridge Parkway in the 1930s partitioned the original route in a number of places. This made it more of a "shut-out" trail. Nearly forty years later an effort to restore it as a hiking trail was made by Jim "Pop" Hollandsworth, a teacher of mountaineering, math, and physics at the Asheville School. He and his prep school boys went weekly to clear the old trail and construct new connecting trails. Contributing to this effort were Gary Everhardt, superintendent of the Blue Ridge Parkway, and members of the Carolina Mountain Club, particularly Arch Nichols, whose goal was to see the trail serve as a connector from Mount Pisgah to Mount Mitchell.

In 1978 Geoffrey Norman, outdoor editor for Esquire *magazine, was a guest of Hollandsworth. Norman's headline for the story on the Shut-in Trail was "Pop Hollandsworth's Secret Hiking Trail." Referring to the story in July 1978, Hollandsworth stated to Nancy Brown, a columnist for the* Asheville Times, *that the trail was not really a secret; the trail was only waiting for attention and care.*

---

always obvious, camping should be planned only where the Pisgah National Forest boundaries are known, or about 11.5 miles ahead at Lake Powhatan Campground. (To access the 1.5-mile Mount Pisgah Trail from the Buck Spring Gap Overlook parking lot, walk 0.2-miles north on the access road to the Mount Pisgah parking lot. The side hike to Mount Pisgah [elevation 5,721 feet] is recommended for the spectacular and panoramic views.)

Steeply ascend steps and the trail to a peak. Descend to a second parking area at 1.3 miles, where you will see signs for the Shut-in Trail and Mount Pisgah Trail. Ascend to a peak at 1.6 miles, from which you will have a scenic view, right, of Laurel Mountain. Descend on ten switchbacks to a flat area with hardwoods and old chestnut logs at 2.3 miles. The U.S. Forest Service boundary is right. There is a scenic view of the Parkway to the right at 2.5 miles. Descend to the junction of NC-151 at Blue Ridge Parkway milepost 405.5, Elk Pasture Gap, at 3.2 miles. Diagonally across the Parkway enter the forest, right, at 3.3 miles. Mills River Valley Overlook (milepost 404.5) is at

4.3 miles; Big Ridge Overlook (milepost 403.6) is at 5.5 miles; Stoney Bald Overlook (milepost 402.6) is at 6.6 miles; and Beaver Dam Gap Overlook (milepost 401.7) is at 7.7 miles.

The forest along this section of trail is chiefly oak/hickory with locust, laurel, rhododendron, and birch. At 8.1 miles there is an excellent view of the city of Asheville and the Craggy Mountains. At Bent Creek Gap (milepost 400.3 miles on the Parkway), at 9.6 miles, there is a U.S. Forest Service road under the Parkway. To the north the road is called Bent Creek Road (FR-479) and to the south it is Wash Creek Road (FR-5000). (Under the Parkway, south, is the north trailhead of the 1.8-mile Bad Fork Trail. It begins off the edge of the Parkway ramp and descends steeply to a network of trails in the North Mills River headwaters of Pisgah National Forest. For more about this trail and other trails in the area, see Chapter 3, section 3, in *North Carolina Hiking Trails*.)

The next Parkway access point is Chestnut Cove Overlook (milepost 398.3), at 12.4 miles. Continuing on through oaks, maples, and dense groves of mountain laurel, you will arrive at Sleepy Gap Overlook after eight switchbacks (milepost 397.3) at 13.3 miles. (Sleepy Gap Trail descends left into Pisgah National Forest to connect with other trails near Lake Powhatan and Lake Powhatan Campground. The fee campground has hot showers, flush toilets, swimming, and outside telephone. It is open from April 15 to November 1.)

Continuing to descend on the Mountains-to-Sea Trail, cross a small stream at 14.2 miles. After nine switchbacks, reach Walnut Cove Overlook (milepost 396.4) at 15.0 miles. For the next 3.5 miles the trail descends gradually and skirts east of Hardtimes Road. After curving around the east side of Glen Bald, it stays east of Shut-in Ridge. In the descent, tulip poplars, dogwoods, ferns, and wildflowers are prominent among oaks and maples. Pass through a gate of the North Carolina Arboretum and descend to the last switchback in a rhododendron thicket at 18.1 miles. To the left is the arboretum fence. A small stream is nearby. (Here also is the former parking lot for the north terminus of the Shut-in Trail.) Follow the trail through rhododendron and pass through another arboretum gate. Exit at the Parkway ramp at 18.5 miles, the new north terminus of the Shut-in Trail. To the left, at 0.1 miles, is the access road to the North Carolina Arboretum and NC-191. (Across NC-191, on the north side, is a large and popular picnicking and fishing area under a canopy of trees and beside the French Broad River. Here is the nearest place to park cars, since no parking is allowed on the Parkway ramp. See "Camping, Lodging, and Provisions" for the Biltmore Square Mall.)

To continue on the Mountains-to-Sea Trail, turn right from the Parkway ramp and after 0.1 miles arrive at the south end of the French Broad River Bridge (milepost 393.6). (On the Parkway, going south, it is 0.1 miles to the French Broad River Overlook.) After hiking across the French Broad River Bridge at 18.8 miles, walk 35 yards and turn right into an open hardwood forest. Pass under a power line at 18.9 miles and enter a white pine grove, but leave it at 19.4 miles. At 19.5 miles cross an old road that goes under the Blue Ridge Parkway. Ascend and descend on gentle hills, cross the Parkway at 20.1 miles, and enter an oak/hickory forest. Join an old woods road and arrive at an overpass of I-26 at 20.4 miles (no vehicular access to I-26). Cross the bridge; turn right into the forest at 20.5 miles. Cross a gravel road at 20.8 miles. In a mixed forest pass through wild orchids, galax, trailing arbutus, wild ginger, and mountain laurel. At 21.0 miles pass a man-made spring, right. Cross a number of used roads (that lead to private property) and cross a small stream at 21.6 miles. Pass through a rhododendron and mountain laurel thicket and cross a vehicle bridge over Dingle Creek at 21.7 miles. Pass under tall oaks and white pines. Songbirds are commonplace here, particularly during spring and fall migration. Cross a gravel road at 22.8 miles (to the left it goes under the Parkway) and other woods roads ahead. Cross a vehicular bridge over Four-mile Branch at 23.4 miles, and go through a grove of tall white pines at 23.8 miles. At 24.0 miles arrive at the US-25 bridge (Parkway milepost 388.8) and access ramps.

(To the left, north, it is 0.2 miles to Biltmore Parkway Shopping Center and another 1.6 miles to the family owned and operated Forest Manor Inn, which serves continental breakfast [telephone: 828-274-3531]. From I-40, exit 50, it is south 1.0 mile to the inn. To the south on US-25 there are a number of small and large shopping malls but not any motels. Past Royal Pines is Airport Road, right, to I-26 and the Asheville Airport. Both highways go south to Hendersonville.)

After crossing the US-25 bridge, stay on the west side of the Parkway, but cross an overpass of Southern Railroad at 24.4 miles (milepost 388.5), and an overpass without ramps of US-25A (milepost 388.1) at 24.8 miles. The forest is a mixture of hardwoods, white pines, ferns, wild orchids, and partridgeberry beds. Cross two streams at 27.0 miles. At 28.4 miles pass under a power line. Arrive at US-74A (milepost 384.7) at 29.3 miles.

(From the access ramp you can go north on US-74A and under I-40 for 0.8 miles to the large River Ridge Market Place. Here you will find department stores, supplies, restaurants, and more. If you turn left at J&S Cafeteria, you will be near a Comfort Inn, which serves continental breakfast and has a swimming pool [telephone: 800-228-5150 or 828-298-9141]. East on US-74A it is 0.7-miles to a Texaco service station.)

Continuing on the MST, switch to the east side of the Parkway once you are on the north side of the bridge; after a few yards descend on steps into the forest. You will soon hear noise from a residential area to the right. After 0.7 miles arrive at the old Hemphill Road (milepost 384.2). To the left the road once passed under the Parkway through a box tunnel. (The use of this passageway for a spur trail to visit the new headquarters building of the Blue Ridge Parkway has been proposed by the Friends of the Mountains-to-Sea Trail.) Ascend a hillside, then hike in and out of coves before descending on a high bank of steps to an I-40 underpass (milepost 383.7) at 30.7 miles. Pass a fence stile at 30.8 miles, cross Southern Railroad tracks, and after 50 yards cross the Swannanoa River bridge and Azalea Road. Enter a fence stile to a meadow and exit through another fence stile. Pass between a private residence and the Parkway at 31.0 miles. Enter a Virginia pine thicket and poison ivy beds at 31.2 miles. Pass under a power line and arrive at the Parkway to walk on the west shoulder. Cross US-70 on a Parkway bridge (milepost 382.6) at 31.7 miles.

(West on US-70 it is 0.2 miles to a service station/snack bar and a nearby restaurant. East on US-70 it is 1.0 mile to a shopping area with restaurants [for example, Poseidon is a steak and seafood restaurant; telephone: 828-298-4121]. There are also a number of motels, such as Econo Lodge [telephone: 800-424-4777 or 828-298-4419]. There is also an easy access to I-40 here, exit 55.)

Cross the Parkway ramp at 31.8 miles, go up an embankment into the forest, and approach the Folk Art and Visitor Center parking lot at 32.1 miles. On the east side of the parking lot, at 32.3 miles, there is a Mountains-to-Sea Trail plaque in honor of Arch Nichols, distinguished leader and trail volunteer worker in the Carolina Mountain Club. Ahead and to the right is the center's entrance road (milepost 382). The MST crosses the parking area to approach the Folk Art and Visitor Center. (The center has a major display and sales of traditional and contemporary crafts of the Southern Highlands. There is also a library and museum. Open daily 9 A.M. to 6 P.M.; telephone: 828-298-7928.)

CAMPSIDE STORIES: One of the most inspiring stores I know is about a wealthy, shy boy educated by tutors who traveled the world to see what he had read in books about the natural environment of trees, birds, and animals. Born on Staten Island, New York, November 12, 1862, he was George Washington Vanderbilt, the youngest son of William and Maria Vanderbilt. He was heir to a family fortune of railroad development. Rather than follow tradition, he devoted himself to forestry, livestock production, landscape gardening, and architecture. He also chose to honor the Asheville area with an everlasting gift of his knowledge.

Henry Arch Nichols

A bronze plaque embedded in granite faces the Mountains-to-Sea Trail at the Folk Art Center on the Blue Ridge Parkway. The plaque design is simple; its message is historically powerful. There is the Mountains-to-Sea Trail logo, and the image of Henry Arch Nichols (1907–89), arms folded and eyes surveying a priceless mountain domain. A resting bench is nearby. There is plenty to contemplate here, because Nichols was more than an unquestionable leader of trail building. He was a dedicated leader in the Carolina Mountain Club and a pacesetter in cultural arts and civic commitment. He dreamed of a 60-mile connecting trail between the towering peaks of Mount Pisgah in the south and Mount Mitchell to the north. Laboring faithfully with teams of fellow workers, their artfully carved and completed trail was dedicated November 15, 1997, eight years after Nichols's death. In 1998 Donald E. Dossey and John I. Hillyer published The Mountains to Sea Trail: Western North Carolina's Majestic Rival to the Appalachian Trail. *Dedicated to Nichols, it graciously honors the legacy of Nichols, his wife Zeffie, and a distinguished list of Carolina Mountain Club leaders and trail associates.*

In love with the North Carolina mountains, he began the purchase of land south of Asheville by 1889 when he was twenty-seven years old. He wished for the most beautiful country home that money could buy, and he chose some of the nation's best designers and architects to build it for him on this land. He named it Biltmore, a combination of part of his last name and the old English name for rolling hills. The Biltmore School of Forestry, which he founded, trained pioneers in scientific forestry, and he brought in Carl Schenk to administer the program. He advanced the science of milk production at his dairy farm and established the Biltmore Nursery for botanical research.

Until his widowed mother's death in 1896, his main home was with her in a Fifth Avenue mansion in New York City. He then moved to Biltmore and two years later married Edith Stuyvesant Dresser of Rhode Island. Vanderbilt also had a home in Washington, D.C., and it was there that he died on March 6, 1914, about one week after an appendectomy. He was survived by his wife and a daughter named Cornelia. Two years later the U.S. government accepted an offer made during Vanderbilt's lifetime to purchase 80,600 acres to form the nucleus of Pisgah National Forest. Vanderbilt's passion for scientific forestry shows in one of his written statements: ". . . no man is a good citizen who destroys for selfish ends a good forest."

SECTION 8. Folk Art Center (Blue Ridge Parkway MP 382) to Balsam Gap (North) (Blue Ridge Parkway MP 359.8)

BUNCOMBE COUNTY: See Section 7.

LENGTH AND DIFFICULTY: 23.0 miles, moderate to strenuous

USGS TOPO MAPS: Oteen, Craggy Pinnacle, Montreat

FEATURES OR EMPHASIS: Rattlesnake Lodge, Lane Pinnacle, Craggy Gardens, Great Craggy Mountains, Glassmine Falls Overlook

TRAIL CONNECTIONS: Rattlesnake Lodge Trail (Blue Ridge Parkway milepost 374.4), Snowball Trail (U.S. Forest Service), Douglas Falls Trail (U.S. Forest Service), Big Butt Trail (Blue Ridge Parkway and U.S. Forest Service)

WEST TRAILHEAD: Parking lot at Folk Art Center

EAST TRAILHEAD: Balsam Gap (North) parking lot (Blue Ridge Parkway milepost 359.8)

CAMPING, LODGING, AND PROVISIONS: Camping is allowed only outside of the Blue Ridge Parkway property boundary, to the west in the Toecane Ranger District of Pisgah National Forest. Easy access would be to choose one of the national forest connecting trails listed above. See Section 8 for lodging and provisions on US-70. For provisions at the east (north) trailhead, the nearest are 1.4 miles down the mountain, west, on NC-80 to the community of Busick. Here you will find a grocery store, Mount Mitchell Restaurant, and Mountain Cove Campground and Trout Pond.

INFORMATION AND SECURITY: Trail Maintenance: Pisgah Task Force of the Carolina Mountain Club (telephone: 828-693-3979). Asheville Area Chamber of Commerce: 151 Haywood Street (P.O. Box 1010), Asheville, NC 28802 (telephone: 828-258-6101). Blue Ridge Parkway: 119 Hemphill Knob Road, Asheville, NC 28803 (telephone: 828-271-4779; for emergencies and accidents, call 800-727-5928). Folk Art Center: 382 Blue Ridge Parkway, Asheville, NC 28805 (telephone: 828-298-7928). Pisgah Ranger District, Pisgah National Forest: 1001 Pisgah Highway, Pisgah Forest, NC 28768 (telephone: 828-877-3350). Buncombe County Sheriff's Office: 393 Hendersonville Road, Asheville, NC 28803 (telephone: 828-277-3131).

DESCRIPTION: At the Folk Art Center (Parkway milepost 382), which features displays of traditional crafts of the Southern Highlands, park in the parking lot section closest to the left after entering. Begin the trail north by crossing the parking area toward the Folk Art Center, and follow the trail sign for a route parallel to the Parkway. Cross a bridge over Riceville Road (SR-2002) at 0.2 miles. Cross a number of old trails and roads; pass over a water line at 0.5 miles, and cross the Parkway at 1.0 miles. Descend and ascend, partly following an old woods road. On an ascent at 2.5 miles is a short spur, left, for scenic views of Northeast Asheville. Ascend on a narrow ridge, then a slope, until you reach the mountaintop at 3.0 miles in an area of mountain laurel, hardwoods, and gentian. Descend, frequently using old logging roads, cross a streamlet at 3.8 miles, enter a mountain laurel thicket at 4.6 miles and a wildflower patch at 4.8 miles. At 5.4 miles arrive at Craven Gap (milepost 377.4) and the juncture with NC-694 (which descends southwest to Asheville).

Cross the Parkway to a parking area, and at the northwest corner of the parking area continue on the Mountains-to-Sea Trail. Ascend on a scenic, rocky east slope of Rice Knob in an oak/hickory forest to encounter large banks of wildflowers—wild geranium, crested dwarf iris, mountain mint, and herbs of the orpine family. Flame azaleas are prominent also. At 6.0 miles a spur trail takes off to the right and descends 0.2 miles to the Tanbark Ridge Overlook (milepost 376.7). At 6.5 miles cross a streamlet, and at 6.9 miles begin a descent on a ridge. Cross the paved Ox Creek Road (SR-2109) at 7.2 miles. (To the right it is 0.1 miles to the Parkway.) Follow the footpath to the end of a ridge and descend on nine short switchbacks to Bull Gap at 7.9 miles. (To the left it is 60 yards to Ox Creek Road.) At the former carriage entrance to Rattlesnake Lodge, begin on the old carriage road and ascend on nine switchbacks for 0.7 miles. This scenic part of the trail passes through rock formations and gardens of wildflowers in a hardwood forest. Deer may be seen in this area, and among the songbirds you may see are scarlet tanager and warblers. Reach remnants of Rattlesnake Lodge (see "Campside Stories," below) at 9.3 miles. A spring is to the left. The Rattlesnake Lodge Trail, to the right, descends steeply for 0.4 miles to the Parkway (milepost 374.4) and a small parking area near the Parkway's Tanbark Tunnel.

At 9.3 miles cross a streamlet and pass the old caretaker's house site, marked by a fallen chimney to the right. Ascend into a mountain laurel thicket at 9.7 miles, and arrive at a spring whose water feeds a patch of bee balm and other wildflowers. There is a spur trail to the left along the mountainside that leads to the Rattlesnake Lodge site. Ascend an old and well-graded trail with switchbacks among hardwoods and wildflowers for the next 0.8 miles to a ridge on the Bull Mountain range. Turn east at Rich Knob and follow the ridge's undulations. At 11.3 miles pass through a buckeye grove and by a rocky ledge, left, at 11.8 miles. Arrive at the summit of Wolfden Knob at 12.0 miles. Rocky ledges and switchbacks continue for the next 0.8 miles. From the summit area of Lane Pinnacle (elevation 5,230 feet) is a scenic view of Beetree Reservoir, to the right (southeast) at 12.8 miles.

More rock walls follow with superb views at 13.2 miles. Lichens, mosses, ferns, sedum, and Virginia spiderwort inhabit the rock crevices and ledges.

Scenic views are also available at 13.5 miles. Descend on switchbacks to a saddle, ascend to a short ridge, and descend again to arrive at the Parkway in Potato Field Gap at 14.4 miles (Parkway milepost 368.2) for views of the Woodfin Watershed. Walk on the west shoulder of the Parkway for 100 yards. Reenter the woods and ascend on switchbacks into a hawthorn grove. Reach a scenic view among rocks, phlox, blueberry bushes, locust, and mountain ash. At 15.1 miles juncture left with the Snowball Trail and cross FR-63 in Beetree Gap (Parkway milepost 367.6). Ahead, northeast, is the entrance road to Craggy Gardens picnic area. Right of the entrance road ascend an embankment, and then pass a spring on the left at 15.5 miles. Pass a juncture for a spur trail, left, to the picnic area parking lot at 15.6 miles. The Mountains-to-Sea Trail ascends right of an old gazebo, and after 0.2 miles reaches the CCC pavilion at Craggy Flats. It then descends on switchbacks and steps to pass behind the Craggy Gardens Visitor Center at 16.4 miles. Curve around Craggy Pinnacle on switchbacks through yellow birch, ferns, and white snakeroot. Arrive at a juncture with Douglas Falls Trail, left, at 17.5 miles. (The Douglas Falls Trail descends steeply 2.5 miles to a scenic gorge, a 70-foot waterfall, and an isolated entrance road and parking area on FR-74. Road access from Barnardsville is off NC-197 onto Dillingham Road [SR-2731] for 5.0 miles to where the pavement ends and the gravel FR-74 begins.)

Continue on the MST around the west slope of the ridge, partially on a rocky treadway to ascend on switchbacks. At 18.6 miles is a spring among rhododendrons. Ascend steps to a service road, pass a U.S. government building, and reach the Parkway at 18.7 miles (milepost 363.6, elevation 5,592 feet). Cross the Parkway at the Graybeard Mountain sign; turn left (north) at 19.2 miles. Follow the blazes along a rocky area and through rhododendron arbors and a dark grove of conifers. Curve west on the slope of Bullhead Mountain.

After coming out on the crest of the Great Craggy Mountains, explore the side trails to the right between 19.6 miles and 21.0 miles. From knob to knob are multiple scenic overlooks that are naturally landscaped with dense blueberry bushes, mountain laurel, mosses, pungent galax, and pastel-colored lichens. Scattered in rocky apertures are yellow birches and chestnut oaks. Unforgettable as may be the views, camping is prohibited. The views to the southeast are of the Asheville Watershed in the valley of the North Fork of the Swannanoa River and Burnett Reservoir. East of the lake is the Blue Ridge Mountain range and Graybeard Mountain, a landmark. To the west is Ivy Creek Valley and the Walnut Mountain range beyond.

Descend to the Parkway parking lot at 21.5 miles (milepost 361.2, eleva-

View of the Blue Ridge Parkway from Great Craggy Mountains

tion 5,197 feet). Here is an overlook for views of Glassmine Falls, to the east. Follow the shoulder of the Parkway; descend on steps to Cotton Tree Gap and then ascend at 21.8 miles. After another knob, descend to begin five switchbacks up the west edge of Walker Knob (elevation 5,482 feet). Descend on three switchbacks among evergreens and hardwoods to Balsam Gap (North) (milepost 359.8, elevation 5,320 feet). Cross the Parkway to a parking lot at 23.8 miles.

CAMPSIDE STORIES: There is a natural amphitheater on the south side of Bull Mountain between Bull Gap and High Knob that could have been named for either. It could have been named Mountain Spring or Wildcat Wilderness. Instead it was named Rattlesnake. The building of Rattlesnake Lodge began in 1900 and within the first three years forty-one rattlesnakes (the largest being 5 feet, 8 inches long) were killed. Others slithered among rocky dens.

The two-story summer home was built on site from cleared native trees and stones for Chase P. Ambler, M.D. (a heart specialist), his wife, two sons, and three daughters, who lived in Asheville. Dr. Ambler was a strong leader for worldwide conservation, and Mount Ambler in Great Smoky Mountains National Park is named to honor him and his role in making the Blue Ridge Parkway possible. Rattlesnake Lodge had three fireplaces downstairs (one with a single stone mantel 11 feet long) and two fireplaces upstairs. Front porches provided space to look down the mountainside toward the Swannanoa River basin. In addition to the house there was a barn, sheds, spring-house, a swimming pool (fed by cold springs), and a guest house for visitors who came to walk the trails. Summer was filled with the laughter of the children and a chorus of vireos, towhees, scarlet tanagers, red birds, indigo buntings, wrens, and sparrows. Wild turkeys, hawks, grouse, bears, and deer were seen in a cleared garden area near purple rhododendron and mountain laurel.

In 1918 Mrs. Ambler died, the property was sold, and in 1925 the lodge was mysteriously destroyed by fire. In the 1930s 223 acres of the property were purchased by the U.S. government for the Parkway. The MST passes by the house ruins and the spring. Some visitors say that if you sit quietly on the rocks by the spring and listen, you can hear the Ambler children running, singing, and playing on the trail.

SIX

PISGAH NATIONAL FOREST
(TOECANE RANGER DISTRICT)
AND MOUNT MITCHELL STATE PARK

**SECTION 9. Balsam Gap (North) (Blue Ridge Parkway MP 359.8) to
Buck Creek Gap (NC-80 and Blue Ridge Parkway MP 344.1)**

YANCEY COUNTY: Yancey County was named for Bartlett Yancey (1785–1828), a
member of the North Carolina General Assembly and of Congress. A scenic
mountain county of 311 square miles, it is bordered by the Blue Ridge
Parkway on the southeast. Its northern boundary adjoins Cherokee National Forest in Unicoi County, Tennessee, where the Appalachian Trail also
takes a turn into Yancey County. The cascading Nolichucky and North Toe
Rivers form the county's northwest border. Both the county and the county
seat, Burnsville, were established in 1833. The town was named to honor
Otway Burns (1775–1850), who served in the War of 1812 and later in the
N.C. General Assembly, where he served as speaker of the Senate.

Encompassed by the county are a number of high peaks including Mount
Mitchell, the highest in the eastern United States, Mount Mitchell State Park,
large sections of Pisgah National Forest, and the Flat Top Mountain Wildlife
Area. The main highways through the county are US-19E and US-19W, both
serving as east-west and north-south routes, and NC-197 and NC-80, which
run north-south.

LENGTH AND DIFFICULTY: 23.2 miles (main route), 22.9 miles (alternate route);
strenuous (change in elevation: 3,091 feet)

USGS TOPO MAPS: Montreat, Mount Mitchell, Old Fort, Celo

FEATURES OR EMPHASIS: Blackstock Knob, Potato Knob, Mount Mitchell, Black
Mountain Campground

TRAILS FOLLOWED: Buncombe Horse Range Trail, Commissary Shelter Trail,
Camp Alice Trail, Mount Mitchell Trail

TRAIL CONNECTIONS: Boundary Trail, Mount Mitchell Summit Trail, Higgins Bald
Trail, Lost Cove Ridge Trail (Green Knob Trail)

WEST TRAILHEAD: Parking lot at Balsam Gap (North) on the Parkway at milepost 359.8

EAST TRAILHEAD: Parking area at the junction of NC-80 and the Parkway at milepost 344.1, on east side of the overpass

CAMPING, LODGING, AND PROVISIONS: Camping is available off the trail in Pisgah National Forest, Mount Mitchell State Park limited camping area, and at Black Mountain Campground. (Camping is prohibited on Blue Ridge Parkway property.) Near the east trailhead, 1.4 miles from the Parkway west on NC-80 to Busick, are Effler Grocery Store (open Monday through Saturday 7:30 A.M. to 7:00 P.M., and Sunday 11:00 A.M. to 6:00 P.M.) and Mt. Mitchell View Restaurant (open Monday through Saturday 8 A.M. to 8 P.M., and closed on Sunday; telephone: 828-675-9599). About 0.3 miles farther is Hammrick Inn (bed and breakfast, telephone: 828-675-5251), and another 0.4 miles is Albert's Lodge (dinner is served from 6:00 to 9:00 P.M., telephone: 828-675-4691). From here it is 3.1 miles south on FR-472 to Black Mountain Campground. It has facilities for tent and RV camping (no hookups, but water and comfort station).

INFORMATION AND SECURITY: Trail Maintenance: Pisgah Task Force of the Carolina Mountain Club (telephone: 828-693-3979) from Balsam Gap (North) to Black Mountain Campground, and by Central Blue Ridge Task Force (telephone: 828-437-6635) from Black Mountain Campground to Blue Ridge Parkway and NC-80. Blue Ridge Parkway: 199 Hemphill Knob Road, Asheville, NC 28803 (telephone: 828-271-4779, for emergencies and accidents call 800-727-5928). Toecane Ranger District, Pisgah National Forest: P.O. Box 128, Burnsville, NC 28714 (telephone: 828-682-6146). Yancey County Chamber of Commerce: 106 West Main Street, Burnsville, NC 28714 (telephone: 828-682-7413 or 800-948-1632). Yancey County Sheriff's Office: East Main Street (P.O. Box 6), Burnsville, NC 28714 (telephone: 828-682-2124).

DESCRIPTION: (The south trailhead for the 6.0-mile Big Butt Trail into the Toecane Ranger District of Pisgah National Forest is also here at the Balsam Gap parking lot. It is 1.6 miles to Mount Misery for outstanding views of Mount Mitchell and the Black Mountain Range.) For the MST, follow the white-dot blazes onto an old railroad grade, but make a sharp right turn. After 75 yards begin to ascend on a series of twenty-two switchbacks and curves among red spruces and hemlocks; there are wooden steps at 0.7 miles. Reach the top of the ridge and site of Old Mitchell Trail (elevation 6,031 feet) at 0.9 miles. At 1.3 miles, left, is an excellent view of Mount Mitchell, and at 1.5 miles, right, are views of the Great Craggy Mountain range to the southwest. Reach Blackstock Knob (6,325 feet in elevation) at 1.6 miles. Descend to views of Mount Mitchell and a network of radio and TV towers on Clingmans Peak, left. Complete the descent to Rainbow Gap

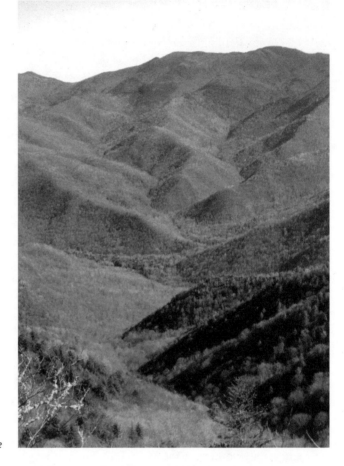

*South view of the
Mount Mitchell range*

at 2.4 miles. At 3.0 miles enter a dense grove of red spruces, some of which are fallen and covered with thick moss. Huge boulders are in this area.

Ascend on two switchbacks among boulders to 3.4 miles where a descent is begun to Promontory Rock at 3.5 miles. Descend on a carefully constructed trail with ten switchbacks over rocks, seeping water, small cascades, mosses, and dense balsam. At 4.1 miles enter an open area of grasses and rocks for views of a spectacular landscape on the south side of Potato Knob. To the southwest is a sweeping view of the Asheville Watershed. Pass through patches of rhododendron, mountain laurel, and birch before turning right on a former trail (Boundary Trail) at 4.6 miles. After a beautiful level area among conifers and hardwoods, turn left at 4.8 miles to descend. Pass through a stile, descend on steps, and arrive at Mount Mitchell Road (NC-128) at 5.0 miles. A roadside parking space for about three vehicles is on

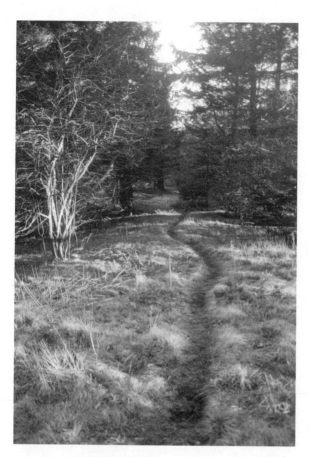

*Mountains-to-Sea Trail on
the east side of Potato Knob*

the opposite side of the road. Left is the entrance road to Mount Mitchell
State Park, and to the right it is 0.6 miles to the Blue Ridge Parkway, milepost
355.4.

Continuing on the MST, cross Mount Mitchell Road at a right angle,
descend, turn left, and go 0.3 miles on an old railroad grade to a juncture
with the Buncombe Horse Range Trail, also an old railroad grade. Turn left
and cross a number of wet areas from mountainside seepage on the easy
grade. Cross a few small streams and pass a waterfall at 6.2 miles. Cross
Lower Creek at 8.2 miles where there is a waterfall. At 8.5 miles turn left on
an old road, the Commissary Shelter Trail (also known as the Old Mount
Mitchell Railway) to leave the Buncombe Horse Range Trail. (If you decide
to continue on the Buncombe Horse Range Trail, it is 0.7 miles to the Mount
Mitchell Trail.) Ascend on the Commissary Shelter Trail to enter Mount
Mitchell State Park, and after 0.3 miles turn right on the Camp Alice Trail.
Continue ascending on switchbacks and at 0.5 miles reach a crest to connect

with Old Mount Mitchell Trail, right and left. (On the left it is 0.5 miles to a tent campground and 1.2 miles to a restaurant and public telephone.) Turn right and meet the Mount Mitchell Trail.

(To the left it is 0.1 mile to a visitor center that has a concession stand and restrooms. The parking lot is accessed via NC-128 from the Blue Ridge Parkway. At the north edge of the parking lot is a picnic area and the south entrance of the rugged 12.0-mile Black Mountain Crest Trail [called Deep Gap Trail for its 3.9 miles within the park to the Pisgah National Forest boundary]. [For detailed information on the challenging Black Mountain Crest Trail see *North Carolina Hiking Trails,* 3rd ed.])

Continuing on the Mount Mitchell Trail (and MST) pass a small museum on the left. The MST blazes continue ahead, but bear right to climb the summit of Mount Mitchell (elevation 6,648 feet) at 9.7 miles. Here is an observation tower with views to rival those of any scenic mountain summit in eastern North America. To continue on the Mount Mitchell Trail pass the Balsam Nature Trail after 0.2 miles (it descends left to the east side of the parking lot). After another 0.5 miles leave the park boundary and reenter Pisgah National Forest. Descend on a rocky trail with switchbacks to the Buncombe Horse Range Trail, right and left, at 11.4 miles. Turn left (a spring is nearby) and after 0.1 mile turn right. At 12.8 miles there is a fork; the Mount Mitchell Trail goes left, and the 1.5-mile Higgins Bald Trail goes right. Follow the Higgins Bald Trail, which is considered to be more scenic with its waterfalls and cascades; it also has campsites. (The 1.2-mile section of the Mount Mitchell Trail can be used as an alternate to the MST.) Follow the Higgins Bald Trail on Flynn Ridge, descend to cross Setrock Creek, and rejoin the Mount Mitchell Trail at 14.3 miles. Continue the descent on nineteen switchbacks and through a virgin forest of hardwoods. At 15.0 miles you will pass by large banks of meadow rue. At 15.8 miles enter the campground of the Black Mountain Recreation Area in the Toecane Ranger District of Pisgah National Forest. Pass Devil's Den Forest Walk at 15.9 miles, and reach an exit on a bridge at the South Toe River at 16.0 miles.

From here, turn left on the gravel forest road FR-472; after a few yards pass the Green Knob Trail (3.3 miles long, also called the Lost Cove Ridge Trail) on the right. After 0.7 miles turn right at a fork (the forest road to the left goes 2.2 miles to NC-80, where there is lodging, a restaurant, and groceries; see "Camping, Lodging, and Provisions" above). The old Neals Creek Information Station is on the left; to the right is the former Neals Creek Heliport. Enter a forest road gate and cross a bridge over Big Lost Cove Creek at 16.8 miles. Ascend and turn left at 17.0 miles. Pass a gate on a timber road and at 17.2 miles turn right on a timber road bordered by young

Mount Mitchell State Park

The 1,677-acre Mount Mitchell State Park was designated in 1915 as the first park in the North Carolina State Park System. It is listed in the National Registry of Natural Landmarks. Mount Mitchell (elevation 6,684 feet), the highest point in the park, is also the highest point east of the Mississippi River. In addition to Mount Mitchell, there are other high peaks over 6,000 feet in the park: Mount Craig (6,648 feet), Balsam Cone (6,596 feet), Big Tom (6,581 feet), and Mount Hallback (6,300 feet).

The park is in the Black Mountain Range and is bordered by Pisgah National Forest except on the west slope. On the range and within the national forest are additional peaks over 6,000 feet. Some of them are Mount Gibbes (6,571 feet), to the south of Mount Mitchell, and peaks such as Cattail Peak (6,583 feet) and Celo Knob (6,327 feet) to the north. Others over 6,000 feet are Potato Hill, Deer Mountain, Gibbs Mountain, Horse Rock, and Winter Star.

The park owes its protection to early environmentalists such as Governor Locke Craig and President Theodore Roosevelt. Named in honor of Elisha Mitchell (see campside story in this chapter), the park is an outstanding location for nature study. Among the fauna, in addition to more common species of wildlife, are the rare northern flying squirrel and saw-whet owl. At least ninety-one species of birds have been recorded in the park vicinity. At various times snow has fallen in every month of the year, and the coldest day on record was at −34°F in 1983.

---

trees. Turn left on another timber road at 17.3 miles, and after 0.2 miles leave the road and ascend right into a mature forest. Ascend on four switchbacks, some among mountain laurel. At 18.0 miles on a ridge curve you can look back and see Mount Mitchell. For the next 1.6 miles the trail curves around ridges and into coves where seeps and streamlets flow down the steep slopes from Big Laurel Mountain. There are patches of ferns and wildflowers, and groves of rhododendron and mountain laurel scattered among a forest of hemlocks, tulip poplars, oaks, birches, and cucumber trees. The trail crosses a few former timber cuts and timber road crossings.

At 19.6 miles fork left where a work access trail ascends right on a slope to the Blue Ridge Parkway. Continuing through a chiefly hardwood forest with scattered hemlocks, curve in and out of coves with large patches of Christmas fern and streamlets. There are a few rock overhangs. At 20.1 miles on a ridge curve are views of Mount Mitchell. The trail begins to parallel the Parkway at 20.7 miles and crosses it diagonally left at 20.8 miles. After four switchbacks descend to the Singecat Ridge Overlook (milepost 345.3) at

21.4 miles. Cross the Parkway and, after 0.4 miles with switchbacks and steps, cross it again at 21.8 miles. From here you will ascend on switchbacks to cross twin Blue Ridge Parkway tunnels that you do not see (mileposts 344.5 and 344.7). Parallel the Parkway on the undulating trail with switchbacks. At 23.0 miles at the top of a ridge, descend on two switchbacks through patches of galax. Arrive at the Parkway bridge over NC-80 at Buck Creek Gap (milepost 344.1) at 23.2 miles. There is a small paved parking area to the northeast of the bridge. (It is 16 miles east on NC-80 down the mountain to Marion, and west it is 14 miles to Micaville. On the way west it is 1.4 miles to Busick, where there are groceries, gasoline, a restaurant, and lodging. See "Camping, Lodging, and Provisions," above.)

CAMPSIDE STORIES: Mount Mitchell is named for Elisha Mitchell, a nineteenth-century explorer, geologist, and professor. A graduate of Yale University, he began teaching math and natural philosophy in 1818, at the age of twenty-five, at the University of North Carolina at Chapel Hill. In 1825 he taught chemistry, geology, and mineralogy. He had been ordained a Presbyterian clergyman in 1821 and during his lifetime divided his energies between the pursuit of clerical and classroom interests. One of his geological interests was the surveying of Black Mountain. He was especially interested in the debate over its altitude: Was it higher than Mount Washington (elevation 6,288 feet) in New Hampshire, and perhaps the highest point east of the Mississippi River? Mitchell's first measurement, 6,476 feet, was taken in 1835; his second measurement, in 1838, was 6,672 feet. As measurement instruments improved in accuracy, he went again in 1844 and measured the peak to be 6,708 feet. By this time citizens in the valley were calling the peak Mount Mitchell.

But one of Mitchell's former students, Senator Thomas Clingman, disagreed and said that the professor had measured the wrong peak: he believed that the highest was 6,941 feet. The disagreement prompted Mitchell to measure the peak once again to retain his academic honor. On June 27, 1857, Mitchell was at Black Mountain with his son and survey guides. While taking a scouting hike alone in a gorge north of Little Piney Ridge he was caught in a thunderstorm. He apparently fell from a waterfall and drowned while unconscious. Though he was first buried in Asheville, the following year, on June 16, 1858, he was re-interred near the observation tower at the summit of Mount Mitchell.

In 1882 the U.S. Geological Survey obtained an altitude measurement of 6,684 feet—only 12 feet less than Mitchell's measurement. Clingman's error was 268 feet, but it was too late for an apology to the professor.

 **SEVEN**

PISGAH NATIONAL FOREST
(GRANDFATHER RANGER DISTRICT)

SECTION 10. Buck Creek Gap (NC-80 and Blue Ridge Parkway MP 344.1) to Woodlawn Park (US-221)

YANCEY AND MCDOWELL COUNTIES: (See Yancey County discussion in Section 9.) McDowell County's 447 square miles were taken from Rutherford and Burke Counties in 1842. Its name honors Major Joseph McDowell (1758– 96), who fought in the Battle of Kings Mountain and later served as a member of Congress. The county seat is Marion, incorporated in 1844 and named for General Francis Marion (1732–95) of Revolutionary War fame. (Francis Marion National Forest in South Carolina is named for him as well.)

On the north side of the county boundary is the Blue Ridge Parkway, and large sections of Pisgah National Forest cover nearly half of the county, all the way down the mountain to the West Fork of the Catawba River and part of Lake James. Some of the natural and historic areas located in McDowell County are Linville Caverns, Old Fort, Lake Tahoma, and Lake James State Park. Through highways are I-40 and US-70 in the east-west direction, and US-221 and NC-226 in the north-south direction.

LENGTH AND DIFFICULTY: 13.1 miles, strenuous (2,016-foot change in elevation)

USGS TOPO MAPS: Celo, Little Switzerland

FEATURES OR EMPHASIS: Chinquapins on Woods Mountain, scenic views of Dobson Knob and Table Rock

TRAILS FOLLOWED: Woods Mountain Access Trail, Woods Mountain Trail, Woodlawn Trail

TRAIL CONNECTIONS: Armstrong Creek Trail, Woodlawn Trail

WEST TRAILHEAD: Buck Creek Gap parking lot on NC-80 and Parkway milepost 344.1 (16 miles west from Marion and 14 miles east from Micaville)

EAST TRAILHEAD: Parking lot at Woodlawn Park picnic area on US-221, 5.7 miles north of Marion and 16.0 miles south of Linville Falls

CAMPING, LODGING, AND PROVISIONS: (See Section 9 for description of camping and provisions near Buck Creek Gap.) Camping is available off the trail in Pisgah National Forest. At Woodlawn Park are picnic tables and a restroom but no telephone. Pizza will be delivered to you if you call Chow-Time in Marion (telephone: 828-652-0219); if you do not have a cellular phone, you may place your call 1.1-mile north at Woodlawn Motel. From Woodlawn Park it is 2.1 miles south on US-221 to a food mart and snack bar, and gasoline; 3.0 miles farther south on US-221, on the left, is Sportsman Inn, a motel that is open all year (telephone: 828-659-7525). Farther south another 0.6 miles, at the juncture with US-70, there is a large shopping center with Wal-Mart, restaurants, and a Comfort Inn (telephone: 800-228-5150 or 828-652-4888) with continental breakfast and heated pool (children free). North of Woodlawn Park on US-221 it is 1.1 miles to the family-owned Woodlawn Motel (telephone: 828-756-0070); and 0.2 miles farther is Wood-lawn Country Store, open every day (6 A.M. to midnight, Monday–Saturday, and 7 A.M. to midnight on Sunday) and offering groceries, grilled food service, and gasoline.

INFORMATION AND SECURITY: Trail Maintenance: Central Blue Ridge Task Force (telephone: 828-437-6635). McDowell County Chamber of Commerce, 629 Tate Street, Marion, NC 28752 (telephone: 828-652-4240). McDowell County Sheriff's Office: 187 Spaulding Road, Marion, NC 28752 (telephone: 828-652-4000).

DESCRIPTION: From the parking lot at Buck Creek Gap ascend to the overpass of the Parkway and follow right on an old Parkway service road (Woods Mountain Access Trail) for 0.7 miles. At a large white oak on the left, turn right off the old road onto a footpath, the Woods Mountain Trail. Skirt south of a knob, leave the Parkway boundary, and at 0.9 miles descend to a gap where there is a left-hand juncture with the Armstrong Creek Trail. (It descends 3.0 miles to the Armstrong Fish Hatchery on SR-1443.) Continue on the remote Woods Mountain Trail along Woods Mountain ridge, where there are outstanding views of Table Rock, Hawksbill, Green Knob, Mount Mitchell, Mackey Mountain, Lake Tahoma, and Armstrong Valley at 1.2 miles and 1.3 miles. Chinquapin, turkey grass, mountain laurel, blueberry, pitch pine, and oaks grow along the ridge. Local wildlife includes deer, grouse, turkey, and black bear.

At 2.4 miles the trail slopes on the north side of the ridge in an arbor of rhododendron, galax, and trailing arbutus. At 2.5 miles you will come to a juncture, right, with an old trail that descends to Singecat Branch. Stay left and ascend to a level area on Timber Ridge at 2.7 miles. Curve right to descend on an old road with switchbacks at 3.0 miles. At 3.3 miles is a shallow saddle, then an open forest. At 3.9 miles is a view left (north) from an outcrop, where you can view U.S. Forest Service clear-cuts. Drop to a wide saddle then ascend at 4.3 miles. Pass through tall hemlocks in an open forest; ignore an old road to the right at 4.5 miles. At 4.9 miles ascend steeply on a rocky ridge for views, to the left at 5.1 miles, of Grandfather Mountain, Table Rock, and Hawksbill peaks. Ascend steeply to a knob at 5.3 miles. After another knob descend, then ascend at an unused FR-104 junction at 5.8 miles, the end of the Woods Mountain Trail. (An old road goes left 0.2 miles to the former Woods Mountain fire tower, at 3,646 feet in elevation.) The Mountains-to-Sea Trail continues right (south) for a descent on Betsy Ridge.

In the descent avoid side timber roads and hunters' trails. At 6.6 miles you will see an old road to the left, an abandoned trail ahead, and a turn right for the MST. Keep left at 6.9 miles at another juncture on an easy treadway. At 7.7 miles the road forks; turn left. (An old road to the right ascends to a knob with views of Mount Mitchell and Lake Tahoma.) Turn left at 8.2 miles, again at 8.6 miles (at a berm) down the north side of a ridge, and again at 9.6 miles (at a berm). At 9.7 miles join a used forest road and keep left. Cross a number of streams, one with a low cement bridge at 10.3 miles. Leave the road at 11.0 miles on a footpath to the right. Pass through broomsedge and briars to cross a creek on a log after 100 yards. Pass through rhododendron, fetterbush, and running cedar; turn left on an old road. Curve right after ascending to a ridge at 11.9 miles. At 12.2 miles reach a wide road; turn left (blaze may be after the turn) through tulip poplars and white and Virginia pines. Turn left at 12.8 miles, then connect with the Woodlawn Trail (a physical fitness trail) at 13.0 miles. Follow it on the ridge to its exit at the parking lot, which is across the road from the Woodlawn Work Center at 13.1 miles. From the parking lot is an access into Woodlawn Park, where there are picnic tables and a restroom on US-221. This section of the MST was designated a state trail in May 1989.

CAMPSIDE STORIES: This is a namesake story about Joseph McDowell, a local hero, born February 25, 1758, at Pleasant Garden near US-70 west of Marion. Woodlawn is about halfway between his birthplace and Ashford, north on US-221, near the route of the march on the Overmountain Victory Trail. McDowell was part of that march. In his youth he received his education in Winchester, Virginia, a home base for the McDowell family. Heroism and success followed the family to what are now Burke and McDowell Counties in North Carolina.

At the age of eighteen McDowell and a second cousin (also named Joseph) enlisted in a local regiment commanded by another cousin, Charles

McDowell. Four years later and now a major, McDowell, his cousins, and other regiment men marched south with the Overmountain Men who had arrived from the northwest of North Carolina, Virginia, and Tennessee to defeat British Major Patrick Ferguson at the Battle of Kings Mountain on October 7, 1780. Following the battle McDowell was given an honorary title of general. He studied medicine and law and passed the bar exams in 1791. A delegate to the Continental Congress, he served as a member of the House of Commons and a four-year term on the Board of Trustees of the University of North Carolina. He married Mary Moffitt, and the couple had three children. McDowell died at the age of 37. When the county was formed in 1842 it was named in his honor.

SECTION 11. Woodlawn Park (US-221) to Ripshin Ridge (NC-181)

MCDOWELL AND BURKE COUNTIES: (See McDowell County discussion in Section 10.) Burke County and the city of Morganton, county seat, were founded in 1777. The 517-square-mile county honors Dr. Thomas Burke (1747–83), a representative of the Continental Congress and state governor. Morganton was named to honor General David Morgan (1736–1802) of the Revolutionary War. The Linville Gorge Wilderness is in the upper northeast corner of the county and includes Linville Falls, the Linville River, and panoramic peaks on the gorge's east rim—Hawksbill and Table Rock. The Linville River flows into Lake James, a large lake of which about half is in McDowell County. At the south border of the county is the large South Mountains State Park. Highways through the county are the east-west routes I-40, US-70, US-64, and NC-126, and the north-south routes NC-181 and NC-18.

LENGTH AND DIFFICULTY: 33.3 miles, exceptionally strenuous (see "Description," ahead)

USGS TOPO MAPS: Little Switzerland, Ashford, Linville Falls, Chestnut Mountain

FEATURES OR EMPHASIS: North Fork of Catawba River, Bald Knob, Dobson Knob, Pinnacle, Linville River, Shortoff Mountain, Linville Gorge Wilderness, Table Rock, Steels Creek

TRAILS FOLLOWED: Overmountain Victory Trail, Shortoff Mountain Trail, Table Rock Summit Trail, Table Rock Gap Trail, Upper Steels Creek Trail

TRAIL CONNECTIONS: Cambric Branch Trail, Little Table Rock Trail, Greentown Shortcut Trail, Persimmon Ridge Trail

WEST TRAILHEAD: Woodlawn Park picnic area on US-221, 5.7 miles north from Marion and 16.0 miles south of Linville Falls

EAST TRAILHEAD: On NC-181 at a parking lot for the Greentown Trail, 0.4 miles south of Barkhouse Picnic Area. This location is 21.4 miles northwest from US-70 in Morganton, and 7.4 miles southeast from the Blue Ridge Parkway (milepost 312.2).

CAMPING, LODGING, AND PROVISIONS: (See Section 10 for services at west trailhead.) Camping is allowed throughout Pisgah National Forest, except on private property that you will cross as you ascend Bald Knob, in a section of the national forest near the Linville River, and in sight of the Table Rock Picnic Area. From the east trailhead there are light provisions and gasoline up the mountain on NC-181 for 4.5 miles.

INFORMATION AND SECURITY: Trail Maintenance: Central Blue Ridge Task Force (telephone: 828-437-6635). McDowell County Sheriff's Office: 187 Spaulding Road, Marion, NC 28752 (telephone: 828-652-4000). Burke County Sheriff's Office: 150 Government Drive (P.O. Box 219), Morganton, NC 28680 (telephone: 828-438-5500). Grandfather Ranger District, Pisgah National Forest: Route 1, Box 110-A, Nebo, NC 28761 (exit 90 on I-40) (telephone: 828-652-2144).

DESCRIPTION: This section is the most difficult and challenging of all the sections of the Mountains-to-Sea Trail. For example, there are steep climbs without switchbacks up Bald and Dobson Knobs and Shortoff Mountain. It also has some of the most spectacular scenery. Careful preparation is required for wading the North Fork of the Catawba and Linville Rivers at regular depths. Steeles Creek is not as wide as the rivers, and is less challenging. The streams may have high or flood-stage water levels in late winter and early spring, or from summer storms. You should try to avoid flooding, icy, or snow-melting seasons. Trail construction is complete in this section of the MST except for the part after crossing the North Fork of the Catawba River and ascending to Dobson Knob (this may be under construction by the time this book is published). Meanwhile, a temporary route is partly on private property. Because of the long ascents and descents on this route, adequate time should be allowed and a backpack with complete gear should be carried.

From the Woodlawn Park picnic area parking lot, cross the four-lane US-221 at a southeast angle to enter a paved forest road at 0.1 mile. Pass a trail sign and gate and follow the main gravel road. Pass an intersection at 0.4 miles, a U.S. Forest Service helicopter site on the left at 0.5 miles, and leave the road, left, at 0.6 miles. Enter a wildlife field and after 100 yards turn right into the forest. Ascend on nine well-designed switchbacks among pines, mountain laurel, rhododendron, and young hardwoods to exit at another gravel forest road on Bald Mountain at 1.6 miles.

Turn right and descend, then rejoin the main gravel forest road by turning left. Turn left again at 1.9 miles to ascend on a less traveled road. To the right

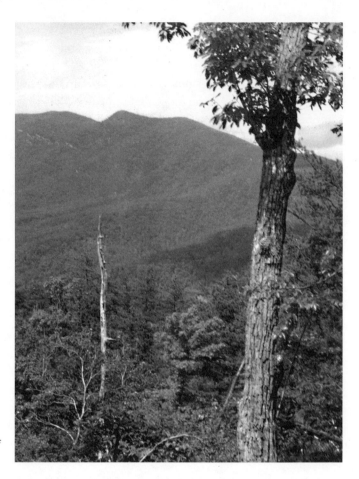

Northeast view of
Bald Knob

are views of the city of Marion. Reach a cul-de-sac at 2.0 miles, and begin a descent on a spur ridge of Bald Mountain. After you leave the woods, enter a clear-cut, where for the next 0.3 miles you will find outstanding views of the North Fork of the Catawba River gorge. Beyond is the massive ridge of Bald Knob on the right, a twin knob in the middle, and Dobson Knob, the highest, to the left. Lake James can be seen to the southeast. On this open space along the trail in early July are rosebud orchids. In early September chinquapins are ripe along the trail.

Reenter the forest, descend steeply, and pass through mountain laurel, hardwoods, and bear grass, all naturally decorated with a base of quartz. Arrive at the main forest road embankment at 3.0 miles. Turn left. Follow a pleasantly graded forest road that meanders by a stream to a large and flat wildlife grazing field. At 3.6 miles pass under a power line and by a national forest road gate. Curve left and at 3.8 miles leave the road by turning right

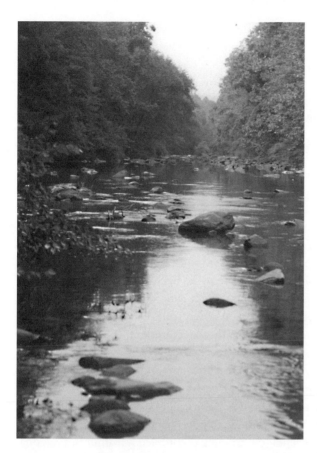

Mountains-to-Sea Trail crossing of the North Fork of the Catawba River

into the woods. (Watch for white blazes.) Descend 120 feet to rock-hop a small stream. Pass through an island floodplain with poplar, sycamore, spice bush, and scouring rush. After 100 yards wade the 205-foot-wide North Fork of the Catawba River. There are three forested islands to the right. (When fording the river be alert to slippery rocks, wear some kind of shoes, loosen your backpack at the waist, and carry a staff for stabilizing your balance. There are plans to construct a footbridge across the river.)

After fording the North Fork of the Catawba River, follow the MST north 0.1 mile to cross the Clinchfield Railroad at 4.0 miles near railroad sign #2117. Across the railroad is an old forest road, right and left. The MST goes right on a temporary route. (To the left on the old forest road a new MST route is planned to reach Bald Knob entirely within the boundaries of Pisgah National Forest. The route would partially follow the road 1.3 miles before turning right to ascend a combination of ridges for an additional 2.3 miles. A scenic route with overlooks, there would be approximately thirty-five switchbacks. There would be a water source and camping would be allowed. For a progress report, telephone the Central Blue Ridge Task Force at 828-437-6635.)

On the temporary route, ascend easily a few yards on the old forest road and turn left off the road onto an ATV trail. Follow the ATV route, first in a flat area and then on an exceptionally steep, eroded trail through scattered pines, hardwoods, mountain laurel, and rhododendron. Level off at 4.2 miles on a ridge gap, but gradually ascend to enter the south boundary of Champion International Corporation's property at 4.6 miles. The location is marked by swatches of white paint on the trees. A sign should indicate the boundary and access restrictions on the private property. For example, camping and campfires are not allowed. (In 1999 the Friends of the Mountains-to-Sea Trail [FMST] signed a contract with Champion for the MST right-of-way until the new MST on Pisgah National Forest property is constructed and open, or at which time Champion sells the 4,500-acre trace of timberland to another owner. For information, telephone FMST at 919-496-4771.) Arrive at an old and rocky road, to the right and left. Turn left and ascend steeply 300 yards to the end of an eroded road at an unauthorized campsite.

Ascend past the trashy campsite into a forest of hardwoods with patchy sections of mountain laurel, hemlock, and blueberries. Ascend northeasterly to stay on the ridgeline. The higher the altitude the more narrow becomes the ridge among rock outcroppings. At 6.1 miles exit the boundary of the Champion property. (On the left at 6.3 miles may be the juncture with the new MST route that ascends the mountain completely within the national forest.) Reach the panoramic summit of Bald Knob (elevation 3,495 feet, and 2,175 feet above the North Fork of the Catawba River) at 6.6 miles. Plan to rest at this isolated and scenic spot. There is almost always a cool breeze, and the faint sounds of the freight trains at the bottom of the canyon seem dreamy and far away. The knob is rugged and windswept, and mountain laurel, rhododendron, and galax are tightly clustered in the sharp rock crevices. Views west include Bald Mountain, Graveyard Mountain, Woods Mountain, and the Black Mountains range, including Mount Mitchell. To the northwest are the lowlands of Turkey Cove, and beyond are multiple ridges, such as Pompey and Chestnut, that ascend to the Blue Ridge Mountains and Blue Ridge Parkway. To the north is Dobson Knob (elevation 3,685 feet), and to the northeast are views of Pond Ridge, Paddy Creek Gorge, and Linville Gorge Wilderness. Views to the south and southeast include sections of Lake James and the towns of Morganton and Marion. Backtrack to a level portion of the trail and turn right (west) for an easy descent to a gap at 6.7 miles.

Ascend among white oaks, red spruces, hemlocks, and witch-hazel to an old forest road. At 7.4 miles the passage becomes mainly level on the east edge of Dobson Knob. Descend on the old road to a level, small open area at 7.8 miles. (There is a spur trail to the right, which may show evidence of ATV use.) You are now on Linville Mountain; continue on the old road, descend, pass a wildlife field on the left, and arrive at a cul-de-sac of FR-106 at 8.2 miles. (There is a desirable campsite here; the headwaters of Black Fork are 250 yards down a narrow old road beginning at the east corner of the cul-de-sac.)

Follow FR-106, which tracks up and down and along the ridgeline of Linville Mountain. At 8.7 miles, pass a wildlife field to the left. There is a radio tower on the right at 10.0 miles and a cellular relay carrier at 10.1 miles on the left. Arrive at a crossing of the yellow-blazed Overmountain Victory Trail (OVT) at 11.2 miles. There is space for about three vehicles to park here. (To the left the OVT descends 2.0 miles to private property at Old Linville Road [SR-1560]. Permission for entrance is required from the landowner at the gated trailhead. [From the trailhead it is 2.5 miles north on Old Linville Road to US-221 and the community of Ashford.]) Forest Road 106 continues ahead 1.0 mile to a juncture with the Kistler Memorial Highway (SR-1238), but FR-106 is gated and locked except during hunting season.

Turn right on the OVT, an old wagon road, and at 11.7 miles cross Yellow Fork in a rhododendron thicket. Cross another small stream at 12.4 miles. Pass through a forest of hardwoods, white pine, and mountain laurel to reach the gravel Kistler Memorial Highway (SR-1238) at 12.7 miles, the section end of the OVT. (It is 4.1 miles to the right, steeply down the mountain to NC-126, where with a right turn it is 7.6 miles to Nebo and the US-70 junction; a left turn takes you 16.3 miles to Morganton.)

To continue on the Mountains-to-Sea Trail, turn left on the Kistler Road to a parking area on the left; at 13.5 miles arrive at a small parking area on the right. Turn right on an old road with mounds of dirt. (The Kistler Road continues ahead 12.3 miles to the Linville Falls community.) (The cumulative mileage for this long section of trail ends here, and mileage restarts at zero for another long and rigorous section.)

After 0.2 miles on the dirt road you will come to a spur trail on the right. (The U.S. Forest Service plans a restructure of this route, and below the Pinnacle will be an observation deck for bird watching.) It ascends to the Pinnacle (elevation 2,816 feet) for a panoramic view of Linville Gorge and Shortoff Mountain (east), Lake James (south), Table Rock (northeast), and Dogback Mountain (north). Return to the main trail and follow the white blazes down the mountain through a hardwood forest with understory of

The Overmountain Men

In celebration of the bicentennial (1780–1980) of the "Overmountain Men," the yellow-blazed Overmountain Victory Trail was planned, constructed, and designated a National Historic Trail in 1980. During the American Revolution, Major Patrick Ferguson (made a colonel by the British near the time of his death) of the Loyalist Army sent word to the frontier mountain men that he would destroy them, "hang their leaders, and lay their country waste with fire and sword." The men responded by mustering a troop of one thousand men from Virginia, Tennessee, and North Carolina to seek out Major Ferguson. On the way the men passed along this route on September 30, 1780, twelve days after they left Sycamore Shoals in Tennessee.

The men found Major Ferguson at Kings Mountain, South Carolina (now Kings Mountain National Military Park). It was a one-hour battle, today remembered as the Battle of Kings Mountain, lasting from three to four o'clock on a Saturday afternoon, October 7, 1780. Americans were pitted against Americans; Major Ferguson was the only Englishman. Patriot losses were 28 killed and 62 wounded; Loyalist losses were 225 slain (including Major Ferguson), 163 wounded, and 716 taken prisoner. Major Ferguson's decision to ensconce his troops on a hilltop where he could be surrounded was a deadly mistake, though he had said "God could not drive him from it."

mountain laurel. Turn left on an old logging road at 0.5 miles. Reach a clear-cut at 0.8 miles. Follow an old logging road, cross Sandy Branch twice, at 1.2 miles and 1.5 miles. Ascend to a knob and pass through patches of bristly locust. Descend, turn sharply left off the logging road at 2.3 miles, and reach a road and gate to private property at 2.4 miles. Turn left and after 0.3 miles turn sharply right off the road in a descent to the Linville River (elevation 1,280 feet). Vegetation near the river includes ironwood, doghobble, sycamore, hemlock, gums, and yellowroot.

Wade the 60-foot-wide river, which has deeper water and stronger currents than the Catawba. Turn right on low ground that is easily flooded. (For your safety, remember to follow the suggestions offered above for fording the North Fork of the Catawba River.) After walking 0.2 miles downstream, turn left. Ascend through a rhododendron thicket, and then cross a ravine at 3.2 miles. Ascend in a forest of oak, pine, mountain laurel, and turkey beard. When you reach a juncture with an old woods road at 3.4 miles turn left. Ascend gradually to a juncture with a foot trail at 4.5 miles. (The old road ahead is a longer route to the top of Shortoff Mountain, and the foot trail right is a private access route from Old Wolf Pit Road.) Turn left on the

Shortoff Mountain Trail. You will soon gain scenic views of the Linville Gorge Wilderness from the precipitous west side of the mountain. A small spring is in a crevice at 4.9 miles. (The spring usually has water but is not dependable in a long dry summer.) There are more scenic views to the left on short spur trails. There are thick patches of sand myrtle, chestnut oak, and blueberry. Reach an entrance to an old jeep road (elevation 3,000 feet) at 5.0 miles. To the left are spectacular views of Linville Gorge, Table Rock, and Hawksbill. To continue follow the old jeep road, but turn left on another old woods road at 5.2 miles. Pass a water hole to the left at 5.5 miles. Reach a knob at 7.9 miles in a forest of large white pines and oaks. Leave the ridge crest, turn right, and at 8.4 miles enter a bed of galax, where to the right is a 60-yard spur trail to an intermittent spring. On the main trail, in a gap at 8.5 miles, the obscure Cambric Ridge Trail takes off to the left. (It descends 1.3 miles to a dead-end at the Linville River.) Reach Chimney Gap at 8.9 miles.

Ascend, steeply in spots, to the Chimneys at 9.5 miles. Pass through dense evergreens on the west side of the Chimneys at 9.8 miles and to scenic areas for views at 10.2 miles. (There may be posted off-limit signs to restrict your use of the spur trails to the Chimneys if peregrine falcons, an endangered species, have been seen here.) Chinquapins grow here among the blueberries. Arrive at Table Rock Picnic Area at 10.6 miles. The area has picnic tables, a garbage stand, and vault toilets, but no water. It is for day use only; camping is not permitted. (Paved road access is from NC-181 in Jonas Ridge on Old Gingercake Road [SR-1264] for 0.3 miles, before turning left on Gingercake Acres Road [SR-1265], which becomes FR-210 (gravel) for 5.9 miles. Then turn right on FR-210B and ascend for another 2.9 miles, partially on a steep paved road near the end, to reach the Table Rock Picnic Area.)

Cross the parking area and follow the Table Rock Summit Trail. The Little Table Rock Trail joins from the left at 10.9 miles. Turn right, ascend 100 yards, and take a sharp left on the Table Rock Gap Trail. (The Table Rock Summit Trail continues the ascent of 0.4 miles to panoramic views at 3,909 feet elevation.) (See "Campside Stories, below.) Follow a rocky treadway, and at 11.6 miles begin a steep descent. Reach an unmaintained road cul-de-sac at 11.8 miles, the end of the wilderness boundary. Cross the road, turn right, and descend on an old logging road to the gravel FR-210 at 12.0 miles. Turn right on FR-210 and go 0.1 mile to make a left turn off the road. Descend, steeply in spots, on an old woods road among rhododendron, white pine, and oak to reach the gravel FR-496 at 12.5 miles. A small stream is to your right. (It is 5.6 miles left on FR-496 to the north terminus of the

Upper Steels Creek Trail and continuing Mountains-to-Sea Trail.) Turn right on FR-496 and reach a gate and parking area at 12.6 miles. (It is 35 yards ahead to FR-210, and 65 yards right on FR-210 to the Table Rock Picnic Road, FR-210B, left.)

Continue on the MST by turning left from the gate onto an old jeep road with hummocks. Pines, rhododendron, and trailing arbutus are prominent. The headwaters of Buck Creek can be heard from the left. Turn sharply right on a foot trail at 13.1 miles. Follow an erratic trail, which is partly on footpaths and partly on old logging roads, up and down grades in coves, across streamlets, and over ridges, for 2.2 miles to an exceptionally steep descent at 15.3 miles. Arrive at the base of the ridge and a trail junction at 15.7 miles in an area of Devil's walking-stick, white pine, and ferns. Turn left (right is a fisherman's trail downstream), and rock-hop Buck Creek. Come to a junction with the Upper Steels Creek Trail, from the right. (To the right the Upper Steels Creek Trail crosses the creek and follows an old four-wheel-drive route downstream for 0.2 miles to FR-228 and a parking area. From here it is 3.9 miles out to NC-181.)

Continue upstream, jointly with the Upper Steels Creek Trail, and ascend next to rapids and pools. To the right at 16.2 miles is a waterfall. Cross an intermittent stream at 16.3 miles. Turn sharply left at 16.5 miles (easy to miss) and ascend steeply. Follow a combination of old logging roads and railroad grades, cross a deep chasm, and pass cascades and pools. Arrive at a beautiful flat area at 16.8 miles where campsites in fern beds are shaded by tall maples, poplars, locusts, and hemlocks. Enter a wildlife field and follow its east edge to a forest road; turn right, rock-hop Gingercake Creek, and after 70 yards rock-hop Steels Creek. Walk on an easy forest road amid tall tulip poplars, white pines, and hemlocks. At 17.5 miles rock-hop Steels Creek again and then once again at 17.6 miles. Continue on the old forest road and gradually ascend to a ridge at 18.3 miles. Enter a cut in the ridge and come to a juncture with an old road on the right, the Mountains-to-Sea Trail route, at 18.4 miles. (Here the Upper Steels Creek Trail goes ahead for 120 yards to the locked gate and access with FR-496. Right on FR-496 it is 1.3 miles to NC-181.) Follow the MST on the old road and cross a scenic and high cascading tributary to Steels Creek at 18.5 miles. Reach a parking area on FR-496 at 18.9 miles; turn right on the road and pass a grassy field at 19.2 miles. Arrive at NC-181 at 19.8 miles, and cross the highway to a parking area for the Greentown Trail. (This section of the MST was designated in October 1986.) Up the mountain on NC-181 it is 4.5 miles for gasoline and light provisions. Down the mountain on NC-181 it is 0.7 miles to the Brown Mountain Lights parking area on the left. (See "Campside Stories" in Section 12.)

CAMPSIDE STORIES: This section of the MST crosses legendary territory from the history of the Catawba and Cherokee Indians. In fording the Catawba River you may imagine why they called it *Catawba*, meaning "people of the river." There is evidence that these people fished, hunted, and camped along the river valleys and both forks. When you ford the Linville River you may think of the name William Linville and his son John, who were ambushed and murdered by the Cherokee in 1766. With them was sixteen-year-old John Williams, who was injured but played dead until the Cherokee left. Then, despite his broken leg, he climbed onto one of the horses and rode for five days "from near the mouth of the Wataga [*sic*] to the Hollows in Surry before coming to a House." Folk historians are not certain where the massacre took place because the records show the site was "below the falls," or "in the gorge," or "near the headwaters above the falls." The Linvilles were pioneer explorers and hunters. In addition to the Linville River, the name is honored in the name of a town, two townships, two creeks, the falls, the gorge, a lake, and a mountain.

The Cherokee called the Linville River *Eeseeoh*, "river of cliffs." Table Rock was called *Namonda* and was used for ceremonial worship of the great spirits. Contrary to some folklore, historians do not think the stories are true about the Cherokee using Table Rock for human sacrifices.

SECTION 12. Ripshin Ridge (NC-181) to Beacon Heights (Blue Ridge Parkway MP 305.3)

BURKE AND AVERY COUNTIES: (See Burke County discussion in Section 11.) Avery County, with 247 square miles of mountainous terrain, is shaped like an arrow pointing north. At its western border with Tennessee are Big Yellow Mountain (6,189 feet in elevation) and the Appalachian Trail. Its eastern border with Watauga County crosses the Grandfather Mountain range (elevation 5,964 feet). The Watauga River flows along the county's northern border, and Pisgah National Forest is at its southern border. In between is Beech Mountain—the Tennessee Valley Divide where the rivers flow north.

The county was named for Colonel Waightstill Avery (1741–1821) of the Revolutionary War, who also served as state attorney general. Avery County was formed in 1911 from parts of Mitchell, Watauga, and Caldwell Counties. Its county seat, founded in 1913, is Newland, named for William C. Newland (1860–1938), lieutenant governor of North Carolina from 1909 to 1913. Highway access is on US-221, US-19E, NC-194, and NC-181 (north-south) and NC-194 (east-west).

LENGTH AND DIFFICULTY: 24.2 miles (main), 21.5 (alternate), strenuous

USGS TOPO MAPS: Chestnut Mountain, Grandfather Mountain

FEATURES OR EMPHASIS: Harper Creek Falls and North Harper Creek cascades, South Harper Creek Falls, Hunt-Fish Falls, Lost Cove Creek, Gragg Prong Falls and cascades, Beacon Heights scenic views

TRAILS FOLLOWED: Greentown Trail, Raider Camp Trail, Harper Creek Trail, North Harper Creek Trail, North Harper Creek Access Trail, Hunt-Fish Falls Trail, Lost Cove Trail, Beacon Heights Trail

TRAIL CONNECTIONS: Greentown Shortcut Trail, Phillips Branch Trail, Persimmon Ridge Trail, Timber Ridge Trail

CAMPING, LODGING, AND PROVISIONS: Camping is allowed throughout Pisgah National Forest, off of roads and trails; it is prohibited on the Blue Ridge Parkway property at Beacon Heights. (The Mortimer Recreation Area, described below, has limited facilities and is off the MST route.) From Beacon Heights at the Blue Ridge Parkway, it is 3.0 miles southwest on US-221 to the town of Linville, where there are groceries, a post office, and a Texaco service station. Also in Linville are the Pixie Inn and Tartan Restaurant at the corner of US-221 and NC-105. The inn is open from April through October (telephone: 828-733-2597). Linville Cottage Bed and Breakfast, on Ruffin Street, is open all year (telephone: 828-733-6551).

WEST TRAILHEAD: The Greentown Trail parking area on NC-181 is 0.4 miles south of Barkhouse Picnic Area, or 4.2 miles southeast from the Jonas Ridge community; it is 7.4 miles on NC-181 through Jonas Ridge from the Blue Ridge Parkway at milepost 312.2. From Morganton, at the junction of US-70, follow NC-181 for 21.4 miles northwest to the Greentown Trail parking area on the right. (At the MST crossing of NC-181, you cross the Mountains-to-Sea Bicycle Route #2 that is on NC-181. The bicycle route will not be crossed again until you cross NC-98, north of Raleigh and west of Wake Forest.)

EAST TRAILHEAD: At the Beacon Heights parking lot on the Blue Ridge Parkway, milepost 305.3

INFORMATION AND SECURITY: Trail Maintenance: Central Blue Ridge Task Force (telephone: 828-437-6635). Burke County Chamber of Commerce: 110 East Meeting Street, Morganton, NC 28655 (telephone: 828-437-3021). Grandfather Ranger District, Pisgah National Forest: Route 1 Box 110-A, Nebo, NC 28761 (telephone: 828-652-2144). Burke County Sheriff's Office: 150 Government Drive (P.O. Box 219), Morganton, NC 28680 (telephone: 828-438-5500). Avery County Sheriff's Office: 1 Jail Street (P.O. Box 426), Newland, NC 28657 (telephone: 828-733-5855).

DESCRIPTION: Begin this section at the Greentown Trail parking area as described above. (If you have a vehicle you may find it interesting to drive 1.1 miles up the mountain on NC-181 to the Upper Creek Falls Trail parking lot, right. The 1.6-mile loop trail descends to spectacular waterfalls in a rugged chasm.) For the next 18.3 miles, the white-blazed Mountains-to-Sea Trail follows trails in the Grandfather Ranger District of Pisgah National Forest. Another 3.2 miles is on an old, rocky forest road, and 2.3 miles is on a foot trail constructed specifically for a climb to Blue Ridge Parkway property and Beacon Heights. Hikers have reported some difficulty in determining trail identity through the interconnecting trail system ahead, particularly in the Harper Creek and Lost Cove Creek wilderness areas. You may wish to purchase a small folding map titled "Wilson Creek Area Trail Map" (1996) from Pisgah National Forest if you plan to hike more than just the MST. The map also indicates authorized trail usage and lists safety/security tips and forest regulations. The Forest Service has numbers for all of its trails, and the names and numbers are listed on the map. I have listed some trail numbers in the event that the trail name is missing and the numbers remain. The MST number, if shown, is 440.

On the Greentown Trail (#268) descend steeply on an old logging road that has berms to prevent erosion. After 1.0 miles rock-hop Upper Creek in a rhododendron grove. At 1.8 miles the Greentown Shortcut Trail is on the right, near the confluence of Upper Creek and Burnthouse Branch. (The Greentown Shortcut Trail [#268A] descends in a gorge on the east side of Upper Creek to scenic Lower Upper Creek Falls at 0.7 miles. Another 0.5 miles leads to a parking area on FR-197.)

Continuing on the Greentown Trail, weave in and out of coves that have small streams. The forest is mainly hardwoods, rhododendron, and mountain laurel. Arrive at a USFS gate at 3.7 miles. A juncture with FR-198 is at 3.8 miles. Turn left, pass a parking area (left) and another gate at 3.9 miles. Ascend through a forest of oaks and white pine with roadside borders of Devil's walking-stick and trailing arbutus. At 4.2 miles, right, on the roadbank is a freshwater pipe spring. At the top of a ridge watch for the MST blazes at a network of forest roads. In a curve at 5.5 miles leave the road and descend left to another old road. Turn sharply right. At 5.8 miles intersect with Raider Camp Trail [#277], right and left, in a halfmoon curve. The main MST route curves right.

(To the left in the curve an alternate MST gently follows a ridge 0.2 miles to high cliffs over the Harper Creek gorge. From this spectacular view can be seen the 200-foot South Harper Creek Falls. Left of the cliffs, the alternate MST descends on switchbacks for wading or rock-hopping Harper Creek. At 0.6 miles intersect with Harper Creek Trail, right and left. [To the left Harper Creek Trail ascends 1.3 miles to its west end at FR-58.] Turn right and descend on switchbacks to the base of the waterfall. At the creekside begin the first of eight crossings [wading or rock-hopping]. Although the crossings are generally in low water, the creek has sections of falls, rapids, flumes, and large boulders. On the sylvan creek banks the trail has a canopy of hardwoods, hemlock, and rhododendron. There are frequent patches of ferns and fedderbushes. At 2.2 miles rejoin the main MST at an intersection with North Harper Creek Trail, left.)

At the junction of the Greentown Trail and Raider Camp Trail, continue right on Raider Camp Trail. Follow a ridge but descend to eventually parallel Raider Camp Creek where it passes from Avery County into Caldwell County. Come to the juncture with the Phillips Creek Trail, right, at 8.0 miles. Rock-hop Harper Creek at 8.3 miles, and then arrive at the juncture with the Harper Creek Trail, right and left, at 8.4 miles. (To the right, in 1.3 miles, is access to Wilson Creek Road, SR-1328.)

Turn left on the Harper Creek Trail and pass cascades and waterfalls. (A spur trail goes near the base of the falls.) Rock-hop the creek twice before coming to a juncture with the North Harper Creek Trail (#266) at 10.7 miles, and turn right. (The Harper Creek Trail with MST alternate continues left.) Rock-hop the creek twice before crossing the Persimmon Ridge Trail at 11.2 miles. At the juncture with the North Harper Creek Access Trail (#266A), at 12.8 miles, turn right. (The North Harper Creek Trail continues upstream.) Arrive at FR-464 and a parking space at 13.8 miles. Turn right and follow FR-464 for 0.6 miles to a parking area, on the left, at the south trailhead of the Hunt-Fish Falls Trail at 14.4 miles. (On FR-464 it is 3.1 miles down the mountain to NC-90, and to the right it is 1.7 miles on NC-90 to Mortimer Recreation Area.)

Descend steeply on switchbacks for 0.8 miles on the Hunt-Fish Falls Trail to the beautiful three-tiered Hunt-Fish Falls and pools, a popular fishing and sunning area at 15.2 miles. Here is the juncture with the Lost Cove Trail, right and left. Turn right and at 15.9 miles, near the convergence of Lost Cove Creek and Gragg Prong, the Timber Ridge Trail branches off to the left. Continue on the Lost Cove Trail, which follows Gragg Prong upstream. Pass a waterfall and over the next 2.0 miles cross the creek four times. The streambed's sculpted rock has created cascades and pools, and there are excellent areas for sunbathing and campsites in the forest. The forest here consists of white pine, oak, mountain laurel, and rhododendron. At 17.2 miles there is a 0.4-mile spur trail to the left that goes to the Timber Ridge Trail. After passing through a small meadow, follow a short length of old road, and then cross a Gragg Prong bridge on FR-981 to a parking area, right, at 18.3 miles. (Access out of here is 4.0 miles east on FR-981 to a juncture, right, on NC-90 at the south edge of the community of Edgemont. On

NC-90, east, it is 2.0 miles farther to Mortimer Recreation Area. Access out of here going west is 0.4 miles on FR-981 to Roseborough and Roseborough Road [SR-1511], which goes 4.5 miles up the mountain to the Blue Ridge Parkway and the town of Linville.)

Across the road from the parking area is the south entrance to FR-192. Follow this narrow and rocky road 3.2 miles upstream, right of the cascading Gragg Prong. Autumn forest foliage makes this a colorful route. (Any attempt to drive this road in a vehicle should be with high-axle four-wheel drive. Depending on erosion or weather, vehicular passage may be impossible.) Hughes Ridge towers to the right. Arrive at Old House Gap at 21.4 miles. (Out from here on FR-192 it is 3.5 miles to a T-intersection with Edgemont Road [SR-1514]. To the right it is 1.0 mile to the community of Gragg. To the left on Edgemont Road it is 4.2 miles to US-221, where another left will take you 0.5 miles to Beacon Heights and the Blue Ridge Parkway.)

At Old House Gap where FR-192 goes straight ahead, there is a yellow-blazed FR-451 on the right. To the left at a national forest gate the Mountains-to-Sea Trail continues on an old woods road. Ascend through a timber cut and turn off right, at 22 miles. Follow an old logging road 0.1 mile to a foot trail on the left. Pass a natural rock shelter at 22.3 miles. At 22.4 miles are views of Beacon Heights and Grandfather Mountain. Cross two small streams in a forest of tall hemlock and oak. Cross two ravines and at 23.1 miles enter a 0.1-mile rhododendron arbor.

Reach a headwater stream of Andrews Creek at 23.3 miles under tall hemlock and cucumber trees. Ascend on switchbacks to scenic areas on the right at 23.8 miles and 23.9 miles. Pitch pine, laurel, witch-hazel, and blueberries are here. At 24 miles come to a juncture with a wide trail; turn right (left it is 35 yards to a small parking area on Gragg Road [SR-1513]). At 24.1 miles arrive at the juncture with the Beacon Heights Trail. (To the right is a large rock outcrop for panoramic views.) Continue ahead on the Beacon Heights Trail, and at 24.2 miles come to the Tanawha Trail on the right. To the left, go 130 yards to the Beacon Heights parking area on the Blue Ridge Parkway (milepost 305.3). On the Parkway to the right is a juncture with US-221. From here it is 3.0 miles southwest on US-221 into Linville for groceries, restaurant, motel, and supply stores. (This section was designated by the state as a part of the Mountains-to-Sea Trail in October 1986.)

CAMPSIDE STORIES: One of the most familiar mountain mysteries is the phenomenon known as the Brown Mountain Lights. From where you cross NC-181 on the MST, it is less than one mile down the mountain, south, on NC-181 to a parking area on the left, from which you can watch for the Brown Mountain

Lights. You probably will not see anything unusual. Others who tired of waiting left you a sign. Examples are "Dont Waste your Time," and "Lights are a Fake." The U.S. Forest Service has placed an official sign: "The long, even-crested mtn in the distance is Brown Mtn. From early times people have observed weird, wavering lights rise above this mtn. Then dwindle and fade away."

First, you need to visit the parking area on a clear dark night, preferably one without moonlight. Second, you must look east, slightly southeast, beyond the first ridge (which is Old Way Ridge). This may mean you need to arrive before dark to focus on the proper ridge. Witnesses have stated that the lights can also be seen from Grandfather Mountain or the Blowing Rock area. Claims are that the lights flicker, dart back and forth, rise up and down, whirl, and slowly fade. (You might also wish to remember that forest service roads ascend to the ridge, and that there is a 40-mile network of trails for ATVs, OHVs, four-wheel-drive vehicles, and motorcycles at the top and in the hollows.)

Both the Catawba and the Cherokee Indians saw the phenomenon as early as 800 years ago. They believed the lights to be women looking for the souls of their husbands lost in battles. A German scientist, Gerald W. de Brahm, in 1771 explained the lights as nitrous vapors that inflamed upon meeting each other in the wind. The U.S. Geological Survey concluded in 1913 that they were locomotive lights from the valley. Even the American Meterological Society made a study in 1941 without a conclusion. There are opinions that the lights are foxfire or St. Elmo's fire, both claimed by scientists not to be possible. Some claim the lights have to be mirages. Others say it does not matter what they are, but they know the lights are real because they have photos to prove it.

 **EIGHT**

BLUE RIDGE PARKWAY
(NORTH AREA)

SECTION 13. Beacon Heights (Blue Ridge Parkway MP 305.3) to Blowing Rock (Blue Ridge Parkway MP 291.9)

AVERY, WATAUGA, AND CALDWELL COUNTIES: (See Avery County description in Section 12.) *Watauga* is a Native American word meaning "beautiful water" (as in the Watagua River). The county was formed in 1849 from parts of Ashe, Wilkes, Caldwell, and Yancey Counties. In its 320-square miles are parts of Pisgah National Forest, a section of the Blue Ridge Parkway, Beech Mountain, Rich Mountain, Elk Knob Game Land, the Appalachian Cultural Museum, Daniel Boone Native Gardens, Mast General Store, and Blowing Rock. The city of Boone is the home of Appalachian State University. Major highways through the county are US-321, US-221, NC-105, and NC-194 (north-south) and US-421 (east-west and partly south).

Caldwell County was founded in 1841 with 480 square miles and was named for Joseph Caldwell (1773–1835), the first president of the University of North Carolina. The city of Lenoir, in the heart of the county, is the county seat. It was named for General William Lenoir (1751–1839), a hero at the Battle of Kings Mountain. In the west and northwest is a large section of the Grandfather Ranger District of Pisgah National Forest, and in the eastern part of the county are the Brushy Mountains. The southeast tip is along the Catawba River and the city of Hickory in Catawba County. Its most northwestern point, near Grandfather Mountain, touches the Blue Ridge Parkway and the Mountains-to-Sea Trail. Major traffic arteries are US-64 and NC-90 (east-west) and US-321, NC-18, and NC-268 (north-south).

LENGTH AND DIFFICULTY: 24.6 miles, moderate to strenuous

USGS TOPO MAPS: Grandfather Mountain, Valle Crucis, Boone

FEATURES OR EMPHASIS: Blue Ridge Parkway, Beacon Heights, Grandfather Mountain, Tanawha Trail, Linn Cove Viaduct, Upper Boone Fork, Price Memorial Park

TRAILS FOLLOWED: Tanawha Trail, Boone Fork Trail, Rich Mountain Trail, Watkins Trail

TRAIL CONNECTIONS: Daniel Boone Scout Trail, Grandfather Mountain Access Trail, Grandfather Trail, Upper Boone Fork Trail, Cold Prong Pond Trail, Black Bottom Trail

WEST TRAILHEAD: Beacon Heights on the Blue Ridge Parkway, milepost 305.3

EAST TRAILHEAD: US-221/321, 1.0 mile west of Blowing Rock

CAMPING, LODGING, AND PROVISIONS: Price Memorial Park Campground (Blue Ridge Parkway milepost 297.1) has 134 tent sites and 60 trailer sites (no hook-ups), picnic area, trout fishing, boat rentals, and hiking trails (telephone: 828-963-5911 in summer). Campground is fully open May 1 through October. (Camping is prohibited on other Parkway property.) Camping is allowed at designated sites off Grandfather Mountain trails with a fee and permit (telephone: 828-733-4337). (For lodging and provisions in Linville, see Chapter 7.) Across the highway (US-221/321) from the MST in Blowing Rock are the New River Inn (telephone: 828-295-0800) and River's Edge Restaurant (telephone: 828-295-0802). It is 1.0 mile south to downtown Blowing Rock, where there are many restaurants, motels and inns, a post office, and supply stores. On the US-321 Bypass it is 1.1 miles from the New River Inn to Food Lion, and along the way it is 0.1 mile to a Shell gasoline station and snacks. Going north from the trailhead on US-221/321 it is 0.1 mile under the Parkway, then 0.2 miles to the Mount View Motel (telephone: 828-295-7991). It is another 4.3 miles to Boone for a large number of motels, restaurants, a post office, supplies, shopping centers, and groceries. Call chambers of commerce listed below for more specific information.

INFORMATION AND SECURITY: Trail Maintenance: Blue Ridge Parkway staff, 199 Hemphill Knob Road, Asheville, NC 28803 (telephone: 828-271-4779; for emergencies and accidents, call 800-727-5928); Grandfather Ranger District, Pisgah National Forest, Route 1, Box 110-A, Nebo, NC 28761 (telephone: 828-652-2144). Avery County Sheriff's Office: 1 Jail Street (P.O. Box 426), Newland, NC 28657. Caldwell County Chamber of Commerce: 1909 Hickory Boulevard S.E., Lenoir, NC 28645 (telephone: 828-726-0616). Caldwell County Sheriff's Office: 214 Mulberry Street N.W., Lenoir, NC 28645 (telephone: 828-754-1518). Boone Area Chamber of Commerce: 208 Howard Street, Boone, NC 28607 (telephone: 828-264-2225 or 800-852-9506). Watauga County Sheriff's Office: 330 Queen Street, Boone, NC 28607 (telephone: 828-264-3761).

DESCRIPTION: Access at the Beacon Heights parking area on the Blue Ridge Parkway (milepost 305.3, elevation 4,205 feet) is at the juncture of the Parkway and US-221. The Mountains-to-Sea Trail follows the Tanawha Trail, an extraordinary example of trail design and construction by the National Park Service. (*Tanawha* means "fabulous hawk" in Cherokee, and the trail is marked with a feather logo in addition to the MST white-dot blazes.) Cross US-221 at 0.3 miles, and at 0.8 miles arrive at the Stack Rock parking area (Parkway milepost 304.8), left. Approach the Linn Cove parking area (Parkway milepost 304.4), left, at 1.5 miles, and gently descend to an observation deck of the Parkway Linn Cove Viaduct, a highway engineering marvel. Pass under the viaduct at 1.7 miles and cross Linn Cove Branch. At 2.7 miles arrive at the Wilson Creek Overlook (Parkway milepost 303.7), right. Ascend to the Rough Ridge boardwalk at 3.8 miles for superb scenic views in a natural garden of turkey-beard, blueberry, mountain ash, red spruce, and sand myrtle. Descend to the Rough Ridge parking area (Parkway milepost 302.9), right, at 4.0 miles. (The interpretive board carries a story about the botanist Andre Michaux and plant communities.)

Reach Raven Rocks Overlook (Parkway milepost 302.3) on the right at 4.7 miles, and Pilot Ridge Overlook (Parkway milepost 301.8) on the right at 5.3 miles. Pass a juncture with the Daniel Boone Scout Trail on the left at 7.3 miles, and one with the Grandfather Trail Extension on the left at 7.4 miles. (Both trails are commercial trails of Grandfather Mountain, Inc., and fee registration is required to hike on them. Camping is assigned at designated sites. If you are using the Boone Scout Trail for camping or scenic views, ascend 2.3 miles to a shelter for superb scenery of Linn Cove and beyond. It is 0.2 miles farther to Calloway Peak [elevation 5,964 feet].)

At 7.6 miles pass a right-hand juncture with the Daniel Boone Scout Trail, a 0.4-mile access route (named Grandfather Mountain Access Trail by the National Park Service) to US-221. Cross the scenic Upper Boone Fork bridge and pass a right-hand juncture with an access to the Boone Fork parking area at Parkway milepost 299.9 and Upper Boone Fork Trail, which goes 0.5 miles to the Calloway Peak Overlook (Parkway milepost 299.7). At 9.6 miles a right juncture with the Cold Prong Pond Trail leads 0.2 miles to Cold Prong Pond Overlook (Parkway milepost 299). Continue through a mixed forest with a varied understory of rhododendron, flame azalea, and mountain laurel. Arrive at a large pastoral area (first of three) at 10.5 miles. Cross Holloway Road (SR-1559) through the stiles at 11.6 miles. After a section of forest, enter the third pasture at 12.2 miles and descend gently into a forest. Reach a juncture with the Boone Fork Trail at 12.6 miles, right and left, near another stile on the right. (The Tanawha Trail follows the Boone Fork Trail to the right for 0.4 miles before it forks right and reaches the Price Lake parking area [Parkway milepost 297.3] at 13.3 miles.)

The Mountains-to-Sea Trail turns left and jointly follows the Boone Fork

Grandfather Mountain

Grandfather Mountain is a 3,087-acre preserve of global significance, some of which is wilderness with an exceptionally fragile botanical and geological environment. Some sections are not open to the public. A road ascends to a parking area for walking access to its mile-high swinging bridge over a couloir. There is an expansive and scenic network of hiking trails with walk-in campsites. A number of commercial and cultural activities take place here, two of which are the Highland Games in July and Singing on the Mountain in June. There is an entrance fee at the main gate on US-221. Some news reporters have called the preserve "Morton Mountain" because without Hugh Morton and his family, who have owned it since 1885, this natural treasure might not exist. One of the best views of Grandfather's facial profile is from NC-105 south of Boone. Slanted, almost lying down, it appears to be watching the sunsets over Sugar Mountain.

Trail for 0.3 miles before they turn sharply right to leave the pasture and descend to the Bee Tree Creek headwaters. At 14.1 miles cross Bee Tree Creek for the last time and curve to the right around the ridge to follow upstream on Old Boone Fork Road. After a scenic route through birch and rhododendron near cascades, pass an old dam site on the left at 15.1 miles. At 15.3 miles reach a huge rock formation by the river; descend to leave the Boone Fork Trail and rock-hop or wade Boone Fork. (The Boone Fork Trail continues ahead 1.1 mile to the picnic area at Price Memorial Park [Parkway milepost 295.5].)

Across the river ascend steeply to a flat knoll at 15.4 miles covered with mountain laurel, white pine, galax, and running cedar. Follow an old wide, level road to old John Road at 15.8 miles. Turn right and at 15.9 miles turn left, off the road, and into a large pine plantation. To the right is a chimney from a pioneer farmhouse. Ascend in a mixed forest and at 16.2 miles pass left of a spring (the last on the climb to Rich Mountain) near a homestead site. Continue ascending the slope of Martin Knob and reach a cattle pasture at the ridgeline at 16.8 miles. Turn right into Martin Gap and arrive at a gated fence to Shulls Mill Road (SR-1552) at 16.9 miles. (Going left on the paved road, it is 1.7 miles to Parkway milepost 294.6.)

Turn right on the road and after a few yards turn left up the embankment to follow the ridgeline. Pass through white pines and then a hardwood area with a grove of flame azaleas. Reach a fence and a juncture with the Rich Mountain Trail, right and left, at 17.4 miles. (To the left the Rich Mountain Trail ascends to its western terminus at Rich Mountain summit [elevation 4,370 feet].) Turn right on the Rich Mountain Trail and follow the carriage

---

The Denim King

A historic feature in the Moses H. Cone Memorial Park is Flat Top Manor, the former twenty-room summer home of Moses H. Cone (1857–1908), who was known as The Denim King. Originally from Tennessee, he and his brother, Caesar, built a textile manufacturing plant in Greensboro. The popularity of blue denim made the company financially successful. From the success, Cone purchased 3,517 acres, built three lakes, planted conifers and grazing fields, and created 25 miles of scenic carriage trails. His wife, Bertha, died in 1947 and she is buried along with her husband on the manor property. In 1950 the property was donated to the National Park Service as a "pleasure ground" for the public. The 0.6-mile Craftsman's Trail on the property is a self-guided walk in the shape of a figure-8 planted with medicinal herbs. Occupying part of the manor house is the Southern Highlands Craft Guild. On the carriage routes are loops and cross-connections for additional hiking, horseback riding, and cross-country skiing.

---

road (3.2 miles to the Moses Cone Manor) into a cattle and horse pasture. Turn left at the first curve and descend into a forest. At 19.0 miles take the left fork and go under large hemlocks. Reach a trout lake at 19.2 miles. Cross the dam and arrive at Flannery Fork Road (SR-1541). Turn right, but after 0.4 miles leave it, left, and ascend on the carriage road with switchbacks to another pasture. Reach the Blue Ridge Parkway at 20.6 miles, the end of the Rich Mountain Trail. Go under the Parkway (milepost 294) and jointly follow the Watkins Trail. Pass the stables on your right and access steps to the parking area of Moses Cone Memorial Park.

Follow a paved carriage trail to the front of the manor house, but turn sharply at the first left, at 20.8 miles, and descend into a forest of white pine and hemlock. Parallel the Parkway and stay left of other carriage roads. At 22.2 miles keep left in a curve (the carriage road right is the Black Bottom Trail, which connects with other carriage trails in the park). Pass left of a lake and spillway at 24.0 miles, cross Penley Branch in a grove of handsome oaks, maples, and tall hemlocks. At a private road at 24.4 miles turn right, and reach the end of the Watkins Trail at US-221/321 at 24.6 miles. (The Boone Fork/Cone Manor part of this section was designated as a state trail in May 1990; the Tanawha Trail was designated in June 1994.) Across the road is the New River Inn. To the right it is 1.0 mile to downtown Blowing Rock. See "Camping, Lodging, and Provisions" at the beginning of this section.

CAMPSIDE STORIES: He was on his way to his Blowing Rock estate from Greensboro when an automobile accident caused his death on October 25, 1946.

His beloved wife, Ethel, had predeceased him by three years. They had two children, Kathleen and Ralph. The information seemed like an ordinary obituary. But he was not an ordinary individual.

Born November 25, 1867, in Lunenburg County, Virginia, he received his formal education in a one-room schoolhouse. As a teenager he cut wood to fire wood-burning locomotives. Later a telegraph operator for Southern Railway, he moved to North Carolina, first to Durham, then Greensboro. He developed an interest in the business of insurance and began work for the Greensboro Life Insurance Company in 1905. The company consolidated with Jefferson Standard in 1912, and in 1919 he became the president. For the remainder of his life there was one success story after another, one of which was his brilliance in management. He served as the governor's financial advisor during the term of Angus W. McLean (1924–28). In April 1946 he received an honorary doctorate of law degree from the University of North Carolina.

In the early 1940s he had purchased 4,344 acres, most of them on a plateau, south of Blowing Rock. He planned to develop it as a recreation site to which company employees could come to rest and relax. After his death his children in cooperation with Jefferson Standard Life Insurance Company gave the land to the Blue Ridge Parkway. There was an understanding that a lake and park would honor his name—Julian Price.

William A. Blount Stewart has written a biographical portrait of Price in which he cites a story described to him by a granddaughter. It seems that one day when Price was leaving the office, a poor man asked him for $10 with which to buy a pair of shoes. When Price learned that they wore the same size, he took off his shoes, gave them to the poor man, and walked to his car barefooted.

SECTION 14. Blowing Rock (Blue Ridge Parkway MP 291.9) to Deep Gap (Blue Ridge Parkway MP 276.4)

WATAGUA COUNTY: See Watagua County description in Section 13.

LENGTH AND DIFFICULTY: 15.7 miles, moderate

USGS TOPO MAPS: Boone, Deep Gap

FEATURES OR EMPHASIS: Parkway overlooks: Thunder Hill, Yadkin Valley, Raven Rocks, Grandview, Carroll Gap, Osborne Mountain, and Stoney Fork Valley

TRAILS FOLLOWED: None (MST in planning stage)

TRAIL CONNECTIONS: None

WEST TRAILHEAD: On US-321/221 across the road from the New River Inn

EAST TRAILHEAD: Juncture of Blue Ridge Parkway and US-421

CAMPING, LODGING, AND PROVISIONS: The nearest lodging to the southwest trailhead is the New River Inn (and River's Edge Restaurant; P.O. Box 868, Blowing Rock, NC 28605; telephone: 828-295-0800; call for reservations). The nearest campground is Morgan's Mountain Retreat (telephone: 336-264-2170); access is from the juncture of the Blue Ridge Parkway at milepost 291.9 and US-321: north on US-321 3.5 miles, then 0.5 miles north on Niley Cook/Mine Branch Road. There are sixty-six sites (some are full service and some are for tenting), laundry, and a grocery store. It is open May 1 through October 31. (See Section 13 for information on Price Memorial Park Campground, 5.0 miles south on the Blue Ridge Parkway.) The nearest campground to the north (east) trailhead is Hitching Post RV Park (telephone: 336-264-5367); access is from the Blue Ridge Parkway (milepost 276.4) west on US-421 for 2.9 miles to Wildcat Road, then left for 1.2 miles. There are thirty sites, tenting sites, and a laundry. It is open May 1 through October 31.

INFORMATION AND SECURITY: Trail Planning: This section is in the process of being flagged according to Blue Ridge Parkway official routing. After its route is approved and inspected, construction will begin. New task forces are being formed and area volunteers are welcome. Call 919-496-4771 for information and progress report. Boone Area Chamber of Commerce: 208 Howard Street, Boone, NC 28607 (telephone: 828-264-2225 or 800-852-9506). Watauga County Sheriff's Office: 330 Queen Street, Boone, NC 28607 (telephone: 828-264-3761).

DESCRIPTION: From a parking space on the north shoulder of US-321/221 (near the New River Inn), cross the highway and walk northwest 0.2 miles; then cross the access ramp to the Blue Ridge Parkway (milepost 291.9). Turn right and follow the northbound shoulder of the Parkway. Cross the bridge over US-321/221 and ascend gradually through a pastoral setting with blue bird houses on fence posts and horses in pastures. On the way there are forests of hemlock, black birch, rhododendron, serviceberry, and wildflowers such as trillium. Reach milepost 291 at 1.1 miles. Arrive at Thunder Hill Overlook (milepost 290.5, elevation 3,776 feet), right (east), at 1.6 miles, and Yadkin Valley Overlook (milepost 290, elevation 3,800 feet), right (east), at 2.1 miles. At 2.5 miles (milepost 289.6) on the left (west) is Raven Rocks Overlook (elevation 3,834 feet). From here you will have a view to the south of Grandfather Mountain. Residential homes are near the Parkway, and pastureland is abundant to your right and left; there is also a forest of hemlocks and white pines along the way. At 3.1 miles come to milepost 289. Descend to Aho Gap (elevation 3,722 feet) and a public road crossing at 4.0 miles (milepost 288.1).

Continue descending. Cross a bridge over a stream where there are rhododendrons and hemlocks among exposed rock formations. At 5.8 miles (milepost 286.3) cross Goshen Creek Viaduct and a public road. There are cascades in a number of streams flowing north. At 6.6 miles (milepost 285.5) come to a public road with access to Boone (6.0 miles) on the left (west) and a public road to the right that leads to the community of Bamboo. There is a sign for the Daniel Boone Trail at 7.0 miles (milepost 285.1, elevation 3,262 feet) on the right (east) at Boone Trace Overlook. Marked by the Daughters of the American Revolution, this trail represents the western route that Boone took in 1769 from North Carolina to Kentucky. Ascend. There are views of a housing development to the left (west). Cross a public road at 9.0 miles (milepost 283.1) in an area of white pines. Pass through a community development; ascend and then descend a hill for scenic views, right and left. To the right (east) is a large castle-like building. At 10.1 miles (milepost 282.0) the Parkway parallels US-421. A sign indicates that this is the Eastern Continental Divide. Grandview Overlook (milepost 281.7, elevation 3,240 feet) is at 10.4 miles on the right (east).

At 11.3 miles, to the left, there is an access spur to a rest area with picnic tables and grills on US-421 (milepost 280.8). (On US-421, Boone is 7.0 miles west and Deep Gap is 4.0 miles east.) This section of the Parkway is scenic with its stands of white pines, cattle farms, and Christmas tree farms. Cross a bridge over Wildcat Road at 12.9 miles (milepost 279.2). Parkway banks have crested dwarf iris, trailing arbutus, and bellwort in the springtime. Carroll Gap Overlook (milepost 278.1, elevation 3,430 feet) is at 14.0 miles on the left (west). After passing through pastureland, you will reach Osborne Mountain Overlook (milepost 277.7, elevation 3,500 feet) on the right (east) at 14.4 miles. Continue descending to reach Stoney Fork Valley Overlook (milepost 277.1, elevation 3,405 feet) on the right (east) at 15.0 miles, where there are scenic views of the valley 900 feet below. Arrive at Deep Gap (milepost 276.4, elevation 3,142 feet) to access US-421 at 15.7 miles. (It is 11 miles west to Boone from here and 23 miles east to North Wilkesboro.) Toward Boone it is 0.6 miles to the Deep Gap community and the junction with US-221. Here there is a food mart/gasoline station. (A former motel has been demolished to make space for the widening of US-421/221.) See "Camping, Lodging, and Provisions" for the nearest campground.

DIVERSIONS: In Boone you can see *Horn in the West*, an outdoor drama that tells a story of pioneer exploration in the movement west. The role of Daniel Boone is predominant, and one of the highlights is the Native American fire dance. The drama is usually staged at night from late June through August (telephone: 336-264-2120; or call the Chamber of Commerce: 828-264-2225 or 800-852-9506).

CAMPSIDE STORIES: In many of the mountain gaps between Blowing Rock and the remainder of the MST in the mountains, you will be crossing historic paths followed by Daniel Boone, the legendary pioneer leader, expert hunter, explorer, negotiator of Indian treaties, and colonial legislator. Three states have cities that bear his name. His name is also on creeks, coves, ridges, gaps, crossroads, parks, and townships.

Born in Pennsylvania in 1734, he was one of eleven children in the Quaker family of Squire and Sarah Boone. In the early 1750s the family moved to the Forks of the Yadkin Valley near the current Boone Cave State Park in Davie County, North Carolina. From this base he explored the most remote western areas of Virginia (West Virginia was part of Virginia then), eastern Tennessee, and Kentucky (the area claimed by Virginia). He journeyed as far south as Florida in 1765 and probably went all the way west to the Yellowstone River in 1814. Soon after 1755 he married Rebecca Bryan. Born to them were eight children. One of his teenage sons, James, and another boy were tortured and murdered (some records show as many as five boys were killed) by Shawnee Indians near Ewing, Virginia, in 1773. The occasion was Boone's efforts to move his family to Kentucky, but after the loss of his son the family returned home.

With John Finley and others Boone went on a hunting trip for furs and hides during 1769–71. He was robbed twice of his furs and captured once by Indians but managed to escape. Boone was captured again in 1778 by the Shawnees, whose chief, Blackfish, claimed him as his son. He escaped after five months.

Boone negotiated a treaty between Richard Henderson's Transylvania Company and the Cherokees in 1775 for the purchase of almost all of Kentucky and Tennessee. Their plans were to make Kentucky the fourteenth colony, but the territory became a county of Virginia. This was the same year that Boone finally moved his family to Kentucky. Three years later his daughter and two other girls were kidnapped by Indians, but Boone rescued them.

With others he led in building a Wilderness Road on the Warriors' Path through the Cumberland Gap in 1777. More than 100,000 pioneer settlers passed through for frontier homes. He established Boonesboro in Kentucky and powerfully led its defense during the Revolutionary War. He served in the Virginia state legislature during the 1780s. (Kentucky achieved statehood in 1792.) Boone, and others in his family, followed his adventurous son, Daniel Morgan, west in 1799 to settle in Spanish territory (which became Missouri). On September 26, 1820, Boone died a natural death, like a mountain lion with nine lives, in St. Charles County, Missouri, about one month before his eighty-sixth birthday.

SECTION 15. Deep Gap (US-421 and Blue Ridge Parkway MP 276.4) to Horse Gap (NC-16 and Blue Ridge Parkway MP 261.2

WATAUGA, ASHE, AND WILKES COUNTIES: (See Watauga County description in Section 13.) Capping the northwest corner of the state, Ashe County shares its western boundary with Tennessee and its northern boundary with Virginia. Its 427 square miles were taken from Wilkes County in 1799. Ashe County was named in honor of Samuel Ashe (1725–1813), governor of North Carolina from 1795 to 1798. The county seat, Jefferson, was incorporated in 1803 when Thomas Jefferson was president of the nation. At the northeast corner of the county is the confluence of the North and South Forks of the New River. Two state parks were created within the county: New River State Park is on the South Fork of the New, and Mount Jefferson State Park is near the town of Jefferson. Highway access through the county is on NC-194, US-221, and NC-16 (north-south) and NC-88 and NC-163 (east-west).

The 765-square-mile Wilkes County was established in 1778. Part of it was formerly in Surry County. It was named in honor of John Wilkes (1727–97), an English leader who supported American rights for independence. Wilkesboro, the county seat, was established in 1847 on the south side of the Yadkin River. Across the river is North Wilkesboro. Upstream and nearby is the W. Kerr Scott Dam and Reservoir, a 49,800-acre impoundment constructed in 1952 for flood control. In addition to the reservoir's recreational areas, the county encompasses the historic Rendezvous Mountain (northwest of Wilkesboro), Thurmond Chatham Game Land, and part of Stone Mountain State Park to the north. The major east-west highway is US-421, and major north-south roads are NC-16, NC-18, and NC-115.

LENGTH AND DIFFICULTY: 15.2 miles, easy to moderate

USGS TOPO MAPS: Deep Gap, Maple Springs, Glendale Springs, Horse Gap

FEATURES OR EMPHASIS: Jesse Brown's log cabin, Cool Spring Baptist Church, E. B. Jeffress Park, Betsy's Rock Falls, Mount Jefferson, The Lump, Daniel Gap, hundreds of scenic views, numerous species of wildflowers

TRAILS FOLLOWED: Tompkins Knob Trail (MST in planning stage; see "Information and Security" at the beginning of Section 14)

TRAIL CONNECTIONS: Cascades Trail

WEST TRAILHEAD: Deep Gap (US-421), Blue Ridge Parkway milepost 276.4

EAST TRAILHEAD: Horse Gap (NC-16), Blue Ridge Parkway milepost 261.2

CAMPING, LODGING, AND PROVISIONS: From Deep Gap it is 11.0 miles west on US-421 to downtown Boone for motels, outdoor sports stores, and shopping centers. Along the way at 0.7 miles is Dollar Mart with telephone, gasoline, snacks, and limited groceries. Another 2.2 miles will take you to the Hitching

Post RV Park (telephone: 336-264-5367), where you would turn left and go 1.2 miles. There are thirty sites as well as tent sites and a laundry. It is open May 1 through October 31. In another 0.9 miles is Greene's Grill (breakfast, lunch, and dinner), which is also accessible from the Parkway at milepost 280.8.

Continuing north on the Blue Ridge Parkway for 8.2 miles (milepost 268.0), turn off at Benge Gap, west, to the Park Vista Restaurant and Motel. The restaurant, serving home-style food, is open daily from 7 A.M. to 8 P.M. (telephone: 336-877-4473); the motel is seasonal (telephone: 336-877-2750). Also here is Bill Watson's Country Store. Farther north at Horse Gap (milepost 261.2), turn on NC-16 and drive 0.3 miles west to the Parkway Restaurant (telephone: 336-982-2344). Farther west it is another 0.1 miles to a Phillips 66 with gasoline and groceries, and another 2.5 miles north to Glendale Springs, where you will find the Glendale Grocery, a post office, and Lee's Lodge and Restaurant. From the Parkway it is 22 miles southeast on NC-16 to North Wilkesboro.

INFORMATION AND SECURITY: Trail Planning: See "Information and Security" in Section 14, and call 919-496-4771 for an update. Boone Area Chamber of Commerce: 208 Howard Street, Boone, NC (telephone: 828-264-2225 or 800-852-9506). Watauga County Sheriff's Office: 330 Queen Street, Boone, NC 28607 (telephone: 828-264-3761). Wilkes County Chamber of Commerce: 717 Main Street (P.O. Box 727), North Wilkesboro, NC 28697 (telephone: 336-838-8662). Wilkes County Sheriff's Office: 201 Curtis Bridge Road, Wilkesboro, NC 28697 (telephone: 336-651-7368). Ashe County Sheriff's Office: 205 Academy Street (P.O. Box 395), Jefferson, NC 28640 (telephone: 336-246-9745).

DESCRIPTION: From the Blue Ridge Parkway junction with US-421 (elevation 3,141 feet), ascend north on the Parkway in a forest of hardwoods, white pines, and wildflowers. Arrive at Elk Mountain Overlook (milepost 275.6, elevation 3,786 feet) on the right (east) at 1.8 miles. Tompkins Knob parking area (milepost 273.6, elevation 3,657 feet) is at 2.8 miles. From here it is 500 feet to Jesse Brown's log cabin (ca. late 1800s) and spring. Nearby is Cool Spring Baptist Church, where on summer Sundays local residents would gather to hear sermons by circuit riders such as Willie Lee and Bill Church. From the parking area the 0.5-mile Tompkins Knob Trail runs north, paralleling the Parkway, to the E. B. Jeffress Park picnic area and restrooms at milepost 271.9. Along the well-designed trail you may see many wildflowers, including bloodroot, toothwort, and yellow violet.

The 600-acre park was named in honor of E. B. Jeffress, who was influential in making the Parkway possible during his term as chairman of the state

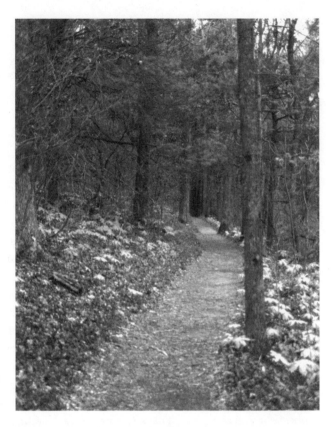

Mountains-to-Sea Trail following the Tompkins Knob Trail on the Blue Ridge Parkway

Highway Commission in 1934. At the parking area for Cascades Overlook (milepost 271.9) at 4.5 miles you can access the Cascades Trail. The 0.9-mile self-guided trail uses botanical markers to inform hikers and descends to platforms from which you can view the cascades on Falls Creek. At 6.2 miles (milepost 270.2) on the right (east) is Lewis Fork Overlook (elevation 3,290), and at 6.6 miles (milepost 269.8) a public road crosses in Phillips Gap (elevation 3,221).

At 8.4 miles (milepost 268), at an intersection in the community of Benge Gap, you will find a motel and restaurant on the left (see "Camping, Lodging, and Provisions"). At 8.6 miles (milepost 267.8), to the right (east), is Betsy's Rock Falls Overlook (elevation 3,400 feet). The slender cascade received its name from Betsy Pierce, who lived with two children on a ledge near the falls during the Civil War. At 9.6 miles (milepost 266.9) on the left is Mount Jefferson Overlook. The view here is one of a number of views you will have of Mount Jefferson as you continue north on the Parkway. You may see signs indicating two different altitudes for the peak—either 4,550 feet or 4,515 feet, as listed by the N.C. Division of Parks and Recreation.

Mount Jefferson

Mount Jefferson towers 4,515 feet in elevation near the town of Jefferson, the county seat for Ashe County. The town was formed in 1803 and named for Thomas Jefferson, who was president of the United States during that time. The mountain was named Jefferson in 1956 when it became a 451-acre state park and preserve. A paved road winds to the scenic and lofty top for picnicking and hiking on a nature trail. Previously, as early as 1810, it was called Negro Mountain, because of the black rocks on the mountainside. Another story dates its name later, but before the Civil War the mountain was known as a temporary haven for African-American slaves attempting to use a northwestern escape route. Although the local citizens were divided in their loyalties, it is reported that some of the white families who opposed slavery provided protection and food supplies.

Descend to Calloway Gap (milepost 265.2, elevation 3,439) at 11.2 miles; a public road crosses here. The gap is named for Elijah Calloway, who moved from Tennessee to settle here before the Civil War. At 12.0 miles (milepost 264.4) come to The Lump Overlook on the right (east). This is an off-Parkway parking area at the base of the mountain. (If you wish to observe The Lump, ascend a grassy mountainside for 0.2 miles for views at the windswept and panoramic summit [elevation 3,465 feet]. To the east are excellent views of the Yadkin Valley, Pilot Mountain, and the Brushy Mountain Range. To the northeast is Stone Mountain and to the south is the South Mountain Range. Western views toward Tennessee take in the areas of Elk Knob and Old Field Bald.)

From The Lump descend to Gilliam Gap (milepost 263.6, elevation 3,238 feet) at 12.7 miles. Along the way are good views east, and patches of mountain laurel, rhododendron, dogwood, and white pine garnish the roadside. Ascend a short way to the top of a ridge at milepost 263 for more views left of Mount Jefferson. Descend on the ridge's east slope. To the left (west) are wet walls of rock with foam flower, meadow rue, saxifrage, and wild hydrangea. After coming into pastoral open views both east and west, you will see Mount Jefferson again to the left. Farther northeast are the light blue rims of mountains in Virginia.

Descend to Daniels Gap (milepost 262.2, elevation 3,170 feet) at 14.2 miles. (Named for Daniel Long, the historic gap once served as a wagon road crossing from Wilkesboro to Mount Jefferson. Long had a country store here for about twenty years during the 1890s and early 1900s.) Continue on an easy walk to Horse Gap (milepost 261.2, elevation 3,108 feet) at 15.2 miles. Here the Parkway bridges NC-16. (If you travel west on NC-16 for

0.2 miles you will come to a restaurant; at 0.4 miles, at the junction with NC-163, left, is Run-In Groceries, a service station, and Don's Seafood and Steak. To the right and farther northwest on NC-16 it is 2.6 miles to the Glendale Springs community, which has a grocery store and Lee's Lodge and Restaurant. After another 9.0 miles is Jefferson, where there are motels, restaurants, shopping malls, and Mount Jefferson State Park. West Jefferson and Jefferson can also be reached by heading northwest on NC-163. Down the mountain, southeast, it is 22 miles to US-421 and Wilkesboro.)

CAMPSIDE STORIES: When you cross over US-421 in Deep Gap, you can think of a true and tragic love story that happened in the 1860s. This story led to a number of legends about who murdered pretty Laura Foster in a lover's triangle. Convicted, overturned, convicted again, and then hanged May 1, 1868, was a twenty-three-year-old Confederate Army veteran named Tom Dula. The other woman in the triangle was pretty Ann Melton, also tried for the murder but acquitted. Some residents claimed that the verdict for Ann would have been different if women had been on the jury. East and down the mountain near Bates Place off Stony Fork Road is where Laura's body was found in a shallow grave on June 18, 1866. Local residents suspected that Ann murdered Laura. Others claimed it was Sheriff Grayson, who was known to be jealous of Dula.

If you go west 1.4 miles on US-421 from the Parkway you will see a road sign to the famous folk musician Doc Watson, who in 1964 recorded the song "Tom Dooley" on Vanguard Records. The ballad was written and sung by others before Dula's hanging, and Watson's ancestors passed the song on to their children. A few miles west of Watson's home lived another folk singer, Frank Proffit, in the Beaverdam Creek area. Proffit promoted the song "Hang Down Your Head Tom Dooley," which the Kingston Trio made famous in 1959.

According to Doc, his great grandmother, Betsy Triplett Watson, was called years later after Dula's hanging to Ann's death bed. With them were Ora Watson and Rosa Lee, and all heard strange sounds like steam from hot rocks in water. Ann is reputed to have said that she "could see the flames of Hell at the foot of her bed."

SECTION 16. Horse Gap (NC-16 and Blue Ridge Parkway MP 261.2) to Laurel Springs (NC-18 and Blue Ridge Parkway MP 248.1)

ASHE, WILKES, AND ALLEGHANY COUNTIES: (See discussions of Ashe and Wilkes Counties in Section 15.) Formerly a part of Ashe County, Alleghany County was formed in 1859 with 230 square miles. Its north border is with Grayson County, Virginia. In the heart of the county is Sparta, the county seat, named for the ancient city of Greece and incorporated in 1879. The New River State Park is in the northwest corner of the county and the Blue Ridge Parkway forms its southwest and eastern boundaries. Part of Doughton Park on the Parkway is inside the county. Stone Mountain State Park is located in the northeast part of the county. Alleghany County has excellent fishing streams. Its major north-south highways are US-21 and US-221, NC-113, and NC-18. East-west routes are NC-93 and, in part, NC-18.

LENGTH AND DIFFICULTY: 16.3 miles, moderate

USGS TOPO MAPS: Horse Gap, Laurel Springs, Whitehead

FEATURES OR EMPHASIS: Jumpinoff Rocks, Cherry Hill, Jess Sheets Cabin, Laurel Fork Viaduct

TRAILS FOLLOWED: None (MST in planning stage)

TRAIL CONNECTIONS: Jumpinoff Rocks Trail

WEST TRAILHEAD: Horse Gap (NC-16) on the Blue Ridge Parkway, milepost 261.2

EAST TRAILHEAD: Laurel Springs (NC-18) on the Blue Ridge Parkway, milepost 248.1

CAMPING, LODGING, AND PROVISIONS: (See Section 15 for this information.) North on the Parkway for 3.4 miles (milepost 257.7) and then left on Raccoon Hollow Road for 0.2 miles is the eighty-acre Raccoon Hollow Campground. The private campground offers 189 sites, most with full service, tenting, laundry, and a limited grocery store. It is open April 15 until November 1 (telephone: 336-982-2706).

INFORMATION AND SECURITY: Trail Planning: See information in Section 14 and call 919-496-4771 for an update. Alleghany County Chamber of Commerce: 348 South Main Street (P.O. Box 1237), Sparta, NC 28675 (telephone: 336-372-5473). Alleghany County Sheriff's Office: 40 Alleghany Street, Sparta, NC 28675 (telephone: 336-372-4455). Wilkes County Chamber of Commerce: 717 Main Street (P.O. Box 727), North Wilkesboro, NC 28697 (telephone: 336-838-8662). Wilkes County Sheriff's Office: 201 Curtis Bridge Road, Wilkesboro, NC 28697 (telephone: 336-651-7368).

DESCRIPTION: Ascend on the Parkway into a cut of the ridge with forests on both sides at milepost 261. After you emerge from the woods, there are good views of Mount Jefferson to the west and Mount Rogers in Virginia to the northwest. At 4.1 miles you will come to the Jumpinoff Rocks parking area (milepost 260.3, elevation 3,165 feet), which features a picnic area and nature trail. The Jumpinoff Rocks Trail is a 0.5-mile round-trip to rocky cliffs. Along the way it ascends, then levels, among patches of galax, trailing arbutus, and cinnamonbush. Continuing on the Parkway there is open space for scenic views, both right and left. Dogwood and white pine are prominent. Cross a public road at 4.6 miles (milepost 259.8). If you look back at 5.4 miles (milepost 259), you can see Grandfather Mountain again. There is another public road crossing (old NC-16) at 5.8 miles (milepost 258.6) near Glendale Springs (Northwest Trading Post is in southwest corner).

After milepost 258 there are borders of rhododendron on both sides of the Parkway, a dense sub-forest under hardwoods and white pines. A large grazing field follows on the right. At 6.7 miles (milepost 257.7) there is a junction with Raccoon Hollow Road, left, and Cherry Hill Road, right. Raccoon Hollow Road takes you to Raccoon Hollow Campground (see "Camping, Lodging, and Provisions"). Ascend and at 7.5 miles (milepost 256.9) is the Parkway's Cherry Hill restaurant and gasoline station on the left. At the top of the hill is a public road crossing. Ascend on another hill among white pines and come to an open area with views west to Phoenix Mountain, and White Top Mountain and Mount Rogers in Virginia. Go through a cut in the ridge at 8.4 miles (milepost 256) and cross a public road (Dan Baer Road). Ascend to a ridge top in a cut where forests are on both sides. Cross another public road (Roe Hunt Road) at 9.3 miles (milepost 255.1). Enter an S-curve and another cut in the ridge before leveling. A cove filled with wildflowers is on your left. Come to a long sweeping curve in an area called Rattlesnake Mountain.

At 10.4 miles (milepost 254) gradually ascend through hardwoods, then come to a scenic open space on your right. If you look south and southwest, you can see Jeffress Park and beyond to Grandfather Mountain. Reach the top of a ridge in a cut, descend, and observe splendid scenery to the west. Level out among white pines, birches, and maples. Descend to Sheets Gap Overlook (milepost 252.8, elevation 3,342 feet), right, at 11.6 miles. Frazier magnolia grows at the edge of the forest. Views here are of the Yadkin Valley nearby and the Brushy Mountains on the horizon. Descend to 11.9 miles (milepost 252.5) to pass Jess Sheets Cabin, left. Sheets built the cabin in about 1815, and his descendants lived there until the 1920s, when the U.S. government purchased the area for the Blue Ridge Parkway. His father, Andrew Sheets, came to America from Europe near the time of the American Revolutionary War.

Reach Alder Gap (milepost 251.5, elevation 3,047 feet), where there is a public road crossing, at 13.0 miles. The gap's name is from a common shrub, tag alder, whose reddish brown catkins appear early in the spring before its leaves. It grows in stream and lake borders and marshy places. On the right is a long bed of skunk cabbage and skullcap. A wooden serpentine fence is on the left. In a long curve pass through white pines. Descend beside the familiar guard railing, left, and notice scenic views west. Enter an open grassy area where both sides of the Parkway are bordered with more of the serpentine fencing and a stream with tag alder. Pass milepost 251. At 13.6 miles (milepost 250.8) is a public road crossing at Peak Creek Road, left, and Darnell Woodie Road, right.

Ascend from the crossroads through a beautiful hardwood forest where crested dwarf iris and fragrant pinxter-flower bloom at the forest edges in the springtime. At the top of the ridge, at 15.1 miles (milepost 249.3), is a crossing of Hiram Bare Road. Descend among white pines, ferns, mints, and thick groves of hemlock. The Parkway levels out, and you will cross Laurel Fork Viaduct at 15.5 miles (milepost 248.9). Ascend gently to reach a cut in the ridge, then pass through tall white pines on both sides of the Parkway. You are likely to see squirrels here and the sound of birds is a prominent feature. On the left is a meadow with skunk cabbages, and tall rhododendrons are on the right. Arrive at a junction with NC-18 (milepost 248.1, elevation 2,851 feet) at 16.3 miles. A general store, restaurant, and the Station's Inn (telephone: 336-359-2888) are 0.2 miles to the left (northwest). (The future MST is planned to pass the Station's Inn and turn northeast on the country road at the corner of the store.) Beyond the store and motel on NC-18 it is 1.8 miles to the community of Laurel Springs and 12.0 miles farther to Sparta. South on NC-18 it is 24 miles to North Wilkesboro.

CAMPSIDE STORIES: On May 10, 1997, when Alan Householder and I were hiking across the state, we could see Mount Rogers (the highest point in Virginia for the Appalachian Trail) from the Parkway in the Doughton Park area. At separate times we both had hiked the AT and the sight of Mount Rogers brought memories of many hikers I had met. I thought about my thick notebooks of copied messages, jokes, and unique comments on shelter walls and the frequent exchanges of jokes and stories that happen around the campfires. Here are a few wall notes from my notebooks: "I have gone to find myself on the AT, if I should return before I get back, wait for me." "I could not find God in Georgia but I did in Tennessee." "Please feed the mouse, it is hungry," to which another hiker wrote, "Feed the mouse? You mean the mice. . . ." to which another hiker wrote, "If I don't find a grocery store tomorrow, I am going to eat the mice." "Kilroy was here." "A nature lover is one who when treed by a bear loves the view." "Hikers are like tea bags, they don't know their strength until they get into hot water," to which another hiker left this note: "I know my strength. I am as strong as a lion, haven't had a hot bath since Damascus, but I smell like a mountain rose."

Here is a sample of some of the many jokes I've heard on the trails. Two hikers spotted a panther stalking them. One hiker quietly took off his hiking boots and put on his tennis shoes. The other hiker said that would not help outrun the panther. "But I don't have to outrun the panther, I just want to be ahead of you."

Once upon a time a backpacker lost his way and came up to a farmer's house to ask if he could have some food and stay in his barn. The farmer said his barn was full of cows, but he could sleep in the corn pen or stay with the baby. The backpacker preferred to sleep in the corn pen rather than with a baby, but next morning at the spring he asked a pretty young woman who she was. "I am Baby, and who are you?" she asked. "I am the fool who slept in the corn pen."

SECTION 17. Laurel Springs (Blue Ridge Parkway MP 248.1) to Devil's Garden Overlook (Blue Ridge Parkway MP 235.7)

ALLEGHANY AND WILKES COUNTIES: See Alleghany County description in Section 16, and Wilkes County description in Section 15.

LENGTH AND DIFFICULTY: 13.9 miles, moderate

USGS TOPO MAPS: Laurel Springs, Whitehead, Glade Valley

FEATURES OR EMPHASIS: Doughton Park, Meadow Fork Valley, and Parkway overlooks: Basin Cove, Bluffs View, Alligator Back, Brinegar Cabin, Air Bellows Gap, and Devil's Garden

TRAILS FOLLOWED: Bluff Mountain Trail

TRAIL CONNECTIONS: Flat Rock Ridge Trail, Grassy Gap Trail, Basin Cove Trail, Bluff Ridge Trail, Cedar Ridge Trail

WEST TRAILHEAD: Laurel Springs (NC-18), Blue Ridge Parkway milepost 248.1

EAST TRAILHEAD: Devil's Garden Overlook, Blue Ridge Parkway milepost 235.7

CAMPING, LODGING, AND PROVISIONS: At the NC-18 exit (milepost 248.1), going northwest, is the Station's Inn (telephone: 336-359-2888), which is open all year. Here is also Woody's General Store. (On NC-18 it is 1.8 miles northwest to Laurel Springs and its post office; 12.0 miles farther north is Sparta. South on NC-18 it is 24.0 to North Wilkesboro.) At 0.8 miles (milepost 247.3) in this section, on the left, is Miller's Campground. It has sixty-five sites, most with full hook-ups, tenting, laundry, and limited groceries. It is open April 1 through November 1 (telephone: 336-359-8156). Doughton Park campground (milepost 240), a National Park Service facility, has 136 sites, no hook-ups, tenting, and no showers. It is open May 1 through October 31 (telephone: 336-372-8877). Doughton Park also has a motel, The Bluffs Lodge (telephone: 336-372-4499), and a restaurant, souvenir shop, and gas station complex.

INFORMATION AND SECURITY: Trail Maintenance: This section has been flagged and the route is in the process of being approved by state and Parkway officials. (To join or form a volunteer task force, call Friends of the Mountains-to-Sea Trail at 919-496-4771.) The state trails specialist is Dwayne Stutzman, DENR Regional Office, 59 Woodfin Street, Asheville, NC 28802 (telephone: 828-251-6208). Alleghany County Chamber of Commerce: 348 South Main Street (P.O. Box 1237), Sparta, NC 28675 (telephone: 336-372-5473). Alleghany County Sheriff's Office, 40 Alleghany Street, Sparta, NC 28675 (telephone: 336-372-4455). Wilkes County Chamber of Commerce: 717 Main Street (P.O. Box 727), North Wilkesboro, NC 28697 (telephone: 336-838-8662). Wilkes County Sheriff's Office: 201 Curtis Bridge Road, Wilkesboro, NC 28697 (telephone: 336-651-7368).

DESCRIPTION: From milepost 248.1 at NC-18 and the Blue Ridge Parkway, enter a uniquely flat plateau known as Meadow Fork Valley for 1.6 miles. To the right is a historic scene: an old silo and barn and remains of an old house and truck. There is a serpentine wooden fence on Parkway property and a Parkway sign that indicates it is 8 miles to Doughton Park and 132 miles to Roanoke. Cross a small stream among fertile meadows with Christmas trees and cabbage farms. Cross another stream fringed with willows. At 0.8 miles (milepost 247.3) is Stillhouse Branch Road to the left. It crosses Laurel Fork Creek to Miller Road and to Miller's Campground on the hillside (see "Camping, Lodging, and Provisions"). Pass Pruitt Cove Road on the left and tall white pines on the right. Parallel the gravel Miller Road on the left, and pass Elk Knob Drive, left, at 2.1 miles. Here is a large serviceberry tree at the entrance to a historic white house. At 2.6 miles (milepost 245.5), to the left, is the Parkway's Bluffs Maintenance Area and ranger's office.

Enter into Doughton Park at 3.3 miles (milepost 244.8), and within 0.1 miles reach Basin Cove Overlook, right (elevation 3,312 feet). Table mountain pines are on both sides of the Parkway. Views below are of Cove Creek draining into Basin Creek, which originates beyond Bluff Ridge, to the left. In the far left can be seen some of the domes of Stone Mountain State Park.

At Basin Cove Overlook, the Mountains-to-Sea Trail leaves the Parkway shoulder and connects with the south end of the 7.5-mile yellow-blazed Bluff Mountain Trail. After 100 yards pass the light-blue-blazed Flat Rock Ridge Trail that begins on the right. (It descends 5.0 miles to Long Bottom Road, where it makes a junction with the 4.3-mile Cedar Ridge Trail and 6.7-mile Grassy Gap Trail.) At 4.5 miles (1.1 miles since leaving the Parkway shoulder) join the Grassy Gap Trail (a fire road) and follow it left for 0.1 mile before bearing right off the fire road. Ascend and at 5.0 miles connect left with the Bluff Mountain Overlook (milepost 243.4). Here are views of the rock wall and cliffs of Bluff Mountain.

Continue on the Bluff Mountain Trail and parallel with the Parkway to

Doughton Park

The 6,000-acre Doughton Park was known as The Bluffs before 1951. Then its name was changed to honor Robert Lee (Muley Bob) Doughton, a North Carolina Congressman from 1911 to 1953 from the 9th District and a strong Parkway advocate. The park is the largest single tract of the Parkway in North Carolina. It has a triangular boundary with the Parkway to the northwest, Cedar Ridge on the northeast, and Flat Rock Ridge on the south. On the outside of the park to the south and east is the state's Thurmond Chatham Game Land.

Pioneer families and descendants with the names Brinegar, Caudill, and Blevins lived in the area before the U.S. Government purchased the property. One example was Harrison Caudill, born February 3, 1839, who lived to be nearly eighty-six. Outliving a first and second wife, he fathered twenty-two children. One of Harrison's sons, Martin, who fathered sixteen children, built a cabin in a cove of Basin Creek. The cabin can be seen from the Fodder Stack Trail northeast from the lodge parking lot.

The Brinegar Cabin is accessible at milepost 238.5. Martin Brinegar lived to be seventy, and his child bride, Caroline Jones, lived to be eighty-one. They moved into their cabin about 1885, and Martin did all the work except lifting the heavy logs into place. He and Caroline raised a family, farmed for food, wove material for clothes, faithfully attended Pleasant Grove Baptist Church, and gathered herbs for medicinal purposes. The sale of herbs and work as a cobbler was Martin's cash money. He sold shoes for about $1 a pair.

reach Alligator Rock Overlook (milepost 242.2) at 6.1 miles. A color-coded map signboard here shows Doughton Park's trail system. There is also information about raptors. Ascend on switchbacks in a rugged and scenic area to a shelter (elevation 3,796 feet) at 6.6 miles, where there is also a juncture with the red-blazed Bluff Ridge Trail, right. (It follows the main ridge of the park to descend 2.8 miles to juncture with the Basin Creek Trail.) Turn left at the shelter and follow the Bluff Mountain Trail through a picnic area, and heath and grassy meadows. Descend to cross a park road, then cross the Parkway for a right turn. Pass the souvenir shop, service station, and restaurant at 8.2 miles (milepost 241.1).

Follow the trail on the west side of the Parkway to a crossing of the Parkway. At 9.2 miles cross the Parkway again at Low Notch (milepost 239.9). Parallel the tent and small-RV section of the campground before crossing the Parkway for the fourth time in Doughton Park. Pass the campground for large RVs at milepost 239.4. From here you will pass through

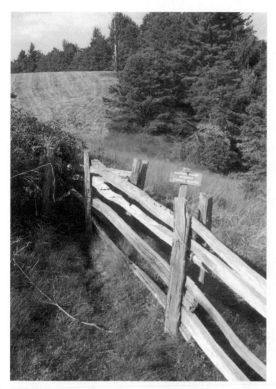

Bluff Mountain Trail in Doughton Park

groves of white pines and grassy fields with wildfowers, and next will arrive at a juncture with the Cedar Ridge Trail at 10.9 miles. (The Cedar Ridge Trail goes right for a descent of 4.3 miles to Long Bottom Road [SR-1728].) Turn left and exit at 11.1 miles to the parking lot of the historic Brinegar Cabin (milepost 238.5, elevation 3,508 feet).

After a visit to the cabin area, return to the Parkway and follow it north, ascending. (The MST is flagged and partially completed from a shed behind Brinegar Cabin, left, for 1.0 mile to a level grassy area. Until the trail is complete you may turn left and walk out to the Parkway for another 0.3 miles. Call 919-496-4771 for an update.) At 12.5 miles reach Air Bellows Gap (milepost 237.1, elevation 3,929 feet). Air Bellows Road runs underneath the Parkway. It was on this old road (east) that Martin Brinegar once traveled by horse, or horse and wagon, to Wilkesboro. The gap receives its name from frequent and strong winds. After another 0.2 miles you will come to Air Bellows Gap Overlook, left (elevation 3,744). Views from here are of mountain ridges paralleling the New River. The town of Sparta can be seen in the near distance, and Grayson Highlands and Mount Rogers may be visible on the far northwest horizon.

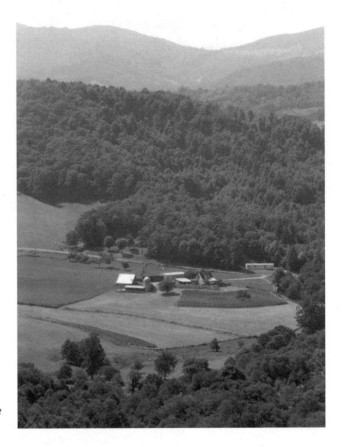

Pastoral view from the
Blue Ridge Parkway

Patches of wild azalea, galax, and trillium can be seen in the woods on the descent to Devil's Garden Overlook, which is on the right at 13.9 miles (milepost 235.7, elevation 3,428 feet). The gap received its name from folk stories. One is that there are enough serpents (rattlesnakes and copperheads) among the flowering shrubs on the rocky slopes to please the Devil; another states that only the Devil could navigate the headwaters of Garden Creek. The views from here show at least four levels of foothill ridges. One of the closest is Greenstreets Mountain; the farthest distance is the Brushy Mountains.

CAMPSIDE STORIES: You have been following the Blue Ridge Parkway, or not far from it, since the Smokies. Because you are only 6.8 miles from where the first 12.0 miles of Parkway were constructed, I repeat here a true campside story of how some of the landowners, right-of-way officials, and claim adjusters made settlements in the early 1930s. Parkway land was being purchased by both Virginia and North Carolina, and each state had authorized their respective highway commissions to deed the property to the Department of Interior.

North Carolina built the first 12 miles from the Virginia border near Cumberland Gap south because the land was easy to purchase. Work began on September 19, 1935. Of course preceding this was considerable government red-tape, a number of logistical nightmares, and dealings with uncooperative landowners. The majority of the landowners were eager to sell. It was during the Great Depression and they needed the money. Land valued at $7 an acre was selling for $25 to $45 an acre. Other landowners opposed the Parkway and responded as follows. At one period of time in Ashe County there were forty suits in court that related to right-of-way. One farmer claimed his hens had a specific place to hatch their eggs and the Parkway would disturb them. Another farmer would not give up his barn, so a settlement was made to cut off a corner and pay him for it. Another farmer halted construction by guarding his property with a shotgun. One farmer claimed the Parkway would take the only land he had that would grow cabbage. Some were successful with delays; the most notable was a right-of-way gap at Grandfather Mountain that was not settled until 1968.

To some the land and their cabins were very sentimental. An example was Caroline Brinegar, whose log cabin is described above. The claim adjuster solved this problem by granting her a life-term lease. Another widow said that she had lived in the same cottage since her late-husband carried her over the doorsill on their wedding night. Because the whole cottage could not be moved in one day, it was agreed that the construction crew would cut half of the building and move it off the right-of-way the first day. This would not interrupt her sleeping schedule, and they would move the other half the next day.

NINE

STONE MOUNTAIN STATE PARK
AND BLUE RIDGE FOOTHILLS

SECTION 18. Devil's Garden Overlook (Blue Ridge Parkway MP 235.7) to Stone Mountain State Park Visitor Center

WILKES COUNTY: See Wilkes County description in Section 15.

LENGTH AND DIFFICULTY: 8.5 miles (moderate to strenuous)

USGS TOPO MAPS: Laurel Springs, Whitehead, Glade Valley, Traphill

FEATURES OR EMPHASIS: Devil's Garden Overlook, aerial tram site, Widow's Creek Water Fall, Stone Mountain Creek, Stone Mountain, Wolf Rock, Stone Mountain Falls

TRAILS FOLLOWED: (Louise Chatfield Trail), Widow's Creek Trail, Stone Mountain Trail, Stone Mountain Spur Trail

TRAIL CONNECTIONS: Aerial Tram Spur Trail, Widow's Creek Trail

WEST TRAILHEAD: Northeast corner of parking lot at Devil's Garden Overlook, Blue Ridge Parkway milepost 235.7 (6.1 miles south from intersection with US-21)

EAST TRAILHEAD: Parking lot at the Stone Mountain Ranger's Station and Visitor Center. To access from US-21 (near Thurmond) turn west on Traphill Road (SR-1002), go 4.3 miles to John P. Frank Parkway (SR-1784), and turn right (north). Follow the road 2.3 miles to gate and entrance to Stone Mountain State Park. After another 0.3 miles turn right into the parking lot.

CAMPING, LODGING, AND PROVISIONS: Camping is available at Stone Mountain State Park. From the park ranger's office and visitor center go west on the main road 0.3 miles and turn right. Go 0.7 miles. There are thirty-seven sites, tenting, picnic tables, hot showers, but no hook-ups. It is open all year, but water is turned off from December to mid-March (telephone: 336-957-8185). (See "East Trailhead," below, for access to ranger's office.)

INFORMATION AND SECURITY: Trail Maintenance: For an update on the continuing development of the MST through this area, contact the Friends of the Mountains-to-Sea Trail at 919-496-4771. Stone Mountain State Park: 3042

> ### Stone Mountain State Park
>
> *More than 300 million years ago Stone Mountain and many other mounds like it were formed beneath the earth's surface by molten lava. The result was a 25-square-mile area of intrusive igneous rock. Today Stone Mountain State Park encompasses two major medium-grained biotite granite domes accessible by hiking trails. The largest dome, usually called Stone Mountain, rises 600 feet above its base and is 2,305 feet above sea level. To this dome's south and across a meadow is Wolf Rock's pockmarked dome. Here and elsewhere aging and weathering processes have created fissures on the slopes and small craters with pools of water and mats of mosses and lichens.*
>
> *The park was established in 1969 and was designated a National Natural Landmark in 1975. Its development began in the early 1960s through the efforts of local citizens, followed by state purchases of North Carolina Granite Corporation property and the company's gift of 418 acres, which included the major dome of Stone Mountain. Other purchases and land donations have increased the park's area to 13,550 acres.*

Frank Parkway, Roaring Gap, NC 28668 (telephone: 336-957-8185). Wilkes County Sheriff's Office: 201 Curtis Bridge Road, Wilkesboro, NC 28697 (telephone: 336-651-7368).

DESCRIPTION: This section of the MST is the last in the Blue Ridge Mountains and the last to parallel the Blue Ridge Parkway. It turns east and remains east and southeast until it takes a turn north on the beaches of the Atlantic Ocean. This section stays exclusively in Stone Mountain State Park, with the exception of the first 0.5 miles, which is on Blue Ridge Parkway property. No camping is allowed in the Parkway property; that includes the old tram site. Camping is not allowed anywhere in Stone Mountain State Park except at the Widow's Creek walk-in campsites (where permits are required) and in the park's campground near the visitor center. When this section of the trail is completed it will be officially named the Louise Chatfield Trail in honor of her leadership during the initial stages of making the MST dream a reality (see Section 24, Chapter 10, for more information).

The major activities available in the park are picnicking, fishing, hiking, climbing, and camping. Walk-in campsites are also available in the backcountry at designated areas, and advance permits with fees are required. Climbing is allowed on the south face of Stone Mountain, and climbers are requested to receive information on the regulations and routes from the ranger's office. Access is by way of the Stone Mountain Trail, described below, to the mountain base where a panel diagrams the twelve climbing routes. The mountain is closed to climbing when the rocks are wet, and all climbers as well as all hikers must be out of the area a half-hour before closing. There are eight hiking trails in the park: Stone Mountain Trail (4.5 miles), Wolf Rock Trail (1.2 miles), Cedar Rock Trail (0.7 miles), Blackjack Ridge Trail (1.4 miles), Stone Mountain Nature Trail (0.5 miles), Middle and Lower Falls Trail (1.6 miles round-trip), and a connecting trail between Stone Mountain Trail and the picnic area. Widow's Creek Trail (1.7 miles) is separate from the others.

At the northeast corner of Devil's Garden parking overlook, enter the forest and follow ribbons that flag the trail route (you may not see any white blazes of the MST until construction of this section is completed). It ascends gradually to a ridge where it turns right at 0.1 miles. At 0.2 miles it turns left of the ridge to meet with the old aerial tram road. Turn right and ascend. At 0.4 miles the tram road goes left and the MST goes straight into the forest. (The tram road goes 150 yards to a cement landing-platform for a former aerial tramway. Offering panoramic views, the Mahogany Knob Cable Car came from the north side of the mountain over a deep hollow (see "Campside Stories," below).

Follow the trail in its gradual descent along a flat ridge, occasionally over layers of rocks. On the way enter the boundary of Stone Mountain State Park. After hiking through dense rhododendron, arrive at an old road juncture, right and left, at 1.0 mile. Turn left and soon descend steeply on the old road (or use switchbacks if the trail is completed). Arrive at a juncture with another old road, right and left, in a level area at 1.8 miles. Turn right and follow the old road among hardwoods and rhododendron. At 3.2 miles begin a steep descent, turn right of a small stream to parallel it to a juncture with another old road, right and left, at 3.3 miles. This is the Widow's Creek Trail for accessing walk-in campsites upstream. (These campsites are not available to hikers unless they have the necessary permits.) Turn left, cross a small stream, and follow the old road. Cross Widow's Creek three times before an ascent. After the ascent, make a descent to the gravel Stone Mountain Road at 4.3 miles. Turn left. After a brief distance, notice the parking area on the left, from which you can easily access the Widow's Creek Falls.

Continue walking on the gravel road, which becomes a paved road, to the first parking area on the right at 5.3 miles. Walk to the restroom area. Next to the restrooms is the entrance to Stone Mountain's trail system. Enter the forest on the entrance trail. After 107 yards the Stone Mountain Trail forks to make a loop of 4.5 miles. The main MST follows the right fork and the alternate route follows the left fork. On the main MST descend to a footbridge among rhododendron, then ascend to another fork at 5.5 miles. (The

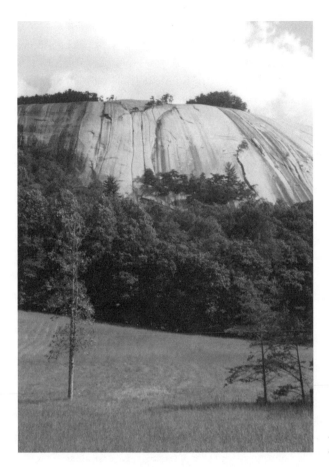

Stone Mountain in Stone
Mountain State Park

right fork is Wolf Rock Trail, which ascends 1.0 mile to the scenic and pockmarked dome of Wolf Rock.) Continuing on Stone Mountain Trail descend to cross four more footbridges, pass a picnic area and parking area for mountain climbers, and enter a large meadow. At 5.9 miles are spectacular views of the south face of Stone Mountain. A plaque describes the dome as a registered landmark. At 6.1 miles, near the edge of the woods, is a juncture with the 0.5-mile Stone Mountain Nature Trail, left. (Forming a loop, it crosses the meadow to the base of the mountain where an information panel shows the mountain-climbing routes.)

Continuing on the Stone Mountain Trail for 25 yards, pass Cedar Rock Trail, which connects from the right. Cross a stream and pass Middle Falls Trail and Lower Falls Trail connection at 6.8 miles. (Both of the falls trails dead end. Wading or rock-hopping Big Sandy Creek is necessary to view the cascades.) On Stone Mountain Trail the route becomes a footpath through a grove of rhododendron. Arrive at the beautiful 200-foot, tumbling Stone Mountain Falls (also called Beauty Falls) at 7.1 miles. Stay on and carefully ascend the stairway to the fall's summit. At 7.4 miles there is a fork. To the left is the alternate MST route on the Stone Mountain Trail loop. On the right fork the MST continues past an old chimney.

(If you choose to follow the alternate MST after entering the forest from the parking lot, ascend to cross a narrow entrance road to the meadows; then ascend on switchbacks among chestnut oaks, pines, rhododendrons, and blueberries. At 6.3 miles the trail ascends steeply on barren granite with yellow trail blazes. Near the top are large patches of lichens, mosses, pines, and more blueberries. Reach the summit [elevation 2,305 feet] at 6.6 miles. At 7.1 miles arrive at Hitching Rock for magnificent views south of Wolf Rock and Cedar Rock. Begin to descend and at 7.7 miles notice an old standing chimney and trail junction to the left. Here is a rejoining of the main MST route that has followed part of the Stone Mountain Trail loop.)

Continuing on the MST follow an access trail out of the forest to a large meadow where deer are frequently seen. Cross a footbridge over Big Sandy Creek and ascend to the park's largest picnic area. Pass through the picnic area and reach the paved park entrance road. Across the road is the park headquarters and visitor center at 8.2 miles if you are following the main MST route, and 8.5 miles if you are following the alternate MST route. If you wish to stay at the park's campground, turn left on the paved road, go 0.3 miles, turn right, and arrive at the campground after another 0.7 miles.

CAMPSIDE STORIES: Worth Folger of Sparta served in Europe during World War II. After the war he had an opportunity to see how cable car systems operated in the Alps, where they were used by sightseers and skiers. He dreamed of having something similar in the Blue Ridge Mountains. Mahogany Rock Mountain, in sight of Sparta, could be the place. That dream came true in the fall of 1967. Worth, his cousin Fred from Mount Airy, and Bailey Glenn Jr. of Winston-Salem formed Mahogany Rock Cableways, a corporation that would build "the world's longest and highest gondola span." They obtained a loan of $300,000 from NCNB with the approval of the Small Business Administration. The investors claimed that at fifty cents a ride it would pay for itself. Equipment made by Bell and Von Rolle in Switzerland arrived with engineers to assist Jim Osborne, the local contractor. There were twenty cars, each ready to carry six or eight passengers. The span was 2,800 feet over Bullhead Creek chasm, a drop of 1,052 feet. On the ride were views of Stone Mountain to the southeast and to Sparta and beyond to Mount Rogers in Virginia in the northwest. Access from the Blue Ridge Parkway was at milepost 234.1.

Jim Osborne rode with the engineers on the first car up. The system functioned as perfect as a Swiss watch. For nearly five years, from April through October, visitors had breathtaking views from Mahogany Rock Mountain (elevation 3,621 feet) in Alleghany County to the high peak of Scott Ridge (elevation 3,762 feet) in Wilkes County. "It was a harrowing ride, not for anyone who had any acrophobia," said Folger's son, Barney, who now lives in Atlanta. Visitors to the high peak of Scott Ridge found a gift shop, refreshments, and restrooms. Because of its altitude and cleared forest, views of Stone Mountain were better than any available from the Parkway.

By 1971 the dream was fading. There were fewer visitors; the Small Business Administration foreclosed on the bankrupt corporation and advertised for a sale with sealed bids in 1972. Immediately there were efforts by the Blue Ridge Parkway, the Stone Mountain Park and Preservation Committee, and other organizations to preserve the land as a scenic area and prevent further encroachment by private or commercial development. The Nature Conservancy purchased 402 acres of the property on September 22, 1975, and transferred it to the Blue Ridge Parkway on January 27, 1977, for $1,322.600 (one newspaper reported it as $1,168,000). And what happened to the cables and cars? The federal government gave them to the city of Biloxi, Mississippi. The system would transport tourists across the Mississippi Sound to a parklike island. (The cable car system was never developed.) And what about Worth Folger? "Folger Made $500,000 in Sale of Property" was the headline in Sparta's *Alleghany News*. Staff reporter Jesse Poindexter wrote, "And his is a story of riches to rags to riches if ever there was one."

SECTION 19. Stone Mountain State Park to I-77

ALLEGHANY, WILKES, AND SURRY COUNTIES: (See Section 16 for discussion of Alleghany and Wilkes Counties.) Surry County was founded in 1771 during the time William Tryon was governor. Because the governor's birthplace was in the County of Surry in England, Surry County was named to honor him. With 538 square miles taken from Rowan County, Surry is bordered on the north side by Grayson, Carroll, and Patrick Counties in Virginia. Its complete southern boundary is traced by the Yadkin River. The county seat is Dobson, named either for William Dobson (a local justice of the peace in 1776) or William P. Dobson (who served in the state legislature in 1814). The town was incorporated in 1891.

Cumberland Knob Recreation Area of the Blue Ridge Parkway is in the northwest corner of the county, and Pilot Mountain State Park is in the southeast corner. The county's largest city is Mt. Airy, the hometown of Andy Griffith, who played the part of Sheriff Andy Taylor of Mayberry in a long-running television series, "The Andy Griffith Show." Major north-south highways are I-77, US-21, US-601, and US-52; east-west routes are NC-268 and NC-89.

LENGTH AND DIFFICULTY: 19.7 miles, easy to moderate

USGS TOPO MAPS: Glade Valley, Traphill, Thurmond, Elkin North, Bottom, and Dobson

FEATURES OR EMPHASIS: Foothills and rolling hills, farms and pastureland, views of the Appalachian Mountains

TRAILS FOLLOWED: N.C. Department of Transportation North Line Trace Bicycle Route #4

TRAIL CONNECTIONS: None

WEST TRAILHEAD: Stone Mountain State Park Visitor Center

EAST TRAILHEAD: Juncture of Zephyr Road and I-77, exit 93

CAMPING, LODGING, AND PROVISIONS: Stone Mountain State Park campground (see Section 18). (See below for information on lodging and provisions in Roaring Gap.) Surry Inn at exit 93 of I-77, a family-owned motel (telephone: 336-366-3000). (See names and some telephone numbers of grocery stores in the description ahead.)

INFORMATION AND SECURITY: Trail Maintenance: For an updated report on a task force for this area, call 919-496-4771; Stone Mountain State Park, Route 1, Box 15, Roaring Gap, NC 28668 (telephone: 336-957-8185). Wilkes County Chamber of Commerce: 717 Main Street (P.O. Box 727), North Wilkesboro, NC 28697 (telephone: 336-838-8662). Wilkes County Sheriff's Office: 201 Curtis Bridge Road, Wilkesboro, NC 28697 (telephone: 336-651-7368). Surry County Sheriff's Office: P.O. Box 827 (218 North Main Street), Dobson, NC 27017 (telephone: 336-386-9253).

DESCRIPTION: Whether you are hiking or bicycling from Stone Mountain State Park, pass the ranger station and visitor center and descend into a young forest of oak, locust, poplar, and Virginia pine to exit at the park gate. At 0.4 miles leave the park boundary at Elk Spur Church, at a junction with Oklahoma Road (SR-1100) from the left. (Oklahoma Road ascends 3.1 miles to US-21, where it is 1.3 miles west to motels, food, grocery store, and post office.)

Continue on the wide John P. Frank Parkway. Ahead are views of the Brushy Mountains. Along the way you leave Alleghany County and enter Wilkes County. Among deep cuts in the hillsides grow wild white roses, Catalpa trees, blackberries, and Devil's walking-sticks. Arrive at the juncture with Traphill Road (SR-1002) at 3.0 miles. Turn left, and for the next 4.2 miles ascend and descend on rolling foothills of the Blue Ridge Mountains. The infrequent dwellings are typically well cared for, with beds of irises, lilacs, and peonies. Most of the farms are small, and some meadows are filled with yellow buttercups. At 5.1 miles is the Stone Mountain Store and Cafe (telephone: 366-957-2839, open all year). At 7.2 miles arrive at the junction with US-21 and North Line Trace Bicycle Route #4, and turn right (east). (West on US-21 it is 5.7 curvy miles up the mountain to Roaring Gap, where there are motels, restaurants, and a post office; it is 4.5 miles farther to the Blue Ridge Parkway.)

(You will follow Bicycle Route #4 to Danbury before leaving it to take a direct route to trails in Greensboro. Watch for the green and white bicycle sign at key points for turning or going straight ahead.) After turning right on US-21, go 0.2 miles and turn left on Thurmond Road (Old US-21). Follow it through a small community and reach the Thurmond Post Office, right, at 9.8 miles. (The postmaster has offered to give directions to places that have groceries, restaurants, and possible overnight camping for through-hikers or bicyclists. For example, on US-21 near the post office are two BP service stations 0.6 miles apart; you will also find Thurmond Grocery [telephone: 336-874-2795] and Foothills Grocery, which has deli, pizza, full meals, and groceries [telephone: 874-7339] and is open from 5 A.M. to 9 P.M.)

At 10.9 miles turn left on Zephyr Mountain Park Road (SR-1315) into Surry County. (To the right it is 0.2 miles to US-21 and 7.0 miles south to Elkin.) Along the way are small farms with clover pastureland for cattle and horses; crops of corn, barley, and soybeans; and small fields of tobacco. There are a few large and highly cultivated farms, such as Pine Ridge Farm, Hill Top Farm, Double J Farm, and Wayside Farm. Some of the fields are bordered with white pines. Churches along the way are (a few are unnamed) White Rock Methodist, Mountain Park Baptist, Full Gospel Tabernacle Association and Campground, and Salem Fork Christian. At 14.1 miles pass through the rural community of Mountain Park with school and playground, and Mountain Park Grocery (telephone: 336-874-2347, open every day except Sunday). Looking east you may begin to see the tops of Pilot Mountain and Hanging Rock State Parks. In the community of Zephyr, turn left at 16.4 miles on Zephyr Road (SR-1001). One mile before I-77 is Lowes Grocery Store on the right. After crossing a bridge over I-77 you will come to the Surry Inn at 19.7 miles (see "Camping, Lodging, and Provisions"), the Fast Track Restaurant, Dairy Queen, a diner, and service stations.

CAMPSIDE STORIES: It is not known where the following story began in the Appalachian Mountains. I first heard it from my grandfather (from my father's side of the family) in Patrick County, Virginia, but I have also heard

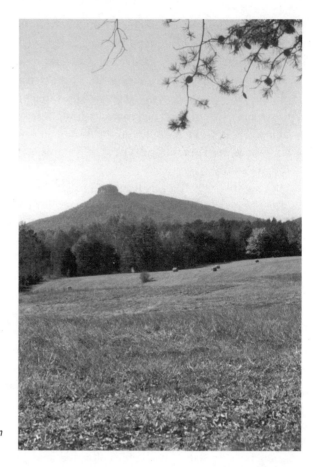

Pilot Mountain as seen from the Mountains-to-Sea Trail

that it happened somewhere in the foothills of the adjoining county of Surry in North Carolina. Storyteller Arthur John Harden called his characters in this story Asa Meters and Henry Holt. I heard them as Caleb Lackey, his brother Aaron, and neighbor John Agee.

It seems there was some jealousy between the brothers who lived together on a hillside farm. One day they had been sheering sheep and Caleb claimed Aaron fell off a wagon with the shears piercing his heart. The community people suspected Caleb of murder, but there was no one to prove it. Caleb secretly buried Aaron in a shallow grave on a rocky hillside. A suspicious neighbor, John, was tilling the soil and accidentally unearthed the skull of Aaron. While Caleb was away from his cabin, John placed the skull on the mantle over the fireplace. When Caleb returned and saw the skull, John accused him of killing Aaron.

The story has different endings, but one of the most common is that Caleb began to tremble and eventually, lacking a desire for food, he withered away to his death. Another ending is that the neighbors said the ghost of his dead brother snatched the food away and he died of starvation. And another ending (with hints of Cain and Abel in Genesis) is that Caleb was banished, taken over the mountains, and never allowed to return. My grandfather added another part to the story. In the mountains Caleb met a Native American bride.

SECTION 20. I-77 to US-52 near Pilot Mountain

SURRY COUNTY: See discussion of Surry County in Section 19.

LENGTH AND DIFFICULTY: 23.3 miles, easy to moderate

USGS TOPO MAPS: Bottom, Dobson, Mount Airy South, Pilot Mountain

FEATURES OR EMPHASIS: Scenic views of Pilot Mountain, Fisher and Ararat Rivers, farmland, country stores

TRAILS FOLLOWED: North Line Trace Bicycle Route #4

TRAIL CONNECTIONS: None

WEST TRAILHEAD: At junction of I-77 and Zephyr Road

EAST TRAILHEAD: At junction of US-52 and NC-268

CAMPING, LODGING, AND PROVISIONS: Motels include Surry Inn at exit 93 of I-77 (telephone: 336-366-3000), Holiday Inn at US-52 (telephone: 336-368-2237) and Mountain View Restaurant. There are stores and shops in the towns of Dobson and Pilot Mountain.

INFORMATION AND SECURITY: Trail Maintenance: Sauratown Trails Association, Route 1, Box 5217, Pinnacle, NC 27043 (telephone: Emily Grogan, 336-983-3250, or R. M. Collins, 336-368-2673), for information on hiking and equestrian trails, camping, and amenities. Surry County Sheriff's Office: P.O. Box 827 (218 N. Main Street), Dobson, NC 27017 (telephone: 336-386-9253).

DESCRIPTION: Alan Householder and I walked through this area on May 14, 1997, on our hike across the state. After crossing I-77 and having refreshments at the Fast Track Restaurant and Exxon Station at 0.1 mile, we turned right off the main road to Twin Oaks Road (SR-1110) for continuing on the North Line Trace Bicycle Route #4. The countryside was serene and scenic. We could look back and see the rim of the Blue Ridge Mountains and ahead to see the dome of Pilot Mountain. There were hayfields and silos, cattle, and farm homes with family names. Manicured church lawns, such as the one by Salem Fork Baptist Church, were pleasant sights along the way.

At 1.5 miles you will turn left on Turkey Ford Road (SR-1100). On the road banks and near patches of forest you may see bristly locust, pinxter-flower, and daylilies. Pass a junction with Brindle Road, right, at 2.7 miles. Cross several bridges over small streams. Arrive at a grocery store as you enter the town of Dobson on Atkins Sreet. In the heart of the historic town is Surry County Courthouse at 4.8 miles. The clean town has a post office, laundry, restaurants, pharmacy, variety stores, service stations, and grocery stores such as Lowes Foods. Cross US-601 and continue on Turkey Ford Road; at 5.8 miles cross US-601 Bypass. (It is 5.5 miles north on US-601 to Mount Airy.)

Pass through both residential and farming areas, and pass by Wayne Farms, a Division of Continental Grain Company. At 7.8 miles cross a bridge over the Fisher River where there are cascades. At the end of the bridge is Sweet Water Sugarsweet Tavern. Ascend (Turkey Mountain Road is left) to the top of a hill where houses are on both sides of the road. Pass Turkey Ford Baptist Church. Farms have mainly grain fields and some tobacco. You may notice different ages and varieties of tobacco barns. A log cabin sits at the corner of the Simpson Mill Road junction. Descend and cross a wooden bridge before passing Johnson Road to the left. There is a fenced-in AA Farm. Pass Hidden Valley Archery Club and ascend to an intersection with Siloam Road at 10.8 miles. Here is Watson Phillips Country Plaza and Grocery (telephone: 336-374-2345), a special place. This is nearly halfway the length of this section, and a rest stop here could be worthwhile. For such a small place out in the countryside it is surprising to see the varied services it provides. In addition to food, it offers such amenities as money orders, UPS shipping, and tanning beds.

Turn left (north) on Siloam Road (SR-1003) for 1.0 mile to a right turn on Ararat Road (SR-2019) at Blackwater United Methodist Church. There is a good view of Pilot Mountain ahead. At 15.0 miles is a sandwich shop on the left. At 16.1 miles is Mount Zion Church, and shortly after that you will come to a one-room schoolhouse built in 1880. Pass Stoney Creek Farm and descend to a crossing of the Ararat River. It has cascades and shady over-hanging trees upstream. Cross a railroad into the community of Ararat. In another 0.2 miles you will come to the Ararat Post Office (27007). From here (18.0 miles) you will have an impressive view of Pilot Mountain directly to the southeast. From Ararat follow Toms Creek Road (SR-2022), descend, cross the railroad, then cross Toms Creek at 20.2 miles. At 21.0 miles turn left on NC-268. Arrive at Tucker Grocery at 22.9 miles. Cross over US-52 at 23.1 miles. At 23.3 miles come to the Holiday Inn and Mountain View Restaurant (telephone: 336-368-2237), an ideal place to rest and sleep after this long section. (It is 10.5 miles north on US-52 to Mount Airy, and 2.5 miles south on US-52 to the entrance of Pilot Mountain State Park.)

CAMPSIDE STORIES: When you arrive in Dobson you will see a state marker by the sidewalk on the east side of Surry County Court House. It reads "Tabitha A. Holton (1854–86), First licensed female attorney in N.C. Was admitted to bar in 1878. Lived 20 yards NW." This is a true story that took place among

Pilot Mountain State Park

Pilot Mountain State Park offers a spectacular view of the countryside from the Blue Ridge Mountains in North Carolina and Virginia in the west and north to Winston-Salem in the south. The Saura Indians used its peak (elevation 2,420 feet) as a pilot from which to navigate their surroundings. Geologically it is a quartzite monadnock, and its peak has been closed to climbers for a number of years for safety reasons. Formerly the peak was privately owned as a tourist attraction, but area residents wanted it to be preserved. It finally became a state park in 1968. There are thirteen trails spanning a total of 23.9 miles. The park covers 3,703 acres in two sections, which are connected by a 300-foot-wide connector for 6.5 miles. The park has a campground with hot showers but no hook-ups (closed December 1 through March 15), picnic areas, and canoe camping. The 20-mile Sauratown Trail (equestrian) from the Hanging Rock State Park area has its western terminus here.

siblings in the home of a Methodist minister. Tabitha, the well-educated sister, tutored her three brothers for their state law examinations. She learned so much about law in the process that in January 1878 when one of her brothers, Samuel, went to Raleigh to take the exam, she requested to take the exam also.

The surprised state Supreme Court, which administered the exam, requested she come back the next day with an attorney for counsel. She chose attorney Albion W. Tourgee. The Court argued that such a southern lady should not be "permitted to sully her sweetness by breathing the pestiferous air of the courtroom." But Tourgee won the request and she passed the bar exam. Not all the press agreed, but the *Greensboro Patriot* congratulated the decision and in an editorial stated, "Blast the prejudice that puts women down as only fit to be men's slaves or playthings."

Samuel and Tabitha set up a law office across the street from the courthouse in Dobson. By choice she did more of the research and left the court appearances mainly to the men, but she had already made history with this landmark decision. She died at age thirty-two and is buried in the Springfield Friends Meeting cemetery in High Point.

SECTION 21. US-52 near Pilot Mountain to Hanging Rock State Park

SURRY AND STOKES COUNTIES: (See Surry County discussion in Section 20.) The 458-square-mile Stokes County is one of six counties in the state that have all square corners. It was formed from parts of Surry County in 1789, and was named in honor of Captain John Stokes (1756–90), who was a Revolutionary War officer and member of the Continental Congress. The county seat is Danbury, by the Dan River, which was founded in 1852.

The county is bordered on the north by Patrick and Henry Counties, Virginia, and on the south by Forsyth County. Part of Belews Lake is in the southeast corner of the county, east of the town of Walnut Cove and southeast of Sauratown Plantation Game Land. The major natural attraction is Hanging Rock State Park, located in the central part of the county and west of Danbury. Main highways east-west are NC-268, NC-704, and US-311. North-south routes are NC-89, NC-772, NC-8, NC-66, and US-52.

LENGTH AND DIFFICULTY: 19.5 miles, easy to moderate

USGS TOPO MAPS: Pilot Mountain, Hanging Rock

FEATURES OR EMPHASIS: Views of the Sauratown Mountains, South Double Creek, Hanging Rock State Park

TRAILS FOLLOWED: Part of Sauratown Trail, Tory's Den Trail, Moore's Wall Loop Trail, Lake Trail, and Indian Creek Trail

TRAIL CONNECTIONS: Sauratown Trail, Cook's Wall Trail, Upper Cascades Trail, Hanging Rock Trail

WEST TRAILHEAD: US-52 at the town of Pilot Mountain

EAST TRAILHEAD: Campground of Hanging Rock State Park

CAMPING, LODGING, AND PROVISIONS: One motel is the Holiday Inn at US-52 (telephone: 336-368-2287). Camping is available at Pilot Mountain State Park, Route 3, Box 21, Pinnacle, NC 27403 (telephone: 336-325-2751), and at Hanging Rock State Park, P.O. Box 278, Danbury, NC 27016 (telephone: 336-593-8480). (See the list of restaurants and grocery stores in the section description, below.)

INFORMATION AND SECURITY: Trail Maintenance: Sauratown Trails Association (volunteers), Route 1, Box 527, Pinnacle, NC 27043 (telephone: 336-983-3250, and staff of Pilot Mountain State Park and Hanging Rock State Park (see above). Surry County Sheriff's Office: P.O. Box 827 (218 North Main Street), Dobson, NC 27017 (telephone: 336-386-9253). Stokes County Sheriff's Office: 118 Main Street, Danbury, NC 27016 (telephone: 336-593-9253).

DESCRIPTION: Walking through the town of Pilot Mountain on NC-268 (Bicycle Route #4), you will pass Food Lion, Lowes Food, restaurants, and a pharmacy. Cross a railroad track at 0.6 miles. At 1.0 mile pass First United Methodist Church, and at 1.1 miles cross Main Street. After another 0.1 mile, Hanging Rock is in view, blue in the distance. Turn right at 1.4 miles. There is a barbecue and pizza place at 2.0 miles. You can see Pilot Mountain again. It will appear to the right of the main or central part of the Sauratown Mountain Range. Enter Stokes County at 2.7 miles. Pass through residential areas, followed by farms, some of which have tobacco.

Saura Indians

The high range of mountains (elevation 2,465 feet) you see between Pilot Mountain and Hanging Rock is part of the Sauratown Mountains, named for the Saura Indians. They lived here and in villages by the Dan River. Examples of these village sites have been identified northeast of Walnut Cove and southeast of Eden in Rockingham County. Jomeokee, meaning the "Great Guide," was the name they gave Pilot Mountain. Historians believe the Saura Indians were driven out of the area by the Cherokee Indians.

Pass a service station at 4.8 miles. There is a log cabin at 5.0 miles, and Jeff's Grocery is at 6.5 miles. After passing White Church Cemetery you will see mainly forested land. Through openings among the trees you will get views of Hanging Rock State Park; its western rock face, Moore's Wall and Moore's Knob, will become more defined. At 8.0 miles, on the right, is Rock House Road (SR-1187), a potential alternate route to Hanging Rock State Park via at least 5.6 miles of the Sauratown Trail. The trail is well graded and follows scenic stream banks among hardwoods, rhododendron, and mountain laurel, and crosses hillsides and meadows of ferns and wildflowers.

(If you are using this route, follow the paved Rock House Road. After 0.7 miles be alert to any signs on the left for the gravel Marshall Road, a future access to the Sauratown Trail. Otherwise, continue on Rock House Road, pass the remnants of the Rock House, a colonial home built in 1770 by Colonel John Martin. It is between Thore Road [SR-1185] and Flat Rock Road [SR-1175] on the right at 1.3 miles. [In 1999 the Sauratown Trail's western route followed Flat Rock Road from Rock House Road before reentering the forest on its way to Pilot Mountain State Park.] Continue on Rock House Road to arrive at a Sauratown Trail parking, restroom, and picnic area, on the right at 2.6 miles.

Leave the road, left, and enter the forest to descend on switchbacks. Pass a waterfall at 3.4 miles, cross the paved Taylor Road at 4.0 miles, and cross NC-66 at 4.2 miles. Descend on switchbacks and rock-hop South Double Creek. Pass Tucker Trail at 6.4 miles and cross Moore's Springs Road (SR-1001) at 6.6 miles. Cross Mickey Road (SR-1481) at 7.9 miles. Ascend and pass the James Booth Trail, left, on your way to access the paved Charlie Young Road (SR-2028) at 8.2 miles. [To your left it is 300 yards to the Tory's Den parking area.] Cross the road to follow the Sauratown Trail that connects with hiking trails through Hanging Rock State Park. [See description ahead if you are arriving at this point on the highways.])

If you are continuing on NC-268, turn right when you come to the junc-

Rock House Road, a Mountains-to-Sea Trail access to Hanging Rock State Park via the Sauratown Trail

ture with NC-66 at 10.5 miles. Descend on a crooked road and cross South Double Creek, which flows northeast about 5 miles to its confluence with the Dan River. Pass the Old Orchard Primitive Baptist Church at 12.7 miles. At 13.0 miles cross the Sauratown Trail on the right and left of the highway. Descend and cross a tributary to South Double Creek in a scenic and pastoral area with an old house on the right at 13.9 miles. Ascend into a forested area with scattered residences, and arrive at Moore's Springs Road (SR-1001), crossing right and left, at 14.3 miles. There is a small parking area here.

Turn left (north). (If you are bicycling, continue to follow North Line Trace Bicycle Route #4 on Moore's Springs Road for 4.8 miles to the entrance of Hanging Rock State Park and turn right if you will be staying at the campground. Do not bicycle on any of the foot trails. To continue bicycling on the MST follow it from the park entrance east to NC-8/89.)

If you are hiking the MST, turn left (north) also on Moore's Springs Road, but after 0.4 miles turn right on the steep Mickey Road (SR-1481). After 0.8 miles turn right again on the steep Charlie Young Road (SR-2028). The grade will level out, and at 15.7 miles notice the Sauratown Trail on your right (Section 5) and left (Section 6). Turn right on Section 5 (Tory's Den Trail). Parking space is not provided here, but 300 yards up the road and to the left is an official parking area (for day-use only) with access to the western terminus of the Tory's Den Trail or for hiking the Sauratown Trail. (Hikers should remember that if they are continuing on the part of the

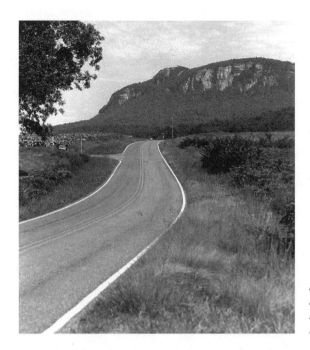

Moore's Wall, seen from the Mountains-to-Sea Trail access route to Hanging Rock State Park on Charlie Young Road

MST that follows the old Sauratown Trail through part of Hanging Rock State Park, camping is not allowed anywhere in the park except at the campgrounds.)

Continuing on Section 5 of the Tory's Den Trail, you will come to a juncture with an unmarked horse trail at 15.9 miles; turn left. At 16.7 miles a horseback riding loop intersects the trail; go straight bearing left. A sign on the trail says "hiking begins," and other signs say "hikers only." At 17.6 miles turn left on the Moore's Wall Loop Trail. Ascend and pass through mountain laurel, hemlock, turkey grass, oak, and dogwood. Arrive at Moore's Knob and observation tower at 18.1 miles. These outstanding views of the Blue Ridge Mountains in North Carolina and Virginia, and as far as you can see to the south and east, are the finale to the major mountain views you first had on Clingmans Dome. Descend past Balanced Rock and Indian Face on an old road. Cross Cascade Creek and enter the camping area at 19.7 miles.

CAMPSIDE STORIES: The hike through Hanging Rock State Park brought back some childhood memories for me. From Moore's Knob I again saw the Blue Ridge Mountains in Patrick County, Virginia, less than 20 miles north of where I was born. My older brother Moir took me with him to explore Hanging Rock and Pilot Mountain (before they were state parks) in North Carolina, and Rocky Knob, Rock Castle Creek, and the Pinnacles of Dan and Lovers Leap in Virginia. My grandfather, Green DeHart, had explored

Hanging Rock State Park

This park encompasses 6,000 acres and its highest point is Moore's Knob, at 2,579 feet elevation. There are more than 18 miles of named trails and side trails that reach scenic heights, waterfall areas, rocky ridges, and caves. There are at least 300 species of plants known from the park, including the mountain camelia. Canadian and Carolina hemlock grow together here, and a number of rare botanical species have been found. The park has camping (also cabins), picnicking, swimming, fishing, mountain climbing, and a parking area for canoeing the Dan River. Hanging Rock State Park is open all year, but the campground water is shut off from December 1 through March 15.

these magnificent places before us and he frequently mentioned them in his ghost stories. Some of his stories were retold according to the weather. For example one snow-bound night that I was at his home I heard this version of "Raw Heads and Bloody Bones."

"Once upon a time a long time ago in the Dan River Gorge, Alfred the Hunter was going home with food and furs for his family when he was caught in a snow blizzard. It was not a flaky kind up to his knees; it was going to be over his head. Now to save himself he went into an old house."

Grandpa stopped. He leaned close to me and in a low heavy whisper said "Alfred the Hunter did not know it was a haunted house full of ghosts." Grandpa stared at me, waiting for the shock to increase my imagination.

"He built a fire to keep warm. Suddenly, a man's bloody leg bone fell down the chimney. Alfred picked it up and threw it in the corner of the room. Soon another bloody leg bone fell and Alfred picked it up and threw it in the corner of the room. Then a bloody arm bone fell, and thigh bones, and foot bones, and finger bones, and ribs one by one, until there was a big pile of bones in the corner. Just as Alfred thought the grizzly scene was over, down fell a raw head. He threw it in the corner." Grandpa stared at the corner behind me, he trembled and groaned. I looked at the fire in the fireplace near me and I looked behind me.

"Just about the time Alfred was about to go to sleep, he heard a scary rattle and he looked to the corner. All the bones had come together, walking toward him." I was holding my breath. My Grandpa was now making eerie sounds of rattling bones and said slowly, at the moment he protectively wrapped his large arms around me, "And the ghost grabbed Alfred and ate 'em up."

TEN

HANGING ROCK STATE PARK
AND WESTERN PIEDMONT AREA

SECTION 22. Hanging Rock State Park near Danbury to Walnut Cove

STOKES COUNTY: See Stokes County discussion in Section 21.

LENGTH AND DIFFICULTY: 16.7 miles, easy to moderate

USGS TOPO MAPS: Hanging Rock, Danbury, Walnut Cove

FEATURES OR EMPHASIS: Hanging Rock State Park, Historic Danbury, Dan River, Walnut Cove

TRAILS FOLLOWED: Part of Moore's Wall Loop Trail, Cook's Wall Trail, and Indian Creek Trail

TRAIL CONNECTIONS: Upper Cascades Trail, Hanging Rock Trail

WEST TRAILHEAD: Hanging Rock State Park campground

EAST TRAILHEAD: South Walnut Cove at junction of US-311 and NC-65

CAMPING, LODGING, AND PROVISIONS: Camping is available at the Hanging Rock State Park campground, P.O. Box 278, Danbury, NC 27016 (telephone: 336-593-8480), and at the private Sunset Park and Campground, 6.5 miles south of Danbury on NC-8/89 (no telephone number). Grocery stores and restaurants can be found in Walnut Cove.

INFORMATION AND SECURITY: Trail Maintenance: Sauratown Trail Association, Route 1, Box 527, Pinnacle, NC 27043 (telephone: 336-983-3250). Stokes County Sheriff's Office: 118 Main Street, Danbury, NC 27016 (telephone: 336-593-8783).

DESCRIPTION: To leave the Hanging Rock State Park campground, follow the lake trail to the left until the junction with the Moore's Wall Loop Trail at 0.8 miles. Turn left and for a few yards follow the Cook's Wall Trail. Pass the swimming area out toward the parking area and follow the road (or a side trail off the road) to the parking area for the park office and visitor center at 1.3 miles. (To the left near the entrance to the parking area is the paved Upper Cascades Trail.) After a stop at the visitor center, go toward the northeast end of the parking lot, but on the way watch for the Hanging Rock

Lewis David von Schweinitz

He was an internationally known and honored botanist and Moravian clergyman (1780–1834). Born in Bethlehem, Pennsylvania, to immigrant parents from Germany, Lewis David von Schweinitz was educated at the Moravian School for Boys in America and the Moravian Theological Seminary in Lusatia, Germany. Although he worked as an administrator of the Moravian Southern Province in America at Salem at the age of thirty-two, his studies of the flora of the Hanging Rock area are most significant to the hiker. Schweinitz received international recognition for his studies of plant life and mycology, and for his publication, in 1831, of a list of more than 3,000 fungi, 1,200 of which he had discovered. A rare species of sunflower is named after him. He died in Bethlehem, Pennsylvania. You will see a state marker dedicated to Schweinitz at the intersection of Moore's Springs Road (SR-1001) and NC-8/89.

Trail on your right. This is the park's most used trail to the legendary rock. On the way the trail connects with the Wolf Rock Trail.

Continue to the end of the parking lot where there is an information board and the trailhead for the south end of the Indian Creek Trail. Follow it through a hardwood forest with scattered pines and patches of mountain laurel. Arrive at a spur trail, right, to Hidden Falls at 2.1 miles and another spur at 2.2 miles to Window Falls, right. At 2.7 miles pass a spur trail left to the group campground. Cross Indian Creek and descend to a more level area with greater undergrowth density. Cross a footbridge over Indian Creek and arrive at Moore's Springs Road at 3.5 miles. (The entrance to the park is a few yards left, and the Indian Falls Trail crosses the road to descend. After 2.0 miles it accesses a parking area at Dan River for canoeing and fishing access.)

Turn right on Moore's Springs Road and ascend to the top of a ridge at 3.9 miles. Descend and arrive at a junction of NC-8/89 right and left; turn right. Across the road is the Stokes Reynolds Memorial Hospital. Pass a sign "Welcome to Danbury, Gateway to the Mountains," and enter the charming community that received its name in 1852. Pass the Danbury Library, left, at 4.9 miles, and pass among historic houses, shops, and churches. Debbie's Diner is on the right at 5.5 miles. On the left you will pass the old Stokes County Courthouse and a number of heritage buildings (some about 150 years old). At 5.8 miles is Pace Grocery and service station, and Booth's Grill. Here is a highway juncture with Moir Farm Road (SR-1606), left, where the North Line Trace Bicycle Route #4 continues. The MST route stays on NC-8/89 to cross a bridge over Mill Creek, which empties to the left into the Dan River.

Ascend to an Amoco station, left, and Manuel's Market and Dan River Restaurant at 6.2 miles. On a descent watch for a sign, left, for Sunset Park and Campground. It has hot showers and is a quiet location in a grassy area by a stream. Pass by a large Department of Transportation office at 7.3 miles. In the community of Meadows arrive at a busy intersection at 8.6 miles, where NC-8 goes right, Dodgetown Road goes left, and NC-89 with the MST goes straight ahead. Oakley's Grocery and Grill is on the right at 8.8 miles. At 10.8 miles come to Betty's Country Grocery and Amoco Station with fishing supplies. At 8.8 miles is a grocery store and gasoline. Pass Willow Oak Baptist Church. Arrive at the junction of US-311 and NC-89 at 15.1 miles. Left is US-311, and the MST continues ahead on NC-89. Walnut Cove Center is here, and you will find a Food Lion, Hardees, Olympic Restaurant, a bank, and a local newspaper office. (Walnut Cove, named for a grove of black walnut trees, was first settled in 1883; it was known as the community of Lash until 1889.)

Continue through Walnut Cove and a mile-long strip of residences, variety shops, clothing stores, hardware stores, drug stores, bookstores, service stations, and grocery stores. There are also banks and business offices. Cross a bridge over Town Fork Creek. Arrive at the Town Fork Seafood Restaurant and the Cove Grill and Restaurant, right, at 16.7 miles. Here the MST turns left on NC-65 to cross the railroad.

CAMPSIDE STORIES: An adventurous youth from the Hanging Rock/Danbury area heard the call, "go west young man." Your hike along the MST has probably crossed territory that he explored. Gabriel Moore, the eighth child of Matthew and Letitia Moore, was born in sight of the Sauratown Mountains in 1785. A year later the family moved into a brick home, known as Moore Castle, near the Dan River. As a boy Gabriel was exposed to the farms and ironworks owned by his father in Double Creek Valley. His father died in 1801.

By the time he was twenty years old Gabriel Moore followed some of his older brothers and sisters west to Tennessee and the new territory that became Alabama. By 1808 he was commissioned as an attorney by the governor of Mississippi, and he settled down in a community now called Huntsville, Alabama. Moore quickly rose to prominence in land speculation and political efficacy. He was elected governor of Alabama in 1829 and during his tenure was influential in creating the University of Alabama. In 1831 he left the post of governor to become a U.S. senator. He personally knew Andrew Jackson and supported his political agenda, but later leaned more toward the Whig Party against Jackson. Gabriel was called home from the Senate by 1835.

While his political career was fading he learned that his irresponsible nephew, Benjamin, who he had entrusted to handle his financial interests while in Washington, had defrauded him of his wealth. This tragedy, combined with his failure to be honored with a political position in the Whig Party, was a terrible blow. Moore left Huntsville in 1844 to go west and live on the new frontier in Texas; he died on the way, at Caddo, Texas. (A state highway marker on Main Street in Danbury stands in Gabriel Moore's honor.)

SECTION 23. South Walnut Cove at US-311/NC-65 to South Summerfield at US-220

STOKES, FORSYTH, AND GUILFORD COUNTIES: (See Stokes County discussion in Section 21, above.) Colonel Benjamin Forsyth, who lived for about seventy-four years, was a native of Stokes County and was killed in the War of 1812. Forsyth County, named in his honor, encompasses 424 square miles. The city of Winston-Salem, the county seat, was formed in 1913 from the adjoining towns of Winston and Salem. Winston was named for Major Joseph Winston (1746–1814), a Revolutionary War officer, and Salem was founded and settled in 1766 by Moravians.

The county is flanked on its west side by the Yadkin River and by Yadkin and Davie Counties. Some of the major attractions in the city of Winston-Salem and vicinity are the Old Salem Historic District, Reynolda House Museum of American Art, and Historic Bethabara Park. To the west of the city is the county's outstanding Tanglewood Park, formerly the estate of Will and Kate Reynolds. The Tanglewood Steeplechase is held each May. Winston-Salem is home to a number of colleges and universities, including Wake Forest University, Salem College, and the North Carolina School of the Arts. One of the state's four largest cities, the highway system carries east-west traffic on I-40, US-421, and NC-67, and north-south traffic is routed on NC-150, NC-8, US-158, US-52, US-311, and NC-6.

Guilford County, founded in 1771 with 652 square miles, is named for Francis North, first Earl of Guilford (1704–90) and member of the British Parliament. Its county seat is Greensboro, one of the state's four largest cities. Its name honors General Nathanael Greene (1742–86), who led the Battle of Guilford Courthouse in 1781. Some of the area's historic sites are Guilford Courthouse National Military Park, Greensboro Historical Museum, and, east of Greensboro, the Charlotte Hawkins Brown Memorial. High Point features the High Point Museum and High Point University. Greensboro is also home to the University of North Carolina at Greensboro, Bennett College, Greensboro College, Guilford College, and N.C. Agricultural and Technical University.

The Deep River runs through the southwest corner of the county, where there are also two lakes: Oak Hollow Lake and High Point Lake. North of the city of Greensboro are Lake Higgns, Lake Brandt, Townsend Lake, and Richland Lake. Major east-west highways are I-40, I-85, US-70, NC-62, and US-421. North-south highways are US-220, NC-68, NC-61, and US-29.

LENGTH AND DIFFICULTY: 19.5 miles, easy to moderate

USGS TOPO MAPS: Walnut Cove, Belews Lake, Belews Creek, Summerfield, Lake Brandt

FEATURES OR EMPHASIS: Belews Lake, farmlands, and historic homes and other buildings, particularly Summerfield

TRAILS FOLLOWED: None

TRAIL CONNECTIONS: None

WEST TRAILHEAD: Junction of NC-65 and US-311 at Cove Grill and Restaurant in Walnut Cove

EAST TRAILHEAD: Junction of South Summerville Road with US-220 northwest of Greensboro's Lake Brandt

CAMPING, LODGING, AND PROVISIONS: There are not any campgrounds along this section of the MST. The currently known option is at the former Circle M Motel (now weekly or monthly rentals) at the east trailhead, where with advance permission you may be able to set up a tent in a grassy area under shade trees. Call Joe Williams at 336-643-5121 or 336-913-2341. If camping at the former Circle M Motel is not permitted, call the following for assistance in arranging a shuttle or in finding a place to stay overnight: Mike Simpson, Lakes, Trails and Greenways Director, Parks and Recreation Department for the City of Greensboro (telephone: 336-545-5955 or 336-202-1346), or MST trail leaders Don and Kathy Chatfield (telephone: 336-292-4120). If you decide on a motel, the nearest is Journey's End Motel, 7.0 miles south on the east side of US-220 (2310 Battleground Avenue; telephone: 336-288-5611). Beyond it, in another 0.5 miles, is Battleground Inn on the west side of US-220 (1517 Westover Terrace; telephone: 336-272-4737). On the way to these motels are a number of shopping centers and numerous single stores that can serve all your needs. Across US-220 (on the east side) from the former Circle M Motel and The "Sporters" Choice store is Sissy's Family Restaurant (telephone: 336-643-9131). A Phillips 66 gas station is nearby.

INFORMATION AND SECURITY: Greensboro Area Chamber of Commerce: 125 South Elm Street #100 (P.O. Box 3246), Greensboro, NC 27402 (telephone: 336-275-8675). Forsyth County Sheriff's Office: P.O. Box 21089, Winston-

Salem, NC 27120 (telephone: 336-748-4100). Guilford County Sheriff's Office: 400 West Washington Street (P.O. Box 3427), Greensboro, NC 27401 (telephone: 336-373-3694).

DESCRIPTION: From the intersection of NC-89/US-311 and NC-65 in South Walnut Cove (the Town Fork community), follow NC-65 east toward Stokesdale. Cross the railroad tracks. Friendly Food Mart is on the right in a partially residential area with rolling hills. Leave the town limit at 0.8 miles. Fogg Road is on the right at 2.0 miles; on the left is a heavy equipment business. At 2.8 miles Tucker Road comes in from the right and Fisher Road, to Metts Farm, is on the left. Among the farming areas are tobacco fields and scattered forests of Virginia pine. Leave Stokes County and enter Forsyth County at 3.2 miles. To the left is Hill Billy Hide-A-Way Restaurant and Sandy's Play School. Pine Hall Road is right and left at 3.6 miles. Descend and pass White's Grocery store. Pass sections of forests and flowering wild pinks on the roadsides; there are cattails and white fragrant roses in the swampy areas right and left at 4.1 miles. Ascend, and if you look backward you can see the tops of Pilot Mountain and Hanging Rock state parks.

Come to a junction with County Bicycle Routes #17 and #18 at 4.9 miles. Pass an old cemetery on the left at 5.1 miles and Belews Church of Christ at 5.3 miles. Descend and reach Belews Creek Post Office, left, at 5.5 miles. Cross a bridge over beautiful Belews Lake. Descend and cross a bridge over an emerald green lake at 6.3 miles. There is a Duke Power Company boat ramp at 6.4 miles. Fish in the lake are carp, sunfish, and crappie. Ascend. Enter Guilford County at 7.4 miles. There is a grocery store at 8.7 miles.

Pass Stokesdale Christian Church, Disciples of Christ, on the right at 10.0 miles. Arrive at the junction with US-158, from the right, at 10.1 miles. NC-65 veers left. Follow US-158 or cross over US-158 to follow Stokesdale Street, which parallels US-158 through the town of Stokesdale. (Stokesdale was formerly known as the community of Pine. Residents claim that the town was later renamed in honor of Governor Montford Stokes [1762–1842]). To the left is a large Bi-Rite grocery store on Lyman Street (US-158). There is a telephone, followed by a bank and a farm supplies and hardware store on the left. If you are following Stokesdale Street in late spring or summer, notice a house (address #8405) on the right with a large, fragrant, multi-colored rosebush near the street at 10.2 miles. After 0.1 mile turn left on Mulberry Street to go a few yards to Lyman Street and turn right. At 10.4 miles is the Stokesdale Fire Station, right, and at 10.6 miles is Stokesdale United Methodist Church. At 10.9 miles arrive at a juncture with NC-68, right (south) and left (north). Turn right to a grocery and BP service station and Family Dining restaurant with home-style cooking. The restaurant is open 24-hours daily (telephone: 336-643-9935). (There are no motels or campgrounds in this area. The closest motel is 10 miles south on NC-68 at I-40.)

After walking 0.1 mile south on NC-68, watch carefully to turn left on Athens Road (SR-2101). Pass a school. The area has manicured residential lawns and some farms. Parallel US-158, and pass a historic house on the right at 11.3 miles and a large white oak on the left at 11.9 miles. Pass Truline Landscaping and Nursery, right, at 12.0 miles, where you turn sharply right on Eversfield Road (SR-2109). The countryside has new and old homes among horse farms, tobacco fields, patches of forest with poplar, beech, yellow pine, white and red oak, and cedar. Wildflowers include daisy, aster, horse nettle, and twayblade. The roadway undulates, and at 13.5 miles you will cross the Haw River near its western headwaters. Ascend through a scenic forest of pine, oak, sourwood, and black gum at 13.5 miles.

Arrive at a junction with NC-150 (Oak Ridge Road) at 14.5 miles; turn left (east). Pass through a residential area of old and new homes to enter the town of Summerfield at 14.7 miles. (Summerfield was settled in 1769 by Charles Bruce, a Patriot of the American Revolution. For some time the community was known as Bruce's Crossroads. It was later named in honor of John Summerfield [1798–1825], a religious leader.) Pass a building with unique wood carvings at 17.0 miles, right. At 17.1 miles cross a bridge over an abandoned railroad. Arrive at a crossroads at 17.2 miles where there are some old and historic buildings in the heart of Summerfield. (Ahead it is 0.1 mile to US-220.)

Turn right on Summerfield Road (SR-2117). The Summerfield Elementary School is right at 17.9 miles and the post office is left. Pass the fire station, left, at 18.1 miles. At 18.2 miles is a special ceramics museum/ workshop on the right (7309 Summerfield Road), near the Full Gospel Tabernacle. Jean Nance has been providing this creative experience for twenty years in an "old fashioned family-type atmosphere." (Closed Sunday and Monday; you can call her in advance at 336-643-7821.) Pass Rose's Day Care and After School Care on the right; on the left you will see Summerfield Feed and Hardware at 18.4 miles. At 18.9 miles there is a passageway left to Food Lion and a pharmacy near US-220. There is also a gravel road passageway left to the former Circle M Motel at 19.3 miles. Watch carefully for the descending passageway across the highway from a neighbor's mailbox with the address #6935. (The ownership is currently renting rooms weekly or monthly, but also may permit you to set up your tent with limited options. You must have permission, so call in advance. See "Camping, Lodging, and Provisions," above.) Exit the former motel site to the corner of US-200 and Summerfield Road. Here is The "Sporters" Choice store at 19.5 miles and access to traffic going into the city.

CAMPSIDE STORIES: About 14 miles southwest of Walnut Cove is Winston-Salem, a city with thousands of legendary and honorable heroes, and inspirational citizens of history. One of them was a teenager, Keith Jackson, who as an adventurer did what none had ever accomplished before him. Keith was born October 28, 1955. His mother said that her over-nine-pounds baby came into the world with his fists clenched ready for life's challenges.

He became an Eagle Scout, was admitted to the Order of the Arrow, graduated from The Principia, and enrolled at the University of North Carolina in Charlotte at the age of seventeen. Keith had an adventurous dream—to bicycle solo the 18,000 miles from Anchorage, Alaska, to Tierra del Fuego at the tip of South America. His journey would be through fourteen countries, and in Columbia he would travel 300 miles in a perilous jungle. Those who went as a group before him into the jungle warned of the danger of being alone. Keith persuaded his professors and the deans to offer academic credit for his expedition.

On his nineteenth birthday, while passing through part of the Panama Canal, he wrote in his diary that the previous four months had been "complete freedom" for his destiny and existence. On April 1, 1975, he completed the grueling odyssey at the cold waters where the Pacific and Atlantic Oceans wash together. If you read the book, *Keith's Incredible Journey*, you will live the journey with him, every day, mesmerized by the risk he was taking. It is an inspiration for bicyclists, for Boy Scouts, for any of us who yearn to dream, dare, and achieve. Keith came home to Winston-Salem, where he was welcomed with the Key to the City and a memorable celebration of "Keith Jackson Day." The public had followed him on his journey from reading Tom Sieg's reports in the *Sentinel* (now the *Winston-Salem Journal*). He was the youngest to complete the passage, and he did so in the shortest time. It was the longest bicycle solo on record.

One year and four months later, at the age of twenty-one, Keith Jackson died when his motorcycle crashed into a stalled motor vehicle in Winston-Salem. In May 1977 the University of North Carolina at Charlotte graduated him posthumously.

SECTION 24. South Summerfield Road / US-220 Junction to Entrance to Bryan Park, North of Greensboro

GUILFORD AND ALAMANCE COUNTIES: (See Guilford County discussion in Section 23.) As with many other counties in the state, larger counties were divided to make new ones. The 434-square-mile Alamance County was formed from Orange County in 1849. Except for a sinuous boundary line at the southeast corner, along the Haw River, it has square boundaries as do Guilford County to the west and Caswell County to the north. Alamance's namesake may be from either Alamance Creek or the Battle of Alamance, which occurred on May 16, 1771, when local farmers called "Regulators" had a skirmish with Governor William Tryon's British troops southwest of Burlington. The county seat is Graham, incorporated in 1851 and named for William Graham, who was governor of the state from 1845 to 1849.

The Haw River, popular for canoeing, runs southeast through the county. Its headwaters derive in part from Stony Creek, which is impounded in two places: Burlington Lake and Stoney Creek Reservoir. The county's largest recreational park is the 414-acre Cedarock Park, located south of Burlington. North-south highways are NC-87, NC-49, NC-119, NC-54, and NC-62; east-west routes are I-85/40 and US-70.

LENGTH AND DIFFICULTY: 20.2 miles, easy to moderate

USGS TOPO MAPS: Lake Brandt, Browns Summit, Ossipee

FEATURES OR EMPHASIS: Lake Brandt, Lake Townsend, woodlands, wildflowers

TRAILS FOLLOWED: Piedmont Trail, Owl's Roost Trail, Nat Greene Trail, Laurel Bluff Trail, Peninsula Trail, Osprey Trail, Townsend Trail

TRAIL CONNECTIONS: Big Loop Trail

WEST TRAILHEAD: Junction of South Summerfield Road and US-220

EAST TRAILHEAD: Entrance to Bryan Park on Townsend Road north of Greensboro off US-29

CAMPING, LODGING, AND PROVISIONS: There are no campgrounds on this section of the MST or at the east trailhead. Therefore through-hikers must hitchhike a ride south on US-29 to a motel on I-40. Call the chambers of commerce listed below for the options nearest to you, or call one of the following contacts for a shuttle to a motel or to camping on the back lawns of friends of the MST: Mike Simpson, Lakes, Trails, and Greenways Director, Parks and Recreation for the City of Greensboro (telephone: 336-545-5955 or 336-202-1346); MST trail leaders Don and Kathy Chatfield (telephone: 336-292-4120).

INFORMATION AND SECURITY: (See the list of maintainers at the end of each trail description.) Greensboro Area Chamber of Commerce: 125 South Elm Street #100 (P.O. Box 3246), Greensboro NC 27402 (telephone: 336-275-8675). Alamance County Area Chamber of Commerce: 610 South Lexington Avenue (P.O. Box 450), Burlington, NC 27216 (telephone: 336-228-1338). Guilford County Sheriff's Office: 400 West Washington Street (P.O. Box 3427), Greensboro, NC 27401 (telephone: 336-373-3694). Alamance County Sheriff's Office: 109 South Maple Street, Graham, NC 27253 (telephone: 336-570-6300).

DESCRIPTION: The city of Greensboro operates thirty-three parks and recreation areas, nature museums, and gardens; expansion of existing parks and additional parks are in the planning and completion stages. In one of the parks, Bur-Mil, the 2.0-mile Big Loop Trail runs jointly with the 4.2-mile Owl's Roost Trail for 0.4 miles. On September 19, 1998, the Greensboro Parks and Recreation Department in cooperation with the North Carolina Parks and Recreation Division dedicated this 0.4-mile trail and nearly 20 other miles in the Greensboro Watershed Trails System as part of the Mountains-to-Sea Trail. To completely hike these newly dedicated trails you will need a full day. For the purpose of following the longest route of combined trails, I will describe the south side of Lake Brandt and Lake Townsend. All of the other dedicated trails and other Greensboro trails are described in my book *Trails of the Triad*, published by John F. Blair Publisher.

From the juncture of South Summerfield Road and US-220, come downhill slightly as you travel south on US-220. At the juncture with Strawberry Road, at 0.7 miles, turn left. After 0.2 miles notice the small parking lot on the right for the west trailhead of the Piedmont Trail, maintained by the Piedmont Hiking and Outing Club. Follow the Piedmont Trail on an old railroad grade for 0.2 miles to a juncture with the Owl's Roost Trail, which continues ahead. The 2.8-mile Piedmont Trail goes left. Follow the Owl's Roost Trail through an open field of wildflowers, grasses, and blackberries. Tag alder, oak, and pine grow closer to Lake Brandt. At 1.3 miles the trail crosses more open space, then crosses a 295-foot old railroad bridge at 1.5 miles. Across the lake, to the west, you can see traffic on US-220.

Ahead the trail passes through an arbor of pines, oaks, birches, and elms to a juncture with Bur-Mil Park's Big Loop Trail, right and ahead. Continue ahead with trail options by a fishing pier, left, and picnic shelters on the right. At 1.9 miles the Owl's Roost Trail/MST goes left and the Big Loop Trail goes right. (The Big Loop Trail goes to Fishing Lake, connects with the Little Loop Trail, passes the golf course and park headquarters, and accesses a parking area for the trailhead on Owl's Roost Road near the Bur-Mil Park entrance. From there it completes its loop as described above.) At 2.2 miles there is a boggy area. There are intermittent views of the lake, but at 3.7 miles there are open views of the Lake Brandt Dam and the nearby marina to the right. Cross a small stream at 4.3 miles. Here and elsewhere on the trail you will notice a mixture of pine and hardwoods. With the oak and pine species are hickory, ironwood, and elm. There are frequent patches of running cedar, mosses, and lichens. Among the wildflowers are rattlesnake orchids. Enter a pine grove, after which, at 5.0 miles, you will cross a railroad bridge. Arrive at a juncture with the Nat Greene Trail at 5.3 miles; turn left

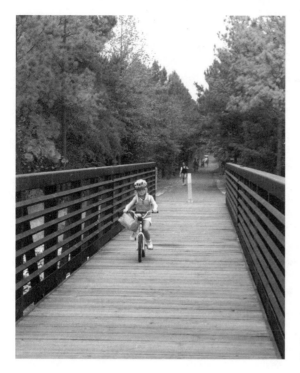

*Mountains-to-Sea Trail on the
Owl's Roost Trail in Greensboro*

(to the right the Nat Greene Trail goes 0.7 miles to its southwest trailhead at Old Battlefield Road, and 0.7 miles farther to us-220). (The Owl's Roost Trail is maintained by the Sierra Club.)

Follow the Nat Greene Trail to cross a small stream at 6.5 miles. Continue to weave in and out of coves for periodic views of Lake Brandt. You are likely to hear songbirds here and throughout the lake trail system, and there should be ducks and herons in the lake. Canada geese are also seen during the migratory season (and sometimes at other times). The forest here is composed of oak, Virginia pine, beech, and poplar. At 7.9 miles pass the parking area for Lake Brandt Marina. Arrive at a small parking lot on Lake Brandt Road at 8.1 miles.

(There is a state highway history marker about the Battle of Guilford Courthouse at the corner of us-200 [Battleground Avenue] and New Garden Road. Also, if you choose to visit the Battleground, access from here is south [right] on Lake Brandt Road to New Garden Road, right [west]. Maintainers for the Nat Greene Trail are members of the Piedmont Hiking and Outing Club.)

To continue on the MST walk north on Lake Brandt Road for a few yards and turn off right before reaching the former Dillard's Store. Follow the

---

Nathanael Greene

The city of Greensboro adopted its name in 1808 to honor General Nathanael Greene, one of General George Washington's most able military leaders. Without him the American Revolution for independence might not have been won. About 3.0 miles south of the trailhead of the Nat Greene Trail is Guilford Courthouse, a location wisely chosen by General Greene as the site for a battle with Lord Charles Cornwallis on March 15, 1781.

General Greene used a military style that involved separating troops in waves among the trees. He had about half as many troops, many of whom were untrained, as did Lord Cornwallis. The Americans fought bravely, and although they lost at Guilford Court-house, Lord Cornwallis's troops were so weakened that he abandoned his efforts to conquer North Carolina.

Later, General Greene turned down the offer to be secretary of war; instead, in 1785, he chose to live at his Mulberry Grove estate north of Savannah, Georgia. He lived only a year. What the gunfire of the British did not accomplish, the Georgia sun did. He died of sunstroke at the age of forty-four on June 19, 1786.

Laurel Bluff Trail near a fence into the woods. This area is part of the Roger Jones Bird Sanctuary. Pass an old barn and cross a gas pipeline at 8.1 miles. At 8.4 miles pass through a large beech grove. Pass an unnamed spur trail, right, at 8.5 miles. Bear left at a fork at 8.9 miles. There is a boggy area at 9.1 miles and a small brook near the edge of the lake at 9.2 miles. This section, as in parts of all the trails in the lakes area, has many species of flowering shrubs such as beauty-berry, mountain laurel, redbud, dogwood, filbert, button bush, redroot, strawberry bush, and sourwood. Among the wild-flowers are wood betony, green-and-gold, wild geranium, and black cohosh. Pass the boundary of a field at 9.6 miles. At 11.1 miles pass through a river birch grove. Arrive at Church Street at 11.2 miles. (The Laurel Bluff Trail is maintained by the Audubon Society.)

Cross the street and enter the Peninsula Trail through a grove of young Virginia pine. At 11.8 miles is an open area from which you can view Lake Townsend. After passing through an area that is sometimes wet from runoff, you will come to a mixed pine and magnolia grove at 12.1 miles. Exit at North Church Road at 12.4 miles. Turn left and follow the road for 300 yards to a roadside parking area on the left (east). The Osprey Trail begins here. At 12.8 miles pass the remains of an old cabin, and after another 0.1 mile pass close to the lake's lapping shoreline. You will ascend a slight ridge among oak and pine and descend to parallel a cove before rock-hopping a stream at 13.4 miles. Return to the lake's edge, and then cross under two power lines to follow a rim of a former pond. At 14.7 miles you will have an excellent view of the lake. Arrive at Yanceyville Road at 15.1 miles.

Across the road begins the Townsend Trail. Pass a gate and enter a grassy slope by the lake to a berm at the edge of the forest. On the left at 15.5 miles is an old well in a forest of oak, beech, and dogwood. You will curve around a long cove, cross a stream, and return to the lakeside at 16.1 miles. At 16.7 miles you may wish to walk the sandy edge of the lake to avoid any dense growth under the power line. Here in the open are button bush, filbert, and tag alder. Reenter the forest and follow the edge of another cove. Cross a footbridge and enter a grove of Virginia pines above clubmoss. You may notice slight ridges in the treadway at 17.8 miles; these indicate a former tobacco field. Pass under a power line at 18.2 miles and again at 18.5 miles, then curve right of a farm pond and ascend at 18.8 miles. At 18.9 miles cross Southshore Road (SR-2524) to reenter the woods. Follow an old road, but watch carefully for a right turn. Ascend gently, and then exit to a field with bluebird houses in Bryan Park. Cross the field and turn right at a fence. After a few yards, turn left to enter the fence opening and forest. Pass through pines, cedars, oaks, and persimmons. Arrive at the paved Townsend Road (SR-2525) at 19.3 miles, the trail's end. Parking is not allowed here. (The Peninsula Trail, Osprey Trail, and Townsend Trail are maintained by the Sierra Club.)

(To the right [south], and past a soccer field, it is 0.2 miles to a large gravel parking area for Bryan Park visitors. After a few yards ahead, there is a Townsend Road gate that is opened at 6:30 A.M. and closed at dusk. Beyond the gate Townsend Road crosses railroad tracks to the left. Southshore Road, to the right, has an immediate entrance road to an outdoor sports area. [The community is known as Rudd, but its former name was Sippanaw until 1898, when it was changed to Morehead. Later it was finally named Rudd to honor local residents Senaca and Cicero Rudd.] You may need to describe this parking location if you have planned for someone to pick you up. Otherwise, I suggest that you follow the directions in the next paragraph.)

From the Townsend Trail trailhead turn left on Townsend Road and follow through an exceptionally scenic golf course. Canada geese may be seen in the lake to the left or, even more likely, munching on the manicured green grass. Arrive at the Bryan Park main entrance at 20.2 miles. Here you have access to a telephone to call for a ride to a campground or motel. Use the telephone numbers listed above under "Camping, Lodging, and Provisions."

CAMPSIDE STORIES: Louise Merony Chatfield was born May 19, 1920. By the time of her death on June 20, 1986, she had earned the honorable title of the "first lady of trails in North Carolina." A naturalist and believer in the value of greenways and hiking trails, she was the state's most influential "mover and shaker in conservation of the state's natural resources," wrote Bodie Mc-Dowell, a reporter for the *Greensboro News & Record* in 1986. It was during this decade that she and her family, particularly her two sons Don Jr. and Bill, with Don's wife Kathy, planned and successfully completed a trek of hiking, biking, horseback riding, and canoeing parts of a potential Mountains-to-Sea Trail across the state.

Chatfield's leadership began much earlier. She led campaigns and lobbied for the preservation of the New River in the 1960s, was influential in the creation of the North Carolina Trails Act of 1973, and served as the first chairperson of the North Carolina Trails Committee. She also assisted in forming the North Carolina Trails Association in 1977. In addition she saw the need for maintenance on sections of the Appalachian Trail and was influential in creating the Piedmont Appalachian Trail Hikers (PATH) for the purpose of caring for 42 miles of the AT in Virginia.

A brilliant student, she graduated from what is now the University of North Carolina in Greensboro at the age of twenty. She later taught at Livingston College and Greensboro College. A close friend, Hollyce Kirkland, who wrote an article in tribute to her in the March/April 1996 edition of *Appalachian Trailway News*, said "she introduced walking to thousands . . . and taught them to be in touch with the natural world." At a memorial service in Greensboro for "Ma Chatfield," Kirkland cited an 1858 quote by Chief Seattle. ". . . Teach your children that the Earth is our mother. What-ever befalls the Earth befalls the children of the Earth. If we destroy the land and the water and foul the air, we destroy ourselves." On July 30, 1998, President Bill Clinton and Vice President Al Gore designated the New River as one of the 14 American Heritage Rivers. Many of us thought about Louise Chatfield at this time because it might never have happened without her. Furthermore, I would not have written this book about the Mountains-to-Sea Trail if not for her personal influence and legacy.

SECTION 25. Bryan Park (off US-29) North of Greensboro to Arrowhead Inn on US-501 North of Durham

GUILFORD, ALAMANCE, ORANGE, AND DURHAM COUNTIES: (See discussions about Guil-ford and Alamance Counties in Section 24 above.) In 1752, when Orange

County was formed, it was probably named in honor of William V of the British House of Orange, whose grandfather was George II. Today Orange County encompasses 398 square miles. The county seat, Hillsborough, was incorporated in 1759 at Childsburgh, but the name was changed to Hillsborough in 1766 to honor Wills Hill, Earl of Hillsborough (1718–93), who was the British secretary of state for colonial America. For a period of time the city's name was spelled Hillsboro, but in 1965 it was officially returned to its original spelling.

The Eno River State Park is in Orange County, and the Eno River flows through it on its way east through Durham County. Northwest of Hillsborough, and west of Durham and north of Chapel Hill, is the magnificent 7,700-acre Duke Forest. (Its trail system is described in detail in *Trails of the Triangle*, published by John F. Blair Publisher.) At the southwest corner of the county is the city of Chapel Hill with its exceptional concentration of historic sites, educational landmarks, and cultural and recreational opportunities. The University of North Carolina Board of Trustees authorized real estate to be sold for a town development in 1792. The university opened January 16, 1795, and the town was incorporated in 1819. The town was named for New Hope Chapel of the Church of England. East-west highways in the county are I-85/40, US-70, and NC-54; north-south routes are US-15, US-501, NC-86, and NC-157.

Durham County has 300 square miles and was formed in 1881 from Wake County on the east and Orange County on the west. The county seat is Durham, which was called Durhamsville from 1851 to 1855. Both names honor Dr. Bartlett S. Durham (1922–1858), a local citizen who contributed land for the railroad station. The city is internationally known for Duke University and Duke Hospital. The city and nearby areas are also home to North Carolina Central University, the North Carolina Museum of Life and Science, Bennett Place, Sarah B. Duke Memorial Gardens, Duke University Museum of Art, Duke Chapel, West Point on the Eno, Research Triangle Park, and part of Falls Lake. Major east-west highways are I-40/85, US-70, NC-54, and NC-98; north-south highways are US-501, NC-157, US-15, NC-751, NC-55, and NC-147.

This long section of MST, spanning two full counties and parts of two others, is broken into three parts—A, B, and C— which resemble each other in terms of terrain, geology, and rural environment. Because it is difficult to find camping locations or motel facilities on or close to the trail in this region it did not seem possible to provide a trail section of less than 20 miles for each day. This means that if you are hiking, you may wish to hitchhike on the state roads south to the motels listed under "Camping, Lodging, and

Provisions." Alternatively, you could call one of the task force leaders for assistance. Camping is a little easier if you are biking, and you can request information from staff of the state Office of Bicycle and Pedestrian Transportation listed below. Whether you hike or bicycle, never trespass or camp on properties without permission.

LENGTH AND DIFFICULTY: 56.9 miles (Part A: 17.1 miles; Part B: 22.1 miles; Part C: 17.7 miles), easy to moderate

USGS TOPO MAPS: Ossipee, Lake Burlington, Burlington NE, Cedar Grove, Caldwell, Rougemont

FEATURES OR EMPHASIS: scenic farms, historic churches, Lake Burlington

TRAILS FOLLOWED: Part of Alamance County Bicycle Route #74

TRAIL CONNECTIONS: Alamance County Bicycle Route #73

WEST TRAILHEAD: Bryan Park entrance at Lake Townsend west of US-29

EAST TRAILHEAD: Arrowhead Inn at corner of Mason Road and US-501 north of Durham

CAMPING, LODGING, AND PROVISIONS: There are no campgrounds along or near this long section of the MST. There are store owners and farmers who have stated that they would provide an overnight campsite for through-hikers, but they have requested that they be contacted through officials or task force leaders of the Friends of the Mountains-to-Sea Trail. Lodging and large shopping centers for hikers or bicyclists are available on the I-40/85 exit for Elon College (exit 141). The exit area is accessible from the MST at Ossipee/Altamahaw, south on NC-87 and Saint Mary's Church Road. (See more detailed highway directions below in "Description.") Lodging possibilities for the Elon College area include Best Western (telephone: 336-584-0151), Hampton Inn (telephone: 336-584-4447), and Mariott (telephone: 336-585-1888).

At exit 145 of I-40/85 (to NC-49), you will find a Days Inn (telephone: 336-227-1270) and Motel Six (telephone: 336-226-1325). In Graham at exit 148 from I-40/85 there is an Econo Lodge (telephone: 336-228-0231). Near Mebane at exit 153 from I-40/85 (at NC-119) there is a Hampton Inn (telephone: 919-563-5400). Near Hillsborough at exit 164 from I-85 you will find a Holiday Inn Express (telephone: 919-644-7997) and the Southern Country Inn and Campground in the Daniel Boone Shopping Center (telephone: 919-732-8101), accessed from NC-86 and NC-57. Arrowhead Inn is at the corner of Mason Road and US-501 north of Durham (telephone: 919-477-8430). South of Arrowhead Inn it is 8.5 miles on US-501 to a Super 8 (telephone: 919-268-8888) and the Chesterfield Motel (telephone: 919-220-4132), both at exit 177B from I-85.

INFORMATION AND SECURITY: For county bicycle route information in Alamance County, call Dean Coleman (telephone: 910-570-6760) in Graham. For other information contact the following—Alamance County Area Chamber of Commerce: 610 South Lexington Avenue (P.O. Box 450), Burlington, NC 27216 (telephone: 336-228-1338); Hillsborough Area Chamber of Commerce: 150 East King Street, Hillsborough, NC 27278 (telephone: 919-732-8156); Greater Durham Chamber of Commerce: 300 West Morgan Street #1400 (P.O. Box 3829), Durham, NC 27702 (telephone: 919-682-2133). If there are security needs, contact the following—Guilford County Sheriff's Office: 400 West Washington Street (P.O. Box 3427), Greensboro, NC 27120 (telephone: 910-373-3694); Alamance County Sheriff's Office: 109 South Maple Street, Graham, NC 27253 (telephone: 336-570-6300); Orange County Sheriff's Office: 144 East Margaret Lane, Hillsborough, NC 27278 (telephone: 919-644-3050); Durham County Sheriff's Office: 201 East Main Street, Durham, NC 27701 (telephone: 919-560-0900).

DESCRIPTION:

PART A: From the clubhouse at Bryan Park, exit the park's main gate at 0.1 mile on Bryan Park Road (SR-2641). Cross a bridge over railroad tracks at 0.2 miles. Pass through scenic landscaping of an industrial park to Summit Avenue (SR-2526) at 0.6 miles. Turn left, pass through more industrial park sites and reach a bridge crossing US-29 at 1.4 miles. (Access to the City of Greensboro and I-85 is 9.6 miles south on US-29.)

After descending on the forested Eckerson Road (SR-2790) and crossing a small stream, begin to ascend. Reach the top of a hill, descend, and cross a tributary to Reedy Fork at 2.1 miles. A lake is to the right. Ascend and pass through a residential area with a historic home on the left at 2.7 miles. At 3.1 miles turn left on Hicone Road (SR-2565). Continue ascending and descending. There is a soccer field on the left at 3.5 miles. Cross Hines Chapel Road and pass by fine homes of the Northwoods subdivision. Tobacco fields follow at 4.4 miles, right. Northeast High School is left at 5.0 miles, followed by an oak and Virginia pine forest. At 6.0 miles is Country Hills Village. At 6.5 miles come to an ideal country store—Sam's Stop and Shop—at the corner of Friendship Church Road and Hicone Road. The store is open weekdays from 6 A.M. to 9 P.M. (telephone: 336-621-2910).

Continuing on Hicone Road pass Country Hills Golf Club and lake, right, followed by new homes. Turn left on Huffine Mill Road (SR-2770) at 7.2 miles. Pass through farmlands and scattered homes. At 8.4 miles cross High Rock Road (SR-2719). Descend and cross Buffalo Creek, a tributary to Reedy Fork, at 9.3 miles. (From High Rock Road to Buffalo Creek is the south boundary of a planned and large City of Greensboro park. Its area will include the confluence of Buffalo Creek from the south and another tributary from the north with Reedy Fork. Among the recreational activities will be trails and a campground. Contact Greensboro Trails and Greenways Information [telephone: 336-545-5961] for an update.) Ascend to the top of a ridge; descend steeply at 10.7 miles; ascend and descend to cross two more small tributaries to Reedy Fork. Virginia pine and hardwood forests alternate with farmlands along the way.

At 11.2 miles, at the juncture with NC-61 in the Friedson Church community, turn left. There is a volunteer fire station on the right corner. (South on NC-61 it is 4.4 miles to the town of Gibsonville.) There are large farms right and left. Riverside Dairy Farm is at 12.2 miles. After another 0.1 mile, turn right and ascend on Sockwell Road (SR-2735). At the top of the hill is one of the most scenic farming areas in this section. Among the rolling hills of grasses are patches of forest, fences bordered with cedars, meandering streams, and farm buildings. You may see dairy and beef cattle. Road traffic is sparse. After a descent, ascend to pass through Reedy Fork Farm. A farm barn, right at 13.2 miles, bears the name of F. J. Teague and Son. At the top of the ridge and among shade trees is a brick farm home, right.

The road continues to undulate. You will cross a small tributary flowing left (north) to nearby Reedy Fork. Leave Guilford County and enter Alamance County on Shepherd Road (SR-1554) at 14.4 miles. Cross another stream and ascend to a juncture with Gibsonville-Ossipee Road (SR-1500), Alamance County Bicycle Route #74, right and left, at 15.6 miles. Keep left on Gibsonville-Ossipee Road to arrive at Old NC-87 at 15.8 miles in a residential area of the community of Ossipee. (The word *Ossipiee* is Native American, but its meaning is not known.) There are not any stores here or public telephones. Turn left. (To the right it is 8.4 miles to motels at I-40 south of Elon College. If you plan to bicycle or make a car shuttle to the motels, turn right and arrive at NC-87 at 0.4 miles. After another 0.3 miles you will come to North Crest Market, which sells food and gas. At 2.9 miles watch for Saint Marks Church Road, right, and follow it, leaving NC-87. Pass through farmland and forests to a residential area where Saint Marks Church Road (SR-1301) becomes North Williamson Street. Stay on it in your passage through a combination of Elon College the town and Elon College the campus. Cross a railroad track at 5.4 miles (a post office is left) and notice that your route has become South Williamson Street. At 6.8 miles there is a shopping center. Cross Church Street. Notice that your route has again become Saint Marks Church Road, and watch carefully that you leave it at 7.1 miles by turning left on Garden Road (SR-1436). After 1.1 miles you are in a dense shopping center with choices of restaurants and motels (such as those listed above in "Camping, Lodging, and Provisions").

Continue on the MST north on Old NC-87. Ossipee Baptist Church is left.

On the right at 16.1 miles is a partially camouflaged private club. Cross a bridge over Reedy Fork at 16.3 miles. Ascend and curve right among tall red oaks between Berea Christian Church, left, and a school, right. Descend to a juncture with NC-87 on the left at 16.8 miles. Turn left. (To the right it is 0.4 miles up a hill to a service station on the left.) Cross a high bridge over the Haw River, then cross a smaller bridge. Turn right at 16.9 miles on Altamahaw Road (SR-1002) and Alamance County Bicycle Route #74. Ascend; on the right is Glen Raven Milling Company in Altamahaw. At the top of the hill, left, at 17.1 miles is a post office and a couple of shops. There is also a shady grove, a good place to wait for someone you have contacted to pick you up for a motel or private home. Across the street (south) from the shade trees is the entrance to the historic milling company. (The town of Altamahaw, a Native American name, was founded about 1860 beside the Haw River.)

PART B: Leave the shady grove in Altamahaw and continue east on the Altamahaw Road (SR-1002). At 0.2 miles cross an intersection where Altamahaw Baptist Church is right and Bethlehem Christian Church is 0.3 miles on the left. At 0.6 miles pass under a large powerline system, followed by tobacco and grain fields. At 1.8 miles pass an abandoned school on the right. Cross Paget Town Road at 2.1 miles. There is an Exxon service station with groceries. A scenic farm is on the left at 3.2 miles. Pass a picturesque farm and barn at 4.2 miles. Descend and cross Buttermilk Creek at 4.4 miles. Ascend through a forest, then descend to cross Stoney Creek Road at 5.0 miles. There are Virginia pine groves and tobacco fields ahead. Cross a bridge at 5.5 miles over beautiful Lake Burlington. At 5.6 miles Vernon Church Road and North Center Fire Station are on the left. Cross another bridge over the lake at 5.7 miles; sycamore and sumac border the causeway. Reach the top of a hill at 6.1 miles; you will see old tobacco barns on the right. At 6.6 miles, historic Union Ridge United Church of Christ and a large cemetery are on the left at Union Ridge Road. On the southeast corner of the intersection is Union Chapel United Church of Christ (African-American). Also at the intersection is Alamance County Bicycle Route #73. (The name Union Ridge was first given to a church on a ridge between Tom's Creek to the west and Jordan Creek to the east. Both streams flow south.)

Continue east on Jeffries Cross Road (SR-1999) to descend from a ridge at 7.0 miles. For the next 2.0 miles ascend and descend to cross Jordan Creek and Owens Creek and through patches of Virginia pine. At 9.1 miles are historic buildings, log tobacco barns, and roadside wildflowers. You will arrive at an intersection with NC-62, right and left, at 10.1 miles. Jeffries

Cross Road Baptist Church is here. Stay left. (It is 11.5 miles right [south] on NC-62 to US-70, NC-87, and NC-100 to I-40, exit 145, for motels.) At 11.1 miles NC-49 comes in from the right (south). Turn left on both road numbers (NC-49 and NC-62) and pass through a residential area. Pleasant Grove Fire Station is on the right at 11.6 miles. At 11.8 miles, at a fork in the road, Pleasant Grove Recreation Center is on the left. A Shell service station is 0.2 miles to the right on NC-49. (The community of Pleasant Grove was established in 1822 with a post office for the farms and cattle ranches.) (It is 9.5 miles south [right] on NC-49 through the towns of Haw River and into Graham, where a turn left on NC-54 takes you another 1.0 mile to Econo Lodge at exit 148 at I-40/85.)

Continuing east on NC-49, descend to cross Quaker Creek, and then ascend at 13.3 miles to a ridge. There are tobacco barns on the right. Cross NC-119 and Alamance County Bicycle Route #74 at 14.4 miles. There are not any stores here. On a straight 1.3 miles, still on NC-49, cross Stagg Creek, then go uphill to turn right on Mount Zion Church Road (SR-1113), opposite a service garage. Horses and a scenic lake are on the right. Enter Orange County at 16.1 miles. Cross a tributary to Stagg Creek. Mount Zion Christian Church is on the right at 16.6 miles. Turn left on Lynch Store Road (SR-1364) at 17.0 miles. Pass a large white frame house on the right at 17.3 miles. At 17.6 miles turn right on a secondary gravel road named Pentecost Road (SR-1361), formerly named Parker Road. Keep right at a fork at 18.0 miles. Descend into a forest to cross Back Creek at 18.3 miles. Ascend. There are large white oaks on the right near Lib Road and an abandoned house on the left. At 18.9 miles pass tobacco and grain fields to the right and left, followed by Cedar Grove Fire Station, left, at 19.5 miles. At 19.6 miles arrive at the paved Cedar Store Road, right and left. Turn right and pass tobacco barns. Tinnin Grocery Store is right at 20.7 miles. Cross West Fork River in a forest at 20.8 miles. Arrive at Efland–Cedar Grove Road, right and left, at 22.1 miles. To the left is the historic C. H. Pender Grocery/Post Office. (Make this store a must-stop on your journey.)

PART C: From the store continue east on Hughes Road (SR-1352) into a forest. Cross a stream at 0.4 miles that flows right (south) into Lake Orange. At 1.3 miles pass a state marker for the Old Eno Church and Cemetery (Presbyterian). The church was founded in 1755 when Henry Pattillo (1726–1801) was the first pastor. It was moved to Cedar Grove in 1893. (In Granville County, north of Stovall, there is another state marker honoring Pattillo for his legislative service, his work as a clergyman in Virginia and North Carolina, and his work as a teacher and author of textbooks.) Cross the East Fork of the Eno River at 1.4 miles. At 2.0 miles cross NC-86. At the southeast

---

Little River Presbyterian Church

For those who walk or bicycle the country road past the Little River Presbyterian Church, there is peace and rest for the weary under its shade trees. A spiritual experience is available here simply by knowing that this church celebrated its 238th anniversary in 1999. In an area settled by the Scotch-Irish, the community began worship services as early as 1755. It is likely that Hugh McAden, a young circuit-rider on horseback from Pennsylvania or New Jersey, preached in the community during that period.

In 1761 John Wright organized church meetings in homes and arbors. The first pastor was the Reverend Henry Pattillo in 1765. (See information in this chapter on honors by the state.) William Murdock gave land for a church site, and a log church was built. When it later burned, a white frame church replaced it. The current sanctuary was erected between 1889 and 1893, during the pastorate of the Reverend W. S. Wilhelm. Other additions followed. The most recent are educational and office facilities completed in 1993. One of the church's important celebrations is the annual homecoming on the second Sunday in May.

---

corner you will see R. L. Snipes Grocery. (For motels you can go south on NC-86 for 7.8 miles through Hillsborough; then leave the state route for 1.0 mile on South Churton Street, where you will find a motel and campground, as well as fast-food restaurants and groceries, near exit 164 of I-85. See "Camping, Lodging, and Provisions.")

Cross NC-86 onto Sawmill Road (SR-1545) and through a residential area. At 3.4 miles cross Wilkerson Road (SR-1507). Stop at a T-intersection at 3.9 miles; turn left on Walnut Grove Church Road (SR-1507). Oakley's Drapery Outlet is on the left at 4.0 miles. Cross the South Fork of the Little River at 4.2 miles. At 4.3 miles turn right on Little River Road (SR-1543) into a forest. Ascend. Pass through a farm with soybeans and other crops. At 5.7 miles you will see large oaks and a historic house. There is a large house and lake at 6.7 miles, followed by more farmhouses. At 7.7 miles on the right is Little River Presbyterian Church.

Arrive at the intersection of NC-57 at 8.1 miles. Turn left, pass under a large electrical transmission line, and turn right on Green Riley Road (SR-1579) at 8.5 miles. At 8.9 miles pass Jackson Road and continue straight ahead, but turn left at a pine plantation. Arrive at and turn right on NC-157 at 10.5 miles. There is a scenic area of pastureland and forest near Norman's Stables at 10.6 miles.

Descend, cross a road at 11.3 miles. You may see Arabian horses on the left at Hollow Oaks. Enter Durham County at 12.9 miles. Cross the South

Fork of the Little River again at 13.2 miles. NC-157 is now called Guess Road. Arrive at a Citco service station at 13.7 miles, and at a B.P. service station with groceries and snacks at 15.2 miles. It is on the left at an intersection with St. Mary's Road/Mason Road. Turn left on Mason Road. Pass a Catholic Church on the right at 16.3 miles, and pass Johnson Mill Road, left, at 16.6 miles among new houses. Cross a tributary to the Little River at 17.3 miles. The Arrowhead Inn, a historic home built in 1778, is on your left shortly after. (Reservations for elegant overnight and breakfast service can be made by calling 919-477-8430.) At 17.7 miles come to a juncture with US-501, which goes north to Roxboro and south to Durham. (The nearest motels are 8.5 miles south on US-501 to I-85, exit 177B.)

CAMPSIDE STORIES: When Alan Householder and I walked across the state in the spring of 1997, we saw vacant and abandoned homes throughout the central and coastal regions. Some were old pioneer cabins, others were one-story clapboard dwellings, and others were large two-story mansions. A few were almost invisible behind clinging honeysuckle, grape vines, and kudzu. Occasionally we stopped and talked about imaginary history of the places and speculated on the lives and deaths of the families. A few houses fit the stereotype of haunted house; others were mysterious but inviting. Occasionally there would be "danger" signs or "no trespassing" signs. I remember one old house on Pentecost Road in Orange County.

In September 1998 I bicycled solo through this remote section of the current MST. I stopped to rest under a large white oak across the road from the house. I thought about how ghostly my surroundings were and how it reminded me of the many haunted house stories I had heard from my grandfather when I was a child. Without much effort I could imagine it being the "House of the Opening Door" on Salola Mountain, where at midnight an interior door latch would mysteriously open without human touch. In that legendary home tools moved around by themselves, too. One story claims the spirits of former owners were looking for money left under the floorboards.

While resting and drinking fresh water I had acquired at Pleasant Grove, I also thought about the haunted house described by Nell Lewis in Raleigh's *News and Observer*. At this home there were inexplicable noises of unseen visitors opening locked doors, and sounds of footsteps coming down from upstairs but never going upstairs. At first the sounds were in the daytime, but later they became nocturnal. There were other strange noises of dishes being moved in the kitchen when no one was there. The owner accepted the noises as a friendly ghost of a former resident.

While noticing how tranquil and naturally beautiful my resting spot was, I may have dozed a few minutes. How else could I explain the sounds of two people coming up a narrow back road, their conversation mixed with the sound of steps on the gravel? I looked in the direction of the sounds but did not see anyone. Their talking about the farm and their family continued as they invisibly walked past me. Then there was a period of silence before the locked door of the house opened and I heard children laughing and greeting their father and a brother. I stared at the silent abandoned house. Mounting my bicycle, I told myself that I had been resting too long.

ELEVEN

CENTRAL PIEDMONT AND
FALLS LAKE RECREATION AREA

SECTION 26. Arrowhead Inn at US-501 North of Durham to
Shinleaf Recreation (Campground) Area at Falls Lake

DURHAM, GRANVILLE, AND WAKE COUNTIES: (See Durham County discussion in Section 25.) Granville County, established in 1746, was named in honor of John Carteret, Earl of Granville (1690–1763). The county was formed from part of Edgecombe County. Oxford, the county seat, was incorporated in 1816 and its name honors Samuel Benton's "Oxford" plantation. Edgecomb County encompasses 543 square miles. Some of its historic landmarks are Oxford Orphanage, Horner Military School Site (1851–1914), Oxford College Site (1851–1924), and Camp Butner, the site of World War II infantry training and incarceration of European enemy prisoners. The camp was named for North Carolina general Henry W. Butner. Granville County is bordered by Virginia to the north, by Person and Durham Counties to the west, by Wake County to the south, and by Vance and Franklin Counties to the east. Its major east-west highways are US-158 and NC-56, and its north-south highways are I-85, US-15, and NC-96.

Wake County may be the only state county named for a woman. She is Margaret Wake (1733–1819), the wife of Governor William Tryon. In 1771 Wake County's territory was carved from Johnston, Cumberland, and Orange Counties. A large county with 867 square miles, its county seat is the capital city of Raleigh, named for Sir Walter Raleigh (ca. 1552–1618). Before the title of Raleigh was selected in 1792, the city was called Wake Court House. There are seventy-four highway history markers in Wake County, more than any other county in the state.

The Neuse River, source for Falls Lake, flows southeast through Wake County. Other lakes in the county are Wheeler, Crabtree, Benson, McGregor Downs, Johnson, Raleigh, Lynn, and a large part of Harris. Between the Raleigh/Durham International Airport and the western edge of Raleigh are William B. Umstead State Park (5,080 acres) and Carl Schenck Forest. Among the city's educational institutions are North Carolina State University, Shaw University, Saint Mary's College, Peace College, and Meredith College. A few of the major historic sites are the N.C. Museum of Art, N.C. Museum of History, N.C. Museum of Natural Science, the Capitol Building, and the Governor's Mansion. Major highways east-west are I-40, US-70, US-64, and NC-98; major north-south routes are US-401, NC-50, US-1, and NC-96.

LENGTH AND DIFFICULTY: 29.8 miles (main MST), 33.5 miles (alternate MST); easy to moderate

USGS TOPO MAPS: Rougemont, Lake Michie, Northeast Durham, Creedmoor, Bayleaf

FEATURES OR EMPHASIS: Historic places, Falls Lake Recreation Area

TRAILS FOLLOWED: Falls Lake Trail

TRAIL CONNECTIONS: None

WEST TRAILHEAD: Arrowhead Inn on US-501 north of Durham

EAST TRAILHEAD: Shinleaf Recreation Area (walk-in campground) of Falls Lake Recreation Area

CAMPING, LODGING, AND PROVISIONS: Camping is allowed in the secluded hardwood forest of Shinleaf Recreation Area, part of Falls Lake Recreation Area. It can be accessed by the Falls Lake Trail of the MST or by a short drive into a parking area from New Light Road, 0.5 miles north of the intersection of NC-98 and Six Forks Road. Facilities include level camping spaces with grill, lantern post, and picnic table. There is a large bathhouse with hot showers and restrooms. Outside the building are trashcans, an information and registration board, and telephone.

Lodging is available at Arrowhead Inn and motels south from there on US-501 to I-85 in Durham (see above). In the Butner area at the intersection of I-85 and NC-56, exit 191, are four motels: Econo Lodge (telephone: 919-575-6451), Comfort Inn (telephone: 919-528-9296 or 800-228-5150), Holiday Inn (telephone: 919-575-5942 or 800-HOLIDAY), and Sunset Inn (telephone: 919-575-6565). For provisions there are shopping centers 8.5 miles south of Arrowhead Inn on US-501, and at exit 191 of I-85 near Butner.

INFORMATION AND SECURITY: Falls Lake Trail Maintenance: Triangle Greenways Council, Sierra Club Capital Group, Oconeechee Boy Scouts Lodge 104, and Falls Lake Task Force. Durham County Sheriff's Office: 201 East Main Street, Durham, NC 27278 (telephone: 919-560-0900). Granville County Sheriff's Office: 143 Williamsboro Street, Oxford, NC 27565 (telephone: 919-693-3213). Wake County Sheriff's Office: 330 South Salisbury Street, Raleigh, NC 27602 (telephone: 919-856-6900).

DESCRIPTION: From the Arrowhead Inn go north on US-501. Pass Bahama Road, on the right at 0.3 miles, and Preston Andrews Road, left at 1.3 miles. Cross a bridge over the Little River at 1.7 miles. Cross US-501 at 2.0 miles onto Johnny Jones Road (SR-1618). Before the trail begins to descend steeply there are large residential houses. Cross a bridge over Mountain Creek, which flows into Little River Lake at 2.6 miles. Ascend. After crossing the top of a ridge at 2.9 miles, descend and pass through a forested residential area. At 4.3 miles come to the juncture with Staggwell Road (SR-1615) and turn right, but leave it when you reach Old Oxford Road (SR-1004) to turn left. At 8.3 miles cross a bridge over the Flat River, which flows from Lake Michie, from the north, to the Neuse River and Falls Lake, south. Pass Cassam Road and later Amed Road, which are on the left. At 9.3 miles enter Butner town limits. Here you will find sobering views of large buildings belonging to the federal Bureau of Prisons. Enter Granville County at 9.7 miles where Old Oxford Road's name becomes Butner Road (SR-1004). Here are more prisons, including a Corrections Complex on the left. Enter a forest at 10.2 miles. Turn right at a sign for West Butner on Veasy Road (SR-1120) at 11.7 miles.

Cross a narrow bridge over Knapp of Reeds Creek and ascend. Patches of sundrops are on the right bank of the road. Pass the Polk Youth Institute at 10.5 miles. Pass right of a large water tower, constructed in 1942, and reach a juncture at 11.6 miles. Keep right. There are restaurants (Ron's Grill, Bob's Pizza) and service stations such as Jack's Phillips 66. At 14.7 miles there is a juncture with Central Avenue and NC-56, left, at a Texaco service station with groceries. Here you have an option on directions. Either continue straight on Central Avenue, which becomes Gate #2 Road (SR-1103) for 2.5 miles to a juncture with Lyons Station Road (SR-1104), without restaurants and motels, or turn left off Central Avenue onto NC-56 and go 2.2 miles to at least four motels and six chain restaurants.

(If you choose to take NC-56 to the motels, cross a railroad track at 2.0 miles. To the left are Econo Lodge, Sunset Inn, and Holiday Inn [see telephone numbers in "Camping, Lodging, and Provisions"] and restaurants. To the right cross the bridge over I-85 [exit 191] to Lyons Station Road (SR-1104), where you will turn right at 2.3 miles. Surrounding you are restaurants, a bank, a shopping center, and a Comfort Inn. To return to the MST follow Lyons Station Road south through a variety of industrial buildings, residential areas, and farms to juncture with Gate #2 Road at 6.2 miles. Here you would continue on the main MST route, left. [It is 2.5 miles right to the Texaco station in Butner.])

If you are following the main MST route from the juncture with NC-56 at

*Upper Barton Ramp
at Falls Lake in Raleigh*

the Texaco station in Butner, go southeast to pass a bank, a service station with groceries, and a National Guard Center. Cross the railroad tracks at 15.1 miles and continue on what has become Gate #2 Road (SR-1103). Cross I-85 at 15.9 miles. Arrive at the juncture with Lyons Station Road (SR-1104) at 16.8 miles. Continue ahead and cross US-15 at 17.5 miles. Continue on what is now called Cash Road (SR-1728) and pass through sections of a forest. Cross the intersection with North Side Road (SR-1724) at 18.4 miles. Ahead is a residential area with wide lawns and a lake to the right. Ascend to a T-intersection, where you leave Granville County and enter Wake County at 20.2 miles. Turn left on Old Weaver Road (SR-1901). A heritage cemetery is on the left. Descend to pass a causeway through a swampy area of Falls Lake Dam at 20.6 miles. At 21.8 miles, to the left, is a historic two-story white clapboard house and a juncture with NC-50.

Turn right on NC-50 and follow its shoulder at first through a residential area and then past Sandy Plain Mini-Mart and BP station at 23.3 miles. Pass entrances to Falls Lake Recreation Area, Sandling Beach, on the right, and Beaver Dam Beach and Picnic Area, on the left, at 23.8 miles. Cross a Falls Lake causeway and bridge at 25.7 miles, after which you will arrive at a guardrail to the Falls Lake Trail (hiking only) of the MST at 25.9 miles. Turn left into the forest. (It is 1.6 miles south on NC-50 to a juncture with NC-98.)

After 0.2 miles cross a paved road to the State Management Center, left;

then cross another paved road that descends left to a state usage boat dock and access to Falls Lake, and right to the center's garage. After more distance through the forest enter an open area and follow a grassy road. On each side are young pine forests with sections of cow-itch vine. Because logging activities could alter the appearance of the area, watch closely for the white-dot blazes at a left turn and then a right turn. Arrive at an old road at 27.0 miles and turn left. At 27.4 miles pass left of an unnamed cemetery near an old home site. On a hillside you may notice former tobacco field ridges on the treadway under a young forest. Pass around a rocky knoll at 27.6 miles. Cross the dam of a small pond at 28.1 miles. In the springtime there are banks of may-apple, foamflower, and crested dwarf iris in a low and damp area. Ascend to cross the paved Ghoston Road (SR-1908) at 28.7 miles. Descend to enter a low area with large ironwood and patches of yellowroot at 28.9 miles. Continue to descend and reach New Light Road (SR-1907) at an embankment at 29.2 miles. Turn right, follow the shoulder of the road for 0.1 mile, and turn left into the forest. (It is 1.5 miles right to NC-98.) After some descending and ascending in a hardwood forest arrive at the Norwood Cemetery, right. Exit the forest at the Shinleaf Recreation (Campground) Area entrance road and parking area, on the left at 29.8 miles. (If you take the entrance road right, it is 0.5 miles to New Light Road.)

CAMPSIDE STORIES: On February 5, 2000, NBC-TV premiered a show called *The Others*. Following the story, Raleigh's TV Channel 17 interviewed Colleen Ray of the Rhine Research Center, Institute for Parapsychology, in Durham. The interview topic was extrasensory perception (ESP), the phenomenon of gaining knowledge without the known human senses. Included within ESP are telepathy (mind-to-mind communication), clairvoyance (knowledge of distant places or events), and precognition (awareness of a future event). According to Ray it has been difficult to define ESP because we do not know what it is. She believes public suspicion of these forces comes from fear of the unknown, but that they are common powers to many people. *The Others* exaggerated, in a dramatic manner, the subjects of ESP and psychokinesis (PK), the movement of objects without physical means.

J. B. Rhine and his wife Louisa began their pursuit of psychic phenomena under the guidance of Professor William McDougall, chairman of the Duke University Psychology Department, in 1927. In 1962, after his retirement from the university, Rhine and other benefactors of the research projects created the Foundation for Research on the Nature of Man (FRNM). This was the parent organization for the Institute for Parapsychology. In honor of the Rhines, the FRNM was renamed the Rhine Research Center in 1995.

In *The Others*, a seven-year-old boy named Adrian is kidnapped and not found until three years later, when a psychic visits the boy's vacant room. The psychic, a woman, touches a windowpane, where the mother had seen Adrian's image, and the glass shatters. The psychic receives a visual image in her mind of Adrian in an abandoned warehouse near a dock. When she investigates she discovers that Adrian might have had paranormal mental powers before his capture; his captor, who also has extrasensory powers, has trained Adrian to see while blindfolded and also cause levitation. In the end of the story Adrian becomes aware that his captor's mental force is influencing him to kill his mother and that in the process he will die also. The result is that Adrian uses his psychic powers to kill his captor.

SECTION 27. Shinleaf Recreation (Campground) Area on Falls Lake Trail to Falls Lake Dam at Falls of the Neuse Road

WAKE COUNTY: See Section 26 above for discussion of Wake County.

LENGTH AND DIFFICULTY: 22.4 miles (main MST), 22.2 miles (alternate MST); easy to moderate

USGS TOPO MAPS: Bayleaf, Wake Forest

FEATURES OR EMPHASIS: Falls Lake, wildlife and wildflowers, recreation

TRAILS FOLLOWED: Falls Lake Trail of the MST, Upper Barton Wildlife Trail

TRAIL CONNECTIONS: Sandy Point Trail, Laurel Trail, Blue Jay Point Trail

WEST TRAILHEAD: Shinleaf Recreation (Campground) Area in Falls Lake Recreation Area (off New Light Road)

EAST TRAILHEAD: Falls Lake Dam Tailwater Fishing Access Area parking lot at Falls of the Neuse Road

CAMPING, LODGING, AND PROVISIONS: Shinleaf Recreation (Camping) Area (see "Camping, Lodging, and Provisions" for Section 26)

INFORMATION AND SECURITY: Trail Maintenance: Triangle Greenways Council, Capital Group of the Sierra Club, Falls Lake Task Force. Greater Raleigh Chamber of Commerce: 800 South Salisbury Street (P.O. Box 2978), Raleigh, NC 27602 (telephone: 919-664-7000). Wake County Sheriff's Office: 330 South Salisbury Street, Raleigh NC 27602 (telephone: 919-856-6900). Falls Lake Recreation Area: 12204 Creedmoor Road, Wake Forest, NC 27587 (telephone: 919-676-1027).

DESCRIPTION: At the south end of the parking lot at Shinleaf Recreation (Campground) Area, follow the MST blazes east on a slight descent. After some footbridges pass infrequent Indian pipe at 0.4 miles and pine-sap a few yards ahead. At 1.5 miles, near lake cove waters, is a skillfully designed footbridge with steps. Hurricane Fran destroyed many of the large beech trees in this area in 1996. The resulting increase in sunlight has revealed additional wild-flowers. Pass scattered views of the lake and through an understory of dogwood, holly, and sparkleberry. At 2.3 miles enter a grove of large beech and tulip poplar trees, followed by more footbridges in the coves. You will cross under a power line among redbud, sumac, and blackberry at 2.9 miles. Deer and wild turkey have been seen in this forest opening. Reenter the woods and exit to NC-98 near the guardrail of a bridge over the lake at 3.0 miles. (N.C. Bicycle Route #2 passes through here, west on NC-98 for 1.5 miles to Six Forks Road, and east 1.2 miles to Stoney Hill Road.)

Cross NC-98 and walk west along a guardrail 145 yards to a sharp left on the road bank. You are now entering property administered by the North Carolina Wildlife Commission. As elsewhere on the Falls Lake Trail, no bicycles or horse traffic are allowed, and hunting is only permitted in season, with a license, on wildlife property. Pass through a former home site with large white oaks. At 3.2 miles arrive at the paved old NC-98 and turn right. (To the left is an open field where deer may be seen grazing.) At 3.3 miles turn left and off the old road at MST blazes. Descend through a patch of clubmoss. This part of the trail travels by quartz rock and small streamlets in a forest of oaks, hickories, tulip poplar, black walnut, holly, loblolly pine, ironwood, and red cedar. Wildflowers include pinxter-flower, cranefly orchid, trillium, yellow jessamine, wild quinine, and blazing star.

At 4.2 miles exit the woods at a power line to pass a small beaver dam before reentering the woods. Pass under the powerline again at 4.4 miles. Cross an old farm road that leads to a sandy beach, left at 4.6 miles. There are two bridges in a scenic cove with large trees, fern beds, and wildflowers at 4.8 miles. Pass under the power line again at 5.0 miles where there are more species of wildflowers, particularly asters, goldenrod, and daisies. Arrive at a gravel parking area for the Upper Barton Creek Boat Ramp at 5.2 miles. Cross the parking area to a parking sign and enter the woods at an MST blaze. After 125 yards exit to roadside parking on Six Forks Road (SR-1005). Keep left, cross the causeway by the guardrail, and enter Blue Jay Point Park (a Wake County Park) to the left.

Although you may not see MST blazes, watch for all trail signs and follow the trail that parallels the lake. The trail frequently undulates on small ridges and coves, all descending to your left. In a forest of hardwoods and loblolly pines, cross footbridges, then a paved road, and at 6.7 miles come out of the forest to a display board and parking lot between a ball field and park lodge. The park office and museum is accessible to the right. Pass rock piles made by early farmers at 7.0 miles. Watch for connecting trails in the next 0.7 miles: Sandy Point Trail (0.2 miles), a trail that leads right to a trail for the physically handicapped, Laurel Trail (0.2 miles), and Blue Jay Point Trail (0.2 miles). All these and the MST are accessible from the park's parking area, the entrance to which is on Six Forks Road (SR-1005). At 8.1 miles are patches of spice bush, wild ginger, and hepatica. Cross more footbridges and arrive at Six Forks Road at 9.0 miles.

Turn left and cross the Lower Barton Creek causeway. Look to the left at the end of the guardrail and descend on steps at 9.2 miles. At 10.4 miles cross Bayleaf Church Road (SR-2003). To the left is the Yorkshire Center of the N.C. Division of Parks and Recreation. Housed here are the headquarters of the administrative offices for the superintendent, state trails coordinator, piedmont district trail specialist, and some of the other state park officials not housed in the Archdale Building in downtown Raleigh. The staff welcomes visitors.

Continue on a slight ascent, then descend to enter a mountain laurel thicket and cross a new bridge. (Hurricane Fran destroyed a former bridge.) Pass in and out of more mountain laurel patches and arrive at views of the lake, left, at 11.7 miles. Cross a footbridge at 12.2 miles, then enter a scenic area among large beech trees. There are remnants of an old homestead on the left at 12.3 miles. Come out of a pine and cedar forest with honeysuckle at 13.2 miles. At 13.3 miles arrive at Possum Track Road (SR-1974). Turn left and cross a causeway. Cross a footbridge at 13.9 miles. After crossing a couple of ravines pass views of the lake to the left at 13.9 miles. Enter another pine grove and exit at Possum Track Road at 16.3 miles. To the left the road is barricaded; to the right it is 1.4 miles to Raven Ridge Road (SR-2002).

Cross the road and follow a residential road briefly before entering the forest at a cul-de-sac. At 17.4 miles pass an old farm pond and old farming area. From here the trail is close to a residential area on the right. There is a clear-cut area at 18.0 miles. Exit the woods at 18.9 miles to Raven Ridge Road (SR-2002). Turn left to cross Honeycut Creek Causeway at 19.0 miles. Ascend a bank to enter the forest. On the hill there are good views left of the lake among tall beech, oak, and hickory trees. There are also scattered dogwood, redbud, and hazelnut bushes. Patches of Christmas fern are commonplace. Curve around the hill and descend to a cascading stream on the left at 19.6 miles. New homes are close to the park boundary on the right. Cross a bridge in a scenic area of stream and rock formations at 19.7 miles. Wildflowers are prominent here and on the hillside ahead. Among the plants are wild geranium, wood betony, and crested dwarf iris. At the ridge top curve right and descend to a cove at 20.0 miles.

At 20.8 miles cross an open forest where the City of Raleigh has a water pipeline to its filtration plant on Falls of the Neuse Road. When you reenter the forest you are on U.S. Army Corps of Engineers property. For the next 0.8 miles you will notice evidence of timbering and prescribed burning by the Corps after Hurricane Fran. At 21.4 miles you will arrive at a fork with trail signs. (To the right is an alternate blue-blazed route of 0.6 miles that avoids the Corps of Engineers Management Center. If you are using this route, cross the management center's entrance road at 0.2 miles and descend into a dense forest. Cross a wet area with jewelweed at 0.4 miles, and parallel a stream to rejoin the main trail.)

If you are following the main white-blazed Falls Lake Trail, descend and at 21.5 miles cross a paved access road to a boat ramp, left. Arrive at the parking lot for the Corps of Engineers Management Center at 21.8 miles. Visitors are welcome. To the left are outstanding views of the lake and the dam. You will also find picnic tables and a descriptive sign on the anatomy of an earth dam. Pass a restroom, telephone, and drinking fountain to the right. Be alert to a trail sign, left, off the road near a timber cut. Follow it, cross the paved road that crosses the dam, and descend to a juncture with the blue-blazed alternate trail at 22.2 miles. Near the juncture is a unique twin tulip poplar tree. At 22.3 miles turn right on a grassy road and follow it to the dam's tailrace parking area at 22.4 miles. Here is a restroom and drinking fountain. To the right is an entrance gate and beyond it is Falls of the Neuse Road (SR-2000). To the right, at the corner, is Pedal and Paddle, a store for renting or purchasing canoes and bicycles (telephone: 919-844-2930). If you take a right on Falls of the Neuse Road (south), it is 12.0 miles to downtown Raleigh. (See Diversions below.)

DIVERSIONS: If you have the time to take a break for a few days or week to visit one of the cities on your walk across the state, I recommend you choose Raleigh, the capital city. Some advance planning would be helpful and the Greater Raleigh Chamber of Commerce would assist you with information to fit your time and budget. Some of the diversions from the MST could be visiting the State Capitol, State Legislative Building, Executive Mansion, North Carolina Museum of History, North Carolina Museum of Natural Sciences, and North Carolina Museum of Art. The variety of entertainment—from sports events to concerts and plays, and nightlife in the city—is exceptionally diverse. In addition, the sports and cultural programs at N.C. State University and other universities and colleges in the city, Duke University in nearby Durham, and the University of North Carolina in Chapel Hill, provide options unavailable to you anywhere else on your MST journey.

CAMPSIDE STORIES: On December 29, 1808, Andrew was born in a log kitchen now located one mile northeast of Morgan and Wilmington Streets near the

Mordecai House in Raleigh. His father, Jacob, was a poor porter who died when the little boy was age three. His poverty-stricken mother, Mary, sold the boy when he was ten years old as an indentured servant (a type of white slavery legally allowed for up to seven years of work) to James J. Selby, a prosperous tailor. At age fifteen Andrew ran away by walking 75 miles to find a job in Carthage as a tailor. Later he worked in Laurens, South Carolina, where he earned enough money to buy a horse and a cart.

He used his new transportation to secretly (still as a legal fugitive) return to Raleigh to see his mother and stepfather, a factory weaver. With their meager belongings they slipped away to Greeneville, Tennessee. At the age of seventeen Andrew set up his own shop as a tailor. At age nineteen he married Eliza McCardle (1810–76), who was well educated. Because Andrew had never attended a day of school, his wife taught him arithmetic and how to write and improve his reading, something he voraciously did the rest of his career. Soon Andrew became interested in politics, and before he was twenty-one years old he had organized a workers' political party. He was elected an alderman, then mayor of Greeneville. At age twenty-seven he began a political career for two terms in the Tennessee House of Representatives and one term in the state Senate. He left the Whig Party and joined the Democrats. He spoke for the poor, the farmers, the common laborers, and the uneducated. In 1853 at the age of forty-five he was elected governor of Tennessee.

By now you probably know he was Andrew Johnson. Governor Johnson became a United States senator in 1857. Unlike other southern governors and senators, he opposed the secession of the Union, and when Tennessee seceded in 1861 he was the only southern senator to remain in Congress. President Lincoln appointed him military governor of Tennessee in 1862. In 1864 he was elected vice-president on the ticket with President Lincoln. After the assassination of President Lincoln, Vice-President Johnson took the oath of office on April 15, 1865. Three turbulent years followed with the president and Congress disagreeing on matters of constitutional interpretation, and policies on reconstruction and readmission of the seceding states. When President Johnson removed his disloyal secretary of state Edwin M. Stanton in 1866, it triggered impeachment proceeding by radical Republicans. He was the first president to be impeached, but the weak claims of high crimes and misdemeanor failed in the Senate on May 26, 1868. The seventeenth presidency ended in March of 1869; Johnson's life ended from a stroke on July 31, 1875. He, like the eleventh president, James Knox Polk, who was born in North Carolina as well, is buried in Tennessee.

 TWELVE

EASTERN PIEDMONT AND
WESTERN COASTAL PLAIN

SECTION 28. Falls Lake Dam to Harris Crossroads on US-401

WAKE AND FRANKLIN COUNTIES: (See Wake County discussion in Section 26.) Franklin County, with 494 square miles, was named for Benjamin Franklin (1706–90) in 1779, when Bute County was divided to form Franklin and Warren Counties. The town of Louisburg, through which the Tar River flows, was also founded in 1779 as the county seat. Its original spelling was Lewisburg, though it was named for King Louis XVI of France. Louisburg College, first chartered in 1787, opened in 1803 as Franklin Academy. It is the nation's oldest private two-year church-related college. Among other historic sites in Franklin County are Casine Plantation, Person Place, Laurel Mill, Franklinton Railroad Station, Green Hill Place, and the Thomas Bickett House. The county's major north-south highways are US-401, NC-581, NC-39, US-1, and NC-58; east-west highways are NC-98, NC-561, NC-56, and US-64.

LENGTH AND DIFFICULTY: 20.3 miles, easy

USGS TOPO MAPS: Bayleaf, Wake Forest, Grissom, Franklinton, Rolesville

FEATURES OR EMPHASIS: Neuse River Cascades, historic homes and churches, hill ridge farms

TRAILS FOLLOWED: None

TRAIL CONNECTIONS: None

BICYCLE ROUTE FOLLOWED: N.C. Bicycle Route #2 (MSBR)

WEST TRAILHEAD: At the parking area of the east trailhead of Falls Lake Trail at the Falls Lake tailrace off of Falls of the Neuse Road in North Raleigh.

EAST TRAILHEAD: At a parking area near an old store at the northwest corner of the intersection of US-401 and Tarboro Road at Harris Crossroads.

CAMPING, LODGING, AND PROVISIONS: Lodging is available at the Hampton Inn at the shopping center at the northwest corner of the NC-98 and US-1 junction in Wake Forest (12318 Wake Union Church Road, telephone: 919-554-

0222). Camping is available at the Franklin County Nature Preserve, 2.4 miles north from the US-401 and Tarboro Road (SR-1100) intersection at Harris Crossroads. (Call the nature preserve, 919-496-4771, at least a day in advance for location information and for free shuttle service.) Provisions are at 2.5 miles north on US-401 at Royal Crossroads, and 6.0 miles farther north in Louisburg. A small store, J.C.'s, that sells snacks is 0.9 miles south on US-401 from Harris Crossroads. In addition to the shopping center in Wake Forest, notice the places for groceries and restaurants described ahead.

INFORMATION AND SECURITY: Trail Maintenance: Friends of the Mountains-to-Sea Trail, 3538 US-401 South, Louisburg, NC 27549 (telephone: 919-496-4771). Oconeechee Boy Scouts Lodge 104 (telephone: 919-512-0163). Wake Forest Chamber of Commerce: 350 South White Street, Wake Forest, NC 27587 (telephone: 919-556-1519). Wake County Sheriff's Office: 330 South Salisbury Street, Raleigh, NC 27602 (telephone: 919-856-6900). Franklin County Chamber of Commerce: P.O. Box 62, Louisburg, NC 27549 (telephone: 919-496-0422). Franklin County Sheriff's Office, 285 T. Kemp Road, Louisburg, NC 27549 (telephone: 919-496-3332).

DESCRIPTION: From the parking area at the base of Falls Lake Dam turn left, north, on Falls of the Neuse Road (SR-2000). (To the right is Pedal and Paddle, a center for sales and rentals of mountain and street bicycles and canoe trips down the Neuse River.) Access to the put-in can be seen from the road. Cross a bridge over the Neuse River. Here you can see the cascades, cold and clear, from the Falls Lake Dam tailrace. Shrubbery grows among the boulder crevices. After crossing the bridge ascend on a narrow and curvy road with expansive farmland on the left and a public school on the right. Farther ahead are expensive residences. At 1.2 miles on the left is the historic house called Wakefield (1805), surrounded by pastureland and large oaks. At 2.3 miles pass a group of large oaks that provide summer shade. At 2.4 miles on the left is The Falls Lunchroom (open 6:30 A.M. to 2:30 P.M., telephone: 919-556-0263), serving home-cooked food. Next to it is Keith's Exxon and Bar-B-Q, and outside telephone.

Turn right on Old NC-98; after 0.2 miles turn left on Thomson Mill Road (SR-1923). (To the right on Old NC-98 it is 0.5 miles to NC-98, where to the right it is another 0.6 miles to Wake Forest Market, a shopping center for restaurants, groceries, a photography shop, clothing stores, and Hampton Inn on Wake Union Church Road (SR-1929) [telephone: 919-554-0222]. Adjoining the market area is US-1; on its east side is the town of Wake Forest.) After 0.3 miles on Thomson Mill Road cross NC-98. (To the right it is 1.1 miles to the shopping center listed above.) Continue on Thomson Mill Road by descending and then crossing Horse Creek. Ascend through a residential area to a juncture with Purnell Road (SR-1909), on which is the Mountains-to-Sea Bicycle Route #2, right and left. Turn right. (The bicycle route left goes west to Stoney Hill Road [SR-1917], where it turns left and then reaches NC-98 after 5.3 miles to turn right.)

Descend on Purnell Road, cross two small streams, and turn left on Jackson Road (SR-1925) at 7.0 miles. Pines are on both sides of the road. You will leave Wake County and enter a dairy farm area in Franklin County at 7.6 miles. Arrive at Holden Road (SR-1146) at 9.0 miles and turn right. Cross a stream bordered with honeysuckle and then cross Horse Creek among large poplar and sweet gum trees. At 10.3 miles you will cross the wide and busy US-1. Continue on Holden Road (which becomes US-1A) to reach the town of Youngsville. Pass the Faith Baptist Church, on the right, and at 12.3 miles arrive at a juncture with College Street (which becomes Tarboro Road [SR-1100]). Turn right at a Subway and gasoline station to cross Seaboard Railroad tracks. Passing through town you will pass a laundry, post office, bank, and hardware store. On the right is Griffin's Restaurant, where home-cooked style food is served 6:00 A.M. to 8:30 P.M. Monday through Friday, and 6:00 A.M. to 1:00 P.M. on Saturday and Sunday (telephone: 919-556-4747). Pass Youngsville Baptist Church, left, and Wildwynn Stables (telephone: 919-556-9070), left. Continue on Tarboro Road.

Arrive at Huff's Cash and Carry (gasoline and groceries) at 14.8 miles. At 16.2 miles there are picnic tables at Hill Ridge Farms, a plant nursery and fresh vegetables market. You may notice that the red clays of the piedmont are becoming loams and sandy soils. Arrive at Harris Crossroads and US-401 at 20.3 miles. (To the left on US-401 [north] it is 2.6 miles to Royal community, where there is a Citco convenience store and outside telephone. To the right on US-401 it 1.4 miles to a junction with NC-98; on the way it is 0.8 miles to a small grocery and gas station.)

CAMPSIDE STORIES: Six miles north of the community of Royal on US-401 is the historic town of Louisburg. Its widest street is named Bickett Boulevard in honor of Thomas Walter Bickett, who in his lifetime of fifty-two years proved to be one of the state's most humane elected officials. Born in Monroe on February 28, 1869, he was a graduate of Wake Forest College, received his law degree from the University of North Carolina in Chapel Hill, and married Fannie Yarborough of the distinguished Yarborough Family in Franklin County.

Bickett was a mesmerizing public speaker and persuasive politician. During World War I he persuaded a group of draft dodgers hidden in the mountains to surrender without penalty and go fight for their country. And once while serving as governor he walked into a lynch mob gathered at a courthouse and persuaded them to dissipate. But the power of Bickett's life story is what this leader of good causes accomplished and left as a legacy. He served as a state legislator in the House, then two terms as attorney general (1908–16), and followed all of this by winning a landslide victory in his run for the governor's post. He improved the state's mental health facilities; created the East Carolina Teacher's Training School (now Eastern Carolina University); raised the standards of living for farmers and tenants, and training for those without jobs; brought agriculture into the school system as an educational discipline; increased teachers' salaries; helped create better hospitals for the mentally and physically disabled; improved tax reform; worked for better and safer highways; improved education facilities and curriculum for African-Americans; established sanatoriums for African-Americans; and provided a reformatory for African-American delinquent boys. He led campaigns against racism and was kind, loving, and fair to all. He was active in the Episcopal church and was a devoted husband and father. His Louisburg home, a graceful three-story Victorian house on North Main Street in Louisburg, was purchased by Louisburg College in 1973 to become the college's presidential home.

SECTION 29. Harris Crossroads on US-401 (near Franklin County Line) to Lamm at US-264

FRANKLIN, NASH, AND WILSON COUNTIES: (See Franklin County discussion in Section 28.) Nash County and Nashville, the county seat, were formed in 1777 from parts of Edgecombe County. The county's name honors General Francis Nash of Hillsborough, who died in Germantown during the Revolutionary War. Its 552 square miles encompass widespread farmlands, but a more urban environment anchors its eastern side, where more than half of the city of Rocky Mount (incorporated in 1867) lies. The city, home to North Carolina Wesleyan College, gets its name from the mounds of rock formations at the Tar River rapids. The Tar River crosses the southern part of the county to form the Tar River Reservoir, and Fishing Creek forms its north boundary with Halifax County. Near the county's south boundary, in the town of Bailey, the Country Doctor Museum displays books and records of early physicians, and medical and pharmaceutical instruments. North-south traffic arteries are I-95, US-301, NC-58, NC-48, NC-581, NC-231, and NC-43; east-west routes are US-264, US-64, and NC-97.

Wilson County has 373 square miles and was formed in 1855 from parts of Edgecombe, Nash, Johnson, and Wayne Counties. Both the county and the county seat, the city of Wilson, were named in honor of Louis D. Wilson (1789–1847). An officer in the U.S. Army, Wilson died at Vera Cruz in the Mexican War. The city of Wilson's origin can be traced to a community called Hickory Grove. Adjoining it was a railroad community with the name of Toisnot, and together both settlements became Wilson in 1849. Barton College (formerly Atlantic Christian College) is here.

A number of swampy streams run from northwest to southeast through the county. Passing through the city of Wilson is Hominy Swamp, on the northeast side is Toisnot Swamp, and southwest of the city is Contentnea Creek, a source for Wiggins Mill Reservoir. Major highways north-south are I-95, NC-581, NC-222, NC-58, US-117, US-301, and NC-91; east-west routes are NC-42 and US-264.

LENGTH AND DIFFICULTY: 31.2 miles, easy

USGS TOPO MAPS: Rolesville, Bunn West, Bunn East, Middlesex, Bailey

FEATURES OR EMPHASIS: Historic homes and churches, large farmlands

TRAILS FOLLOWED: None

BICYCLE ROUTE FOLLOWED: N.C. Bicycle Route #2 (MSBR)

TRAIL CONNECTIONS: None

BICYCLE ROUTE CONNECTION: N.C. Bicycle Route #7 (Ocracoke Option)

WEST TRAILHEAD: Harris Crossroads on US-401, 1.4 miles north of its juncture with NC-98 and 2.6 miles south of the community of Royal (where there is an access road east to the Franklin County Airport).

EAST TRAILHEAD: Intersection of US-264 and Lamm Road near I-95 in the community of Lamm

CAMPING, LODGING, AND PROVISIONS: For camping, take US-401 north to the community of Royal, where the private Franklin County Nature Preserve offers free primitive camping (with access to restroom and showers if reservations are made in advance, telephone: 919-496-4771). Camping is also available at a Daddysville private home (see description ahead) and at Kampers Lodge of America (north of Wilson on US-301, 2.5 miles north of juncture of US-301 and US-264 [see description ahead in Section 31]; this full-service campground is open all year). Lodging is available at Lamm (Hayes Place), where at least three motels are located on US-264 near I-95 exit 121: Holiday Inn (telephone: 252-234-7900 or 1-800-HOLIDAY), Sleep Inn (telephone: 252-234-2900), Microtel Inn (telephone: 252-234-0444 or reservations at 888-771-7171). Provisions, including some snack bars, can be obtained at country stores along the way, and there are restaurants at the US-264 crossing.

INFORMATION AND SECURITY: Trail Maintenance: Oconeechee Boy Scouts Lodge 104 (telephone: 919-512-0163). Franklin County Chamber of Commerce: P.O. Box 62, Louisburg, NC 27549 (telephone: 919-496-3056). Rocky Mount

Area Chamber of Commerce: P.O. Box 392, Rocky Mount, NC 27802 (telephone: 252-442-5111). Wilson Chamber of Commerce: 220 Broad Street (P.O. Box 1146), Wilson, NC 27894 (telephone: 252-237-0165). Franklin County Sheriff's Office: 285 T. Kemp Road, Louisburg, NC 27549 (telephone: 919-496-3332). Nash County Sheriff's Office: Courthouse Annex, Washington Street (P.O. Box 355), Nashville, NC 27856 (telephone: 252-459-4121). Wilson County Sheriff's Office: 1003 Green Street (P.O. Box 1666), Wilson, NC 27894 (telephone: 252-237-2118).

DESCRIPTION: For the next 31 miles this section of MST passes through excellent examples of Eastern Piedmont landscape. You will see fields of grains (corn, wheat, oats, and soybeans), cotton, tobacco, vegetables, and hay as well as livestock. Scattered among the modern farmhouses are some grand examples that represent antebellum, Federal, Greek revival, and Victorian periods. Although you will pass 6 miles south of Wilson, you will not go through a small agricultural town until LaGrange, another 43 miles.

At Harris Crossroads (between the towns of Louisburg, north, and Rolesville, south), cross US-401 and continue east on N.C. Bicycle Route #2 (Mountains-to-Sea). On a curving road pass Harris Chapel, right. At 0.9 miles turn left on NC-98 (Strickland Road). Pass Phelp's Chapel Baptist Church, right, at 1.4 miles. Come to Haywood Groceries at 1.8 miles, right; New Hope Christian Church at 2.6 miles, right; and Floyd's Grocery and Grill, with an outside telephone and a Citco gasoline station, at 2.8 miles on the right.

After another 0.1 mile on NC-98 from Floyd's Grocery and Grill, keep right at the fork and follow Strickland Road (SR-1716). (NC-98 continues to the town of Bunn.) Pass Green Ridge Farm at 4.8 miles, and at 6.2 miles cross Pearces Road onto Brantleytown Road (SR-1720) at Jim Ray's Crossroads. Here is Dean's Grocery, right, with an outside telephone. Continue through farmland and pass some large boulders, right, at 6.9 miles. Poplar Spring Baptist Church, right, is at 8.0 miles. Arrive at the juncture with NC-39, right and left at 8.1 miles, in the community of Sutton. (To the left it is 2.5 miles to the small town of Bunn, named for Green Bunn, a prominent local citizen. Here is a post office, grocery store and grill, bank, medical clinic, and hardware store.)

Turn right on NC-39 and after 0.2 miles turn left on Pine Ridge Road (SR-1736). Pass Chris's Greenhouse, left. Soon you will pass a farm where you may see horses with polka dot coloring. At 9.9 miles pass Pine Ridge Baptist Church on the right. On the left is a white-fenced area followed by old tobacco barns and huge white oaks. Old Bunn Road is left at 11.1 miles. After another 0.1 mile there is a juncture, left and right, with Old US-64 in the

Harris Chapel

On the backroads of the MST you see surprisingly beautiful and historic churches with tall steeples at the sanctuary and multiple expansion buildings. Although they may be prosperous today, possibly having survived economic struggle and rebuilding after fires or hurricanes, these churches may have had simple beginnings. An example is Harris Chapel Baptist Church.

In the mid-1880s there was a one-story clapboard school building at Math Rock, whose name came from its proximity to a one-acre flat rock on which Math Medlin fed his hogs. Jack King used the building as a Sunday school for Baptist, Methodist, and Congregational Christians. After about a year, Gideon Mingas desired to have the Baptists meet separately in the morning or afternoon.

In 1888 the group invited the Reverend Marion R. Pernell from the town of Franklinton to lead them in a bush arbor revival. This event inspired them to build a chapel. A. J. P. Harris (1835–1919) gave two acres of land and material, thus the name Harris Chapel Baptist Church. Reverend Pernell returned as their first pastor and served until 1900. The majority of the charter members came from the Flat Rock community, a few miles west of the new church. A major period of the church's growth was during the pastorate of Reverend Charles W. Howard from 1921 to 1950, longer than any of the church's other pastors. When the church had its centennial celebration in 1990, the occasion was dedicated to the life and work of Reverend Howard.

community of Daddysville. (The community name honors Rod Wells, a beloved father and local citizen.) (To the right on Old US-64 it is 1.0 mile to Tant Road, where to the left it is 1.5 miles to the US-64 interchange and FoyMart and Exxon. This service area also provides a restaurant, groceries, and hardware. It is open from 5 A.M. to midnight every day.) Turn left on Old US-64 and after a few yards notice a school bus stop (waiting shed) with a sign "Victory Lane." If you wish a quiet grassy place for overnight tenting near a water faucet, turn right on the driveway and go to the second house, the home of Dwight Brantley (telephone: 252-478-3969). This private option is open to MST hikers only.

Continuing on Old US-64 you will see part of the large Newcomb Farm, right. At 12.2 miles come to Mulberry Road (SR-1732), left; turn to the right on Saunders Road (SR-1733). Enter Nash County at 12.4 miles and join Fraziers Road (SR-1712). Cross a bridge over the four-lane US-64 at 13.6 miles. Thornhill Farm, where you may see cattle and horses, is on the left. Pass Gold Valley Methodist Church, left, adjoining Gold Valley Crossroads at the NC-231 juncture at 14.7 miles. Pass a horse farm on the right. Among the roadside wildflowers are wild quinine, rabbit pea, and heal-all. At 16.3 miles Old Nash Road is right. Cross Old Spring Road at Frazier Crossroads at 17.2 miles, and reach Bissettes Crossroads and NC-97 at 18.2 miles. (If you are bicycling or wish to walk the extra miles, there is a good place to eat by turning right on NC-97 and going 2.8 miles to Richie's Diner, right, at the crossroads in Samaria [telephone: 252-478-5533]. The price is right and the home-cooked pie is advertised as "dang good." North of Samaria on NC-231 for 0.5 miles is the historic Old Mill at Turkey Creek.)

Continuing from Bissettes Crossroads on Fraziers Road, arrive at a juncture with, but keep left on, Strickland Road (SR-1134) at 19.9 miles. Cross NC-581 at 20.9 miles. (Off the trail to the right it is 3.4 miles on NC-581 south to the small town of Bailey and the intersection with US-264. There are groceries, a Hardees, and The Pantry.) Continue east among some beautiful new houses. Cross Toisnot Swamp, a slow stream that flows into Contentnea Swamp to pass east of Wilson. At 22 miles reach the Strickland Road (SR-1134) and Liles Road (SR-1949) intersection, where you will find Kounty Kwik Pik, a general store. Arrive at a juncture at 23.8 miles and turn right, still following Strickland Road. Cross Whiteoak Swamp after 0.2 miles, and slightly ascend to pass Free Will Baptist Church on the right. At 24.5 miles pass Green Pond Loop Road on the left. Stoney Hill Church Road is right at 24.8 miles, and Glover Milling Company, grain dealers, is left at 25.2 miles. High Crossroads is at 25.8 miles, where a used-car dealership is in the fork of two roads. Follow N.C. Bicycle Route #2 to the left on West Hornes Church Road (SR-1941). After 2.1 miles arrive at a crossroads, the west terminus of N.C. Bicycle Route #7, known as the Ocracoke Option, which comes in from the right beside the Hornes Methodist Church at 27.9 miles. Across the intersection to the left is Hornes Church Road Convenient Mart; N.C. Bicycle Route #2 continues straight ahead on its way to Manteo. Turn right on Lamm Road (SR-1326), pass the church, and later pass a pecan grove. At 28.8 miles cross the Wilson County line. Pass Bloomery Road, right, at 29.1 miles. After seeing new residences among old farms, arrive at the Lamm Road intersection with US-264 at 31.2 miles.

CAMPSIDE STORIES: Where you crossed NC-39, it is 24 miles north on NC-39 to the community of Epsom. On one of its rural roads lived Mrs. C. E. Neal on a 70-acre farm. It was the summer of 1976 that something happened in her large farmhouse that remains unsolved. Mrs. Neal was recovering from a broken hip and was confined to a walker and wheelchair. She was living alone, and there had been an attempted break-in; but that was unrelated to what happened in July when her daughter was present.

They saw furniture in the kitchen and bedroom begin to move around. At first they watched cabinet drawers shifting themselves, then whole pieces of furniture moved. The residents left. Other family members, including her son, made investigations. At times upstairs pieces of furniture would be turned upside down. Curious neighbors offered explanations such as earth tremors and sonic booms. Some youths who had been helping take care of Mrs. Neal were declared innocent of any wrongdoing. A parapsychology team from Durham made a study but did not develop any answers. (See "Campside Stories" in Chapter 11.) Mrs. Neal told a *Franklin Times* reporter that she feared because of the attempted break-in, the spirit of her deceased husband was "warning her to vacate the home."

SECTION 30. US-264 Intersection in Lamm to NC-222 Intersection in Eureka

WILSON AND WAYNE COUNTIES: (See Wilson County discussion in Section 29.) Wayne County encompasses 555 square miles and its boundaries were created in 1779. It was named in honor of General Anthony Wayne (1745–96), a devoted Revolutionary War officer. Goldsboro, the county seat, was incorporated in 1847 and is centrally located near the Neuse River. The city was named for Major Matthew T. Goldsborough, a prominent railroad engineer. To the southwest of the city is Waynesborough State Park, and to the east is Seymour Johnson Air Force Base. Near Fremont, a town in the northern part of the county, is the birthplace of Governor Charles B. Aycock (1859–1912). In the southeast part of the county one of the state's most geologically significant landmarks occurs in the Cliffs of the Neuse State Park by the Neuse River. Major north-south highways are US-117, NC-111, NC-581, and US-13; east-west highways are NC-55, US-70, and NC-222.

LENGTH AND DIFFICULTY: 20.8 miles, easy

USGS TOPO MAPS: Bailey, Lucama, Wilson, Freemont

FEATURES OR EMPHASIS: Historic homes and churches, farmlands

TRAILS FOLLOWED: None

BICYCLE ROUTE FOLLOWED: N.C. Bicycle Route #7 (Ocracoke Option)

TRAIL CONNECTIONS: None

WEST TRAILHEAD: Intersection of Lamm Road and US-264 in community of Lamm

EAST TRAILHEAD: Crossroads of NC-222 and Church Street in the community of Eureka

CAMPING, LODGING, AND PROVISIONS: For lodging, see Section 29 for information on motels at the west trailhead in the community of Lamm and near I-95, exit 121, west of Wilson. The nearest campground is Rock Ridge Camp-ground (telephone: 252-291-4477), 2.0 miles west of I-95 at exit 16. Access from the Mountains-to-Sea Trail is 3.6 miles after leaving US-264 in Lamm, then 3.0 miles west on NC-42 to I-95 and the community of Rock Ridge. Services include full hook-ups, tent campsites, laundry, and swimming pool, and it is open all year. For provisions, several roadside combination grocery stores/gasoline stations are mentioned below in the description; a few of these have snack bars or grills.

INFORMATION AND SECURITY: Trail Maintenance: Wilson County Task Force (tele-phone: 919-291-3560). Wayne County Chamber of Commerce: 308 North William Street (P.O. Box 1107), Goldsboro, NC 27533 (telephone: 919-734-2241). Wilson Chamber of Commerce: 220 Broad Street (P.O. Box 1146), Wilson, NC 27984 (telephone: 252-237-0165). Wayne County Sher-iff's Office: 207 East Chestnut Street (P.O. Box 1877), Goldsboro, NC 27533 (telephone: 919-731-1481). Wilson County Sheriff's Office: 100 East Green Street (P.O. Box 1666)), Wilson, NC 27894 (telephone: 252-237-2118).

DESCRIPTION: Head south on Lamm Road. Pass through mixed residential and farmland areas, and cross a railroad track at 1.1 miles. Cross over I-95 at 1.5 miles. Pass Lamm's Grocery, left, and cross Old Raleigh Road. To the left is a state fire tower. The view from near the top is of farm fields and forests. At 3.1 miles cross James Baxter High School Road. Arrive at an intersection with NC-42 at 3.6 miles. (To the left it is 3.0 miles to US-264 near the west side of the city of Wilson; to the right it is 3.0 miles to I-95 [exit 116] and another 1.0 mile into Rock Ridge community, for a 1.0 mile right on Rock Ridge Road [SR-1142] to Rock Ridge Campground [see "Camping, Lodging, and Provisions."])

Cross a bridge over Contentnea Creek at 3.8 miles. At 5.0 miles turn left on Downing Road (SR-1163), but turn right on Shirley Road (SR-1164) at 5.6 miles. Turn right at 6.3 miles on Wiggins Mill Road (SR-1103) among farm homes and residences. At 6.7 miles turn left on Healthy Plains Road (SR-1129); pass through a loblolly pine forest, wax myrtle, and sweet bay. After a residential area arrive at a junction with Baswellville Road, left, and Saint Mary's Church Road, right, at 7.7 miles. Cross an intersection with US-301 at 8.4 miles. (Going left on US-301 toward Wilson will take you 1.8 miles to a cafe; another 0.4 miles brings you to Village Motor Lodge, Way-side Motel, Quality Inn, and restaurants.)

After crossing US-301 continue on Lely Road (SR-1646), and cross railroad tracks at 8.6 miles. Pass farms of soybeans, wheat, corn, and tobacco. Arrive at Blalock Road (SR-1645) and turn left at 10.3 miles; come to the juncture with US-117 at 10.4 miles. Turn right and after 0.1 mile turn left on Church

> **Cottage Mansions**
>
> *Walking or bicycling the MST on the Ocracoke Option Bicycle Route #7 through the coastal plain counties of Wilson, Wayne, Greene, and Lenoir, you will see a large number of farmhouses that are of the same architectural style. They are simple and functional cottages. Typically, the one-story basic house is rectangular with one or two windows on each side of a central front door. There are brick chimneys at one or both ends. On some there is a central gable. A separate kitchen might be close to the main house, where it would have been constructed at the same time in the nineteenth century, or a kitchen may have been added later along with other rooms in the back to form a T-shape.*
>
> *Some farmers, and now some city residents who have moved to the country, have transformed these simple houses into cottage mansions with Italianate designs. Full-length porches were added, and porch columns were garnished with brackets. Roofs were given overhanging eaves, also supported with ornate brackets. Windows were made fancy with head molds. New landscaping gave the house invitational class and neighborly warmth. Once you see the first house, you will probably be on the lookout to see what changes, if any, other residents have made in these historic homes.*

Loop Road (SR-1619) at Lower Black Creek Primitive Baptist Church (founded 1783). At 10.8 miles enter the town of Black Creek (named for Black Creek, which flows west and south of the town). In the historic town (founded 1840) is a bank, post office, grocery, town hall, and cafes. At 11.3 miles cross railroad tracks. Pass the Black Creek Pentecostal Holiness Church at 11.8 miles and go through farmlands with some vacant houses. Arrive at the juncture with, and turn right on, Frank Price Church Road (SR-1613) at 12.7 miles. You will see more farm fields of soybeans and cotton. Pass the Frank W. Price Presbyterian Church at 13.2 miles. Enter a forested area with wetlands, loblolly pines, river birch, maple, and bay trees. You are likely to see wood ducks and herons. Cross a bridge over Black Creek at 14.2 miles. At 14.6 miles come out of the forest. After crossing into Wayne County turn left on Buck Newsome Road (SR-1508) at Aycock Primitive Baptist Church at 16.4 miles. Enter a forested and swampy area at 16.4 miles and come out of the forest at 16.7 miles. Cross a swamp at 17.2 miles, followed by large flat farm fields.

Arrive at a junction where there is a cemetery both on the right and across the road. Turn left on Davis Mill Road (SR-1505, formerly Pippin Street). Cross a bridge over Aycock Swamp, and at 18.6 miles turn right on SR-1520 (which has two names: Turner Swamp Road and Church Street). Pass some residential homes and Turner Swamp Church at 19.7 miles. At 20.7 miles come to the community of Eureka and the Eureka United Methodist Church. You will arrive at the juncture with NC-222 at 20.8 miles, where you will find Eureka Super Market (telephone: 919-242-4045) and Ann's Cafe (telephone: 919-242-2120). An alternate MST (AMST) begins here, west on NC-222.

CAMPSIDE STORIES: Do you ever think about the enormous record-keeping job carried out by government officials known as archivists? Not only do these specialists in historical documents need to be historians, but they must be trained as well to recognize what records to select and how to safely maintain them. This is the story of the state's first archivist, who, because of his brilliance, became the first official archivist for the nation. He was R. D. W. (Robert Digges Wimberly) Connor (September 26, 1878–February 25, 1950). A state marker honors his birthplace at East Nash Street and NC-58/US-264 in Wilson.

Historian, author, and teacher, he was the first secretary of the 1903 North Carolina Historical Commission, which became the North Carolina State Department of Archives and History in 1943. His services were so outstanding that President Franklin D. Roosevelt, who recognized Connor's pioneering work, appointed him the first archivist of the United States in 1934. As a result Connor served as the first archivist of the state and the nation at the same time. In 1941 he returned to teach at the University of North Carolina (UNC) at Chapel Hill. He retired in 1949, one year before his death.

Connor was one of twelve children by Henry and Kate Connor. His father, an attorney and associate judge of the North Carolina Supreme Court, had also served in the state legislature as senator and member of the House of Representatives. Robert graduated from the public school system in Wilson and at age twenty-one received his doctorate degree at UNC-Chapel Hill. Three years later he married Sadie Hanes of Mocksville. While at the university in his senior undergraduate year, he was editor-in-chief for the campus newspaper, yearbook, and literary magazine. Among his many literary works are such textbooks as *Makers of North Carolina*, and other historical books such as the three-volume *History of North Carolina*.

SECTION 31. Intersection of NC-222 and Church Street in Eureka to Town of LaGrange on NC-903

WAYNE, GREENE, AND LENOIR COUNTIES: (See Wayne County discussion in Section 30.) Although the area was formerly called Glasglow County (founded in

1799), the name was changed to Greene County when James Glasglow, a secretary of state (1777–98), was involved in land fraud. Nathanael Greene (1742–86), considered to be a major hero of the American Revolution, led and won the Battle of Guilford Courthouse (now the site of a national military park) in 1781. The 292-square-mile rural county is chiefly agricultural. Its county seat is at Snow Hill, through which flows the Neuse River. The town was incorporated in 1828. Historians suggest the town's name developed from the white sandy soil in the area. Major north-south highways are US-258 (US-13 diagonally), NC-58, NC-91 (and NC-903 diagonally); east-west routes are US-13 and NC-121.

The county of Dobbs was formed in 1758 from Johnston County and was named in honor of Arthur Dobbs (1689–1765), who was governor of North Carolina from 1754 to 1765. But in 1779 Wayne County was formed from Dobbs County, and by 1791 the entire county was undergoing territorial division. The result was that part of the county went to Glasglow County and the other part was formed as Lenoir County with 399 square miles. It was named to honor William Lenoir (1751–1839), a patriot hero at the Battle of Kings Mountain in the Revolutionary War. The town of Kingston (named in honor of King George III of England) was founded as county seat in 1762. The name was changed to Kinston in 1784. In 1833 the town's name was changed to Caswell (in honor of Governor Richard Caswell), but it changed back to Kinston in 1834. There is a Richard Caswell Memorial on the south side of the Neuse River, southwest of the city.

LaGrange was incorporated in 1869, choosing the name from the Parisian estate of Lafayette. The town was the birthplace of William D. Moseley (1795–1863), the first governor of Florida. The Neuse River flows centrally across the entire county. A silently flowing river, it has multiple ox-bows and a number of swamps and marshes from southwest of Kinston to New Bern. Major north-south highways in Lenoir County are US-258, NC-903, NC-11, and NC-58; east-west highways are US-70 and NC-55.

LENGTH AND DIFFICULTY: 20.9 miles (main MST), easy; 42.5 miles (alternate MST), moderate

USGS TOPO MAPS: Stantonburg, Jason, LaGrange (main MST); Fremont, Northeast Goldsboro, Northwest Goldsboro, Southwest Goldsboro, Southeast Goldsboro, Williams (alternate MST)

FEATURES AND EMPHASIS: Farms and farm homes, some of which are historic residences (main MST); farms, Waynesborough State Park, historic district of Goldsboro, Stoney Creek, Cliffs of the Neuse State Park, Seven Springs (alternate MST)

TRAILS FOLLOWED: None (main MST); Wayne County Trail (alternate MST)

BICYCLE ROUTE FOLLOWED: N.C. Bicycle Route #7 (Ocracoke Option) (main MST)

TRAIL CONNECTIONS: None (main MST); Stoney Creek Trail, Spanish Moss Trail, Galax Trail, Bird Trail (alternate MST)

WEST TRAILHEAD: Intersection of NC-222 and Church Street in Eureka (both main MST and alternate MST)

EAST TRAILHEAD: LaGrange Post Office (main MST); intersection of Hardy Bridge Road (SR-1152) and Davis-Hardy Road (SR-1300) (alternate MST)

CAMPING, LODGING, AND PROVISIONS: For the main MST, the nearest campground to Eureka, Rock Ridge, is described in Section 30. The nearest campground from LaGrange is Cliffs of the Neuse State Park. It is accessible by driving south on NC-903 for 6.8 miles, turning right on Davis-Hardy Road for 0.8 miles to NC-55, and following NC-55 for 1.8 miles to turn off right on Park Avenue. After 2.0 miles turn right on an access route to the park. The park has family and group camping, hot showers, hiking trails, picnic areas, swimming and boat rentals at the lake, and fishing at the river. It also has an interpretive museum with informative displays about the park's geology. It is open daily all year. Contact the coastal region trail specialist (telephone: 910-778-9488) for more information. For information on a private residence, church, or bed and breakfast in LaGrange, contact the pastor of the LaGrange United Methodist Church (telephone: 252-566-3862/3148). For the alternate MST, there are motels and shopping centers in Goldsboro, and a campground in Falls of the Neuse State Park, through which the alternate route passes.

INFORMATION AND SECURITY: Trail Maintenance: Because this section of the main MST is the North Carolina Division of Bicycle and Pedestrian Transportation's Bicycle Route #7, that agency oversees signage maintenance. At the time of the writing of this book, the Friends of the Mountains-to-Sea Trail reported any damage to signs or missing signs to the state office. Wayne County Chamber of Commerce: 308 North William Street (P.O. Box 1107), Goldsboro, NC 27533 (telephone: 919-734-2241). Kinston/Lenoir County Chamber of Commerce: 301 North Queen Street (P.O. Box 157), Kinston, NC 28502 (telephone: 252-527-1131). Waynesborough State Park, 801 Highway 117S, Goldsboro, NC 27530 (telephone: 919-731-5680). Wayne County Sheriff's Office: 207 East Chestnut Street (P.O. 1877), Goldsboro, NC 27533 (telephone: 919-731-1481). Greene County Sheriff's Office: 301 North Greene Street, Snow Hill, NC 28580 (telephone: 252-747-3411). Lenoir County Sheriff's Office: 1305 Queen Street, Kinston, NC 28501 (telephone: 252-559-6100).

DESCRIPTION: For the main MST, beginning on Church Street (N.C. Bicycle Route #7), leave the junction with NC-222 in Eureka on your way south toward the

Stoney Creek Trail in Goldsboro

community of Faro. At 0.3 miles pass an old abandoned school building and some vacant houses. Farm fields are mainly tobacco, wheat, cotton, soybeans, and corn. Pass through the community of Faro. Big Daddy's Road is right. At 2.9 miles pass the Yelverton United Methodist Church. For the next mile you will pass by hog farms, one of which is Beaver Branch Farm with tobacco and grains. At 4.4 miles leave Wayne County and enter Greene County. Enter a forest and swampy area at 5.0 miles. Cross bridges of stillwater streams in a swampy area with river birch at 5.6 miles. Turn left on Bull Head Plantation Road (SR-1201) at 5.9 miles. Turn right, following signs for N.C. Bicycle Route #7 (Shine Road, SR-1210), and pass Cow Branch Farm. False dandelions and orange daylilies grow on the roadsides.

Arrive at Jim's Foods and Games and Cafe on the left at 7.4 miles. Exit from pine forest at 9.5 miles. Cross US-13 in the community of Shine at 11.0 miles, and continue south on Creech Road (SR-1132). You will find the Trading Post Restaurant and Grocery Store here. Pass Free Gospel Church at 11.1 miles. At 13.5 miles cross Pate Road (SR-1130). Among farms are

Waynesborough State Park

Waynesborough State park opened in 1986 on the site of the former town of Waynesborough, incorporated in 1787. The town was situated on the banks of the Neuse River and was the first county seat of Wayne County. The town became a travel station for river boats carrying passengers and freight. It also served as a center for stagecoach travel for passengers and materials between Kinston, New Bern, Raleigh, and Fayetteville.

In 1839 the community of Goldsborough Junction, less than one mile northeast, became favored by Waynesborough businesses when the Wilmington-Weldon Railroad passed through it. Waynesborough began to decline in population, river traffic ceased, and during the Civil War its remaining buildings were burned.

Currently the park has a visitor center and historical exhibits, a picnic area, boat dock at the Neuse River, and a nature trail. Its major emphasis is the creation of a new village with nineteenth-century houses, a law office, a physician's office, a one-room school, and a meeting house. All of these are in sight of the visitor center.

abandoned barns at 14.0 miles. Turn right on NC-903 at 15.2 miles in the community of Jason. Follow through the community and past a large farm where doves, bob-whites, and mockingbirds congregate. Leave Greene County and enter Lenoir County at 16.5 miles. Enter LaGrange at 19.9 miles and intersect with County Bicycle Route #42. Pass First Missionary Baptist Church. Cross railroad tracks at 20.6 miles. There are stores, UCB and Southern Banks, laundry, and Mickey's Restaurant. End this section at the post office and near the United Methodist Church at 20.9 miles.

DESCRIPTION FOR ALTERNATE MST: If you choose to follow the alternate MST, go west from Eureka on NC-222. After 1.5 miles turn left on NC-111. (Ahead on NC-222 it is 5.5 miles to the town of Fremont.) Pass through farmland of cotton, wheat, and soybeans, and cross Nahunta Swamp Creek bridge at 2.7 miles. Pass Northern Elementary School at 4.7 miles. Cross Moccasin Run bridge in a swamp at 5.5 miles. Pass through the community of Patetown at 7.2 miles and the community of Stoney Creek at 9.4 miles. At 12.6 miles arrive at an intersection where US-117 divides, with US-117 Business going left and US-117 Bypass going ahead at a left angle. (To the right of the intersection is Triangle Restaurant; beyond it on US-117 north for 0.3 miles is Carolina Motel [telephone: 919-735-4563].)

Follow US-117 Bypass and after 0.8 miles merge right with US-70 Bypass/ US-13 Bypass. After another 0.5 miles US-70 Bypass exits right, but you continue on US-13 Bypass. (US-70 Bypass, west, becomes US-70 where, within sight of the exit, there is a Ramada Inn [telephone: 919-736-4590], restaurants, and a few stores.) After another 1.9 miles you will arrive at Waynesborough State Park, right, at 15.8 miles. Enter the driveway and turn left to a parking area at the visitor center. (See information on the park in the sidebar and in "Information and Security.") Part of an 8.7-mile section of the MST passes through the park. Here and outside the park the MST follows the Wayne County Trail. A 0.8-mile section of the Wayne County Trail goes upstream beside the Neuse River to a dead-end. (Beyond is a proposed 95-mile section of the MST to connect with the MST at Falls Lake Dam north of Raleigh.)

To continue on the alternate MST route, follow the Wayne County Trail out of the park's driveway and cross US-13 Bypass/US-117 Bypass. Turn left and be alert to turn right at a trail sign on Elm Street. Follow Elm Street until you reach George Street. Turn left, north, and go three blocks on George Street to make a right turn on Chestnut Street. Go three blocks to Ormand Avenue and turn left, north. After one block on Ormand Avenue, turn right on Walnut Street. Go one block and turn left, north, on William Street. After another block turn right, east, on Mulberry Street. (This area is part of Goldsboro's historic district.) Continue east on Mulberry Street to Stoney Creek Park and the end of Mulberry Street at 19.6 miles. (To the left Stoney Creek Trail goes upstream for 1.1 miles to dead-end at Quail Park.)

On the Wayne County Trail turn right, downstream. Plant life along Stoney Creek includes river birch, maple, tulip poplar, laurel oak, ironweed, cardinal flower, beauty bush, and sensitive fern. Cross Elm Street at 20.2 miles. (To the left is an entrance gate to Seymour Johnson Air Force Base.) Continue downstream along Stoney Creek and exit the forest to steps at South Slocum Street at 21.8 miles. (To the left is an entrance to Seymour Johnson Air Force Base.)

(The alternate MST follows the Wayne County Trail across South Slocum Street into a forest of loblolly pine for 1.8 miles to where the trail ends at Arrington Bridge Road [NC-581]. This section has been closed for the past few years because of hurricane damage. Until it is repaired, follow the description below.)

Continuing on the alternate MST, turn right on South Slocum Street and at 22.4 miles turn left on Westbrook Road. Reach Arrington Bridge Road (NC-581) at 23.5 miles. Turn left near a plant nursery farm. Cross the Neuse River on a bridge at 23.9 miles. At 25.9 miles is S & S Foodliner and gasoline station. (Homemade sandwiches are available here.) Leave Arrington Bridge Road on a left curve at 26.4 miles. Cross the Neuse River again on a bridge at 27.6 miles. Arrive at a juncture with NC-111 at 28.5 miles. Turn right, south. In the community of Daly at 31.6 miles is C & T Country Store and restaurant. Again, cross the scenic Neuse River on a bridge at 32.4 miles. Turn left on Park Road (SR-1742) at 33.7 miles. After 0.9 miles turn left into Cliffs of the Neuse State Park at 34.6 miles.

On the left, after 0.7 miles, is the park's campground. There are tent and RV sites, water, flush toilets, hot showers, tables, and grills (no hook-ups). The campground is open from March 15 to November 30. Other recreational activities in the park are picnicking, swimming and boating in the lake, fishing, and hiking. Wide and easy trails are the Spanish Moss Trail (0.5 miles), Galax Trail (0.5 miles), and Bird Trail (0.5 miles). The 350 Yard Trail is between the museum area and Mill Creek. This pathway provides spectacular views of the Neuse River from 90-foot-high cliffs. (See Cliffs of the Neuse State Park sidebar for more information.)

Returning to the park's entrance, continue on the alternate MST by turning left, south, on Park Road (SR-1742). Arrive at Indian Springs Road (SR-1744) at 35.1 miles and turn left. Follow this road to make a left on NC-55 at 37.0 miles. Enter the community of historic Seven Springs at 37.8 miles, but leave NC-55 by going straight (partially left) on Dog Pond Road at 38.5 miles. (The road name changes to Davis-Hardy Road [SR-1300] after 0.4 miles, when you leave Wayne County to enter Lenoir County.) Cross NC-903 at 39.2 miles. Pass through farmland and reach a juncture with Barber Road, but keep left on Davis-Hardy Road at 41.2 miles. Pass through a swampy area of Hardy Mill Run. Arrive at an intersection with Hardy Bridge Road (SR-1152), left and right, at 42.5 miles. Here is a connection with the main MST (left 6.7 miles to LaGrange and another 14.2 miles to Eureka), and an end to the alternate MST. The main MST continues on the Davis-Hardy Road (SR-1300) east at the N.C. Bicycle Route #7 (Ocracoke Option) sign.

CAMPSIDE STORIES: This is the success story of a Lenoir County farm boy, James Joyner, who was orphaned at age two. Born August 7, 1862, he was the youngest of seven children of John and Sarah Joyner. James was reared by his maternal grandfather, Council Wooten. In addition to receiving lessons during childhood from his grandfather, he attend LaGrange Academy. At the age of sixteen James entered the University of North Carolina in Chapel Hill (UNC); he graduated at the age of nineteen. Joyner returned to LaGrange Academy to teach Latin, and at age twenty was simultaneously principal of the academy and public school superintendent of Lenoir County.

While at UNC-Chapel Hill James Joyner developed long-lasting friendships with some of his classmates: Charles B. Aycock, from Wayne County, who served as governor of the state from 1901 to 1905; Edwin A. Alderman, from Wilmington, who served as president of UNC from 1896 to 1900, of Tulane from 1900 to 1904, and of the University of Virginia from 1904 to 1931; and Charles D. McIver, from nearby Sanford, who became president of what is now the University of North Carolina at Greensboro (1891–1901).

Joyner decided he would rather be an attorney, and after obtaining his law degree he moved to Goldsboro. After three years he realized his major interest was still in education. Meanwhile he married Effie Rouse of La-Grange and they had two sons, James Noah and William Thomas. In 1889 Alderman left his post as principal of Goldsboro Graded School and Joyner took his place. Joyner gave thirty years of effort for public education reform (seventeen of which involved service as the state's superintendent of public instruction). With the help of Aycock and McIver, Joyner was a strong crusader for better teacher training and facilities, the availability of secondary education, consolidated schools, rural libraries, adult education, and increased revenue for raising the standards of the state's school system. In 1919, the year of Joyner's retirement to his farm, the state's voters approved a constitutional amendment to make the school term six months instead of four months. For the remainder of his life Joyner was an active leader in agriculture. He died January 24, 1954, at the age of ninety-one. There is a state marker to honor him on South Caswell Street (NC-903) in LaGrange.

THIRTEEN

CENTRAL COASTAL PLAIN

SECTION 32. Town of LaGrange on NC-93 to
Juncture of NC-11 at Albrittons Crossroads

LENOIR COUNTY: See discussion of Lenoir County in Section 31.

LENGTH AND DIFFICULTY: 13.5 miles, easy

USGS TOPO MAPS: LaGrange, Seven Springs, Deep Run

FEATURES OR EMPHASIS: Historic homes and churches, farmlands, Neuse River

TRAILS FOLLOWED: None

BICYCLE ROUTES FOLLOWED: N.C. Bicycle Route #7 (Ocracoke Option) and Lenoir County Bicycle Route #40

TRAIL CONNECTIONS: Alternate MST

BICYCLE ROUTE CONNECTIONS: Lenoir County Bicycle Route #45

WEST TRAILHEAD: U.S. Post Office near the United Methodist Church in La-Grange

EAST TRAILHEAD: Juncture of NC-11 at Albrittons Crossroads

CAMPING, LODGING, AND PROVISIONS: The nearest campground after leaving La-Grange is 11.5 miles away at Cliffs of the Neuse State Park. Its address is 345-B Park Entrance Road, Seven Springs, NC 28578 (telephone: 910-778-9488). The park is on the alternate MST (see Section 31). If you have a vehicle or bicycle for shuttle, follow the description in Section 31, above. To access the other campground, Riverbank Recreation Area south of Kinston, turn left (north) at the intersection of NC-11 and Albrittons Crossroad at Jimmy D's restaurant. After 2.1 miles arrive at the juncture with NC-55/11 at Light-house Food Mart. At 5.3 miles there is a shopping center, then at 5.4 miles you come to a crossroads with US-70/258 Bypass. There is a restaurant and service station here.

(If you turn right [east] on the US-70/258 Bypass, it is 1.1 miles to motels: Holiday Inn [telephone: 252-527-4155], Hampton Inn [telephone: 252-523-1400], Comfort Inn [telephone: 252-527-3200], and Day's Inn [telephone: 252-527-1500]. You will find restaurants here also.)

For the campground, continue north on NC-55/11. After another 0.6 miles cross bridges over a swamp, and by 0.9 miles watch for a sign for Riverbank Recreation Area, at which you will turn left. You will approach a nature center and a campground by the Neuse River. There are picnic tables, electrical hook-ups, and restrooms provided by the Kinston-Lenoir County Tourism Development Authority. You can expect some mosquitoes here in the summertime.

INFORMATION AND SECURITY: Trail Maintenance: Neuse River Association, 170 Quail Drive, Dudley, NC 28333 (telephone: 919-734-1936). Kinston/Lenoir County Chamber of Commerce: 301 North Queen Street (P.O. Box 157), Kinston, NC 28502 (telephone: 252-527-1131). Lenoir County Sheriff's Office: 1305 Queen Street, Kinston, NC 28501 (telephone: 252-559-6100).

DESCRIPTION: After leaving the LaGrange Post Office and LaGrange United Methodist Church on NC-903 (South Caswell Street), pass a state marker that honors William Dunn Moseley (February 1, 1795–January 4, 1863), a North Carolina senator and the first governor of Florida. Pass the La-Grange Freewill Baptist Church at 0.9 miles. Cross US-70 at 1.3 miles, and at 1.5 miles continue ahead on Jenny Lind Road (SR-1324, formerly Old River Road). (To the right on NC-903 is an access highway toward Seven Springs and Cliffs of the Neuse State Park.) Pass through large farms and fine homes right and left. Saint Matthews Freewill Baptist Church is at 2.5 miles. At 3.6 miles, in the community of Jenny Lind, turn left on Kennedy Home Road (SR-1324). (There is a legend that the famous Swedish singer, Jenny Lind, sang here when on her U.S. tour in 1850.) Ahead are forests with pine plantations and soybean fields at 4.0 miles. Turn right on Hardy Bridge Road (SR-1152). At 5.3 miles the road has some curves. To the left is Pine Bush Road (SR-1307) and connection with Lenoir County Bicycle Route #45. Cross a bridge over a swamp at 5.9 miles. Cross the scenic Neuse River Bridge at 6.1 miles. Another bridge is at 6.2 miles, and there is a swamp to the right. At 6.7 miles turn left on Davis-Hardy Road (SR-1300). Here is the south end of the alternate MST, which approaches from the right on Davis-Hardy Road. (To the right it is 4.0 miles to Seven Springs, another 1.8 miles to Park Avenue, right, off NC-55, and another 2.0 miles to turn right for an entrance to Cliffs of the Neuse State Park. See Section 31 for more information.)

Cross a creek at 7.7 miles and pass by farms of cotton, corn, and soybeans. There is a grove of tall trees by a stream at 8.7 miles. At 9.4 miles arrive at NC-55. To the left it is 10.0 miles to Kinston and 8.0 miles right to Seven Springs in Wayne County. Turn left, and at 9.9 miles come to Norwood Grocery store, grill, telephone, and gasoline on the right. The store is

Cliffs of the Neuse State Park

A geological treasure, the Cliffs of the Neuse River is unlike any other place in the state. A state park since 1945, it has 751 acres, some on each side of the river. Its uniqueness is a series of cliffs that have been created by the river's cut into the hill- side. In the process multicolored layers have been exposed. In the ancient layers are fossils, seashells, and shale. The highest cliff is 90 feet, and from it you can view the silent river below. The park's plant life is also unique. Among its 420 species of plants are galax and Spanish moss, a rarity together.

Human history of the area includes occupation by both the Tuscarora and Saponi Indians, who used the area for hunting, fishing, and tribal ceremonies. How remark- ably fortunate that the state was able to acquire the area after Lionel Weil and others generously donated part of the land through the Wayne Foundation in 1944. Other land donations followed in combination with state purchases.

open 5:30 A.M. to 9:00 P.M.; Sunday hours are noon to 9:00 P.M. (the grill is not open on Sundays). There are large white houses at 11.0 miles in the community of Sandy Bottom. Pass Sandybottom Baptist Church, and arrive at Webb Chapel United Methodist Church at 11.2 miles. Here is a sheltered picnic area, a granite tablet honoring the Croom family, and a historic meet- ing house. The Croom Meeting House has a tin roof, clapboard siding, and green shutters.

To continue on the MST (and N.C. Bicycle Route #7) turn right on Greene Haynes Road (SR-1161, across the road from the church and meeting house). Pass the Sandy Bottom fire station and enter into an area of old and new residences at 11.9 miles. At 13.5 miles arrive at an intersection, Albrittons Crossroads, where the trail continues across the road but ends here for this section. In the southwest corner of the intersection is Jimmy D's restaurant, known for its daily lunch special. Among its specialties are homemade bread and pastries such as applejacks. It is open Monday through Friday from 5 A.M. to 7 P.M. and on Saturday 5 A.M. to 1 P.M. (closed on Sunday, telephone: 252-527-9779). From the intersection north on NC-11 it is 6.4 miles to the campground at Riverbank Recreation Area, described above.

CAMPSIDE STORIES: One of the most famous stories about a North Carolina phenomenon is the Ghost of Maco Station (a train stop formerly called Farmers Turnout). Like the Brown Mountain Lights north of Morganton, and Ephraim's Light at Seaboard, there are unanswered questions in this story. During the centuries of sightings of all of these phenomena, a variety of stories have been told, some of which are very imaginary while others are

---

Croom Family

Facing the highway and between United Methodist Church and the Croom Meeting House in the community of Sandy Bottom in Lenoir County is a tablet with the following information:

> *After most careful and intensive research, this family finds that the first Croom came to America from Gloucester England in 1664, and settled in the New England States. The next Crooms left "Croom" in Limerick Ireland, came to Virginia in 1700, or prior to that time took up land grants, and established "houses" in the James River. From there, three Croom brothers moved down and settled in the eastern counties of N.C. in 1741. This site named by the Indians "Sandy Bottom" has been used by the Crooms continuously ever since. Nearby the little meeting house still stands on sacred sod, where many weary souls have met and found their way to God.*

---

the result of scientific study. The legend of the Ghost of Maco Station has its roots about 85 miles southwest of Kinston and about 14 miles west of Wilmington. Ephraim's Light is located about 100 miles north of Kinston and east of Roanoke Rapids. (Its history is that a slave named Ephraim was burned at the stake for murder of his master and the lights from the fire still haunt the living.)

The Ghost of Maco Station may be more believable if only the light is the subject. The story begins in 1867 when Joe Baldwin, a conductor on the Atlantic Coast Line Railroad, was beheaded by a train that crashed into an uncoupled coach. Joe was swinging his lantern in an effort to get the conductor's attention. As a result of his failure and death, the light of his lantern has been swinging regularly since then. Witnesses to the wreck claimed to have first noticed the mysterious light soon after. There is even one claim that President Grover Cleveland saw the light in 1889. (Other stories concerning President Cleveland's visit tell that he inquired about the green and red lantern lights. He was told that colored lights were used for safety reasons. A white ghostly light would confuse the engineers.)

If you plan to visit Maco, it is on US-74/76/NC-86 west of Wilmington and 3.0 miles east from the Columbus/Brunswick County line. The legend is that the best time to see the light is in the summertime without moonlight. The most common description of what people see is that at first it flickers, then becomes brighter and faster as it follows a few feet above the track. It is always on the left rail looking east. As it approaches Maco it stops, glows, and speeds back down the track to vanish. It frequently repeats itself and has dependable timing. Sometimes it swings back and forth. Some maintainers of the story say that Joe Baldwin is swinging his lantern in search for his head.

SECTION 33. Albrittons Crossroads and NC-11 to Cove City on Sunset Boulevard

LENOIR, JONES, AND CRAVEN COUNTIES: (See Lenoir County discussion in Section 31 above.) The 468-square-mile Jones County was established in 1778 from part of Craven County. It was named in honor of Willie Jones (1740–1801), a leader of the American Revolution who later opposed the adoption of the U.S. Constitution. The town of Trenton, the county seat, was organized about 1874 and derives its name from the Trent River, along which it is located. At the north end of the county is the vast Great Dover Swamp. In the south are Hofmann State Forest and White Oak Pocosin, both at the headwaters of the winding and swampy White Oak River. Croatan National Forest spreads over the east boundary from Craven County. Major highways crossing the county are US-17, NC-58, US-258, and NC-41 for north-south routes, and NC-41, in part, for east-west routes.

Craven County, with 785 square miles, was named in 1712; but earlier it probably was known as Archdale County (1696) and was a precinct of Bath County in 1705. Historians have researched which of various Craven names belong to the county. William Craven, Earl of Craven (1606–97), was one of the original Lord Proprietors. Other claims include William's grandnephew, William Lord Craven, who inherited the proprietary title, and the third William, Lord Craven, who was a proprietor at the time of the county's name change.

New Bern, incorporated in 1723, is the county seat. Its name, from Bern, Switzerland, originated by one of the city's founders, Baron Christoph von Graffenried. New Bern was the state capital from 1746 to 1792. In the north part of the county are a number of bays and swamps—the Big Pocosin, marshes along the Neuse River, and Hog Island near New Bern. South of the Neuse is Sunset Boulevard, running from Dover to Clarks, the longest straight 15 miles of the Mountains-to-Sea Trail. The city of New Bern has the longest distance of sidewalks on which the MST passes. On the south of the county is Croatan National Forest with its Sheep Ridge Wilderness, in which are located the crater-like lakes—Great Lake, Long Lake, Little Lake, and Lake Ellis Simon near Carteret County. There are also extensive forest tracts along the Neuse River and adjoining the Cherry Point Marine Corps Air Station. Near the Marine Corps air station is Havelock, the county's second largest town. Its name, received in 1857, honors Sir Henry Havelock (1795–1857), a British major general. The county's main north-south highways are NC-306, NC-43, and US-17; east-west highways are NC-101, US-70, NC-55, and NC-118.

LENGTH AND DIFFICULTY: 23.5 miles, easy

USGS TOPO MAPS: Rivermont, Dover, Cove City

FEATURES OR EMPHASIS: Farms and farm homes

TRAILS FOLLOWED: None

BICYCLE ROUTES FOLLOWED: N.C. Bicycle Route #7 (Ocracoke Option) and Lenoir County Bicycle Route #40

TRAIL CONNECTIONS: None

BICYCLE ROUTE CONNECTIONS: Lenoir County Bicycle Routes #43 and #41

WEST TRAILHEAD: Juncture of NC-11 on Albrittons Road

EAST TRAILHEAD: Sunset Boulevard in Cove City

CAMPING, LODGING, AND PROVISIONS: See description of camping by the Neuse River in Kinston in Section 32. There are no other campgrounds or lodging in this section. There are a few rural grocery stores for provisions in Dover and Cove City. For information about potential camping areas, make an advance telephone call to John Jaskolka, P.O. Box 723, Bridgeton, NC 28519 (telephone: 252-637-6737). Also, you can call the chambers of commerce listed below for information on bus, taxi, or shuttle services.

INFORMATION AND SECURITY: Trail Maintenance: N.C. Division of Bicycle and Pedestrian Transportation, P.O. Box 25201, Raleigh, NC 27611 (telephone: 919-733-2804). Kinston/Lenoir County Chamber of Commerce: 301 North Queen Street (P.O. Box 157), Kinston, NC 28502 (telephone: 252-527-1131). New Bern Area Chamber of Commerce: 316 South Front Street, New Bern, NC 28906 (telephone: 252-637-3111; office not open on weekends). Lenoir County Sheriff's Office: 1305 Queen Street, Kinston, NC 28501 (telephone: 252-559-6100). Jones County Sheriff's Office: Corner of Market & Jones Streets (P.O. Box 267), Trenton, NC 28563 (telephone: 252-448-7091). Craven County Sheriff's Office: 411 Craven Street (P.O. Box 1027), New Bern, NC 28563 (telephone: 252-636-6620).

DESCRIPTION: Continue on the MST and N.C. Bicycle Route #7 from the NC-11 junction at Albrittons Crossroads. Pass Dawson's Christmas Tree Farm on the left at 0.7 miles. Macedonia Free Will Baptist Church is at 1.4 miles, followed by a dense forest. On its borders with the road shoulders are groves of wax myrtle and yellow milkwort. Pass small fields and then arrive at a T-intersection with US-258 at 2.5 miles. (A turn left will take you 4.4 miles to US-70 and the motels near the Neuse River at Kinston, described in Section 32.) Turn right on US-258, cross Southwest Creek at 2.6 miles, ascend, and turn left on Bill Stroud Road (SR-1908) at 2.9 miles. On the right is Amaryllis Garden (telephone: 828-527-5363). Ascend among beautiful home sites and reach a T-intersection with Woodington Road (SR-1909) at 3.2 miles. There is a large white house at the intersection. Turn left. (Lenoir County Bicycle Route #43 begins to the right.)

Descend to a swampy area with tall trees, wild roses, grape vines, and elderberries. At 4.9 miles turn right on Elizabeth Loftin Road (SR-1913) to cross Spring Branch at 4.0 miles. Turn left and pass Parker Fork Road, right. At 6.7 miles arrive at the juncture with NC-58. Here bicycle routes #7 and #40 go straight across NC-58, and Lenoir Bicycle Route #41 goes left into the community of Loftins Crossroads. Kennedy's Korner hot dogs and dip ice cream is here. Pass King's Chapel Church at 7.1 miles. Houses may be seen on the left and an abandoned historic house and large oaks are right. After a pine plantation arrive at 9.0 miles to a juncture with Cobb Road (formerly Fire Tower Road [SR-1903]). (To the left Lenoir County Bicycle Route #40 turns north.) Turn right. After 0.2 miles turn left on Silo Road (SR-1915). There is another abandoned house on the left. At 10.2 miles leave Lenoir County and enter Jones County, where Silo Road becomes Webb Farm Road (SR-1306). At 11.4 miles turn left on Wise Fork Road (SR-1002). After 1.1 miles watch for and make a right turn on Burnett Road (formerly Tucker Town Road [SR-1313]). Holly Branch Free Will Baptist Church and Pilgrim House Free Will Baptist Church are here. For the next 2.7 miles the road is mainly straight through fields of dark fertile soil and areas of exposed ancient sand. Farm crops and loblolly pines are prominent.

Arrive at US-70 (where it is 9.0 miles left to Kinston and 26.0 miles right to New Bern). Cross the highway and turn right. At 15.5 miles turn left on Old US-70 into Dover. Leave Jones County and enter Craven County at 15.8 miles. Cross the stream of Gum Swamp that drains into Tracey Swamp. Cross railroad tracks at 16.1 miles to a divided highway. Stay left. Pass Creel's store on the left and then a pecan grove. At 16.6 miles come to Dover Post Office on the right and a grocery store on the left. The long, straight, and shadeless Sunset Boulevard (SR-1005) has begun. The railroad tracks parallel the highway to the community of Clarks.

Whenever you see fields in this flat but fertile area, they are mainly grassy with cattle or planted in crops such as corn or cotton. You will pass World Wood Corp (wood products) at 21.7 miles, and Cove City Wood Processing at 22.3 miles. Enter the town of Cove City at 22.9 miles. Cove City Community Mart, right, is at 23.4 miles, and the post office is at 23.5 miles. Nearby is a Food Center and Edna's Grill, advertised as "Jones County Cooking, We Got the Beef and Bull."

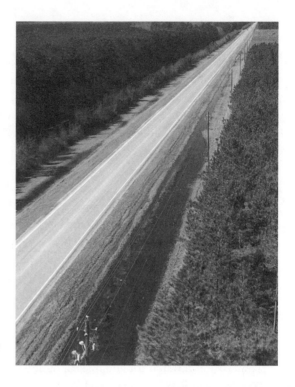

Mountains-to-Sea Trail following Sunset Boulevard (Old US-70)

CAMPSIDE STORIES: As you journey through the northwest corner of Jones County and onto the lengthy Sunset Boulevard at Dover in Craven County, you are at the edges of the territory influenced by New Bern's venerated history long before you arrive in the city. North to Grifton on US-17 and west on NC-118 is one of the state's three markers honoring John Lawson, an explorer and leader in the founding of New Bern. Southeast to the Trent River is the site of a former plantation home of John Martin Franck, who was also a leader in the founding of New Bern (though his legendary life is not honored with a silver-white highway sign). Historians believe Franck was born in 1680 and died at age sixty-five in 1745.

This is a short story about Franck, a German immigrant and highly respected friend of John Lawson. Franck was an outstanding leader in the welfare of Swiss and Palatine immigrants to the New Bern area in 1710. It is likely that he was the overseer of the ship that brought the settlers from England. Although Franck was left out of the journals of Lawson and Baron Christoph von Graffenried, he played an integral part in the establishment of New Bern and in the city's survival. (Graffenried's name is honored at the Neuse River Bridge in New Bern as the sole founder of New Bern.) The respect that Franck received from mercantile companies allowed his ships to exchange wood products and animal furs for food and other needs for the starving colonists after Lawson was murdered in the Tuscarora Indian War of 1711–13. And Frank was there to help the settlers who had been cheated with broken promises on their land grants by the North Carolina Provincial Council and possibly the governor and Graffenried. Franck also stood by the colonists after Graffenried abandoned the colony and left North Carolina in 1712.

Franck started a school on Rocky Run near Mill Creek that lasted for more than 225 years. He was elected to the N.C. General Assembly in 1715 and 1727, served as justice of the county, and served on the parish vestry. He was also known for his White Rock Plantation by the Trent River, where he developed progressive methods of agriculture. Twice married, he had eleven children (all born between 1713 and 1732), the last born of whom was Barbara. She became the wife of Captain Daniel Shine at whose inn she entertained President George Washington on his Southern Tour.

SECTION 34. Cove City on Sunset Boulevard to Juncture of US-17/NC-55 in Bridgeton

CRAVEN COUNTY: See Craven County discussion in Section 33.

LENGTH AND DIFFICULTY: 21.9 miles, easy

USGS TOPO MAPS: Cove City, Jasper, Askin, New Bern

FEATURES OR EMPHASIS: Old US-70 (Sunset Boulevard), Historic City of New Bern, Neuse River Bridge

TRAILS FOLLOWED: None

BICYCLE ROUTE FOLLOWED: N.C. Bicycle Route #7 (Ocracoke Option)

TRAIL CONNECTIONS: None

BICYCLE ROUTE CONNECTION: N.C. Bicycle Route #3 (Ports of Call)

WEST TRAILHEAD: Cove City on Sunset Boulevard

EAST TRAILHEAD: Juncture of US-17 and NC-55 in Bridgeton

CAMPING, LODGING, AND PROVISIONS: At the east end of this section is Curtis Motel, a family motel (113 B Street, Bridgeton, NC 28519 [P.O. Box 217]). Camping is available at the Neuse River Campground: north on US-17 from the junction with NC-55, then left for 2.5 miles. It has laundry and showers (1565 B Street, New Bern, NC 28560 [telephone: 252-638-2556/633-3911]). For hikers and bicyclists who wish to stay in downtown New Bern motels or hotels, here are a few of the ones closest to US-17 and the historic district of New Bern: Days Inn (telephone: 800-325-2525), Comfort Suites (telephone: 252-636-0022), and Bridge Point Hotel and Marina (telephone: 252-636-

3637). Provisions are plentiful at a number of shopping centers and chain grocery stores.

INFORMATION AND SECURITY: Trail Maintenance: Contact New Bern Area Task Force, P.O. Box 723, Bridgeton, NC 28519 (telephone: 252-637-6737) for information on campgrounds or motels in Cove City at the west end and Bridgeton at the east end of this section. New Bern Area Chamber of Commerce: 316 South Front Street, New Bern NC 28906 (telephone: 252-637-3111). Craven County Convention and Visitors' Bureau (same street entrance as Chamber of Commerce, telephone: 252-637-9400). New Bern Historical Society (telephone: 252-638-8558). Jones County Sheriff's Office: Corner of Market and Jones Streets (P.O. Box 267), Trenton, NC 28563 (telephone: 252-448-7091). Craven County Sheriff's Office: 411 Craven Street (P.O. Box 1027), New Bern, NC 28563 (telephone: 252-636-6620). New Bern Police Station: 601 George Street, New Bern, NC 28563 (telephone: 252-633-2020).

DESCRIPTION: This section of the Mountains-to-Sea Trail is considerably different from any other section through which you have passed or will pass. The major difference is your proximity to (and density of) vehicular traffic. While hiking into the city you will notice narrow road shoulders or only a curb. Continue with caution. After entering the business and commercial districts, both hikers and bicyclists share and follow a narrow dirt sidewalk toward downtown. This is followed by paved sidewalks. When you cross the Neuse River Bridge on a walkway you will also be close to heavy traffic. This section of the MST is also different because you are in a historic city with hundreds of magnificent reminders of its heritage, colonial culture, and early influence as the state's capital. There are more than twenty state historic markers, and special tours of the historic buildings and other commercial visitors' services are available (see "Diversions," below).

From Cove City's post office and Food Center continue the long straight hike on Sunset Boulevard. Cross a bridge over the black waters of Core Creek. At 1.3 miles White's Meat Market has a sign indicating it is "Home of Old Fashion Pork Cracklings." There is also a sign stating that the market serves beef, poultry, and barbecued pork. After 2.0 miles there is a dense forest on the left (north) and forest gaps on the right (south of the railroad tracks, with irrigated agriculture beyond). Along the road shoulders are blazing star and colicroot, an orchid with small white flowers on a stalk arising from a rosette of leaves. At 4.9 miles arrive at the Tuscarora Lookout Tower of the Tuscarora Game Land (North Carolina Wildlife Resources Commission), left. The steps are open for ascending to near the top. Panoramic views are spectacular.

Cross Tuscararo Crossroads at 6.0 miles. After passing Hymans Road, left, notice the swamp area and bridge (constructed in 1937) over Batchelder's Creek. (About 300 yards north of here is the site where Generals Robert Hoke and George Pickett captured a Union Army outpost in February 1864.) Finally, you will come to a curve that bends left at 8.9 miles in the community of Clarks. Pass Clarks United Methodist Church, pass Clarks Road, right, and Parker Road, left. At this point there is an increase in highway traffic. Pass a Martin Marietta Quarry, right, at 10.2 miles, followed by large trees and a swamp area, right and left. Cross Caswell Branch and reach a V-shaped juncture with NC-55, right and left, at 10.5 miles. Turn right. (A sign indicates downtown New Bern is 6.0 miles ahead, but the city limits is 1.1 miles.) Walking is difficult in this area because of the lack of highway shoulder space or sidewalk during periods of heavy traffic. In the traffic are logging trucks and large trucks hauling marl. Pass a two-story historic home on the right and a family cemetery to the left. At 11.6 miles enter the city limits where there is an increase in density of residential houses. Pleasant Hill AME Zion Church is at 12.0 miles. Some houses are abandoned. At 12.4 miles is a V-shaped juncture with NC-43, right and left. Stay right.

There is a mini-mart and gasoline station here in the Washington Forks community. To the left at 13.0 miles is a section of the Neuse River Game Lands. Pass Rollerland at 13.2 miles. At 13.9 miles is a shopping center with stores, restaurants, laundry, and pharmacy. There is another shopping center at 14.6 miles with theater, restaurants, and stores. The Craven Regional Medical Center is left at 15.3 miles. If you are hiking you may have noticed that bicycles are using a dirt path on the right (south) side of the street where there is not a paved sidewalk. You may wish to walk on the path. The dirt path eventually becomes a sidewalk after you cross the connecting intersection of US-17/70 Business with NC-55, which is Broad Street. At 16.4 miles there is a Days Inn (telephone: 800-325-2525). At 16.7 miles there is a sign, right, at the corner of Metcalf Street that indicates access to Tryon Palace and Gardens.

Continuing on Broad Street, pass the Craven County Court House on the left at 17.1 miles, and at 17.2 miles turn right on East Front Street (US-17/NC-55 Business). (Ahead is the site of the former Neuse River Bridge.) On the left of East Front Street is Comfort Suites and Union Point Park Complex; to the right at 17.4 miles is Riverfront Convention Center. Cross the Alfred Cunningham Bridge over the Trent River, and pass a state historical marker about the Civil War battle at New Bern. To the right is Bridge Point Hotel and Marina (Ramada Inn, telephone: 252-636-3637). A traffic light is

---

New Bern Historic Area

On the New Bern Historic District Trail are sixty-five historic buildings (business, government, homes, and churches) within a walking, bicycling, or driving distance of 4.5 miles. Because the route is divided into four sections (1.2 miles in the Palace area, 1.1 miles in the Johnson Street area, 1.2 miles in the East Front Street area, and 1.0 mile in the downtown area), which may begin or end in irregular patterns (such as in the middle of a block), it is essential that visitors have a tour map to determine which buildings are in which tour section.

  Maps are available free of charge from the Craven County Convention and Visitors' Bureau, 314 South Front Street (telephone: 800-437-5767 or 252-637-9400). The visitor center is open daily. Tours offered through the tour agency originate at the southeast corner of the Palace Reception Center (George Street and Pollock Street), across from the Tryon Palace main gate.

---

at 17.9 miles; here is a connection with N.C. Bicycle Route #3 (Ports of Call) coming in on Howell Street from the right. Continue straight on US-17/ NC-55 and both N.C. Bicycle Routes #7 and #3 to pass under a highway complex. Stay right to ascend in a loop for merging with traffic coming east on US-70 to go north on US-17/NC-55 at 18.6 miles. Cross the Neuse River with skyline views of New Bern left and downstream to the right. Reach the end of the bridge at 20.4 miles. At 21.3 miles is the Bayboro exit for NC-55 and bicycle signs for routes #7 and #3. (If you are bicycling and not stopping at the end of this section, you could turn right on NC-55 and after 0.8 miles connect with Section 35 at Mallard Food Shop.)

Continue ahead on US-17 north and pass under an overpass. After 0.6 miles turn left at an intersection on South D Street in Bridgeton. Arrive at the Curtis Motel after 0.1 mile. Here is the eastern end of Section 34 at 21.9 miles. The address for Curtis Motel is 113 B Street (P.O. Box 217), Bridgeton, NC 28517 (telephone: 252-638-3011). Nearby is Earl's Country Kitchen, which serves breakfast and lunch and is open Monday through Saturday from 5 A.M. to 2 P.M., and Mrs. Harvey's Cafe, open weekdays, from 5:30 A.M. to 2:00 P.M. Also nearby is Bridgeton Fuel Market, which is open twenty-four hours daily. (North of here it is 2.5 miles on US-17 to Neuse River Campground, which has full hook-ups, tent sites, laundry, and a swimming pool. See "Camping, Lodging, and Provisions" at the beginning of this section.)

DIVERSIONS: Many potential diversions are available in this city full of historic places. In addition to tours through the historic district (see the sidebar), there are singular visits to such places as the New Bern Civil War Museum, Fireman's Museum, and New Bern Academy. For information about other cultural and theater events, seafood restaurants, and fishing, call or visit the Craven County Convention and Visitors' Bureau, listed above under "Information and Security."

CAMPSIDE STORIES: You have crossed the Neuse River for the fourth time on your main MST journey (sixth time if you took the alternate MST through Goldsboro) across the state. Your fifth (or seventh) time will be in the next section when you take the 2.3-mile ferry ride from Minnesott Beach to Croatan National Forest. The first time you crossed the Neuse was on the NC-50 bridge at Falls Lake, north of Raleigh. The Neuse is a historic river. English explorers in the late seventeenth century and early eighteenth century found many Indian villages along the wide riverbanks near New Bern and upstream. One of those explorers was John Lawson, historian, biologist, and humorist. On December 28, 1700, he began an exploratory and meandering expedition of about 1,000 miles from Charles-Town up the coast to the Santee River in South Carolina. From there he went northwest to what is now Waxhaw, High Point, Raleigh, Wilson, Greenville, Washington, and New Bern in North Carolina. He kept a lengthy diary, later published in England and in Germany as *A New Voyage to Carolina*.

Lawson settled in an Indian village called *Chatooka* (now part of New Bern) near a creek that today bears his name. He was influential in establishing both New Bern and Bath communities, and he became the surveyor general for the colony. Lawson wrote detailed information on the biology of his environment. Understanding and generally sympathetic to the natives, he wrote about their culture. For instance, describing their superstitions, he wrote: "Then the Doctor proceeded to tell a long Tale of a great Rattle-Snake, which, a great while ago, liv'd by a Creek in that River (which was Neus) and that it kill'd abundance of *Indians*; but at last, a bald Eagle kill'd it, and they were rid of a Serpent, that us'd to devour whole Canoes full of *Indians* at a time."

During a three-year colonial political power struggle known as the Cary Rebellion, Governor Thomas Cary fled to Virginia and Edward Hyde took his place. With the colonists divided, the Tuscarora Indians attacked the white settlers in September 1711. Although Lawson was politically uninvolved, and had been friendly to the Indians, he and his friend Baron Christoph von Graffenried were captured upstream on the Neuse River by the Tuscarorans. A few days after the natives had tortured and executed Lawson, the baron's ransom offer was accepted for his freedom.

SECTION 35. Juncture of US-17 and NC-55 in Bridgeton to NC-306 in Minnesott Beach

CRAVEN AND PAMLICO COUNTIES: (See Craven County discussion in Section 33.) Pamlico County was established in 1872 from parts of Craven and Beaufort Counties, and was named for the Pamlico Indians. It encompasses 576 square miles, 341 of which are on land and 235 are in water. The county seat is Bayboro, incorporated in 1881 and named for the Bay River. On the south side of its boundary is the Neuse River, and the southeast part of the county borders on Pamlico Sound, the largest sound on the nation's East Coast. The Intracoastal Waterway runs through Bay River and Goose Creek to the Pamlico River, which creates Goose Creek Island. The geography of Pamlico County provides appealing options for boating, fishing, and sailing. There is a free ferry from Minnesott Beach across the Neuse River to Craven County and Croatan National Forest. Almost half of the large Gum Swamp and all of the Light Ground Pocosin are included in the county. Its main east-west highways are NC-55 and NC-304; the main north-south route is NC-306.

LENGTH AND DIFFICULTY: 21.0 miles, easy

USGS TOPO MAPS: New Bern, Reelsboro, Upper Broad Creek, Arapahoe, Cherry Point

FEATURES OR EMPHASIS: Rural area, Neuse River Ferry

TRAILS FOLLOWED: None

BICYCLE ROUTE FOLLOWED: N.C. Bicycle Route #7 (Ocracoke Option)

TRAIL CONNECTIONS: None

BICYCLE ROUTE CONNECTION: N.C Bicycle Route #3 (Ports of Call)

WEST TRAILHEAD: In Bridgeton where NC-55 leaves US-17 and goes east

EAST TRAILHEAD: Campground at Minnesott Beach on NC-306

CAMPING, LODGING, AND PROVISIONS: Motels are available in New Bern and in Bridgeton, and there is a campground north of Bridgeton. (See information in Section 34.) Minnesott Beach Campground (near Minnesott Beach Ferry), Arapahoe, NC 28510 (telephone: 252-249-1225). Provisions can be picked up along your way at country grocery stores and mini-marts.

INFORMATION AND SECURITY: Trail Maintenance: New Bern Area Task Force, P.O. Box 7223, Bridgeton, NC 28519 (telephone: 252-637-6737). New Bern Area Chamber of Commerce: 316 South Front Street, New Bern NC 28563 (telephone: 252-637-3111). Craven County Sheriff's Office: 411 Craven Street, New Bern, NC 28563 (telephone: 252-636-6620). Pamlico County Sheriff's Office: 202 Main Street (P.O. Box 437), Bayboro, NC 28515 (telephone: 252-745-3101).

DESCRIPTION: Begin at Curtis Motel or one of the restaurants described in Section 34. Go 0.1 mile east on South D Street to the intersection with US-17. Cross US-17 to Fisher Street. Proceed about 100 feet to a stop sign at South E Street at 0.2 miles. Turn right on South E Street, then curve left. To the left are blueberry farms. At 0.9 miles connect with NC-55 and N.C. Bicycle Routes #7 and #3. Turn left and pass Mallards Food Shop at 1.0 mile. At 1.3 miles is an intersection where Half Moon Road (SR-1600) goes left and N.C. Bicycle Route #3 (Ports of Call) goes with it. (Its north terminus is at the Virginia border near the Great Dismal Swamp.) Continue on NC-55.

When you cross Upper Broad Creek at 2.6 miles you have left Craven County and entered Pamlico County. There are signs of a beaver dam in the vicinity. Among the plant life in wet areas are cypress, ferns, and lizard tail. Broad Creek Christian Church is on the left in the Olympia community. You will notice an increase in farms by 3.5 miles. Holton Farms, on the right, has strawberries. Cross Deep Run at 4.6 miles.

In the approach to the community of Reelsboro, pass the Reelsboro Christian Church on the right and, on the left, a home with a pecan grove and then New Hope Christian Church. Reelsboro United Methodist Church follows, right. At 6.2 miles come to a Shell service station and a mini-mart. A Dairy Queen follows at 6.3 miles, and a food mart is at 6.6 miles. Here is also Neuse Road (SR-1005), where you turn right. Immediately you will notice less vehicular traffic and residences become more scattered. Pass Reelsboro Pentecostal Holiness Church, left. In the farm fields are corn, soybeans, and tobacco. At 7.5 miles there is a longleaf pine forest with Spanish moss and cypress trees. A crossing of a bridge in a swampy, dark, and remote area is at 9.1 miles.

At the juncture with Scott's Road at 10.3 miles is New Bethlehem Original Free Will Baptist Church. Lionel Willis Grocery is at 13.6 miles. Pass Goose Creek Road and large fields, then continue through mixed forests of oaks, pines, and wax myrtle. Songbirds are prominent. At Amity Christian Church and cemetery there is a tombstone that has the following statement: "An honest man is the noblest work of God." Cross a canal, the home of some wood ducks. At 14.5 miles cross a bridge over Beard Creek, and then at 15.0 miles cross a tributary to the creek. There are a number of abandoned houses, some that may be of historic value.

Arrive at historic Arapahoe's town limits at 16.5 miles. Pass the Belma Lee Taylor Garden and the Anointed Remnant Church of Christ near the post office. At Camp Seafarer Road turn left and promptly face NC-306, right and left. Turn right. There is a First Citizens Bank and Bethesda Christian

Stanly and Spaight Duel

Richard Dobbs Spaight was born from a distinguished colonial family in New Bern on March 25, 1758. He was orphaned at age nine and Governor Arthur Dobbs was one of his guardians. Young Richard was sent to schools in Ireland and to Scotland's University of Glasgow. He returned to New Bern in 1778. From then until his death fourteen years later, on September 6, 1802, he was a superior political activist who followed the political views of Thomas Jefferson. Spaight held honorable roles in civic and educational affairs in New Bern, was a successful farmer, and served as a U.S. congressman as well as three terms as state governor. He was also a military leader and a signer of the U.S. Constitution.

Spaight served in Congress from 1798 to 1801, after which he became a state senator. Taking his place in the U.S. Congress was a Federalist, twenty-eight-year-old John Stanly Jr., also from New Bern. Spaight decided in 1802 to run against Stanly. Serious and hostile campaign rhetoric was exchanged. Spaight challenged his opponent's integrity and charged him as an outright liar. The result was a pistol duel in New Bern on Sunday, September 5, 1802. Senator Spaight was wounded in the fourth round and died the next day. Stanly left New Bern until public feelings against him had declined. When Governor Benjamin Williams learned about all the circumstances, he gave Stanly an official pardon.

Church, founded in 1814. Here, as with other sections of the road shoulders, the centipede grass makes for carpet-like comfortable walking. There is a Clover Farm Food Store at 17.3 miles, and a mini-mart at 17.7 miles. At 19.0 miles is the access road, left, to United Methodist Camp Don Lee and to Camp Carolina. The town limits of Minnesott Beach are at 19.7 miles. A sign directing traffic to Camp Sea Gull is left at 20.8 miles. To the right is Minnesott Beach Campground. You will see some recreation vehicles and campers under the tall pines. Check with Garvin Hardison's office on the street near the river for camping permission (telephone: 252-249-1225). Nearby on NC-306 is the New River Ferry at 21.0 miles. Snacks and drinks are available here. At regular daytime and evening hours the ferry runs every thirty minutes. It takes fifteen minutes to cross the 2.3-mile-wide Neuse River.

CAMPSIDE STORIES: Born in Chinquapin, Duplin County, May 27, 1867, young Caleb Davis Bradham was interested in medicine. At first he attended academies, then the University of North Carolina at the age of nineteen. He transferred to the University of Maryland after three years. Lacking funds he withdrew and came to New Bern to teach at Vance Academy. Later he returned to the University of Maryland and graduated from the College of Pharmacy. Back in New Bern he established Bradham's Pharmacy.

At his soda fountain he enjoyed concocting soft drinks for his customers. One favorite was called "Brad's Drink." In 1898, for no particular reason (unless it was that he believed his concoction with kola nut flavoring would pep up one's spirits), he named it "Pepsi-Cola." He formed the first Pepsi-Cola company in late 1902, had the name trademarked in 1903, and by 1910 there were Pepsi-Cola companies in twenty-four states.

During World War I the price of sugar increased to record high levels and caused Bradham's business to reduce production. After three years of losses, his soft drink company became bankrupt in 1921. He placed the trademark up for sale and returned to his position as a pharmacist. Responding to the sale options was Roy C. Megargel, a New York stockbroker. To save the company he moved it from New Bern to Richmond, Virginia, and later to New York. After eight years of deficits the company experienced a second bankruptcy in 1931. Another effort to save the company was made by Charles Guth, president of the Loft Incorporated chain of stores. He restored financial stability by doubling the bottled drink's volume to twelve ounces for the same price.

From its humble beginnings in New Bern, Pepsi-Cola's 1998 retail sales in 195 countries amounted to $31 billion.

 **FOURTEEN**

CROATAN NATIONAL FOREST
AND CEDAR ISLAND AREA

SECTION 36. Minnesott Beach to Mill Creek in Croatan National Forest

CRAVEN AND CARTERET COUNTIES: (See Craven County discussion in Section 33.) In 1722 Carteret County, with 1,063 square miles (532 on land and 531 of water), the state's third largest county, was formed from part of Craven County. It received its name from John Carteret (1690–1763), one of the area's Lord Proprietors of England. The large coastal county is almost surrounded by water of the Pamlico Sound on the north. On the south are Core and Bogue Sounds and Banks, Onslow Bay, and the Atlantic Ocean. On the west is Croatan National Forest with its Pocosin Wilderness, and on the east is Cedar Island National Wildlife Refuge. The county has multiple rivers, creeks, bays, swamps, marshes, islands, and beaches. Central to the county are many square miles of dense marshes, some canals, and wild and remote tracts labeled as "Open Space" and "Open Grounds" on old maps.

The county seat is at historic Beaufort (not to be confused with Beaufort County farther north, though both are named for Henry Somerset [1684–1714], Duke of Beaufort and one of the Lord Proprietors). Beaufort was incorporated in 1723 on the site of an Indian Village called *Wareicock*, which translates to "fishing village." Among the historic sites are Fort Macon State Park, Cape Lookout National Seashore, and, at Beaufort, the North Carolina Maritime Museum.

LENGTH AND DIFFICULTY: 25.8 miles, moderate (includes 2.3 miles on ferry)
USGS TOPO MAPS: Cherry Point, Newport
FEATURES OR EMPHASIS: Cherry Point on the Neuse River, cypress groves, pocosins, wildlife, remoteness
TRAILS FOLLOWED: Neusiok Trail
TRAIL CONNECTIONS: None
BICYCLE ROUTES FOLLOWED: Part of N.C. Bicycle Route #7 (Ocracoke Option)
WEST TRAILHEAD: Minnesott Beach Campground near NC-36 Ferry

EAST TRAILHEAD: Newport River near Mill Creek in Croatan National Forest

CAMPING, LODGING, AND PROVISIONS: Camping is allowed anywhere in the Croatan National Forest, except at official picnic areas. There are no full-service campgrounds near the Neusiok Trail, except at Military Park (Cherry Point Marine Corps Air Station) in Havelock. Access is 6.7 miles from the trail crossing on NC-101. It has full hook-ups, tent sites, laundry, and motorboat rentals (open all year, telephone: 252-466-4232). Havelock also has motels, of which the nearest (7.0 miles) to the MST is Travel Lodge (telephone: 252-444-2424) on US-70 near the juncture of NC-101 and US-70, a few blocks west of Military Park. In the area you will find a shopping center, grocery stores, and restaurants.

INFORMATION AND SECURITY: Trail Maintenance: Carteret Wildlife Club, 205 Blades Road, Havelock, NC 28532 (telephone: 252-447-4061); Outdoor Adventure Club (OAC, telephone: 252-637-9353); and staff of Croatan National Forest, 141 East Fisher Avenue, New Bern, NC 28560 (telephone: 252-638-5628). (Visiting hours to the forest headquarters are Monday–Friday 8:00 A.M. to 4:30 P.M. It is closed on Saturday and Sunday, but a map rack outside the office has forest information twenty-four hours a day.) New Bern Area Chamber of Commerce: 316 South Front Street (P.O. Drawer C), New Bern, NC 28563 (telephone: 252-637-3111). Havelock Chamber of Commerce: P.O. Box 21, 28532 (telephone: 252-447-1101). Carteret County Chamber of Commerce: 3615 Arendell Street (P.O. Box 1198), Morehead City, NC 28557 (telephone: 252-726-6350). Craven County Sheriff's Office: 411 Craven Street (P.O. Box 1027), New Bern, NC 28563 (telephone: 252-636-6620). Havelock police station (telephone: 252-447-3212). Pamlico County Sheriff's Office: 202 Main Street (P.O. Box 437), Bayboro, NC 28515 (telephone: 252-745-3101). Carteret County Sheriff's Office: P.O. Drawer 239, Beaufort, NC 28516 (telephone: 252-504-4800).

DESCRIPTION: From the beginning of the Mountains-to-Sea Trail concept, the state and the citizen task forces envisioned that the cross-state corridor would have a variety of users. But the major emphasis would be hiking. Some of the back roads could be used for hiking and bicycling. There would be sections in the national forests and parks for hiking, bicycling, and horseback riding on the same trail. For canoeists there could be short sections of the Yadkin River, but more than 200 miles on the Neuse River. Who would be the first canoeists to organize and complete a through-trip adventure on the Neuse? It is now history, chronicled and published (see sidebar).

The Croatan National Forest was designated in 1933 when a purchase unit was established. In 1935, 77,000 acres were acquired. Today it encompasses 159,102 acres and is the most coastal of North Carolina's four na-

Canoeists Chronicle the Neuse

On August 8, 1998, James Eli Shiffer, reporter, and Chuck Liddy, photographer, both of the News and Observer, *began a 235-mile canoeing adventure on the Neuse River. Clothing, maps, food, camping gear, photography supplies, and lap-top computer were packed and ready for the start from Falls of the Neuse Road below the Falls Lake Dam. For eighteen days Shiffer and Liddy maneuvered their canoe through oxbow curves and snake-infested swamps. Their paddling averaged 3 miles an hour, and they camped ten nights on the riverbanks, sand bars, or islands. The major cities along the way were Smithfield, Goldsboro, Kinston, and New Bern.*

There was a climatic ending when Hurricane Bonnie threatened their passage from New Bern to Pamlico Sound. They stored the battered canoe and took a motorboat journey on the remaining 35 miles to a landing in the community of South River. "What we discovered," said Shiffer, "is that the Neuse is a river of multiple personalities, of many faces . . . people told us we were crazy to float down such a stream of pollution . . . a river that runs through everyone's back yard but few consider a pathway to anywhere any more."

Millions of fish have died during recent summers as a result of the microscopic organism Pfiesteria, *mainly in waters between New Bern and Pamlico Sound. Researchers think the organism is linked to the presence of fertilizer, animal waste, human sewage, and other pollutants in the river. But the story of two adventurers from Raleigh had its positives: "peace and quiet," "haven for frogs and herons," "cool refuge," "pink and ivory swamp mallow," and "a living corridor of history."*

tional forests. The forest is almost totally surrounded by the Neuse, Trent, White Oak, and Newport Rivers. Bogue Sound and Bogue Banks separate its southern border from the Atlantic Ocean. The name *Croatan* comes from the Algonquin Indian word for "council town."

Hunting (both big and small game), fishing (both salt- and freshwater), boating, swimming, water skiing, camping, picnicking, and hiking are popular in the national forest. In addition to fishing in the freshwater lakes, saltwater fishing is popular at the lower end of the Neuse River and in the saltwater marshes. Other activities include oystering, crabbing, and flounder gigging. More than ninety species of reptiles and amphibians have been noted in the national forest. Among them are the tiger salamander and the longest snake in the forest, the eastern coachwhip. Poisonous reptiles are the cottonmouth, eastern diamondback, timber, and pigmy rattlesnakes. You should watch for poisonous snakes along the trail, wear hiking boots,

Swamp on a Hill

Within the Croatan National Forest there are 95,000 acres of a vegetation type known as pocosin. Pocosin *is a Native American word that means "swamp on a hill." Actually, a pocosin consists of dense shrubby vegetation over a layer of organic topsoil that has resulted from a series of physiographic and biological changes occurring within the last 9,000 years. Essentially wet upland bogs with black organic muck, pocosins vary in depth from inches at the edge to several feet in the central area. The soil is highly acidic, the vegetation is dense, and generally there is no drainage in at least the lowest sections of a pocosin. In 1984, 31,221 acres of pocosin were designated by Congress as wilderness areas that represent a unique estuarian ecosystem. The largest of these is Pocosin Wilderness (11,709 acres), a tract between NC-24 and the Great Lake area in Craven County. Adjoining the forest is the Cherry Point Marine Corps Air Station. The Marine Corps has proposed twice (1986 and 1994) to establish a combat training base in these wetlands, which are surrounded by wilderness. Both proposals failed when objections were filed by conservationists, with the help of the Southern Environmental Law Center.*

long trousers, and leggings if you are in undergrowth. The bays, swamps, marshes, and creeks provide a haven for migratory ducks and geese. Such birds as egrets, including the snowy egret, flycatchers, woodpeckers, woodcocks, hawks, owls, and osprey may be seen. American alligator, black bear, white-tailed deer, raccoon, gray squirrel, and bald eagle also inhabit the Croatan's forest.

There are large stands of pond, loblolly, and longleaf pines. Common hardwoods are tulip poplar, sweet and tupelo gums, swamp cypress, American holly, and maple. Among the oaks are bluejack, blackjack, and laurel. You will see a wide variety of ferns, mosses, and grasses along the MST route. Wildflowers include the bright red pine lily, orchids, gaillardia, and wild ginger. Some of the shrubs you will see are titi, fetterbush, gallberry, wax myrtle, and honeycup.

Croatan National Forest has eight trails on its inventory, all of which are classified as hiking trails; but some are unused or closed and none connect for longer networking. I have written a detailed description of the forest trails and recreational areas in *North Carolina Hiking Trails*, 3rd edition. In May 1990 the 20.9-mile Neusiok Trail was dedicated by the N.C. Division of Parks and Recreation as a section of the Mountains-to-Sea Trail. Because of the sensitive soft soils and mosses, it is for foot traffic only. For bicyclists and

ATV/ORV riders, the forest roads with dry or hard marl surface provide a recreational option. Equestrians should contact the Croatan National Forest office before riding any of the roads, such as those in current use, abandoned logging roads, swamp roads, or gated roads. Primitive campsites may be set up anywhere along the MST route, with the exception of picnic areas such as Pinecliff Picnic Area. You will need to carry your own drinking water. You should also carry insect repellent and all-weather hiking gear. It is also recommended that you not hike alone, and that you avoid this section during hurricanes. You will see a few MST signs and white-dot blazes, but more often there will be aluminum tags nailed to the trees. Watch for these signs and be reminded that once you are lost, all of nature around you looks alike.

After crossing the Neuse River on the Minnesott–Cherry Branch Ferry for 2.3 miles, follow NC-306 south. At 1.2 miles turn right on Pinecliff Road (FR-132), a gravel road entrance to Pinecliff Picnic Area in Croatan National Forest at 2.6 miles. The gated area is open from 8 A.M. to 8 P.M. April through October, but walking in to use the trail is allowed from November through March as well. Camping is not allowed in the picnic area. From the parking area enter the picnic area, pass a sanitary facility, and follow signs or blazes to a boardwalk. (If the boardwalk is washed away or under water, go right to the beach and continue upriver.) Follow the beach among scenic cypress groves and Spanish moss. Ahead can be seen the Cherry Point U.S. Marine Corps Air Station. Watch carefully to the left; at 4.0 miles leave the beach to ascend steps. Follow an erratic path through hardwoods and pines. Glimpses of Handcock Creek can be seen through the trees, right, at 4.6 miles. Pass left of a bog cove at 4.9 miles, and cross a swamp at 5.3 miles on a boardwalk. This boardwalk and most of the ones ahead were constructed by the Cherry Point and Carteret County Wildlife Club; in more recent years the Outdoor Adventure Club of New Bern's Recreation Department has built bridges. Assistance from national forest staff has been provided to the two volunteer groups. Pass right of a U.S. Forest Service road at 5.5 miles. Cross a boardwalk through another swamp among palmetto at 5.7 miles. You will notice on the banks near the boardwalks that the forest has an unusual display of wildflowers, some that you have seen in the upper piedmont or mountains, such as galax, trailing arbutus, and wild ginger. Others are downy foxglove, partridgeberry, strawberry bush, orchids; more coastal is the marsh pennywort. Mixed with the wildflowers are ferns, highbush blueberry, and witch-hazel. Oak, black gum, dogwood, and beech are prominent hardwoods. To enhance this natural wonder are the sounds and sights of songbirds, hummingbirds, and owls. Make a sharp left at 6.2 miles to

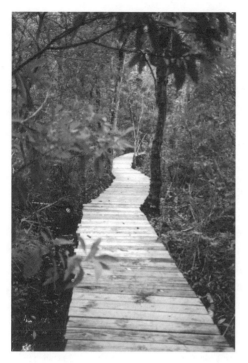

Mountains-to-Sea Trail following Neusiok Trail through Croatan National Forest

avoid a wide swamp, but cross a boardwalk over it and a tributary to Ca-hoogue Creek at 7.0 miles. Turn right on an old field road bordered with loblolly pine at 7.1 miles, and enter a swamp with a boardwalk at 7.9 miles. Follow the edge of a hardwood timber cut and cross two boardwalks at 8.2 miles and 8.3 miles. At 8.6 miles is a grove of large beech trees and holly. For the next 0.6 miles follow an old road through pines; reach a gated forest road that exits to NC-306, right and left, at 9.2 miles. (It is 2.0 miles right on NC-306 to NC-101.) Across the road is a parking area for trail users.

Cross the road and follow a footpath through dense undergrowth and tall pines. At 9.5 miles cross a boardwalk and follow an old field road bordered with loblolly and pond pine. At 10.8 miles turn sharply right onto an old forest road. Cross FR-136 (which goes 1.0 mile right to NC-101) and continue through the forest. At 11.2 miles begin a 0.8-mile section of tall oaks and pines and patches of sensitive fern. Reach NC-101 at 12.0 miles. (It is 6.7 miles right on NC-101 to Military Park [Campground] in Havelock and another 0.3 miles to a Travel Lodge motel and shopping center, as described above in "Camping, Lodging, and Provisions." To the left on NC-101 it is 2.1 miles to North Harlowe, where you will find a store with groceries, gasoline, and telephone.)

After crossing NC-101 and entering a beautiful open savanna of longleaf pine, notice the undergrowth of yaupon, bracken, beard grass, and Christmas fern. Cross a 300-foot boardwalk at 12.8 miles to a hardwood forest. A 150-foot boardwalk is at 13.3 miles. Here is a juncture where the trail continues left through a pine forest (or goes right for 0.1 mile to Billfinger Road [FR-147]). The trail meanders through a former timber cut with tall pines scattered throughout. The dense undergrowth ranges from young pines, weeds, grasses, broomsedge, and wildflowers. In damp sunlit places there are carnivorous plants such as sundews. This strip of the MST is periodically bush-hogged by Forest Service staff. Blazes may be scarce but the cut through the dense growth should be well defined. Exit at Billfinger Road (FR-147) at 14.8 miles. (If at the juncture near the boardwalk you find this section overgrown and not safe to follow, take the 0.1-mile path option to the right to Billfinger Road. Turn left and continue on it for 1.4 miles to juncture with the route mentioned above.) It is 0.2 miles farther to a juncture with Little Deep Creek Road (FR-169) at 15.0 miles. (To the left on Little Deep Creek Road it is 1.1 miles north to NC-101 at North Harlowe. A grocery store is right [east].)

To continue on the Neusiok Trail (MST), turn right on Little Deep Creek Road and hike south on the road for 1.9 miles to where the trail turns left on a footbridge over a ditch at 16.9 miles. (If you come to a gate across the road, you have gone too far; backtrack and look carefully for the footbridge and a sign.) Enter a dense forest of loblolly pine, wax myrtle, bay trees, maple, titi, sweet gum, greenbrier, and yellow jessamine. Trail blazes are small metal tags nailed to trees. After 0.8 miles begin to follow left of a small canal. Pass a damp area that drains into Money Island Swamp at 18.0 miles. After another 0.2 miles enter a more open area with small pines and switch cane. At 19.0 miles turn east (left) to parallel Alligator Tram Road (FR-124) for 0.5 miles before crossing it at 19.5 miles. (This road is gated to the right, west, where it accesses Weyerhauser Paper Company property. To the left, east, the road is 1.8 miles to Old Windberry Road [may be called Bill Road], SR-1155. North from there it is 1.3 miles to a juncture with NC-101; south from there it is 2.3 miles to the community of Mill Creek and a juncture with Mill Creek Road [also called Newport Road], SR-1154.)

After crossing Alligator Tram Road, enter and pass through a dense area of undergrowth for 0.6 miles. Begin passage into an open longleaf pine forest at 20.1 miles. Follow an old road, used frequently by hunters, through sections of switch cane, pitcher plants, bracken, and other ferns. Deer may be seen in this area. Cross two small drains of Mill Creek at 21.1 miles and 21.5 miles. Pass a trash dump, leave the old road, and descend slightly to cross Mill Creek Road (SR-1154) (also called Newport Road or Orange Street) at 21.9 miles. Here you have an option. You could backtrack enough into the forest for camping. You could cross the road to the trail sign and white blazes to complete another 1.6 miles to the end of this section at 23.5 miles. Here at the south terminus of the Neusiok Trail is the isolated Newport River parking area. (Access to the parking area is on FR-181 for 1.1 miles from Mill Creek Road, near where you started the final 1.6 miles of the trail.)

CAMPSIDE STORIES: Your trip on the Neusiok Trail of the MST in Croatan National Forest is the most isolated part of your journey since you passed through Pisgah National Forest in the mountains. Blackwater swamps, Spanish moss, water moccasins, and wildlife noises in the darkness create a good setting for ghost stories. One such story is the one about the Traveling Swamp Girl. She has been seen on back roads of the Great Dismal Swamp in Virginia/North Carolina, near Little Creek Swamp in the Croatan National Forest, in the Congaree Swamp in South Carolina, and in the Okefenokee Swamp of Georgia.

The stories vary in period of history, but the timing is always at night, usually with moonlight. The ghost has a shawl and is carrying a suitcase or traveling bag. The girl in the Croatan originates from 1846, before it was a national forest and before Mill Pond had been constructed on waters from Money Island Swamp. The story goes that two drivers of a covered wagon saw a lonely girl dressed in black and carrying a suitcase. They halted and offered her help. She spoke not a word as she was lifted into the wagon and the flap cords were made secure. But by the time they approached a crossroads near what is now Newport she had vanished.

A similar story was reported in 1891 on the Suwannee Canal Road at the Okefenokee Swamp in Georgia. In 1946 a hunter saw a veiled girl walking west on Yellowjacket Road near Darlington Swamp in South Carolina. When he stopped his truck to ask if she needed help, she disappeared. In 1962 Nancy Roberts described a similar story in *Ghosts of the Carolinas*. In this story a husband and wife meet a veiled girl near the Congaree Swamp who wishes a ride to Columbia. After she is inside the two-door car, she gives the woman an address in Columbia. Later, when the woman notices that the passenger is not responding to her conversation, she looks behind her. The swamp girl has vanished. When the husband goes to the address given him by the girl, a young man comes to the door and says he knows why the driver has come. He says the girl is his sister who was killed in a car crash near Congaree Swamp. She reappears each anniversary of her death.

SECTION 37. Mill Creek at the Croatan National Forest to Cedar Island and the Ocracoke Ferry

CARTERET COUNTY: See Carteret County discussion in Section 36.

LENGTH AND DIFFICULTY: 44.7 miles, easy

USGS TOPO MAPS: New Port, Core Creek, Williston, Davis, Long Bay, Atlantic, North Bay

FEATURES OR EMPHASIS: Marshlands, bays, causeways, islands, hammocks, and Cedar Island National Wildlife Refuge

TRAILS FOLLOWED: None

BICYCLE ROUTES FOLLOWED: N.C. Bicycle Route #7 (Ocracoke Option)

TRAIL CONNECTIONS: None

WEST TRAILHEAD: In community of Mill Creek at juncture with Neusoik Trail

EAST TRAILHEAD: Cedar Island Campground

CAMPING, LODGING, AND PROVISIONS: There are three campgrounds on this long coastal section: In Part A is A and J Avent Park at Otway (no telephone); in Part B is Cedar Creek Campground at Sealevel (telephone: 252-225-9571). The latter has full-service hook-ups, tent sites, picnic area, hot showers, and boat dock. In Part C is Driftwood Campground at Cedar Island (telephone: 252-225-4851). It has tent sites, picnic tables, and hot showers, but no hook-ups. Driftwood Motel is also here (telephone: 252-225-4861). Along the way on all parts of the journey are sufficient but scattered grocery stores.

INFORMATION AND SECURITY: Trail Maintenance: Except for 3.5 miles on Bill Road from Mill Creek to NC-101, this section is part of the Ocracoke Option Bicycle Route #7 east to its end at Cedar Island. Carteret County Chamber of Commerce: 3615 Arendell Street (P.O. Box 1198), Morehead City, NC 28557 (telephone: 252-726-6350). Carteret County Sheriff's Office: P.O. Drawer 239, Beaufort, NC 28516 (telephone: 252-504-4800).

DESCRIPTION: For the next 44.6 miles you will gain an up-close acquaintance with tidal North Carolina. You will cross bridge after bridge over the inlets, see horizon after horizon of water that looks like the Atlantic Ocean. But the water is more tranquil because it is Core Sound, which is protected by Core Banks, a long boundary of beach, yaupon, and cedar, and hundreds of sound side islands. It, like some of the ground under your feet in Cedar Island National Wildlife Refuge, is environmentally guarded by the Cape Lookout National Seashore on Shackleford and Core Banks. You will see marshes, some deep in brackish water, stretching as far as you can see from arched bridges. The breezes will be flavored with degrees of salt and wax myrtle, a type of preparation for your double ferry ride and long hike on the Cape Hatteras National Seashore. Outside of nature's endless sameness and changes you will also see examples of human adaptation. There will be the small houses of citizens with meager incomes and the expensive retreats of the wealthy. There will be fertile fields for limited agriculture, and shrimp boat nets folded at anchor. At the corner service stations you may meet local residents and the state's tourists on their way to fish, hunt, or take a shortcut by ferry to Ocracoke. You may wish to make part of this section a vacation. If so, the section is divided into three parts to offer a campsite or motel for overnights.

PART A: If you are leaving from the south terminus of the the Neusiok Trail at the Newport River, return to Mill Creek Road (SR-1154) and turn right for 0.2 miles to the Mill Creek community. From the intersection turn north on Old Winberry Road (SR-1155) (also called Bill Road) and pass Alligator Tram Road (FR-124), left, at 2.2 miles. Reach the juncture with NC-101 at 3.5 miles. On the left side of the juncture is space for parking if you are arranging a shuttle. (Ahead it is 1.5 miles to Harlowe for groceries, gasoline, and a telephone.) Turn right and cross a bridge over Harlowe Canal to follow a straight road. Pass Coastal Carolina Tree Farm, left, and reach the community of Core Creek at 6.6 miles. Cross a bridge over Adams Creek Canal (the Intracoastal Waterway). Curve south and at 8.4 miles turn left on Laurel Road (SR-1163). There are cabbage farms in this area, scattered residences, and vegetable garden crops such as cabbage and corn. At 10.6 miles reach a T-intersection; turn right on Merrimon Road (SR-1300) and arrive at North River Corner community at 13.0 miles. Here is a juncture with US-70, right and left. Turn left (east), where there is a mini-mart. (To the right, south, it is 4.0 miles on US-70 to the historic town of Beaufort.) Pass through marshland on both sides of the road.

At 14.0 miles is a long bridge over the North River. (The river begins in marshes from the north and flows south about 12 miles to merge with waters of The Straits, north of Harkers Island and Back Sound.) In the community of Bettie is a small medical center. Woodville Missionary Baptist Church (1843) is on the left. To the right is a decoy crafts shop named Lucky Ducks. Also to the right are residences and tomato farms. Bettie Farm Strawberries is left (telephone: 252-726-2678). Cross an inlet bridge over Ward Creek at 16.2 miles. Otway Free Will Baptist Church is left. (One of its signs has been "Love seeks not limits, but outlets.") Arrive at A and J Avent Park, on the left at 16.7 miles. It has hook-ups and tent sites in a pecan grove. (Ahead it is 0.5 miles to a BP service station.)

PART B: Continue from the campground and arrive at a BP service station at 0.5 miles, left. Pass three cemeteries near the road. At 1.1 miles come to Tee Dee Food Store #6, an Exxon service station, a hardware store, and a sign that states "Core Sound Waterfowl Museum, Harkers Island." At 2.1 miles is Smyrna Texaco station, Handy House Convenience Store, S & R Supermarket, and Smyrna Post Office. Smyrna Missionary Baptist Church (1929) is left. Pass Williston United Methodist Church on the left, and then cross a bridge over Williston Creek and cypress groves at 4.9 miles. Pass through marshland at 6.3 miles. Cross another inlet bridge at 7.1 miles. Arrive in the community of Davis at 8.5 miles, where on the left you will find a Texaco/ Handy House Convenience Store. There is a picnic shelter across the road. Ahead at 8.9 miles is Davis Post Office. There is another inlet bridge over Ouster Creek at 10.0 miles. From here you have exceptionally scenic views of the marshland to the horizon. Cross another inlet bridge at Brett Bay at 11.7 miles.

At 12.0 miles enter the community of Stacy (a sign states the population is 305). There is a shop for hand-carved decoys and a post office at 13.0 miles. After crossing a bridge over Salters Creek at 16.1 miles, arrive at a juncture with NC-12, left, at 16.5 miles. US-70 continues to the right. If you are not stopping here to visit the town of Sealevel and Atlantic, or to stay at Cedar Creek Campground, continue left on NC-12. (If you turn right, it is 1.5 miles on US-70 to a right turn on Cedar Creek Road, and another 0.3 miles to Cedar Creek Campground and Marina (telephone: 252-225-9571). (See "Camping, Lodging, and Provisions.") (In Sealevel there is a medical center, pharmacy, and bank.)

PART C: From Cedar Creek Campground and Marina return to NC-12 and turn right. You will notice that vehicular traffic has become light. The straight highway has grassy shoulders for easy walking. At 2.0 miles is a grocery store, followed by marshland in Cedar Island National Wildlife Refuge. Cross a bridge over Thorofare Bay with scenic water and marsh combinations at 2.6 miles. Continue through Cedar Island National Wildlife Refuge. There are places where water laps the shoulder of the road. In the marshes are herons, egrets, and gulls. After the highway turns north to parallel Cedar Island Bay there are more water oaks and white cedars. Residences are more frequent and the highway weaves between them. At 8.0 miles there is less marshland. Eastern red-cedar, Atlantic white cedar, and yaupon grow along the roadside. Arrive at the Cedar Island Ferry area at 11.5 miles. Here you will find the Cedar Island Post Office, a grocery store, a restaurant, and the Driftwood Motel (telephone: 252-225-4861). To the right of the entrance is Driftwood Campground (described under "Camping, Lodging, and Provisions"). Near the campground and at the beach is White Sands (equestrian) Trail Rides.

CAMPSIDE STORIES: Of all the stories about the flamboyant pirate Blackbeard

North Carolina Ferry System

Of North Carolina's nearly 1,000-mile Mountains-to-Sea Trail, 33 miles lie uniquely over coastal waters. Passage is on three of the state's seven ferry routes: 2.3 miles from Minnesott Beach to Cherry Branch near the confluence of the Neuse River and Pamlico Sound, 26.6 miles from Cedar Island to Ocracoke Island, and 4.1 miles from Ocracoke Island to Hatteras near the Atlantic Ocean on the island's south shore.

There are twenty-four ferry vessels in the fleet, which is the largest on the Atlantic Coast. (The state of Washington has the largest fleet on the Pacific Coast.) Each vessel has a name; examples are Kinnakeet, Ocracoke, Herbert C. Bonner, Cedar Island, Governor James Baxter Hunt Jr., Chicamacomico, *and the most recently named,* Southport. *The vessels bear the school colors of the state's sixteen public universities. Ferry size ranges from 122 to 220 feet in length. The general speed is 10 knots (about 11.5 miles per hour). In 1999 the fleet transported 1,032,755 motor vehicles (cars, buses, and trucks), and 2,474,686 passengers. The highest vessel capacity is fifty cars on the Cedar Island to Ocracoke passage, and the lowest vessel capacity is 18 cars on the Currituck to Knotts Island passage. All seven ferry locations have state bicycle route connections, and four of the seven have free fares.*

This method of transportation dates back to 1924 when private ferry owners transported passengers and freight across Oregon Inlet. In 1934 the state Highway Commission began to subsidize and expand the system, and in 1947 the state formed the N.C. Ferry Division of the N.C. Department of Transportation.

(Edward Teach), none is more gruesome than the story of the last day of his life, November 22, 1718. For years Blackbeard, a mercantile byproduct of the War of Spanish Succession, pillaged sea vessels, murdered their crews, and stole cargo from the West Indies and along the coast of the Carolinas and Virginia. He successfully persuaded the British Royal governor Charles Eden of North Carolina to provide him and his minions sanctuary within Pamlico Sound (some stories have it as Ocracoke Inlet) in exchange for stolen goods and gold.

Stories circulated from escaped sailors about the fearsome appearance of Blackbeard: his ebony head of hair and thick beard, his burly and brazen leaps in colorful attire, his blood-curdling screams, his two-foot knife between his teeth, and his flashing sword when capturing ships. Many say that on his last day he and his men boarded the HMS *Pearl*, commanded by Lieutenant Robert Maynard, who had been sent there by Virginia's Governor Spotswood. Twenty-nine crew members were murdered. Unable to find a commander, Blackbeard and his pirates left. They returned later and re-boarded the ship. Lieutenant Maynard, who had been hiding, appeared and shot Blackbeard in the head, cut off his head, and threw his body in the ocean. Another version of the story, one often recounted in history books, says that Lieutenant Maynard boarded Teach's sloop, engaged in hand-to-hand combat, and shot Blackbeard dead.

Some witnesses claimed they saw Blackbeard's headless body swim around the ship before disappearing. As the years passed, the claim was further exaggerated from one to three and even to seven times around the ship.

FIFTEEN

CAPE HATTERAS NATIONAL SEASHORE
AND JOCKEY'S RIDGE STATE PARK

SECTION 38. Cedar Island to Cape Hatteras National Seashore, to Jockey's Ridge State Park

CARTERET, HYDE, AND DARE COUNTIES: (See Carteret County discussion in Section 36.) Hyde County was named about 1712 to honor Governor Edward Hyde, who died in 1712. The county seat, incorporated in 1903, is at Swan Quarter, a village south of Lake Mattamuskeet and on the north side of Pamlico Sound. The name, it is said, honors Samuel F. Swann, an early settler. With 1,364 square miles, of which 730 are in water, it is the state's largest county. On the south of Swan Quarter is Swanquarter National Wildlife Refuge, and across Pamlico Sound are Cape Hatteras National Seashore and Ocracoke Island. To reach the latter, there is a ferry ride of two and one-half hours from Swan Quarter. Lake Mattamuskeet and Pocosin Lakes National Wildlife Refuges are located north of Swan Quarter. Through the county's northern boundary is the Intracoastal Waterway on the Pungo and Alligator River Canals. Major highways north-south are NC-45 and NC-94; the major east-west route US-264.

Dare County has 1,246 square miles, making it the second largest county in the state. It was named for Virginia Dare, the first child born (August 18, 1587) to English settlers in America. Out of that large total, 858 square miles are water. The county is almost surrounded by either sounds and bays or the Atlantic Ocean. Only 10 miles of its western boundary are on land that connects with Hyde County. Its western waters are Pamlico, Croatan, Roanoke, Albermarle, and Currituck Sounds. Its most famous island is Roanoke Island. In 1870 the county was formed from sections of Hyde, Tyrrell, and Currituck Counties. The county seat is Manteo, on Roanoke Island. Permanently settled in 1865 and incorporated in 1899, it was named for the Indian chief Manteo, who was transported to England in 1584 by Englishmen Philip Amadas and Arthur Barlowe of Sir Walter Raleigh's fleet.

Among the county's major historic and environmental sites are Cape Hatteras National Seashore, Cape Hatteras Lighthouse, Pea Island National Wildlife Refuge, Oregon Inlet, Bodie Island Lighthouse, Fort Raleigh National Historic Site, Elizabethan Gardens, Elizabeth II, Jockey's Ridge State Park, Nags Head Woods Preserve, and Wright Brothers National Memorial. Access to the county is on highway NC-10 and part of Alternate US-158, running north-south; the major east-west route is US-64/264.

LENGTH AND DIFFICULTY: 111.4 miles (or option of 111.1 miles), of which 30.7 miles are by ferries; easy to moderate

USGS TOPO MAPS: North Bay, Portsmouth, Ocracoke, Howard Reef, Green Island, Hatteras, Cape Hatteras, Buxton, Little Kinnakeet, Rodanthe, Pea Island, Oregon Inlet, Roanoke Island

FEATURES OR EMPHASIS: Seafowl, plant life, Atlantic seashore, dunes, freshwater lakes, historic sites, lighthouses, bays, inlets, hammocks, shoals, fishing sites, ferries

TRAILS FOLLOWED: Cape Hatteras Beach Trail, Bodie Island Dike Trail

TRAIL CONNECTIONS: Ocracoke Boardwalk Trail, Hammock Hills Nature Trail, Buxton Woods Nature Trail, North Pond Interpretive Trail, Tracks in the Sand Trail

WEST TRAILHEAD: At Cedar Island Ferry Dock

EAST TRAILHEAD: Jockey's Ridge State Park Visitor Center and top of sand dome

CAMPGROUNDS, LODGING, AND PROVISIONS: Cape Hatteras National Seashore has designated campgrounds: Ocracoke, on Ocracoke Island; Frisco and Cape Point, on Hatteras Island; and Oregon Inlet, on Bodie Island. They usually open the last weekend in March and close after Labor Day weekend in September or later. The campgrounds have modern restrooms, potable water, unheated showers, grills, and tables. There are not any utility connections. Reservations can be made only for the Ocracoke Campground (telephone: 800-365-CAMP). Credit cards can be used to pay fees.

There are other, commercial campgrounds. Those near the MST are listed here along with the national park campgrounds. Some of the nearest motels along or near the MST are listed here or on your approach to them. Campgrounds: Driftwood Campground at Cedar Island (telephone: 252-225-9571); Ocracoke, Frisco, and Oregon Inlet National Park Service Campgrounds (telephone: 252-473-2111). Motels: Driftwood Motel at Cedar Island (telephone: 252-225-9571); on Ocracoke Island, the Island Inn (telephone: 252-928-4351) and Blackbeard's Lodge (telephone: 252-928-3421); on Hatteras Island, The Sea Gull Motel (telephone: 252-986-2550); at Buxton, the Cape Hatteras Hotel (telephone: 252-995-5611); at Rodanthe, Hatteras Island Resort (telephone: 252-987-2345 or 800-331-6541); at Nags Head, Quality Inn (telephone: 252-441-7126 or 800-228-5151).

INFORMATION AND SECURITY: Trail Maintenance: Cape Hatteras National Seashore staff and volunteers. Carteret County Chamber of Commerce: 3615 Arendell Street (P.O. Box 1198), Moorehead City, NC 28557 (telephone: 252-726-6350). Carteret County Sheriff's Office: P.O. Drawer 239, Beaufort, NC 28516 (telephone: 252-504-4800). Hyde County Sheriff's Office: P.O. Box 189, Swan Quarter, NC 27885 (telephone: 252-926-3171). Dare County Tourist Bureau: P.O. Box 399, Manteo, NC 27954 (telephone: 252-473-2138). Ocracoke Museum and Visitor Center (telephone: 252-928-4531). Outer Banks Chamber of Commerce: Ocean Bay Boulevard and Mustian Street (P.O. Box 1757), Kill Devil Hills, NC 27948 (telephone: 252-441-8144). Dare County Sheriff's Office: 300 Elizabeth Avenue (P.O. Box 757), Manteo, NC 27954. Cedar Island, Ocracoke, and Hatteras Ferries (telephone: 800-293-3779 for information, routes, schedules, reservations). Cape Hatteras National Seashore: Route 1, Box 675, Manteo, NC 27954 (telephone: 252-473-2111) (Information Center, telephone: 252-441-6644). Hatteras Island Visitor Center (telephone: 252-995-4474). Pea Island National Wildlife Refuge: P.O. Box 150, Rodanthe, NC 27968 (telephone: 252-987-2394). Bodie Lighthouse Station and Visitor Center (telephone: 252-441-5711). Jockey's Ridge State Park: P.O. Box 592, Nags Head, NC 27959 (telephone: 252-441-7132).

DESCRIPTION: This section of the MST includes chains of barrier islands east of Pamlico Sound that are frequently referred to as the Outer Banks. The reefs beyond are often called the "Graveyard of the Atlantic." The offshore areas have two ocean currents near Diamond Shoals that are used as shipping lanes and which are hazardous for those navigating the seas. More than 600 ships have fallen victim to the shallow shoals, winds, and storms over the past 400 years. Cape Hatteras itself has 30,318 acres of sandy Atlantic beaches, dunes, and marshlands. It was the nation's first national seashore. Authorized as a park by Congress on August 17, 1937, the islands are havens for more than 300 species of migratory and permanent shorebirds. Major shore fish are flounder, bluefish, and spot; offshore species are marlin, dolphin, mackerel, and tuna.

For hikers on the MST there are infrequent signs and blazes. If at any time you lose the route described ahead, remember that NC-12 begins in Ocracoke and goes north to parallel US-158 for an entrance to Jockey's Ridge State Park, the Atlantic end of the MST journey.

Other important information about Cape Hatteras National Seashore follows. If you are bicycling on part of this section, use the bicycle space on the shoulders of NC-12 rather than attempting the beach areas. Bicycling is prohibited on nature trails of the national park. Examples are Hammock Hills Nature Trail on Ocracoke Island, Buxton Woods Nature Trail on

Hatteras Island, and Bodie Island Dike Trail on Bodie Island. If you wish to swim on the beaches, it is wise to choose only beaches with lifeguards, such as Ocracoke, Frisco, and Coquina. Tides, rip currents, and strong waves make ocean swimming dangerous. To obtain current weather conditions, telephone 252-473-5665 or 252-995-5610. Hikers using tents should use stronger tents and longer stakes than usual for protection against the sand and wind. Protection against sunburn and insects is essential.

Cape Hatteras National Seashore also administers two other area parks. The Wright Brothers National Memorial (9.0 miles north of the US-64/NC-12 intersection at Whalebone Junction) is a 431-acre memorial museum to Wilbur and Orville Wright, who on December 17, 1903, were the first to successfully achieve air flight with machine power. The other park is the Fort Raleigh National Historic Site (8.0 miles west of Whalebone Junction on US-64). It was designated as a historic site on April 5, 1941, and covers 346 acres, which includes parts of the settlements made in 1585 and 1587. The Lindsay Warren Visitor Center displays excavated artifacts, and other exhibits tell the story of Sir Walter Raleigh's "lost colony." In addition, the park includes a reconstruction of Fort Raleigh, the Waterside Theatre (which in the summer presents Paul Green's symphonic outdoor drama of the "Lost Colony"), an Elizabethan Garden maintained by the Garden Club of North Carolina, and the Thomas Hariot Trail. The trail is a 0.3-mile interpretive loop with signs about the plant life that Hariot found in the area in 1585. It begins at the visitor center.

I have listed this long section's difficulty as easy to moderate. I consider it moderate because there are miles and miles of soft sand that can impede easy walking. Additionally, you are without refuge from inclement weather, gale winds, and storms. Off-beach sections have insects that can make the hike anything but pleasant in hot weather. Other than the beach you will follow short sections that climb dunes with sea oats and beach holly and pass through forests of live and laurel oaks, pine, and sweet bay, salt marshes of sedge and cordgrass, and road shoulders. Although you will have spanned some rivers and inlets on high bridges, none compares to the experience and scenic beauty of the 2.4 miles on the Oregon Inlet Bridge. In viewing waterfowl you are likely to see many species—ones such as swans, geese, ducks, gulls, egrets, terns, herons, and migratory and permanent shorebirds. In the maritime forests some of the songbirds are crested flycatchers, prothonotary warblers, and Carolina wrens.

This section is divided into five parts; each is of a length that I consider adequate for a day's hike. Using a combination of motels and campgrounds, you could extend the journey to include time visiting historic sites and

> **Surf Zone Runners**
>
> There is a special place on the beach that is popular for walking. It is near the surf zone where the impacted sand is sparkling wet from the ebb and flow of waves. It is also a place where for one moment the sand appears lifeless, yet then it is suddenly full of life when a retreating wave reveals scurrying mole crabs. This place is also popular with running flocks of tiny sanderlings (shorebirds) searching for food. Gray and white and weighing only three ounces, the black-legged sanderlings are fast runners and fliers. They usually fly in unison, swinging away up and down the beach like aeronautical gymnasts.
>
> Sometimes you will see sanderlings running with other shorebird companions, ruddy turnstones (also called calico birds because of their black, white, and brown plumage patches). The ruddy turnstones are slightly larger than the sanderlings, and they search a wider zone of the beach for their food. Other areas of the beach may provide worms, small mollusks, and beach fleas. Occasionally, a larger shorebird, the speckled black, white, and brown willets, will be seen with the sanderlings and ruddy turnstones. They will scream and dive toward you when they think you are too close to their nests. Both sanderlings and ruddy turnstones take long remarkable flights to Arctic zones for breeding and nesting.

enjoying the beach environment without walking the full day. Part A begins at Cedar Island.

PART A: The ferry to Ocracoke leaves Cedar Island nine times daily from late May to October 1, the earliest at 7:00 A.M. and the latest at 8:30 P.M. Fall and winter crossings are less frequent, usually ranging between four to six times daily. (In 1998, the fee for a hiker was $1; for a bicyclist it was $2.) After boarding the ferry, which takes about two and one-half hours to cross from Cedar Island to Ocracoke (26.6 miles), you will pass north of Cape Lookout National Seashore. About three-fourths of the distance you may see Portsmouth Island to the south. Upon arriving in Ocracoke you have a choice of lodging, as listed under "Camping, Lodging, and Provisions." There are also restaurants, grocery stores, and beach stores for clothing and beach supplies. Ocracoke Campground is at 4.7 miles ahead. From the Ocracoke ferry dock, walk 1.3 miles to the edge of town and begin the 75.8 miles of the Cape Hatteras Beach Trail. You are on NC-12, but after 0.5 miles turn right to ORV ramp #70 near the Ocracoke Airstrip to the seashore and cross the dunes on a boardwalk. Turn left and reach ORV ramp #68 at 4.7 miles. At the ramp is access to the National Park Service's Ocracoke Campground. At 9.0 miles to

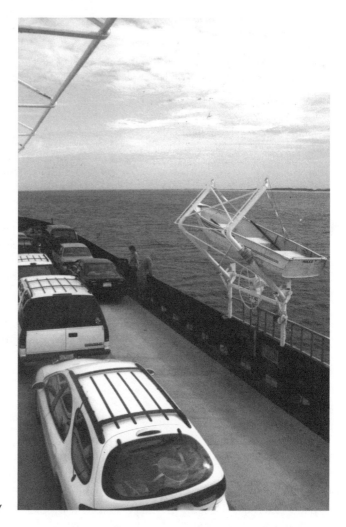

Ocracoke Island Ferry

the left and over the dunes it is 100 yards to a parking area. A short hike on NC-12 leads to the observation deck for the Pony Pen, where you can view the island's wild ponies. (Because an infectious disease outbreak occurred among the ponies in the mid-1990s, and it became necessary to euthanize some herds, you may not see any here at this time.)

There is another parking area on NC-12 for dune access at 10.6 miles. (From that parking area you could go a few yards northeast to another parking area to hike the 0.8-mile-loop Hammock Hills Nature Trail. Along it you can see groundsel, yaupon, and prickly ash. There is also a salt marsh with cordgrass and black needlerush. You may see herons, black skimmers, and woodpeckers.) Watch for an access to leave the beach and dunes at 13.8

miles to a parking area on NC-12. Turn right and walk the shoulder of the road for 0.6 miles to the ferry dock. Crossing the Hatteras Inlet to Hatteras Island on the ferry takes about forty minutes (it is 4.1 miles). Because of the volume of traffic, the ferries leave every half-hour from 5 A.M. to at least 11 P.M. From November 1 to April 30, the ferries leave every hour, or more frequently if necessary. During the crossing you may see a few sand dunes in Pamlico Sound with waterfowl, and to the south you may have views of the southwest tip of Hatteras Island.

After docking, you will have choices of restaurants, grocery stores, and motels. (See "Camping, Lodging, and Provisions.") Access to the beach from NC-12 is in 0.1 mile; turn right at a beach parking lot. Pass ORV ramp #55 at 14.6 miles. On the seashore, hike 6.0 miles, passing a fishing pier on the way, and turn off left to ramp #47 at 20.6 miles. Follow a 0.2-mile boardwalk to the entrance of the National Park Service's Frisco Campground at 20.8 miles. (Once you enter the campground property, it is 0.1 mile left to the campground entrance station. It is another 1.1 miles on a paved road to NC-12 and the Frisco Post Office and restaurants.) If you are staying at the campground, check in at the entrance station. Road and campsite parking are paved. The campsites are not shaded by trees, but there are patches of yaupon and beach holly with ground cover of pennywort and yellow cactus.

PART B: To begin Part B of your beach journey consider the distance from the boardwalk trail near the entrance gate of the Frisco Campground and follow the paved loop road to its easternmost curve at 0.3 miles. Here is a gate and a sign for the Mountains-to-Sea Trail. Enter and follow the sandy Open Pond Road into the island's largest forest. Pines, holly, oaks, and yaupon are prominent. Pass an open area of dunes at 2.6 miles. Pass a lake that is on the north side at 2.7 miles. At 2.8 miles reach a juncture with a road to the right, but continue ahead. Cross a small stream at 2.9 miles. Continue through a dense forest and approach a paved road at 4.2 miles. On the left and in the forest before the road is a cemetery with the following World War II memorials: "Unknown sailor of British Royal Navy, 1942, body found May, 1942" and "Michael Cairns of British Merchant Navy, body found May, 1942." Keep left on the paved road.

(To the right but across the paved road is a camp trailer disposal system. On the right of it the paved road is 0.2 miles to the Cape Hatteras Coast Guard Station, right, followed by an entrance to Cape Point Campground, right, at 0.8 miles. Ahead for another 0.1 mile is ORV ramp #44 and the seashore.) Continuing on the MST, pass the National Park Service maintenance area on the left, which is followed by a picnic and parking area on the

Cape Hatteras Lighthouse

The Mountains-to-Sea Trail passes beside the famous Cape Hatteras Lighthouse. Built in 1870, it is the tallest brick lighthouse in the nation—198 feet from base to tip. Formerly using Fresnel lenses, its high wattage light is similar to an airport beacon now. Signal distance is 20 miles with a white flash every 7.5 seconds. The black and white painted spiral on the outside is in keeping with its inside spiral steps. There are nine staircase landings. For MST hikers this is the highest climb since a shorter fire tower between Cove City and New Bern.

This is not the first Cape Hatteras Lighthouse. In 1803 a 90-foot tower was constructed, and in 1850 another 60 feet was added. The earlier lighthouse had to be abandoned because of ocean encroachment. After the current tower was built, the old one was destroyed; its remains are under the ocean waves. Such would have been the fate of the present lighthouse unless it was moved or a sea wall was constructed to protect it. For more than fifteen years at the end of the century various temporary protective measures were taken, but Hurricanes Emily and Gordon brought the Atlantic to within 100 feet of the lighthouse. Beginning in 1998, the National Park Service contracted the International Chimney Corporation to relocate the 4,800-ton landmark 2,900 feet inland. The relocation of the lighthouse on roller dollies along steel tracks began June 17, 1999. The lighthouse reached its new location on July 9 of that year.

left at Buxton Woods, at 4.6 miles. Here you may wish to visit the Buxton Woods Nature Trail, a self-guided interpretive 0.6-mile scenic loop in the forest. To the right of the parking area is the Cape Hatteras Lighthouse in its new location. Here is also a parking area for Hatteras Island Visitor Center and Cape Hatteras Lighthouse. (From here it is 0.8 miles on the road to NC-12, where you can find restaurants, stores, motels, and service stations.) To continue on the MST, do not take the access road to NC-12, but continue straight toward the Atlantic Ocean beach.

From the beach at the former location of the Cape Hatteras Lighthouse, turn left (north) and follow the beach for the next 1.4 miles, where an alternate route can also be followed. (If you are following it, cross over the dunes, down to NC-12, and cross the highway to enter a gated old beach road. Keep left to parallel Pamlico Sound for 1.5 miles. Although this old road and accesses to it are forbidden for public vehicular use, the signs are typically ignored; you will notice considerable ruts and water holes in the road. There is dense, but usually low, shrubbery on this route. Mosquitoes are frequent in hot weather. Fishing and bathing are more commonplace

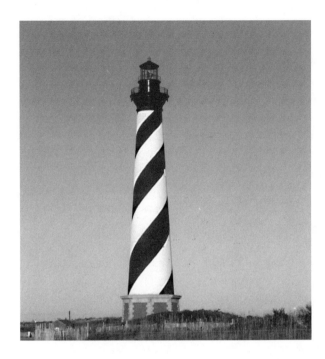

Cape Hatteras Lighthouse

near the ends of the back roads. To return to the seashore veer right and cross NC-12. Turn left and walk the road shoulder for 0.2 miles, then turn right to follow an old beach road for 100 yards to a parking area. Hike over the dunes another 100 yards to the ocean for rejoining the regular MST route. Turn left.) At 10.2 miles there is a beach exit, ORV ramp #38, to a parking area at NC-12. Arrive at Avon Fishing Pier in the town of Avon at 10.4 miles. From the pier there is access to NC-12 for a restaurant and stores. Motels in Avon are the Avon Motel (telephone: 252-995-5774) and Castaway Ocean Front Inn (telephone: 252-995-4440) at 13.0 miles.

PART C: Begin Part C from the motels and continue north on the beach. There are parking areas on the other side of the dunes at 1.2 miles and 5.0 miles. At ORV ramp #27 you have gone 7.7 miles; over the dunes is a boardwalk to NC-12. Beach use may be sparse through this part of the trail because of its isolation. At 10.1 miles it is 0.5 miles from the beach west and across the dunes to the former National Park Service Salvo Campground, now a large picnic area named Salvo Day Use Area. It has restrooms and drinking water. At 10.4 miles come to ORV ramp #23. Here you may take a 0.2-mile access path over the dunes to a paved parking area on NC-12. A United Methodist Church is at 10.8 miles. The new Salvo/Waves/Rodanthe Post Office (27968) is off the beach on NC-12 at 14.4 miles. At 15.0 miles come to Camp

Hatteras, a large campground with more than 300 sites (telephone: 252-987-2777). Cape Hatteras KOA at 15.3 miles has more than 300 sites (telephone: 252-987-2307).

PART D: From these campgrounds, begin Part D of this section of MST. It is 1.0 mile north to the Rodanthe Fishing Pier and Hatteras Island Resort and fishing pier. The water tower is 0.3 miles farther; it can be seen above the sand dunes from the beach for a considerable distance and makes a good point from which to estimate your location. At 1.6 miles is the North Beach General Store and Family Campground (telephone: 252-987-2378). There are also stores and a laundry here. At 1.8 miles off the beach and dunes is NC-12 and the historic Chicamacomico Coast Guard Station, established in 1874 as a lifesaving station (now closed). (The water tower has the name Chicamacomico painted on the ball.)

At 2.6 miles arrive at the south end of Pea Island National Wildlife Refuge, at an exit to a parking area on NC-12. But stay on the seashore. Also stay on the seashore at 7.0 miles where there are off-limits buildings belonging to the wildlife refuge on the west side of NC-12. At 10.3 miles leave the seashore, cross over the sand dunes among sea oats and pennywort, and cross NC-12 at the Refuge Visitor Center, which is located at 10.4 miles. There is a parking area and an office with a bookstore, information, restrooms, and drinking water. At the south end of the parking area is the beginning of the 2.5-mile North Pond Interpretive Trail and a signboard. The dike area was constructed by the Civilian Conservation Corps in the 1930s. Cross a bridge over a moat, where you may see turtles sunning and enter an arbor of yaupon, wax myrtle, and vines. Exit on the dike for views both south and north of the pond. Some of the bird life you may see are yellow-rumped warblers, cardinals, seaside sparrows, yellow throats, and rufous-sided towhees; black ducks, wigeons, and pintails; brown pelicans; and red-tailed hawks. During the late-fall and winter seasons there are thousands of geese, ducks, and other waterfowl. At 0.6 miles reach an observation stand and turn right. From here on the west and north side of the North Pond it is another 1.9 miles on the trail. Be prepared to meet mosquitoes and other insects on hot, wet, or humid days.

Arrive at NC-12 at 12.9 miles. Hike left on the road for 0.3 miles before turning right to cross the dunes for 105 yards to the beach. After 1.9 miles return to NC-12 and pass a ferry schedule on the west side of NC-13. Arrive at the Herbert C. Bonner Bridge at 15.3 miles. Cross the bridge on a narrow (45-inch-wide) pedestrian walk space for 2.4 miles. After another 0.4 miles turn right into the entrance of Oregon Inlet Campground at 18.1 miles. From here there are good views of the marsh, inlet, bridge, and dunes. From

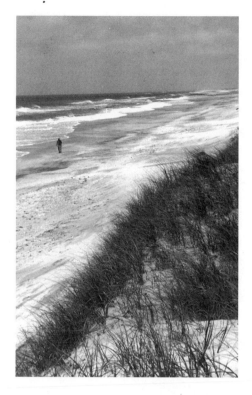

Mountains-to-Sea Trail on Atlantic beach

high dunes with sea oats, the views of the Atlantic for sunrise, or the views of Pamlico Sound at sunset, are magnificent.

PART E: To complete the final part of the Mountains-to-Sea Trail, begin at the Oregon Inlet Campground and walk north on NC-12 for 0.6 miles to connect with the Bodie Island Dike Trail, left. (One way of knowing where to join the trail is to count the power line poles on your left. You should see the trail begin to parallel the road after the twelfth pole from the campground.) Turn left onto the wide Bodie Island Dike Trail. There will be occasional views of the Bodie Island Lighthouse to your right. The trail has numbered markers through wax myrtle, beach holly, cedar, and cordgrass. At 1.2 miles turn right onto a back bay National Park Service road and cross a small cement bridge. Follow the sandy road to a gate, where you may see faint MST blazes on posts or trees. Turn right to a parking area and to the Bodie Island Lighthouse Station and Visitor Center at 1.5 miles. At the northeast corner of the lawn, left of the lighthouse, is the Bodie Island Pond Trail. (It is 0.3 miles round trip through wetlands on a boardwalk to an observation deck for waterfowl. Some of the botanical species are bayberry, salt marsh cordgrass, and black needlerush.)

Jockey's Ridge State Park

Over a period of about twenty-five years, Jockey's Ridge State Park became a 484-acre investment into the state's irreplaceable natural wonders. Soaring to 140 feet, the sand mountain is the tallest in eastern North America. This historic spot is a fitting terminus of the Mountains-to-Sea Trail. To travel from the cool winds of Clingmans Dome in the Smokies to the cool breezes of a sand dune from which you can view the Atlantic Ocean is a true hiker's challenge.

Jockey's Ridge State Park has a museum and nature trail in addition to its main attraction—climbing the sand mountain. Nearly 700,000 people visit the park annually. One of the legends for the name of the park comes from the island horse races that took place as early as 1851 in a flat area on the south side of the ridge top.

Until 1975 the popular park area had been privately owned. Without public knowledge, the owners planned a development on the ridge and began to destroy it in 1973. The shock waves were immediate. Enter Carolista Baum, who defiantly placed herself in front of a bulldozer. This inspired other citizens to raise funds for public acquisition of the property. The North Carolina General Assembly appropriated funds that were matched by the U.S. Bureau of Outdoor Recreation. The sand was saved.

Continue following the paved road through a pine forest to an intersection with NC-12 at 2.5 miles. Cross the road and follow the entrance to Coquina Beach. Here is a large parking area with restrooms, picnic area, boardwalks to the beach, and bathhouse for summertime. Between the parking area and the dunes is the remains of the *Laura A. Barnes*, a 629-gross-ton four-masted schooner wrecked in 1921. Although the original designation of the Cape Hatteras Beach Trail for part of the MST had its eastern terminus at the intersection of US-64/158 and NC-12 at Whalebone Junction, the terminus has changed to Jockey's Ridge State Park. That is another 4.0 miles on US-158. Your option is to access the seashore from Coquina Beach and hike along the beach to a public access at East Conch Street parking area in Nags Head. This route would be within three blocks of the entrance to Jockey's Ridge State Park. Both options are described below.

If you choose to follow NC-12, return to it and walk on the wide shoulder facing traffic. At 3.9 miles pass a National Park Service maintenance center on the right. Pass two wildlife observation decks at 4.2 miles and 4.8 miles to the left. Pass two parking areas on the left at 5.4 miles and 7.1 miles. At 8.5 miles arrive at the Cape Hatteras National Seashore Whalebone Junction Information Center, and at 8.6 miles reach the intersection of US-64/158 and NC-12. Follow US-158 Bypass (South Croatan Highway) and pass a

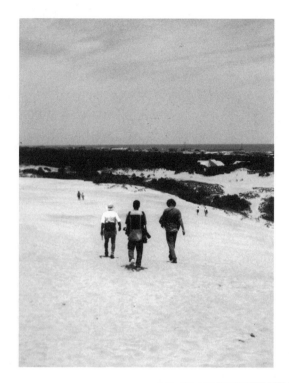

East end of the Mountains-to-Sea Trail at Jockey's Ridge State Park

shopping center to the left at 9.1 miles, Nags Head Water Tower at 10.6 miles, another shopping center on the left at 10.9 miles, and turn left at the entrance to Jockey's Ridge State Park at 13.1 miles. It is another 0.3 miles to the park headquarters. From here you can follow the Tracks in the Sand Trail part of the way before leaving it to ascend the ridge top at 13.8 miles, the eastern end of the Mountains-to-Sea Trail.

If you are following the seashore from Coquina Beach, pass Outer Banks Fishing Pier at 6.7 miles, Jennett's Fishing Pier at 8.4 miles, and a public parking access at East Conch Street at 13.0 miles. A landmark to watch for is the remains of a former pier, where you will turn left off the beach. Walk out to South Virginia Dare Trail (Street), turn right, pass a Shell Service Station, left, to turn left on East Hollowell Street at 13.2 miles. After 0.2 miles you will arrive at US-158 Bypass (Croatan Highway). Across the highway is the entrance to Jockey's Ridge State Park and its headquarters at 13.7 miles. Follow part of the Tracks in the Sand Trail for 0.4 miles to the summit of the ridge at 14.1 miles, the eastern end of the Mountains-to-Sea Trail.

DIVERSIONS: At the intersection of NC-12 and US-264/64/158, if you go north on US-158/NC-12 to milepost 1.5, you will come to the Aycock Welcome Center, the beach headquarters of the Dare County Tourist Bureau. You can obtain maps and printed information here (telephone: 252-261-4644 or

800-446-6262). If you have time for diversions, make sure to visit the Wright Brothers Memorial on US-158/NC-12 north at milepost 8 in Kill Devil Hills (telephone: 252-441-7430). Nearby at milepost 9.5 is the one-thousand-acre Nags Head Woods Preserve with its coastal forest trails and visitor center (call ahead, telephone: 252-441-2525). On Roanoke Island in Manteo you can visit the Fort Raleigh Historical Site, Elizabethan Gardens and Lost Colony Outdoor Drama, and the North Carolina Aquarium. For information call 800-446-6262.

CAMPSIDE STORIES: Theodosia Burr, born June 21, 1783, in Albany, New York, was the only child of Aaron Burr and Theodosia Prevost. Her mother died when Theodosia was eleven. Aaron directed and influenced his beautiful daughter's education and social life, which led to her marriage in 1801 to Joseph Alston of South Carolina, who later became the state's governor. Devoted to her father, she frequently visited him. She was with him after he shot Alexander Hamilton in a political duel in 1804, and she was in Richmond, Virginia, to comfort him when he was tried for treason in 1807. After Burr was acquitted, he exiled himself to Europe, but Theodosia took charge of his American affairs. She persuaded him to return in May 1910.

She desperately wished to see him, but in June her son died of a fever. Seriously depressed and in poor health, she was not able to leave for New York City until December 30. With a maid she left from Georgetown, South Carolina, on the *Patriot*, a ship with credentials from Governor Alston to pass the British blockade of the War of 1810. The ship and its passengers were never seen again.

Although the above story is recorded history, it has acquired a number of questionable endings. According to Charles Harry Whedbee in *Legends of the Outer Banks*, land pirates killed all aboard the *Patriot*, except Theodosia, when the ship was washed ashore in a storm at Nags Head. She was spared because she went insane during the massacre, and the pirates were afraid to harm her. The only item she carried ashore was a painting she had made of herself for her father. During the remainder of her life she was cared for by the islanders. Occasionally visiting her was Dr. William G. Poole from Elizabeth City. On one of his routine calls the neighbors wished to give him the painting for his services, at which time Theodosia hugged the painting and ran out of the cottage into the ocean. She was never found, but the painting washed ashore the next day.

Those who believe in ghost stories may see Theodosia between Christmas and New Year's Day walking on the beach at Nags Head. She will be a specter in ocean mist looking for the painting she was taking to her father.

SIXTEEN

A BRIEF HISTORY OF THE
MOUNTAINS-TO-SEA TRAIL

As early as 1686 English adventurers and traders were following the Native American Occoneechee Trail from the Tidewater area of Virginia to Catawba Indian settlements in the Carolinas, where they then gained trail accesses to the Cherokee Indians in the Appalachians. This was a trading passage both from the Atlantic Ocean area to the mountains and from the mountains to the coast. By 1698 Jean Couture and James Moore, trade adventurers from Charles Towne (Charleston) in the Carolinas, were active in the Appalachian region. Trading records show that they traded "deerskins and furs from the Appalachians to the coast" for shipment to Europe. North Carolina became a royal province in 1729, but the entitlement did not contribute to any major land routes. By the 1740s the younger William Byrd, Abraham Wood, and Patrick Brown were among the principal travelers to and from the James River of Virginia.

Between the 175-mile-long string of islands known as the Outer Banks and the mainland of North Carolina, the Albermarle and Pamlico Sounds constituted a geographical barrier to trade. During the nineteenth century east-west wagon and carriage routes were developing, but not until the twentieth century was there a mountains-to-the-sea highway. The highway, US-64, is the state's longest: 543 miles "from Murphy to Manteo." The highway was made possible by bridges over Croatan and Roanoke Sounds with Roanoke Island as a connector between them. The highway's eastern terminus connects with US-158 at Whalebone on the Outer Banks, six miles east of Manteo; its western terminus extends into Tennessee, 20 miles west of Murphy.

In the early summer of 1977 the Bicycle Program of the North Carolina Department of Transportation used the term "Mountains-to-Sea" in planning its Bicycle Route #2(A) (MSBR) between Murphy and Manteo. The 712-mile route would have termini in the two towns but would only infrequently follow US-64.

In September 1977, the Division of Parks and Recreation in the North Carolina Department of Conservation and Community Development proposed a "Mountains-to-Sea Trail" (MST) that would serve primarily as a hiking trail across the state. That is why in this book I have associated the MST, a hiking trail, with the Division of Parks and Recreation and the MSBR with the Department of Transportation. Their routes cross or follow each other at a few locations. Although the development of the bicycle routes and hiking trails can be traced to state government officials in Raleigh, the capital city, many citizen leaders and groups developed new concepts and participated in the long history of planning for these trails. Neither the government nor citizen leaders announced their dreams and hopes with a dazzling brass band parade on Raleigh's Hillsborough Street. Instead, the concepts evolved quietly and powerfully through the efforts of such bicycle leaders as Tom Yates and Mary Meletiou of Raleigh, and hikers Louise Chatfield of Greensboro and Jim Hallsey of Raleigh. Chatfield, the citizen leader among the hikers, led campaigns for state legislative action to create a network of trails across the state at least four years before the official birth of the Mountains-to-Sea Trail. Those who played roles in developing the concept and planning proposals remember how the foundations were laid for a state trails system.

The North Carolina Trails Act

In 1973 the North Carolina General Assembly ratified the North Carolina Trails System Act. House Bill #436 was introduced by Earnest Messer, Clyde R. Greene, Herbert Hyde, Liston Ramsey, Wade Smith, and John Stevens. Senate Bill #314 was sponsored by Phillip Godwin, Michael Mullins, Staton Saunders, Linwood Smith, McNeil Smith, Mauney Stallings, and Deane Webster. Responsibility for developing and managing the Trails System was assigned to the Department of Conservation and Development Commission, which was later incorporated in the Department of Natural Resources and Community Development (DNRCD), now the Department of Environment and Natural Resources (DENR). Today, the Division of Parks and Recreation, the current state trails management agency, is within the DENR.

Passage of the North Carolina Trails System Act was expected by the Department, and some planning had already begun. A catalyst was *Resources for Trails in North Carolina,* written in 1972 by staff member Bob Buckner, Chief of Planning in the Recreation Division, Department of Local Affairs, which also was merged into DNRCD. Alan Eakes, a planner in landscaping and land purchase for state parks, and Hallsey, a recreation planner in the Recreation Division, were active leaders from the beginning. Their efforts inspired trail leaders in the state's trail organizations and other citizens' groups to move forward in implementing the Trails System Act. One of the Act's statutes created the North Carolina Trails Committee (NCTC). As a seven-member advisory council appointed by the secretary of DNRCD, the committee was directed to meet in a variety of locations in the state at least three times annually to advise the DNRCD "on all matters directly or indirectly pertaining to trails, their use, extent, location, and the other objectives and purposes of this Article." Another statute explains that

> in order to provide for the ever increasing outdoor recreation needs of an expanding population and in order to promote public access to, travel within, and enjoyment and appreciation of the outdoors, natural and re- mote areas of the state, trails should be established in natural scenic areas of the state, and in and near urban areas.

The Trails System Act did not include an initial suggestion for a foot trail that would span the state from its border with Tennessee to the Atlantic Ocean. At that time the longest foot trail in the state was the 305-mile Ap- palachian National Scenic Trail (AT), which followed the high ranges of Stand- ing Indian Mountain, the Great Smoky Mountains, the Unaka Mountains, and Roan Mountain. Those high windswept ridges, balds, and plateaus seemed to be the proper place for part of a 2,160-mile adventure from Georgia to Maine. The AT connected with the Allegheny Trail (a cross-state trail in West Virginia), which connected with the Big Blue Trail (now the Tuscarora Trail into West Virginia, Maryland, and part of Pennsylvania before reconnecting with the AT), and the Long Trail in Vermont. Why not have a hiking trail across North Carolina that connected with the AT?

In the lexicon of trails, the public basically expected long trails to be con- fined to the national and state forests and national and state parks. Short nature trails were more likely to be in city or county parks. But in the late 1970s new words such as "greenways" and "greenspace" were joining "greenbelt" and "greensward" to emphasize belts of grassy parks and undeveloped places.

In 1977 Mecklenburg County began a master plan that would add nearly 10,000 acres to its park system. It would provide the city of Charlotte, the state's largest metropolitan area, with a vast network of trails. Elizabeth Hair (former chair of the Board of County Commissioners) called the network "Charlotte's green necklace." (By 1992, when the city and county parks were merged, there were more than 150 parks, and more were planned. Beginning with the twenty-first century, a visitor will need to visit three different parks a week to see them all within a year.)

Urban and county planners elsewhere in the state were thinking about how trails could bring communities together. The idea was not totally new. The Washington and Old Dominion Trail in northern Virginia passed through dense residential areas for part of its 40 miles. From it were numerous con-

View of Falls Lake from Falls Lake Trail

necting trails to many of the 300 parks and greenspaces in the Fairfax County/ Alexandria/Arlington area. On the north side of the Potomac was the multi-use historic Chesapeake and Ohio Canal Towpath through Maryland.

The metropolitan areas of Raleigh and Durham were creating master plans for more parks and recreational areas in greenspace. Raleigh's greenway system began in 1974 with a master plan to have parks and trails throughout the city. (By 1996 there were 245 parcels of land, of which 130 were parks and greenspace. If all plans could be completed there would be about 200 miles of trails in the city and Wake County combined.) In the 1970s Winston-Salem had a master trail plan to connect trails within the city and other towns in Forsyth County. (By 1995 it had connected the Strollway Trail into the heart of the city.) The combined metropolitan area of High Point/Jamestown/Greens-boro and Guilford County had plans for connecting urban parks with trails (for example, there is the Bicentennial Greenway Trail). Later municipal plans would include options for the Mountains-to-Sea Trail through north Greens-boro that could make connections east to Durham and Raleigh. North of Raleigh members and friends of the Triangle Greenways Council were constructing a proposed 40-mile Falls Lake Trail to be part of the Mountains-to-Sea Trail. East of and near to Ásheville, Arch Nichols of the Carolina Mountain Club proposed a 60-mile foot trail from Mount Pisgah to Mount Mitchell (completed in 1997) on border lands of the Blue Ridge Parkway and Pisgah National Forest. These plans, and many others developed during the 1970s and 1980s, represented exciting challenges for trail planners and trail users. A trail from the mountains to the sea could serve as a flagship to connect many trails along the way.

The North Carolina Trails Committee

The first meeting of the North Carolina Trails Committee took place in January 1974; Louise Chatfield served as the chair. A highly qualified leader, she had already established herself as an ambassador for municipal parks and recreation. Other members of the initial board were Susan Chasson, Jim Cobb, Charles Clampitt (who replaced Fred Ogden), John Falter, Doris B. Hammett, and William Sterritt. In 1975 and 1976 John Falter of Apex was the chair, followed by Doris B. Hammett, M.D., of Waynesville in 1977. An eloquent and persuasive leader in the equestrian program for trails in the mountains and elsewhere in the nation, Hammett believed in plans with strategic values and guidelines to complete them. In one of her plans she arranged for the Fourth National Trails Symposium to be held at Lake Junaluska, September 7–10, 1977. Among the distinguished state and national guest speakers was Howard Lee, Secretary of DNRCD (and former mayor of Chapel Hill [1969 to 1975], now N.C. senator from the Sixteenth District).

Lee's lecture was prepared by his speechwriter and director of public relations, Stephen Meehan. Near the end of an inspiring speech, Lee said, "I think the time has come for us to consider the feasibility of establishing a state trail between the mountains and the seashore in North Carolina." Lee explained that he wanted the North Carolina Trails Committee to plan such a trail that would utilize the National Park System, the National Forest System, state parks, city and county properties, and private landowners who were

> willing to give an easement over a small portion of their land on a legacy to future generations. I don't think we should be locked into the traditional concept of a trail with woods on both sides. . . . I think it would be a trail that would help—like the first primitive trails—bring us together. . . . I would depend on trail enthusiasts for maintenance. . . . Beyond that, how great it would be if other states would follow suit and that the state trails could be linked nationally.

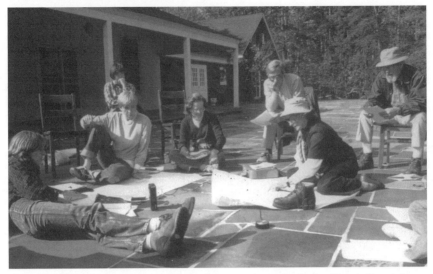

Louise Chatfield (center) discusses plans for the Mountains-to-Sea Trail at Murrow Mountain State Park in the early 1980s. Also pictured are (clockwise from left) Kay Scott, Willie Taylor, Cindy Johnson, Doris Hammett, John Falter, and Jim Maddox. (Courtesy N.C. Division of Parks and Recreation)

The challenge spread quickly from the conference room; it was publicized throughout the state. Leaders of trail organizations, outdoor recreation leaders, and related government officials took notice. The *Asheville Citizen-Times* quoted Lee as saying that the new trail would give the state's citizens and visitors "a real feel for the sights, sounds and people of the state." Some trail leaders did not take it seriously. "A dream trail as vaporous as the fog on the Smoky Mountains," said one doubter. "Too costly" said a state official in Raleigh. But Lee had explained in his speech that he would not be requesting a new state budget item to bear the cost of a cross-state trail. The cost, he said, would be shared by local, state, and federal agencies whose budgets could accommodate the expenses. He also expressed his faith that dedicated volunteer organizations would lead work forces, and that landowners would donate real estate.

The Mountains-to-Sea Bicycle Route

Curtis Yates, bicycle coordinator, and Mary Meletiou, assistant bicycle coordinator, of the North Carolina Department of Transportation, attended the Lake Junaluska conference and heard Lee's speech. "We were surprised," stated Meletiou, "because earlier in the summer we had publicized the same idea for bicycling." Nevertheless, and regardless of the origins of separate but similar visions, Lee's recommendation was a summons to the Division of Parks and Recreation for a hiking trail. Like runners with a flame on an Olympic torch, who would be the leaders, the promoters, and the workers to carry the dream of the Mountains-to-Sea Trail to completion?

Yates, a planner and monitor for federal projects, was transferred from the Department of Administration to the Department of Transportation in 1973 as a bicycle coordinator. In 1974 the state legislature ratified the Bicycle and Bikeway Act (GS136-71.6-12), drafted by Yates and others, and championed by Senator McNeil Smith of Greensboro. Meletiou, who was experienced in national bicycle touring, was employed in 1975. This combination of exceptional leaders ushered in an advanced recognition of bicycling as a means of transportation. Another state legislative bill in 1977 clarified and revised parts of the original bill and mandated the Department of Transportation "to develop and coordinate the bicycle program." In 1979 additional bicycle policies were set for planning, constructing, and maintaining bicycle routes. During the evolution of the bicycle program the North Carolina Bicycle Committee, a citizens' advisory council, was created. Yates became the Director of Bicycle and Public Transportation in 1991.

When asked about the formula for their successful bicycle program, Yates said that "we had an opportunity and an idea, and we allowed it to carefully develop, but we could not have accomplished it without the help of others. An example is the help of Bill Flournoy, in another department, who assisted us in drafting legislative bills and planning. He had vision for potential future problems and needs." In the mid 1970s Flournoy, a bicyclist and hiker, was a senior land use planner in the Wake County Planning Department; in 1980 he became the Environmental Assessment Chief in the Department of Natural Resources and Community Development. Currently he is the Environmental Analysis Program Manager in the Department of Environment and Natural Resources. He has been an active board member of the Triangle Greenway Council from the beginning of the citizens' organization, and was one of the leaders in the design and construction, during the 1980s, of the Falls Lake Trail, a foot trail segment of the Mountains-to-Sea Trail. In addition, he was a leader in the formation of the North Carolina Trails Association.

In 1992 pedestrian responsibilities were added to the bicycle program, and in May 1997 the office became an official division within the North Carolina Department of Transportation. "Division status was conferred to recognize the importance of providing for (both) bicycle and pedestrian transportation," stated *Bike/Ped Notes* in its September 1997 edition. "This seemingly small name change signifies the growth and maturity of bicycling and walking as transportation." By 1998 Yates and program manager Meletiou had developed an astonishing network of more than 5,500 miles of highway and back-road routes. At least 450 miles of official highway bicycle route or back-road routes, described in this book, can be used for either bicycling or on foot in crossing the state on the Mountains-to-Sea Trail. The currently proposed Mountains-to-Sea Trail (MST) follows part of that network. Specifically, Bicycle Route #4 (North Line Trace), from Thurmond to Danbury, and Bicycle Route #2 (Mountains-to-Sea [MSBR]) from Raleigh to Wilson both are cross-state bicycle routes. Bicycle Route #7 (Ocracoke Option), a spur from Bicycle Route #2 near Wilson to Cedar Island, was designed to provide another trail option for cross-country bicyclists or pedestrians. (The Division of Parks and Recreation planners had already recommended the Neuse River as a potential canoe trail from Raleigh to New Bern, with a parallel foot trail on the Neuse River floodplains. Westward, parts of the Eno and Haw Rivers could be used.)

The Mountains-to-Sea Hiking Trail

If there was to be a hiking passageway across the state known as the Mountains-to-Sea Trail, what would be its route? In the beginning of the 1980s, a 20-mile-wide general corridor that would allow for some flexibility and experimentation was determined by the Division of Parks and Recreation. No topographical plans were made, nor were any specific boundaries along roads or county lines outlined, except in a few areas. Examples were about 10 miles on each side of the Blue Ridge Parkway and, the easiest route of all, the narrow islands of Cape Hatteras. From Raleigh to the Croatan National Forest, the Neuse River would be a centerline of the corridor, which would spread 10 miles north and south of its eastward flow. This route would include a passage within or near the cities of Smithfield, Goldsboro, Kinston, and New Bern and would pass through Cliffs of the Neuse State Park and Croatan National Forest.

Because the Mountains-to-Sea Trail was conceptualized as a "flagship trail," it was desirable to have it pass through as many federal, state, county, and city parks as possible along the way. This would include at least seven state parks, a national park, a national wildlife refuge, a national seashore, three of the four national forests, and a number of town and county parks. In early discussions about the Mountains-to-Sea Trail route, the western terminus was uncertain. Suggestions were the town of Murphy (as with the bicycle route), the town of Cherokee at the south end of the Blue Ridge Parkway, Clingmans Dome (on the AT and the boundary of Tennessee), and the Joyce Kilmer Memorial Forest west of Robbinsville. The eastern terminus could be at the town of Buxton near the Cape Hatteras Lighthouse, or at the east end of US-64 at Whalebone, six miles east of Manteo, or in the town of Nags Head, or at Jockey's Ridge

State Park. Currently the western terminus is Clingmans Dome and the eastern terminus is Jockey's Ridge State Park.

The early and undocumented policy about the route was to address location when it became an issue. For twelve years there has been uncertainty about where the Mountains-to-Sea Trail would leave the Blue Ridge Parkway on its descent to Stone Mountain State Park. Ability to change plans also became necessary when the Carolina Mountain Club task forces constructed a new trail on the west side of the Blue Ridge Parkway to make the original route into Davidson Valley an alternate route. When the Sauratown Trail, a combination equestrian and hiking route mainly on private property, was closed between Pilot Mountain and Hanging Rock State Parks, the MST route was temporarily shifted to follow Bicycle Route #4 (North Line Trace). (By 1998 some of the new sections of the Sauratown Trail were opening.) One location issue, about a proposed riverside route on the Neuse River east of Raleigh, developed in 1996 when thousands of fish were poisoned by Pfiesteria. A comprehensive report was published by the *News and Observer* about pollution from feeder streams and farmlands. Pollution in addition to the many problems of crossing feeder streams, frequently flooded areas, and densely populated areas, and issues of riverside space had made the route seem undesirable for the MST. (See a change in proposal at the end of this chapter.) Trail task forces have advocated alternate passages on back-road areas or bicycle routes to widen the Mountains-to-Sea Trail corridor. This issue underscored the fact that a boundary of 10 miles on each side of rivers or ridges is not always practical.

At the request for wider corridor flexibility by the Friends of the Mountains-to-Sea Trail (FMST) in 1997, the North Carolina Trails Committee and the Division of Parks and Recreation suggested the FMST recommend specific boundary changes. Such changes could influence boundary locations in areas with a pollution problem, areas where population is too dense for the desired level of trail quality, or places where safety hazards had developed. This agreement would allow options in cross-state passage. An example would be to use parts of Bicycle Route #2 and Bicycle Route #7 to parallel the Neuse River. Until a riverside trail becomes possible, a connector route could be arranged to include the 8.7-mile Wayne County Trail in Goldsboro (see Chapter 12, Section 31). This trail, which passes through Waynesborough State Park and Goldsboro, had been designated as a segment of the MST in May 1991.

The North Carolina Trails Association

There had always been and continued to be a more serious issue about routing. The dreams of easements from private landowners and adequate financial resources to purchase land for a hiking trail soon clashed with some difficult and realistic facts. Landowners were understandably reluctant to grant land in fee simple or to donate long-term easements. The state did not have the money and neither did the fledging but ambitious North Carolina Trails Association (NCTA), formed by a group of outdoor recreation leaders in 1977, organized in 1981, and chartered February 2, 1982. Acquisition of land and development of trails was a purpose written into the NCTA's charter. Some of the other purposes of the NCTA were as follows:

promote the establishment and conservation of a system of scenic, recreational, and historic trails and related facilities in the State of North Carolina; and to encourage all persons to participate in trail activities for the mental, physical and spiritual well-being which can be derived. To work with federal, state, and local agencies and trail related organizations, landowners, and individuals in planning, acquisition, development, maintenance and proper use of trails and trail related facilities.

The first acting president of the new organization was Bill Flournoy, who guided a steering committee composed of Faye Collins, David Pyles, Ray Rimmer, Ann Davis, Ruth Noonan, and Bill Scott. At their May 20, 1977, meeting in Raleigh they began plans for a major organizational meeting at Morrow Mountain State Park in the summer. From this meeting on August 6 came a list of other acting officers: Doug Henderson of Chapel Hill as vice president, Ruth Noonan of Lexington as secretary, and Bill Sims of Greensboro as treasurer. An eight-member board of directors was also created. When the acting officers called for a president, Louise Chatfield, whose term with the North Carolina Trails Committee was expiring, accepted the position effective February 1, 1978.

After Chatfield took over leadership, a new NCTA Board of Directors convened: Willie Taylor, Bill Sims, Ray Rimmer, Kathy Chatfield, and Don Chatfield Jr. of Greensboro (the organization's base headquarters); Darrell McBane of Danbury; Larkin Kirkman of Raleigh (an attorney and the initial registered agent of the corporation); Allen de Hart of Louisburg; Ann Davis of Apex; Mary Joan Pugh of Asheboro; and Phillip Hurst of High Point. The Association, the North Carolina Trails Committee, and the staff of the Division of Parks and Recreation had lengthy meetings to discuss the issues, to plan sessions with local government boards, to create representative trail task forces along the corridor, to determine how to acquire land and trail easements—all in an effort to keep alive the summons of Secretary Lee. Could it be possible to create such a flagship trail through the heart of the state, where farms are prevalent, forests scarce, and towns offer only a sidewalk? Louise Chatfield said that "one of the things I want us to do is every time we come down the road and see something beautiful is to let someone know about it." She was referring to the need to increase public awareness of the value of trail easements to everyone. Publicity was clearly needed. In a brainstorming session, the NCTA decided that a major trip, from the mountains to the sea, by outdoor enthusiasts would solicit public interest and support.

First Mountains-to-Sea Multi-Use Trek

Planning for the "Mountains-to-Sea Trek" began in 1981. The North Carolina Trails Association would sponsor a combination expedition across the state for hikers, bicyclists, equestrians, and canoeists. The event was highly publicized in the media during the six months leading up to the start date in April of 1982. Newspaper headlines dubbed the event as the "Murphy to Manteo Trek," "Trek Across North Carolina," "Cross-state Trek," and "Trek-A-State" (modeled on the "Hike-A-Nation" during the nation's bicentennial). The NCTA's president at this time was Larkin Kirkman, an attorney from Raleigh. He said the trek would offer "nine fun-filled and educational weeks of good, healthy exercise," and that one of the purposes was to "get people interested in the outdoors through trail-related activities." The two chairpersons for the Trek were Kathy Chatfield, daughter-in-law of Louise Chatfield, of Greensboro, and Kay Scott, the state trails coordinator from DNRCD, of Raleigh. Scott described the purpose of the Trek as "to promote awareness of trails in North Carolina, to motivate local areas to build trails, and to make people conscious of the Mountains-to-Sea Trail." Anne Taylor, director of Regulatory Relations of DNRCD, and a strong supporter of the Trek, said that the state office wished to involve the event with Outdoors North Carolina Expo. "We want to use the Mountains-to-Sea concept and Trek as a highlight of the Expo and the year-long theme" for 1982.

There were four recreational groups in the Trek: bicyclists, chaired by Mary Joan Pugh of Asheboro; hikers, chaired by Phil Hurst of High Point; canoeists, chaired by Don Chatfield, husband of Kathy; and equestrians, chaired by Ann Davis of Apex. Fifteen volunteer trail task forces had been organized (similar to task forces and clubs that maintain the Appalachian Trail) to oversee the trail corridor across the state. Trail user gatherings were scheduled at Asheville, Blowing Rock, Stone Mountain State Park, Pilot Mountain State Park, Greensboro, Sanford, Raleigh, Smithfield, and Cape Hatteras. Each user caravan would have different routes and stops and include different leaders and information personnel. Lee Price was hiking leader from Soco Gap on the

Blue Ridge Parkway to Sanford, where Frank Barringer took over as leader on the Buckhorn Trail. Ruth Ann Chatfield was the information leader from Moncure into Raleigh and on to Clemmons State Forest. Allen de Hart was trail leader from Ocracoke to Cape Hatteras Lighthouse and Visitor Center.

Of the hundreds who participated, one hiker, Lee Price, a twenty-four-year-old electrician from Bristol, Tennessee, and formerly of Greensboro, was especially watched. He would walk from Soco Gap on the Blue Ridge Parkway, near Maggie Valley, to Smithfield. Canoeists would paddle sections on the Yadkin River led by Aaron Tilley, on the Haw River led by Chuck Brady, and on the Neuse River led by Bob Benner. Equestrians started in the town of Murphy with Vincent Parker as trail leader. Other equestrian leaders at selected areas across the state were Troy Whitesides, Woody Hampton, Tommy Stamey, Ron Harris, Gregg Wilder, and R. M. Collins. Kathy Chatfield had an exceptionally well-organized entourage, complete with shuttle services. She arranged for Price to be a continuous backpacker and where possible to have other recreational groups meet him at selected locations across the state. There were long sections on the highways and back roads where Price hiked alone. In Raleigh he was asked by a news reporter why he was participating in the long walk. "If you enjoy it, do it," he said. "There's no great inner searching in me. I don't have to dig deep to find myself . . . I just like to walk."

On April 3, 1982, the Trek began for the hikers at Soco Gap on the Blue Ridge Parkway. Louise Chatfield wrote in her journal "The Trek is off! Amid high winds and cold weather with 15 horsebackers, 10 bicyclists, and 5 hikers we left for the long trek to Raleigh. There was not one bureaucrat from Raleigh in sight! I do hope before this thing is over some of you will be able to leave your desks long enough to get out and meet the people." She probably spoke too soon, because a week later at Bent Creek in Asheville, government representatives were present. Edgar Israel, director of the Western Field Office of DNRCD, offered greetings and praised the hikers for enduring rain and snow over the mountains. Wayne McDevitt, of the governor's western office, called the participants "ambassadors of our state's outdoor programs" and emphasized the importance of community involvement in such activities as the Mountains-to-Sea Trek. He also said he spoke for Governor Jim Hunt. "The governor recognizes the importance of the state's tourist industry and the attention to the state provided by the outdoor trail system." He presented a state flag to be carried across the state. The officials attending were Gary Everhardt, superintendent of the Blue Ridge Parkway, and George Olsen, supervisor of the U.S. Forest Service in North Carolina.

In August 1997 Governor Hunt appointed McDevitt as Secretary of the Department of Environment and Natural Resources, to replace Jonathan

Howes who had served since 1993. In my interview with Secretary McDevitt May 27, 1998, he said "In 1977, when Secretary Howard Lee announced his vision for the Mountains-to-Sea Trail, I had the good fortune of serving on a committee working to bring that vision to fruition." During the conversation we discussed some of the events that marked progress during the past twenty years. While sharing memories of some past trail leaders he stated that he had talked "with folks from the mountains to the sea, encountering again many of those same citizens who were at the forefront of this effort to connect our state and its natural treasures." (Secretary McDevitt was promoted to chief of staff for Governor Hunt on September 1, 1999; assigned to the secretary's position was Bill Holman.)

When the Trek passed through Greensboro on May 14–15, there was a celebration to walk through the city on a historical trail route. "It is time we celebrated foot power," said city council member Dorothy Barolph. Joe Grimsly, secretary of DNRCD, met with the trekkers at a Saturday night banquet. He had earlier made a statement that he viewed "the state trails program and the Mountains-to-Sea Trail project as a challenging and innovative undertaking of state government . . . I will look to our Division of Parks and Recreation to continue its role as coordinator and catalyst of citizen and government trail efforts." At Lake Brandt there was a ribbon-cutting ceremony for a new trail.

On May 22, at Endor Furnace, near Sanford, James S. Stevens Jr., director of the Parks and Recreation Division of DNRCD, and state representative Dennis Wicker of Lee County met with the trekkers. On May 27 Kathy Chatfield led an entourage, including Lee Price, from the State Fairgrounds in Raleigh to visit Governor Jim Hunt at the capitol building. Price received a certificate of appreciation from the governor. That night Price stayed at Clemmons State Forest near Clayton. At Smithfield he ceased his hiking to honor a contract he had with Philmont Scout Ranch in New Mexico for the summer. A group of canoeists continued on the Neuse River and a group of bicyclists continued from Sanford.

On June 5 a group of bicyclists wheeled off the ferry from Ocracoke Island and proceeded to Frisco Campground. The next day, Sunday, a few hikers joined the bicyclists on the Open Pond Road to Buxton Woods and on to the Cape Hatteras Lighthouse and Visitor Center. There Jim Hallsey and Kay Scott of N.C. Division of Parks and Recreation officiated at a ceremony for the ending of the Mountains-to-Sea Trek. This was also the occasion to designate the 75.8-mile Cape Hatteras Beach Trail, the first trail to be designated as part of the Mountains-to-Sea Trail. Anne Taylor, director of the Office of Regulatory Relations, represented the N.C. Department of Natural Resources and

Governor Jim Hunt receives a Mountains-to-Sea Trail T-shirt from Kathy Chatfield (right). Lee Price (center) is the first long-distance MST hiker. (Photograph by N.C. Governor's Office)

Community Development. She presented plaques to Paul McCrary, of Cape Hatteras National Seashore, Ron Height, of Pea Island National Wildlife Refuge, Kathy Chatfield, the Trek's leader, and Larkin Kirkman, chairperson of the N.C. Trails Association, in recognition of their assistance in establishing the Cape Hatteras Beach Trail. In a local news story, a reporter referred to the designation as one for the "Sea-to-the-Mountains Trail." In an interview with Bodie McDowell of the *Greensboro Daily News and Record*, Chatfield said "there was good participation in the trek and it did what we wanted it to do—focus attention on trails. Just seeing so many people taking part in this trek reaffirmed to me that we are doing something worthwhile, so it was worth the time and effort." Chatfield said that she hoped there would be many more trails constructed and designated as a result of the Trek.

In May 1997 Alan Householder and I camped at the residence of Don and Kathy Chatfield in Greensboro on our hike across the state. We swapped memories of the 1982 Mountains-to-Sea Trek and the first segment designation at Cape Hatteras National Seashore. Did she remember her statement about wishing the Trek would inspire more trails across the state? "It must have had an impact, it has been 15 years and we have half the trail completed," she said. "After the (N.C. Trails) Association did not meet anymore I lost track of many of the leaders and workers. As you know, the Association's headquarters was here and most of our business meetings were here for all our planning."

First State Hiking Trails Guidebook

For some time previous to the Cape Hatteras designation, Hallsey and Scott had begun the research for a compendium of the state's trail names, locations (on public or private property), length, and usage. I found their work of great assistance when I began my project in late 1978 to hike and measure all of the state's trails for a guidebook, *North Carolina Hiking Trails* (the first edition was published in 1982). In the book I described sections of the Cape Hatteras Beach Trail, which I had hiked in 1981, and plans for its designation in 1982. This would follow a route on the beach, on a ferry ride, through beach villages and the pristine Buxton Woods, into Pea Island National Wildlife Refuge, and "over dunes with sea oats and sedge; through forests of water oaks, sweet bays, and beach holly; around sound marshes," and past two lighthouses and other historic maritime sites.

Once the Mountains-to-Sea Trail became a recognized concept in park and forest planning, the conversation turned toward potential use of already established trails on public lands. From the beginning, proponents of the Mountains-to-Sea concept realized that private land would be financially difficult to acquire. Free easements or donation of property for the passageway would be the likely approach. A statute in the 1973 Trails Act encouraged this method for establishing and designating trails. Private land was to be "provided fee-simple title, lesser estates, scenic easements, easements of surface ingress and egress running with the land, leases, or other written agreements from landowners through which a State trail will pass."

In the 1980s an equestrian group, the Sauratown Trails Association, a task force of the North Carolina Trails Association, attempted to acquire rights to use some private property for a segment of the Mountains-to-Sea Trail. The property was between Hanging Rock and Pilot Mountain State Parks. After much effort, one mile of a single ten-year easement was officially and legally signed. But the overall goal failed when adjoining landowners would not provide the legal easements required by the state for designation. Not to accept defeat, the The Sauratown Trails Association revised its plans and strategy in the early 1990s. By February 1998 the project was experiencing greater success with some continuous easements on the planned 20 miles. During the life of the North Carolina Trails Association there were a number of sessions and symposiums on how to acquire private land easements for trails. The Division of Parks and Recreation assisted in the effort; it recommended that no easement be less than ten years (with some federal government grants requiring twenty years), an unacceptable length of time for many private landowners. During this period the efforts by state staff to acquire a former railroad grade that passed through the town of Walnut Cove in the piedmont was not acceptable to the adjoining property owners. This rail-trail was within the MST recommended corridor.

The State Designates MST Sections

Within three years after designation of the Cape Hatteras Beach Trail, 63 miles were designated in the South Pisgah section of the Blue Ridge Mountains, including 18 miles of the 30-mile Art Loeb Trail. This section of the MST dipped into the Davidson River valley and followed the Black Mountain Trail to cross the Pink Beds and ascend to the Mount Pisgah area. These plans and results were contagious. At this time the North Carolina Trails Association had expanded its task forces to represent all the counties in the Mountains-to-Sea Trail corridor. In 1986 the Central Blue Ridge Task Force added 45 miles from a spectacular descent and ascent in the Linville Gorge, over multiple streams, and by waterfalls to reach the base of Grandfather Mountain.

In Raleigh, in the piedmont, some board members of the Triangle Greenways Council and other task force volunteers were constructing the 13.2-mile Falls Lake Trail. The trail route curved in and out of coves among tall birch trees, on bridges over rocky streams, and among banks of wildflowers on the south side of Falls Lake from the Falls Lake Dam west to Six Forks Road. The trail construction coordinators were Chris Bracknell and Bill Flournoy, devoted trail leaders. This part of the Falls Lake Trail was designated as a section of the Mountains-to-Sea Trail in April of 1987. Another 6.9 miles of the Falls Lake Trail, between NC-98 and NC-50, was designated as a hiking section of the Mountains-to-Sea Trail in May of 1991. Bill Flournoy, board member of the Triangle Greenways Council, prepared the designation applications for both sections of the Falls Lake Trail. Earlier, in May of 1987, another 9.1 miles were designated after approval of an application presented by Doris B. Hammett, M.D., of the Balsam Highlands Task Force. The section paralleled the Blue Ridge Parkway. In 1988 Bob Benner submitted an application for a section along Woods Mountain for the Central Blue Ridge Task Force. The 12.6-mile route was designated in May 1989. In the same year another 31 miles that involved part of the Arch Nichols Trail of the MST was designated as a result of work by the Pisgah Task Force of the Carolina Mountain Club. The Central Blue Ridge Task Force completed another 12.8 miles to include Boone Fork and Cone Manor near Blowing Rock for a designation in 1990. That same year in May, the Neusiok Trail—21.7 miles in Croatan National Forest, near New Bern—was designated through the efforts of the Carteret Wildlife Club Task Force.

All sections of the MST designated during the years 1991 through 1997 were in the mountains: Old Balsam Gap, 11.1 miles, in September 1992 for the Balsam Highlands Task Force; Arch Nichols Trail (Extension), 8 miles in June 1993 for the Pisgah Task Force of the Carolina Mountain Club; 13 miles of the Tanawha Trail in June 1994 for special crews of the Blue Ridge Parkway; Old Bald to Bear Pen Gap, 12.9 miles, in July 1994 for the Balsam Highlands Task Force; Pisgah Ledges Trail (a new MST route west of the Davidson River and the Pink Beds), 14 miles, in June 1996 for the Pisgah Task Force of the Carolina Mountain Club; South Toe to Buck Creek, 6.5 miles, in May 1997 for the Central Blue Ridge Task Force; and Glassmine Falls Overlook to Black Mountain Campground, 16.9 miles, in November 1997 for the Pisgah Task Force of the Carolina Mountain Club. In September 1998, a 19.1-mile section of the MST was designated from a network of trails constructed by workers of the Greensboro Park System and volunteer groups. Leading this action and making the application was Mike Simmons, county trails coordinator. In December 1999 a 3.8-mile section was designated from Woodlawn Gap to the Catawba River for the Central Blue Ridge Task Force.

As each new section of the Mountains-to-Sea Trail has been designated, the spirits of the trail leaders and task force crews have been lifted. Each designation ceremony, faithfully attended by officials such as director Phillip McKnelly, state trails coordinator Darrell McBane, and others of the Division of Parks and Recreation, has honored those who worked thousands of hours to design, flag, construct, and blaze a trail section. Chairs and board members of the North Carolina Trails Committee, a state advisory board on trails, have participated in the ceremonies as well.

A Memorandum of Understanding between Government Agencies

Early in the Mountains-to-Sea Trail planning process (1979 to 1981), the Department of Environment and Natural Resources (then Department of Natural Resources and Community Development) realized that the cross-state trail would pass through federal properties as well as city and county properties. The most urgent need would be to secure a "Memorandum of Understanding" (MOU) between the U.S. Forest Service (Department of Agriculture), the National Park Service (Department of the Interior), and the North Carolina Department of Environment and Natural Resources. Through this MOU the various agencies agreed to cooperate and to share resources to complete the Mountains-to-Sea Trail; the MOU was renewable every five years. A clause in the agreement allows any of the parties to "terminate this Memorandum of Understanding by providing 60 days written notice." Some of the volunteer leaders felt that this clause undermined the security of long-range planning. Despite these concerns, none of the government agencies or trail task forces has requested to terminate the agreement. The agreement includes Great Smoky Mountains National Park, the Blue Ridge Parkway, Nantahala National Forest, Pisgah National Forest, Croatan National Forest, and Cape Hatteras National Seashore. The following extract from the MOU, which consists of eight parts, illustrates the level of cooperation required by the agreement.

> All parties agree to cooperate and coordinate in the planning, construction, maintenance, administration and use of the Trail. The State will coordinate these activities between the land managing agencies. Implementation will be carried out by the agency administering the lands through which the Trail passes. The selection and approval of the Trail route on-the-ground is the primary responsibility of the land managing agency. All parties will cooperate with and encourage volunteer trail clubs, private organizations and individuals. Funds for Trail planning, construction, maintenance and management activities are the responsibility of the appropriate land managing agency.

A sense of optimism prevailed during this period, when cooperation between government leaders and the task forces had been worked out, an inventory of the many trails that the MST could follow was completed, and plenty of volunteers came out for trail construction. The exuberance and enthusiasm was shown in internal documents of government agencies and on the calendars of the dynamic trail leaders. The enthusiasm of state staff was reflected in an article by the Associated Press in the *News and Observer* dated April 20, 1989:

> "The volunteers do everything with our technical assistance," said Darrell McBane, the state's trails coordinator with the Division of Parks and Recreation, "from the initial scouting, then trying to find out who is the owner of a property to the actual flagging of the trail route and the construction of the trail. They do it all."

"Most of them are hikers," said Bill Flournoy, "whose group is building a section of trail along Falls Lake in Wake and Durham counties."

"The N.C. Trails Committee was formed to plan a west to east trail, using national, state, city and county park land and private land. The Appalachian Trail is the kind of original long-distance trail and a guide for what we are doing," said McBane.

Internal documents in the Division of Parks and Recreation show that the same zeal and faith existed in the early 1980s. In a September 4, 1984, letter from Jim Hallsey, assistant chief of planning and special studies, to Bill Ross, chair of the North Carolina Trails Committee, Hallsey outlined how the MST could be completed "within the next four years." He described a recipe using organization, communication, and determined goals as ingredients. The project was "ambitious but not impossible," said Hallsey, who retained his vision and hope.

Loss of the N.C. Trails Association

A shadow fell over the rosy picture of the MST project and mission at the end of the 1980s. The North Carolina Trails Association, vanguard of the task force movement, began to disintegrate. It held its last general conference at Camp Sertoma near Hanging Rock State Park in late September 1989. Two months later the organization's president, Suzanne Riley, attended the North Carolina Trails Committee meeting at the Falls Lake Corps of Engineers' headquarters in Raleigh. She presented a hopeful and positive report on the purposes and values of the NCTA and distributed the second edition of the Association's trail directory. The directory included the names and addresses of the state's trail organizations and leaders; federal, state, and local government agencies associated with trails; and allied groups involved in outdoor recreation. The first directory of its kind in the state, the publication was of exceptional service to the Mountains-to-Sea Trail program. But Riley's attendance was the last official representation of the NCTA at a Trails Committee meeting, though she remained in contact with Parks and Recreation staff and some of the task force leaders until some business matters were completed. Although Riley had the best in qualities of organizational leadership, her talents came too late to restore the once dynamic and influential trail organization. Some of the State Parks and Recreation officials said to her that they believed the organization no longer had "sufficient representation" of the state's multiple trail organizations. But Phillip McKnelly, newly appointed that year as the Division Director of Parks and Recreation, later stated that the "lack of service and support to the state's trail program by the Association was an irreplaceable loss."

During 1990, and on occasions since then, a number of "autopsies" were conducted on the NCTA's demise. Some concluded that there were "internal conflicts" that resulted from power plays in management. Others thought that "the board of directors wanted to control the Committee [North Carolina Trails Committee]." A former NCTA leader said the staff members of Parks and Recreation "became hostile to Association leaders' efforts to influence DPR [Division of Parks and Recreation] policy." Another diagnosis theorized that the NCTA suffered from a vacuum left by its founder, Louise Chatfield. Chatfield was the matriarch of the organization and the originator of many of its goals and dreams for major trails and recreational projects. Before her death in 1986, her presence was a kind of cementing power that enabled the task forces to keep on course and encouraged the members to keep faith that the MST would be completed. To achieve the founder's dreams, the Association had outstanding leaders in addition to Chatfield and her family. Among them were presidents with special talent and energy: Larkin Kirkman of Raleigh, Willie Taylor of Greensboro, David Drexel of Southern Pines, the late Hazel Monroe of Wadesboro, Frank McNutt of Durham, and Suzanne Riley of Charlotte. The NCTA's board of directors' working relationship with the North Carolina Trails Committee and Parks and Recreation staff was so cohesive that it prompted Committee board member R. M. Collins to remark that "you can't know the difference between who belongs to which."

A Challenge for Volunteer Trail Workers

The early 1990s appeared bleak for the future of the MST. Not only was the loss of the NCTA taking its toll on active task force leadership, but the state's Division of Parks and Recreation did not have a progressive course of action to fill the volunteer leadership gaps. During the life of the NCTA, sixteen active task forces were organized for work within the MST corridor, but after the NCTA's demise the number declined to five (of which three were in the mountain region) by 1993.

The growing lack of interest in the MST was showing among both volunteer workers and Parks and Recreation staff. Some particular incidents illustrate this fact. On the Cape Hatteras Beach Trail signs disappeared as a result of storms and vandalism, and blazes faded from the wear of sand and sun. Park staff no longer published the MST title on sectional brochures of the Cape Hatteras National Seashore. Weeds and fallen trees began to cover the cleared path of the MST along the Blue Ridge Parkway north of Doughton Park, and the task force that once planned to construct the Louise Chatfield Trail from the Blue Ridge Parkway into Stone Mountain State Park was no longer active. Extended construction on the Falls Lake Trail north of Raleigh was halted. A series of events contributed to the latter and prevented the Triangle Greenways Council (a volunteer task force) from continuing work on these parts of the MST. One event happened late in 1991 when bicyclists and equestrians began to violate government regulations on trail usage of the MST. As a result, the U.S. Army Corps of Engineers (which had leased property to the Division of Parks and Recreation and the Wildlife Resources Commission) requested that the Division of Parks and Recreation enforce the restrictions. But the state division had neither the law enforcement officers nor the financial resources for the management of the MST sections. During 1992 efforts were made by the Division of Parks and Recreation to display "foot traffic only" signs, periodically enforce the restrictions with the help of volunteers, and request that bicycle shops inform bicyclists of the regulations.

To further address the multi-use issue, the secretary of the Department of Environment, Health and Natural Resources, William W. Cobey Jr., appointed a twenty-one-member committee (the Falls/Jordan Trails Task Force) in December 1992 to study and recommend action, and to "develop management options that would provide hiker, equestrian, mountain bicycle trails, and hunting opportunities on the Falls and Jordan Lake properties."

There was not a single name of a hiker in the initial list of committee members, but by the time of the first meeting, January 27, 1993, Larkin Kirkman (a long-time volunteer who worked on constructing the Falls Lake Trail and former president of the North Carolina Trails Association) was included. For a year the committee faced difficult decisions—difficult enough that at one point, in the summer of 1993, the group declared an impasse. Secretary Cobey's final report in January 1994 stated that the MST sections would be reconstructed to the width of a single-lane road to accommodate all users. This easy-way-out decision did not show comprehension of the enormous cost, and the committee underestimated the negative reaction from all user groups. Kirkman spoke eloquently for the volunteer workers who had spent ten years constructing this section of the MST. On January 14, 1994, he defended the status quo of the Falls Lake Trail sections of the MST. "As one of the planners and builders of the currently dedicated trail at Falls Lake I believe I speak accurately when I say that the trail was conceived and constructed as a hiking trail, and that its design did not contemplate use either by horse traffic or by cyclists."

He described how such a conversion would require substantial rebuilding and relocation and in the process would destroy the integrity of the trail. "I believe the removal of this lovely public amenity is not necessary, would be equivalent to vandalism, and would alienate numerous persons who have supported the North Carolina Trails System." Kirkman and other volunteer workers recommended a solution that would benefit mountain bikers and equestrian groups. Rather than destroy the MST route, they could construct a more adaptable trail on the north shore of the lake. (The north shore has the potential for more than 100 miles of new trails.) While the issue of destroying the MST route languished, Hurricane Fran swept through the Falls Lake area on September 5–6, 1996. The state closed all Falls Lake Recreation Area trails until professional workers could clear the trails and rebuild the bridges.

Those of us on the Board of Directors of the North Carolina Trails Committee in 1995 (and new board members since) noticed a change in overall Division of Parks and Recreation policy. For example, the following statement was included in the 1994 Division of Parks and Recreation handbook:

> Between 1979 and 1987 the Mountains-to-Sea Trail Plan became the primary focus of the Division of Parks and Recreation and the North Carolina Trails Committee. Since 1987, that focus has been redirected to encourage and assist all federal, state, local governments and volunteer trail organizations who have an interest in planning, construction, maintenance, and management of trails.

This expansion would result in more equitable attention being given to bicycle and equestrian trails, canoe trails, rails-to-trails, and greenways. While accepting this focus as desirable and essential, the NCTC voted on a recommendation June 23, 1995, to "reaffirm our support of the MST concept."

At a meeting of the NCTC called by division director Phillip McKnelly on September 15, 1995, for the purpose of discussing the future of the MST, he explained in detail how public demands for a wide range of park and recreation services had escalated. He also stated that "I would love to see a hiking trail connecting Clingmans Dome in the Great Smoky Mountains National Park to Jockey's Ridge State Park." The NCTC board members again stated they wished "to keep the dream alive . . . that it would be difficult to eliminate the MST name since North Carolina is known for its MST effort, and there is great promotional and economic value in having a completed and advertised MST." Agreement was reached that by combining the overland trail efforts with the N.C. Department of Transportation's Mountains-to-Sea Bicycle Routes, a true multi-use trail from the mountains to the sea can become a reality. The NCTC voted to issue a statement defining the Mountains-to-Sea Trail as the state's flagship trail of the North Carolina Trail System.

But a month later, on October 11, the Division of Parks and Recreation appeared to question the "flagship" image when officials requested that Darrell McBane call meetings with the three major active volunteer task forces in the mountains, who had completed more than 240 miles of the MST. He inquired of their interest in continuing to use the MST name rather than choose other sectional trail names. The separate meetings involved the Balsam Highlands Task Force and the Pisgah Task Force of the Carolina Mountain Club. (A meeting with the Central Blue Ridge Task Force did not materialize, but a telephone conversation was made to the task force leader, Bob Benner.) As chair of the North Carolina Trails Committee I attended the meetings, and another Board member, Anne Alaya, from Waynesville, also attended the Balsam Highlands Task Force meeting. The mountain region trails specialist, Dwayne Stutzman, attended both meetings. Volunteers at these meetings defended the name of the MST. "We do not believe the Mountains-to-Sea Trail should be killed by pessimism at the state level because it has not been built in a day," said Doris B. Hammett, M.D., chair of the Balsam Highlands Task Force. Later in the day a dinner meeting was held at the crossroads of Mills River for the Pisgah Task Force, chaired by Dick Johnson. Although the discussion was less dramatic than with the Balsam Highlands Task Force, the response was to support and retain the MST name.

The Carolina Mountain Club, organized in 1920, is the largest in membership and can be the most productive of any of the MST task forces. It has three organized sections with supervisors or coordinators and more than forty-five sub-task forces. In addition to maintaining about 90 miles of the Appalachian Trail, Carolina Mountain Club volunteers have constructed and maintained more than 93 miles of the Mountains-to-Sea Trail.

Living through the successes and failures of the NCTA and serving fourteen years on the Board of Directors of the North Carolina Trails Committee, I became aware, in the mid-1990s, that the MST program was not only in jeopardy but also might lose its name. I discussed the issue with some of the former and current task force leaders of the MST and associated government officials. The consensus was that the Mountains-to-Sea Trail needed a parent or umbrella organization whose focus was entirely on its defense and promotion. The result was the formation of the Friends of the Mountains-to-Sea Trail.

Friends of the Mountains-to-Sea Trail

The first actions were to resurrect public interest in the MST and to plan the first all-hiking expedition across the state on the designated trails and connector routes, and to form and charter the nonprofit Friends of the Mountains-to-Sea Trail (FMST). Incorporated on August 5, 1997, the FMST's charter stated that it was organized "to promote the concept, research and provide information, advocate cooperative efforts among allied government offices and citizens, and support task forces and trail organizations for the benefit of a cross-state trail known as the Mountains to the Sea Trail." Among its chartered purposes are

> to encourage, sponsor, promote, publicize, and increase public awareness of the Mountains-to-Sea Trail that has a western terminus at Clingmans Dome in the Great Smoky Mountains National Park to its eastern terminus at Jockey's Ridge State Park near the Atlantic Ocean . . . to support task forces . . . to inform and educate the public of the biological, geological, human heritage and natural beauty across the state . . . to publish newsletters and brochures . . . to have meetings and conferences . . . to protect the Trail from neglect or damage . . .

While the charter was going through its legal process, plans for a cross-state hike were completed by March 1997. Alan Householder of Asheville, an experienced hiker who had hiked the Appalachian Trail, the Pacific Crest Trail, the major trails of England, and many other trails, would be my hiking companion. I had previously hiked all the trails and connecting sections from Clingmans Dome to Blowing Rock as well as all other designated sections of the MST and had bicycled the remainder of the state corridor. In preparation for publishing *North Carolina Hiking Trails* and other state guidebooks, I had hiked most of the trails twice and some as many as six to ten times. Householder had also hiked some of the mountain trails, and both of us had separately hiked the Cape Hatteras Beach Trail.

But only Householder has the title of being the first through-hiker, walking every step on a defined route with either a backpack or daypack. He also camped, setting up and sleeping in a tent wherever possible. Householder started on Clingmans Dome in the Great Smoky Mountains National Park on April 18, 1997, met me at Blowing Rock on May 8, and together we walked the remainder of the distance (I had previously hiked to our starting point). We finished at the highest sand dune on the East Coast—Jockey's Ridge State Park—on June 12, 1997. Without Alan Householder or a similarly experienced hiker, I would not have attempted to hike the bicycle route back roads alone.

Among the memories of that springtime journey is the meeting of hundreds of new "friends" for the Mountains-to-Sea Trail. One of the most appreciated events on the journey was when we arrived at the Bayleaf office of the Division of Parks and Recreation in Raleigh. There was a welcome party, consisting of

Darrell McBane, Phillip McKnelly, Jim Hallsey, Smith Raynor, Lola Morrison, and others, waiting for us at a picnic table in the shade. With a welcome cake and refreshing drinks we did not know where to begin our story and how to answer all the questions. Soon, the entire staff took turns coming out of the building to greet us. It was like coming home to a big family reunion.

The first hiker to officially hike across a major part of the state was Lee Price. As a participant in the Mountains-to-Sea Trek, a feat sponsored by the North Carolina Trail Association and referred to earlier in this chapter, he hiked, backpacker style, from Soco Gap on the Blue Ridge Parkway to Smithfield, an erratic distance of approximately 475 miles. On October 18, 1994, Jeffrey Scott and Jarrett Franklin, graduates of Appalachian State University, began at Nags Head on the coast and ended at Clingmans Dome in the Smokies on February 19, 1995. Of the time, they said that seventy-five days had been backpacking with some breaks and nearly a month break during the Christmas period. They did not follow or hike a completely MST-defined route in the official corridor, and their logistical record is not known. Their hike was part of a project to bring attention and funds to the preservation of Howard (Howard's) Knob, a scenic peak at 4,420 feet elevation in sight of the city of Boone.

Revitalizing the Task Force Process

In the late-1990s, the FMST took on the role of presenting requests to state and local government agencies for the advancement of the Mountains-to-Sea Trail. For example, in 1997 after my expedition from Clingmans Dome to Jockey's Ridge State Park, the FMST sent a request to the Division of Parks and Recreation seeking funding to restore the position of the Western Piedmont Trails Specialist, formerly held by John Shaffner. The staff response was that a budget request had been made since 1994, and that a request would probably need to go to the state legislature. For a request in trail construction funds, the staff responded with the encouraging news that an increase had been approved by the state legislature for all areas of trail construction and allied needs through the Adopt-A-Trail Program. Depending on congressional action, there could also be federal funding for trail projects.

In response to the FMST's request that the integrity of completed MST sections (such as the Falls Lake Trail) be maintained and that the Memorandum of Understanding with the federal agencies be secured, the state staff assured the organization that the agreement documents would continue to be signed by the land managers. On the topic of the Falls Lake Trail, the response from state staff was that "The NCTC understands the sensitivity of and the importance of this issue. Because of the State Trails Program overall mission—to promote the development of all trails—we plan to discuss this issue in greater detail in future meetings."

On the issue of MST routing and corridor recommendations, the state trails staff indicated that the route planned in 1989 was not permanent. "We encourage the FMST, based upon your research, to recommend a complete routing of the MST with maps and documentation of reasons for changes in the initial route to the NCTC for consideration." There was also a recommendation by the state that FMST remember that "liability exposure to the State and the Division are too great for us to promote walking road shoulders." Also outlined was the fact that the "North Carolina Department of Transportation and its Bicycle and Pedestrian Program are responsible for identifying and signing safe and acceptable bicycle routes." The FMST was also asked to make efforts to avoid public confusion over where the two mountains-to-sea routes (hiking and bicycling) cross or connect. The FMST assisted in expeditiously preparing the trail segments that were ready for designation, and was asked to present reasonable guidelines and timelines for designation of other sections.

It was not possible to cover every exciting achievement and each episode of failure and disappointment in this brief history of the Mountains-to-Sea Trail. But there is one type of achievement that brings me exceptional pleasure and emotional pride. That is when government officials, task force workers, and visitors gather to officially designate a section of the MST. I well remember November 15, 1997, at Mount Mitchell State Park. Hoarfrost and snow had turned every tree, shrub, and blade of grass into crystal pieces of art, a background showpiece for a celebration at the state's highest peak. My spirits lifted even higher when I met two backpackers, Patrick Hart of Kernersville and Brenton Young of Chapel Hill, who were following the MST, at the intersection of the trail on the park entrance road. "One day we will hike across the state," said Hart.

At the park's visitor center were the honored workers from the Pisgah Task Force of the Carolina Mountain Club who had worked on this section of the MST. Almost all of them senior citizens, they sat in a crescent before the warmth of the large fireplace; they listened to the distinguished speakers, and they had daypacks by their side, ready to show their guests a spectacular segment of their craftsmanship on the rocky Potato Knob. At 11 A.M. Elizabeth Feil, president of the Carolina Mountain Club, gave the welcoming remarks. She praised all who had made "this monumental task" possible. She said credit was due to Arch Nichols, a man "who could motivate people." Nichols was the dreamer and the leader who had envisioned a 60-mile foot trail from Mount Pisgah to Mount Mitchell. Now, eight years after his death, his trail-building coworkers were here to recognize a completed task.

Robert Johnson, the MST coordinator for the Carolina Mountain Club, praised the team, some of whom had worked twenty-one years on the mission. Philip McKnelly, division director of Parks and Recreation, thanked the crew for their hard work and praised the leadership of Arch Nichols. Will Orr, landscape architect of the Division of Resources Planning and Professional Services for the Blue Ridge Parkway, said "this is almost too good an idea for it to happen. Now you need to celebrate your heroes." Mary Noel, recreation staff officer for Pisgah National Forest, remarked that these occasions are one of the best parts of her work; and J. Clark Hipp, chair of the North Carolina Trails Committee, said that "this type of celebration is to show appreciation for who does the work." After lunch the task force leaders led the group on an ascent to the scenic mountainside. Among the open grassy spaces were groves of birch, rhododendron, and balsam fir. The snow had melted, the clouds and fog lifted; the sun began to shine.

More recently, on September 20, 1998, a 19.1-mile section of the MST was designated on Owl's Roost Trail (which partially passes through Bur-Mil Park in northwest Greensboro). That ceremony took place on a new asphalt MST section and rebuilt bridge near Lake Brandt. On its way east from that site the MST joins a combination of connecting trails: Nat Green Trail, Laurel Bluff Trail, Peninsula Trail, Osprey Trail, and Townsend Trail to Bryan Park. Pleasant weather and excitement over the designation of a new segment of the MST in the central part of the state brought many people to the event. In attendance were Triad area citizens; local government officials; members of the North Carolina Trails Council, the Friends of the Mountains-to-Sea Trail, and the Sierra Club; and Division of Parks and Recreation officials. "We are nearly twenty miles closer to our dreams," declared Jeff Brewer, president of the volunteer FMST, to Ethan Feinsilver of the *Greensboro News and Record*.

By 1999 the FMST had restored not only the task forces created by the North Carolina Trails Association, but had added twenty-six new task forces to oversee the continuing development of the MST. The year 1999 was also a turning point in federal funding when the FMST received a $30,000 grant for the purchase of construction equipment, trail signage, and promotional material. On March 17, 2000, the Division of Parks and Recreation and the North Carolina Trails Committee approved a $50,000 grant to begin construction of a footbridge over the Catawba River in McDowell County, and another $20,000 for much needed trail-work equipment and signage. Private foundations were also beginning to provide cash gifts for construction costs of the MST.

Highlighting the dreams and goals of the FMST for the end of the decade was an announcement by Division of Parks and Recreation director Phillip McKnelly on November 19, 1999, at an NCTC meeting in Cary. He proposed that the state legislature "authorize the creation of the Mountains-to-Sea Trail

State Park; specify that the initial trail through eastern North Carolina follow the Neuse River corridor from Falls Lake to the Pamlico Sound; and the Neuse River corridor should be established as both a state hiking and canoe trail." He summarized a three-page document in stating "the concept of a mountains-to-sea trail was conceived during Governor Hunt's first term in office in 1978. It is appropriate that steps necessary to make the trail a reality should be initiated during the final year of the governor's fourth term."

On July 12, 2000, the North Carolina General Assembly ratified House Bill #1603 and Senate Bill #1311 (with some modifications). The bills authorized the Department of Environment and Natural Resources to incorporate the Mountains-to-Sea Trail into the state park system of the Division of Parks and Recreation. "The Division shall promote, encourage, and facilitate the establishment of dedicated connecting trails through lands managed by other governmental agencies and nonprofit organizations in order to form a continuous trail across the State" is an example of statements in the enaction. The House bill was introduced by representatives Daniel Barefoot, Arlie Culp, George Goodwin, Pryor Gibson III, and Joe Hackney. The prime sponsor was Representative Gibson. In the Senate, the bill was introduced by Robert Carpenter, Howard Lee, and T. LaFontine Odom. Senator Lee was the prime sponsor for the Senate bill.

Friends of the Mountains-to-Sea Trail officers and board members in 2000 were Jeff Brewer, president (Raleigh); Chris Bracknell, vice-president (Raleigh), Allen de Hart, treasurer and projects director (Louisburg), Elaine Marshall, secretary (Wilson), Charles Yarborough, attorney (Louisburg), Ray Benedicktus (Fayetteville), Bob Benner (Morganton), Mark Gatehouse (Greensboro), Emily Grogan (Pinnacle), Alan Householder (Asheville), Glenn McLeroy (Charlotte), and Mike Simpson (Greensboro).

Officers and board members of the North Carolina Trails Committee in 2000 were Mary Barry, chairperson (Cary), J. Clark Hipp, immediate past chairperson (Wilmington), Anne Ayala (Waynesville), Dean Coleman (Burlington), Allen Poole (Manteo), Mike Price (Ellenboro), and Brian Sears (Granite Falls).

MOUNTAINS-TO-SEA TRAIL: STAGES OF DEVELOPMENT

LOCATIONS (WEST TO EAST)	DESIGNATION BY DPR	USAGE	CONDITION	MILEAGE	
				MAIN	ALTERNATE
Clingmans Dome in Great Smoky Mountains National Park to west terminus of the Blue Ridge Parkway at Cherokee (MP 469.1)	Designated	Hiking (and partly equestrian)	Complete	27.4	28.7
Blue Ridge Parkway (MP 469.1) to Balsam Gap (South) (MP 443.1) jct with US-23/74	Undesignated	Hiking (and Parkway bicycling)	Under construction	26.0	—
Balsam Gap (South) (MP 443.1) jct with US-23/74 to Blowing Rock at Blue Ridge Parkway (MP 291.9)	Designated (except for 9.6 miles)	Hiking	Complete (except for Bald Knob area)	227.9	241.2
Blowing Rock and Parkway (MP 291.9) to Laurel Springs (MP 248.1)	Undesignated	Hiking (and Parkway bicycling)	Planning stages	47.2	—
Laurel Springs (MP 248.1) jct NC-18 to Devil's Garden Overlook (MP 235.7)	Undesignated	Hiking	Nearly complete	13.9	—
Devil's Garden Overlook (MP 235.7) to Stone Mtn. State Park Visitor Center	Undesignated	Hiking	Nearly complete	8.2	8.5
Stone Mtn. State Park Visitor Center to Hanging Rock State Park (West)	Undesignated (except 4.0 miles designated)	Hiking (or bicycling)	Official DOT bicycle Rt #4, complete	62.7	63.2
Hanging Rock State Park (West) to Bur-Mil Park, North Greensboro	Undesignated (except 3.5 miles designated)	Hiking (or bicycling)	Unofficial DOT bicycle Rt, complete	36.2	—

LOCATIONS (WEST TO EAST)	DESIGNATION BY DPR	USAGE	CONDITION	MILEAGE	
				MAIN	ALTERNATE
Bur-Mil Park, North Greensboro, to Bryan Park entrance	Designated	Hiking	Complete	20.2	—
Bryan Park entrance to Falls Lake State Rec Area (West), at NC-50	Undesignated	Hiking (or bicycling)	Partial official county bicycle Rt, complete	82.8	86.3
Falls Lake State Rec Area (West) at NC-50, to Falls Lake State Rec Area (East) at Falls of Neuse Road	Designated (except 3.4 miles at Blue Jay Point)	Hiking	Complete	26.2	26.0
Falls Lake Rec Area (East) at Falls of Neuse Road to Croatan National Forest (North)	Undesignated (except 8.7 miles designated)	Hiking (or bicycling)	Official DOT bicycle Rt #2 & #7, complete	173.1	195.0
Croatan National Forest (North) to Croatan National Forest (South)	Designated	Hiking	Complete	25.8	—
Croatan National Forest (South) to Cedar Island and Ocracoke Island Ferry	Undesignated	Hiking (or bicycling)	Official DOT bicycle Rt #7, complete	44.7	—
Cedar Island Ferry to Ocracoke Island and Cape Hatteras National Seashore, to Jockey's Ridge State Park	Designated	Hiking	Complete	112.0	111.7
Total				934.3	974.6

Legend:

DPR (Division of Parks and Recreation)
DOT (Department of Transportation)

MOUNTAINS-TO-SEA TRAIL: DISTANCES BY SECTION

CHAPTER AND SECTION	MAIN ROUTE (MILEAGE)	ALTERNATE ROUTE (MILEAGE)	CUMULATIVE TOTALS	
Chapter 1. Great Smoky Mountains National Park				
Section 1	27.4	28.7	27.4	28.7
Chapter 2. Blue Ridge Parkway (West and South)				
Section 2	13.4	—	40.8	42.1
Section 3	12.6	—	53.4	54.7
Chapter 3. Nantahala National Forest (Highlands District)				
Section 4	24.2	—	77.6	78.9
Chapter 4. Pisgah National Forest (Pisgah District)				
Section 5	8.5	—	86.1	87.4
Section 6	21.4	37.8	107.5	125.2
Chapter 5. Blue Ridge Parkway (Central)				
Section 7	32.3	—	139.8	157.5
Section 8	23.0	—	162.8	180.5
Chapter 6. Pisgah National Forest (Toecane District)				
Section 9	23.2	22.9	186.0	203.4
Chapter 7. Pisgah National Forest (Grandfather District)				
Section 10	13.1	—	199.1	216.5
Section 11	33.3	—	232.4	249.8
Section 12	24.2	21.5	256.6	271.3
Chapter 8. Blue Ridge Parkway (North)				
Section 13	24.6	—	281.2	295.9
Section 14	15.7	—	296.9	311.6
Section 15	15.2	—	312.1	326.8
Section 16	16.3	—	328.4	343.1
Section 17	13.9	—	342.3	357.0
Chapter 9. Stone Mountain and Foothills				
Section 18	8.2	8.5	350.5	365.5
Section 19	19.7	—	370.2	385.2
Section 20	23.3	—	393.5	408.5
Section 21	19.7	20.2	413.2	428.7
Chapter 10. Hanging Rock and Western Piedmont				
Section 22	16.7	—	429.9	445.4
Section 23	19.5	—	449.4	464.9

CHAPTER AND SECTION	MAIN ROUTE (MILEAGE)	ALTERNATE ROUTE (MILEAGE)	CUMULATIVE TOTALS	
Section 24	20.2	—	469.6	485.1
Section 25	56.9	—	526.5	542.0
Chapter 11. Central Piedmont and Falls Lake				
Section 26	29.8	33.5	556.3	575.5
Section 27	22.4	22.2	578.7	597.7
Chapter 12. Eastern Piedmont and Western Coastal Plain				
Section 28	20.3	—	599.0	618.0
Section 29	31.2	—	630.2	649.2
Section 30	20.8	—	651.0	670.0
Section 31	20.9	42.5	671.9	712.5
Chapter 13. Central Coastal Plain				
Section 32	13.5	—	685.4	726.0
Section 33	23.5	—	708.9	749.5
Section 34	21.9	—	730.8	771.4
Section 35	21.0	—	751.8	792.4
Chapter 14. Croatan National Forest and Cedar Island				
Section 36	25.8	—	777.6	818.2
Section 37	44.7	—	822.3	862.9
Chapter 15. Cape Hatteras National Seashore				
Section 38	112.0	111.7	934.3	974.6

MAPS

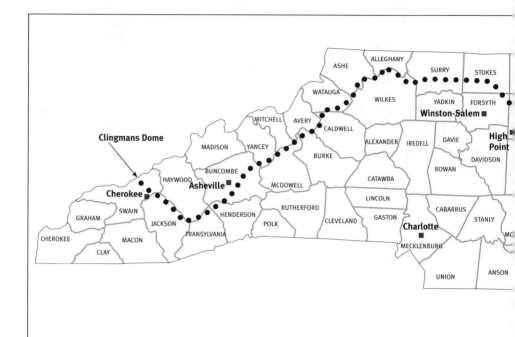

MAP LEGEND

TRAIL CLASSIFICATIONS

Mountains-to-Sea Trail ● ● ● ●

Alternate Mountains-to-Sea Trail route ○○○○○

Sauratown Trail ᴐ ᴐ ᴐ ᴐ ᴐ

Ferries — — — —

Scale for inset maps 1 0 1 2 miles

Scale for topographic maps 0 .5 1 mile

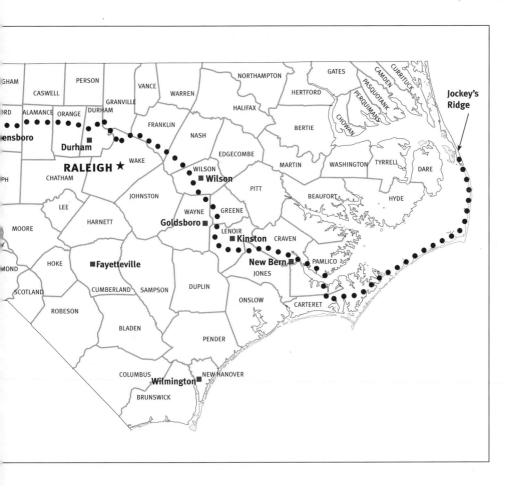

Jockey's Ridge

SYMBOLS (used on inset maps)

77	Interstates	▲	Campgrounds
601	U.S. highways	✚	Hospitals
66	N.C. highways	●	Towns or communities
7	N.C. bicycle routes	■	State parks or points of interest

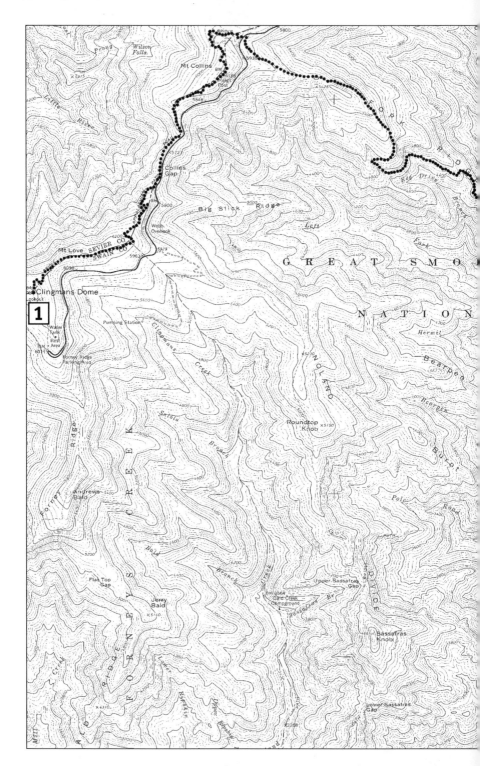

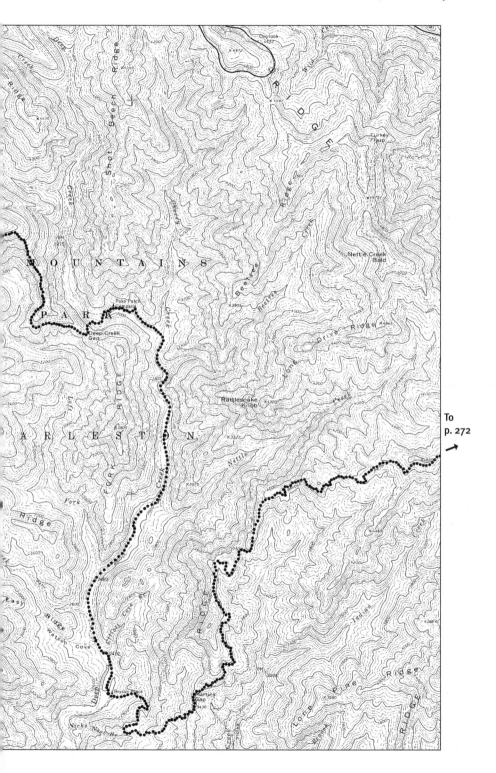

To
p. 272

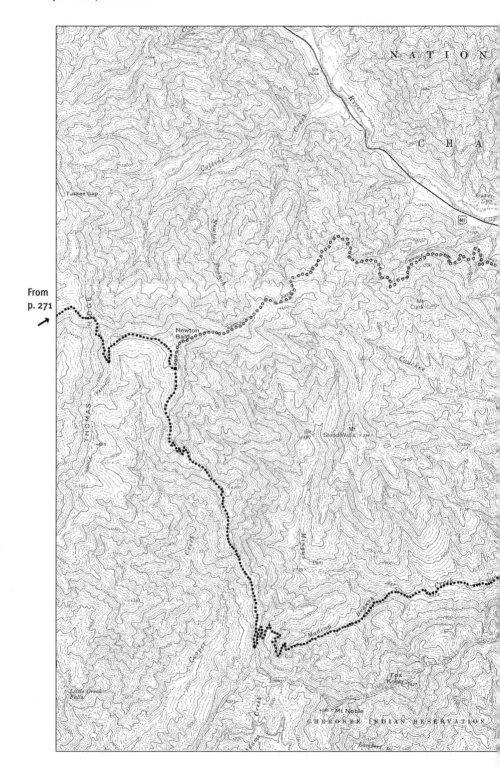

From
p. 271

To
p. 274

2

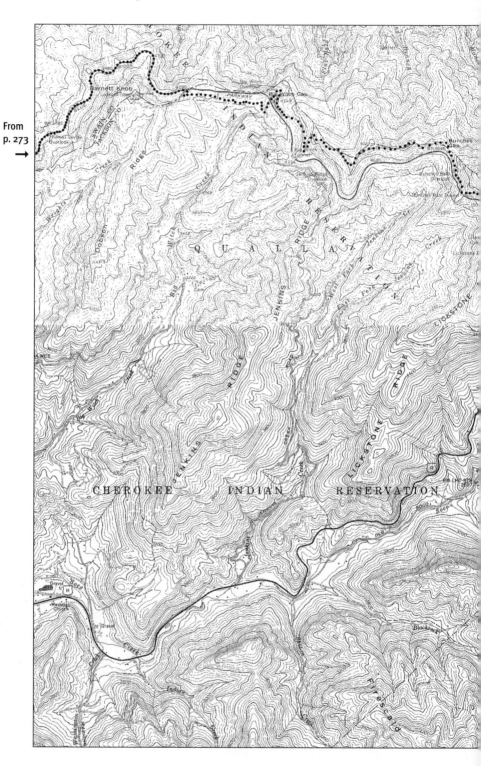

From
p. 273
→

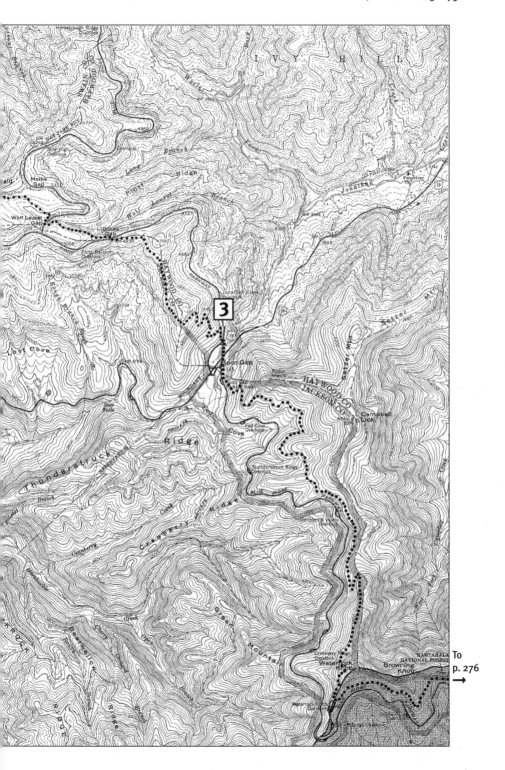

To
p. 276

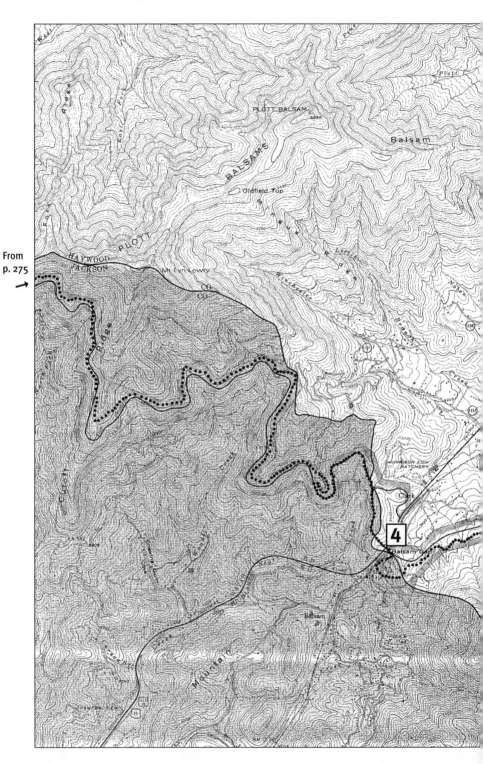

From p. 275

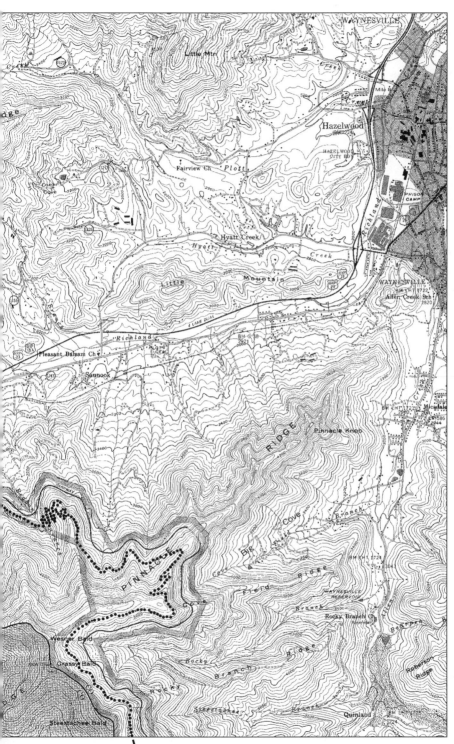

↓ To p. 279

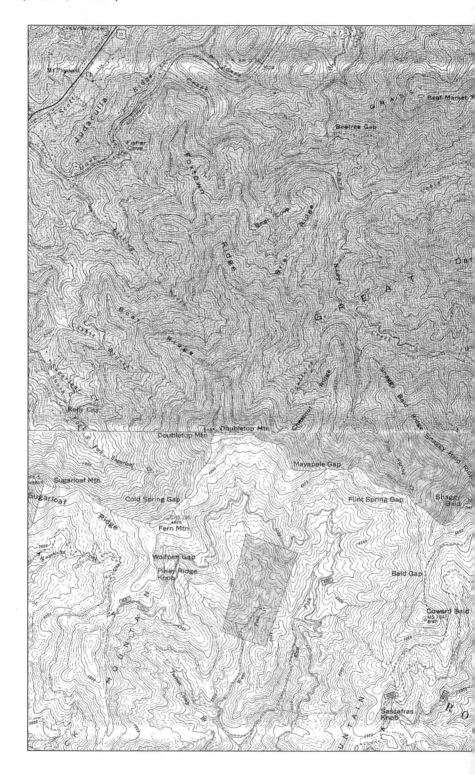

From p. 277

To
p. 280

From
p. 279
→

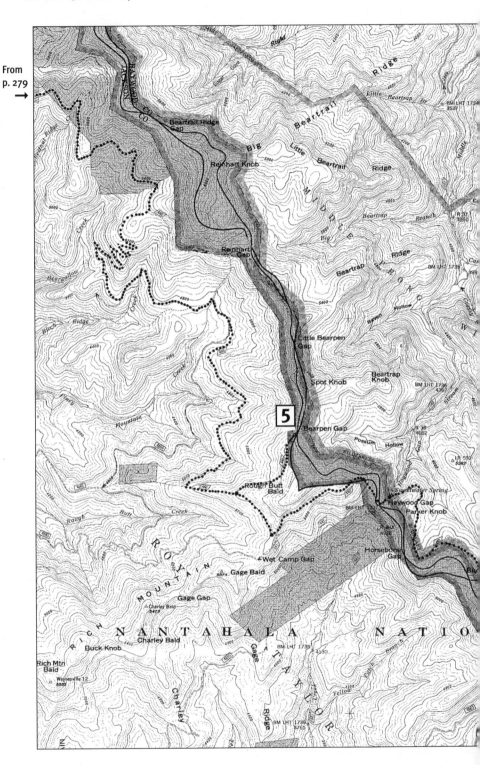

To
p. 282

6

6a

To
p. 284

6a

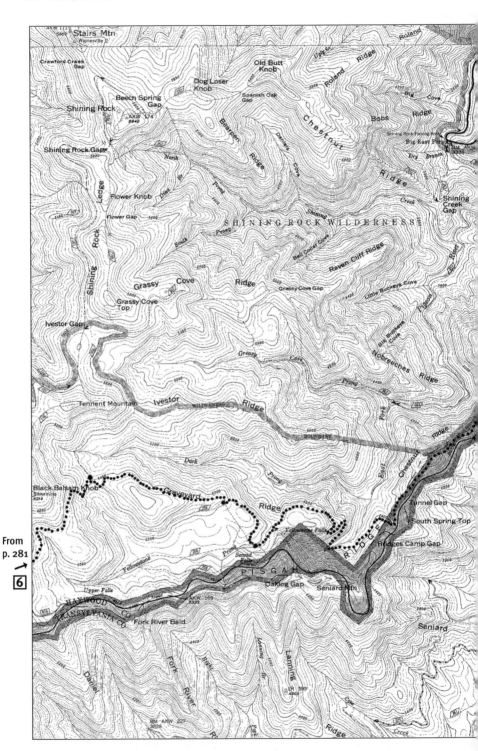

From
p. 281

To p. 287 ↑

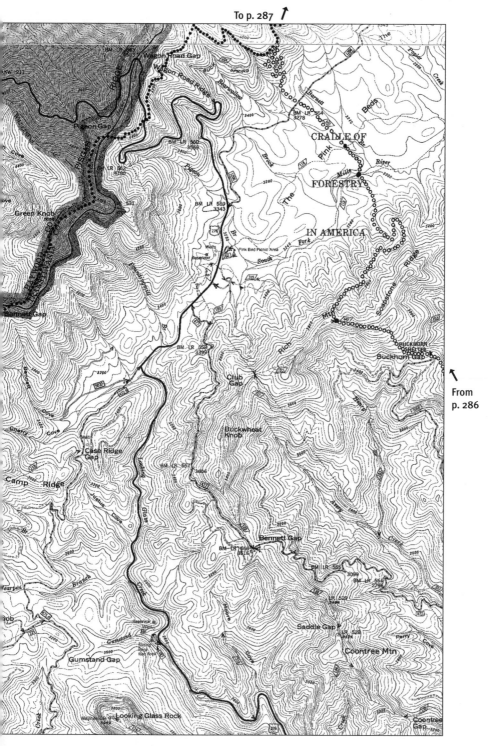

From
p. 286

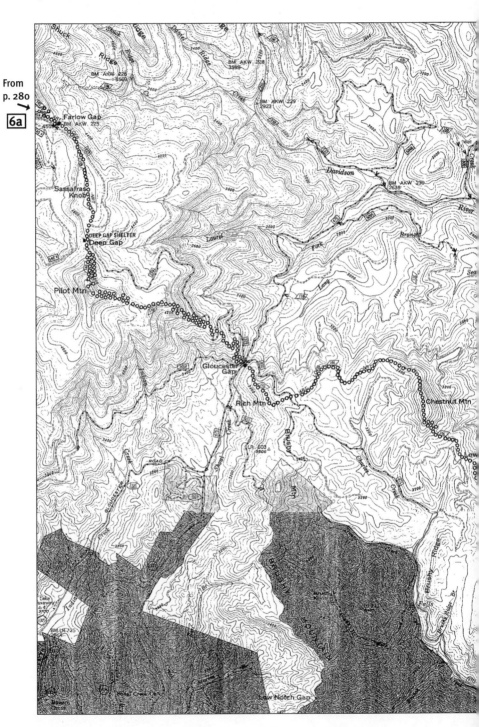

From
p. 280

6a

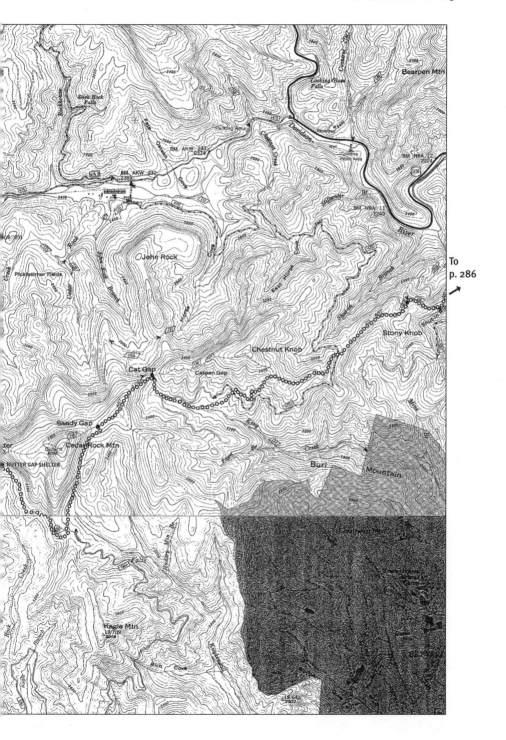

To
p. 286

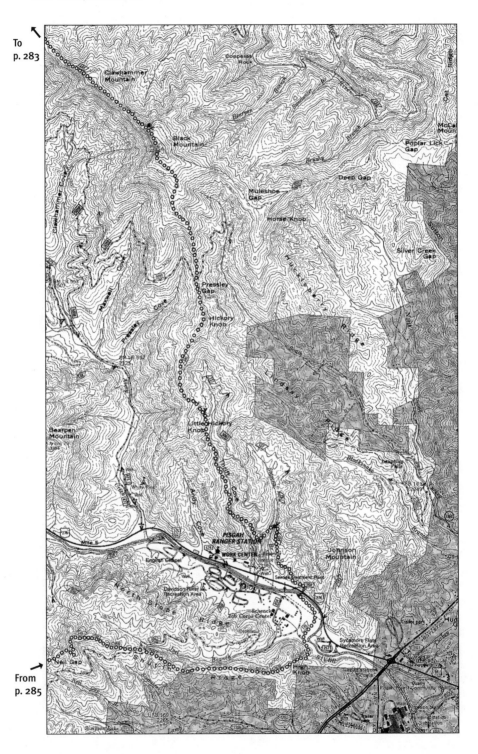

To
p. 283

From
p. 285

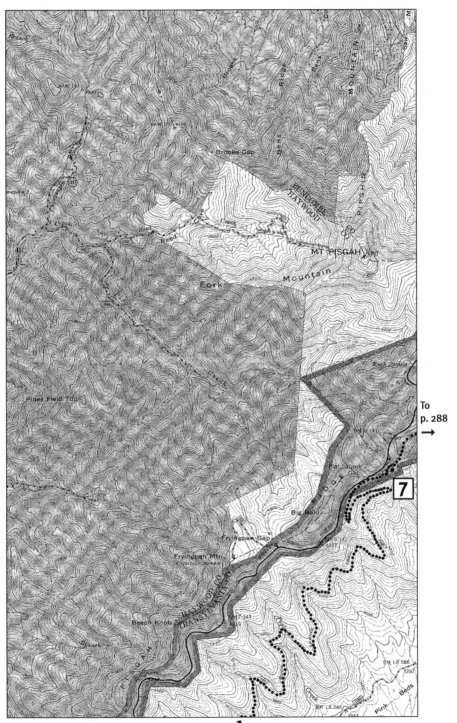

To
p. 288
→

7

↗ From p. 283

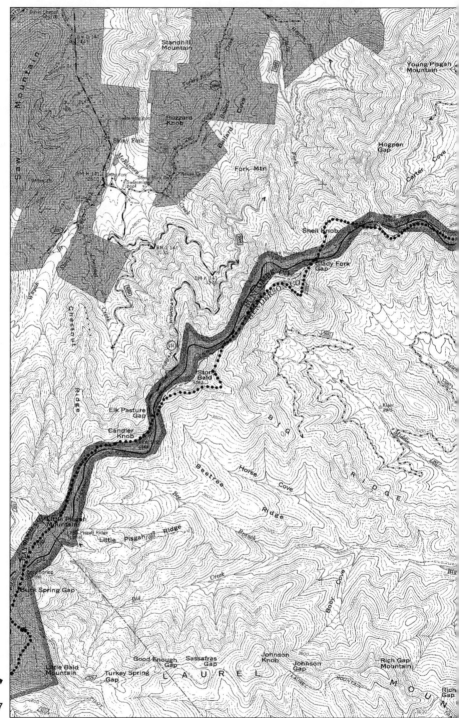

From
p. 287

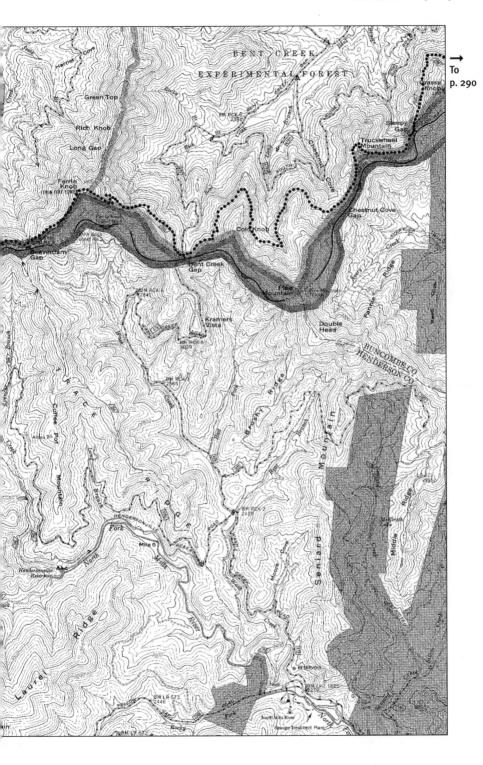

To
p. 290

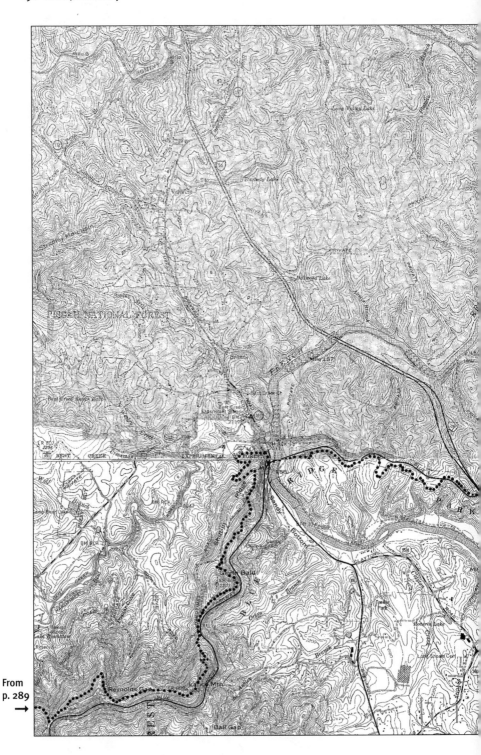

From
p. 289
→

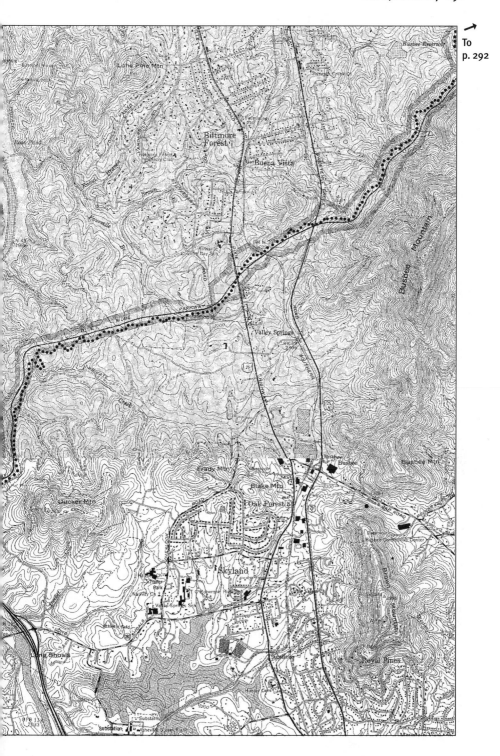

To
p. 292

To p. 293

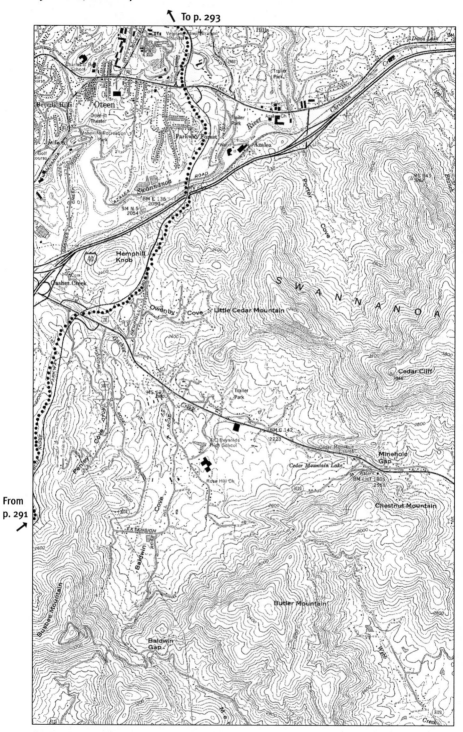

From
p. 291

↑ To p. 294

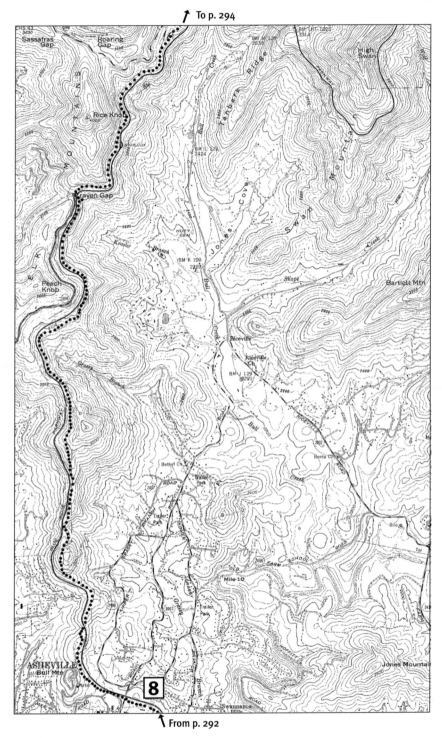

8

↑ From p. 292

↑ From
p. 293

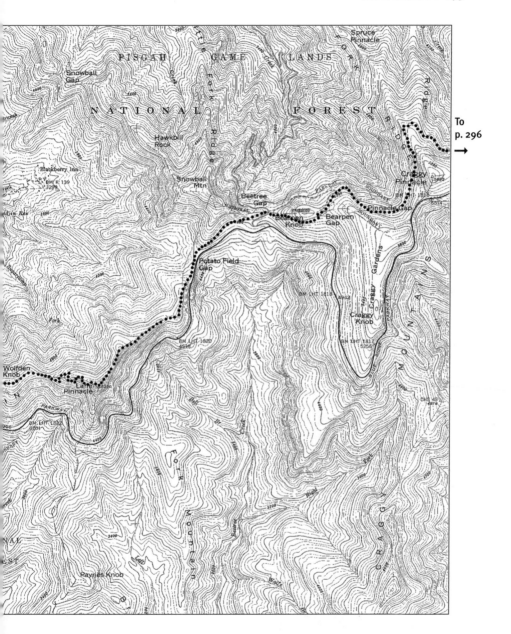

To
p. 296
→

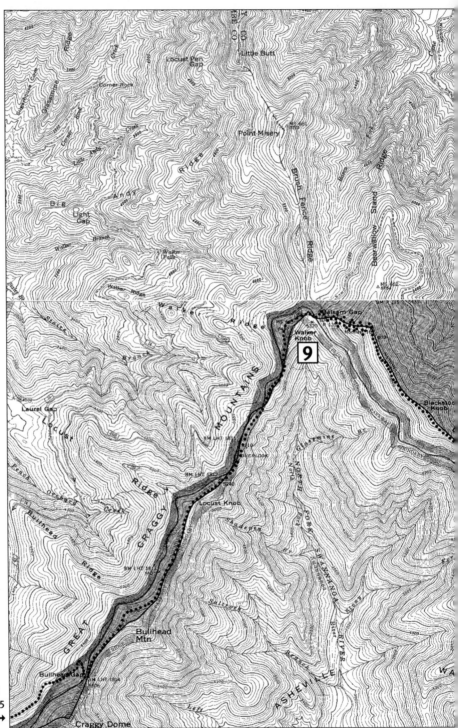

From
p. 295
→

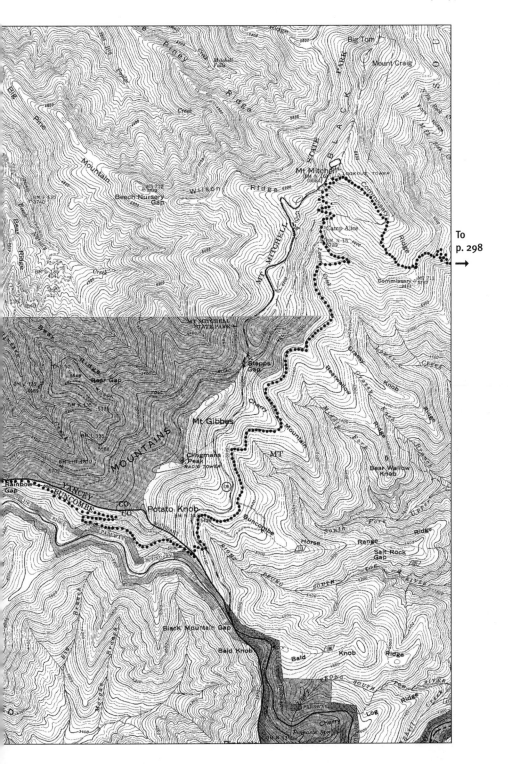

To
p. 298
→

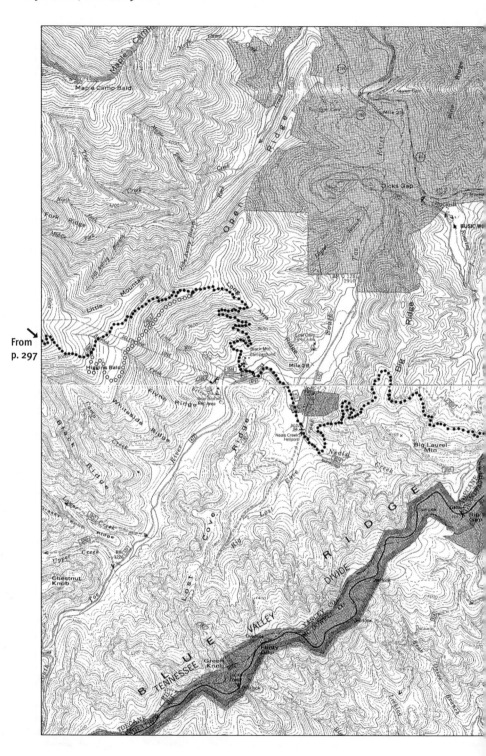

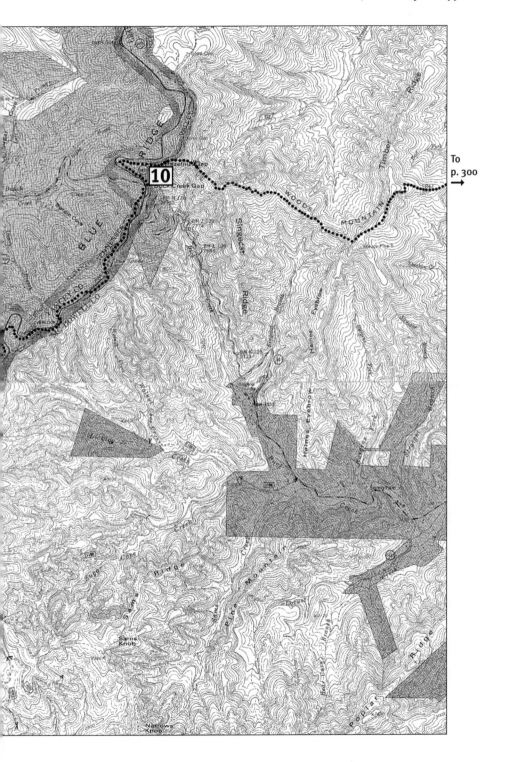

To
p. 300
→

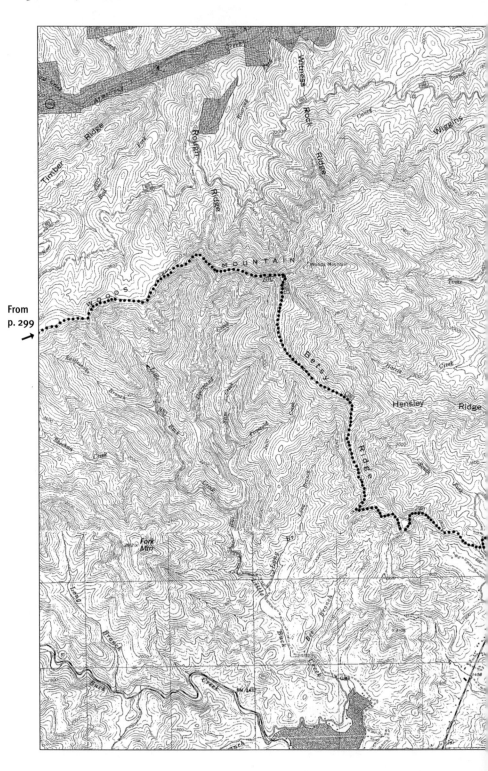

From
p. 299

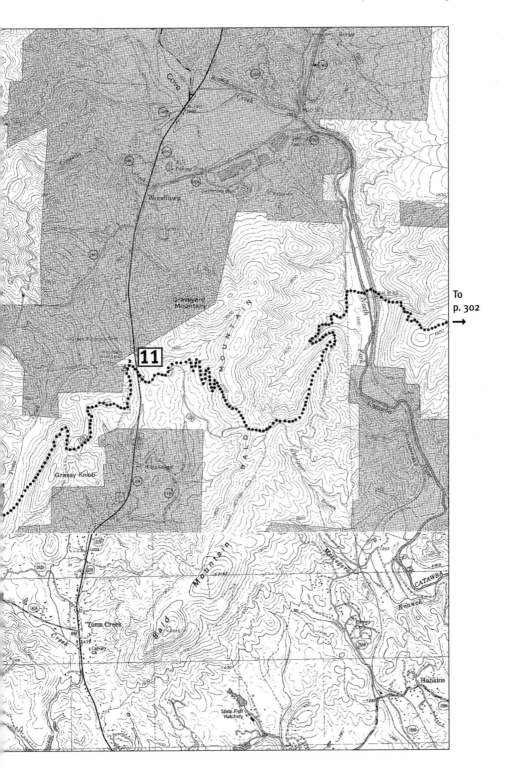

To
p. 302
→

To p. 303

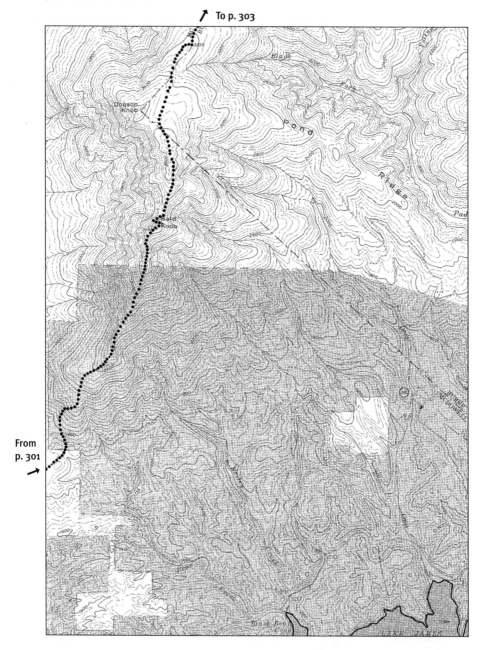

From
p. 301

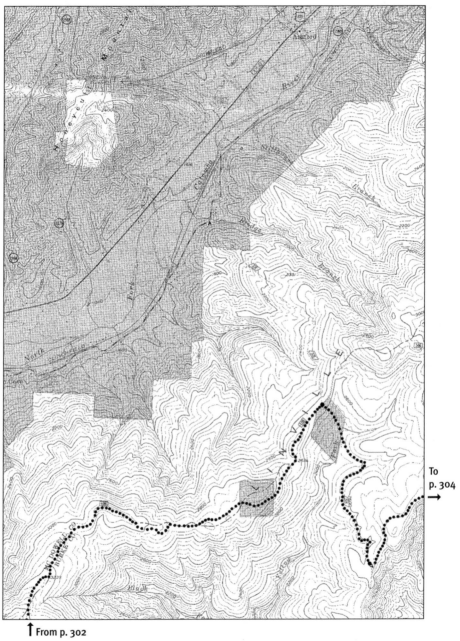

To
p. 304

From p. 302

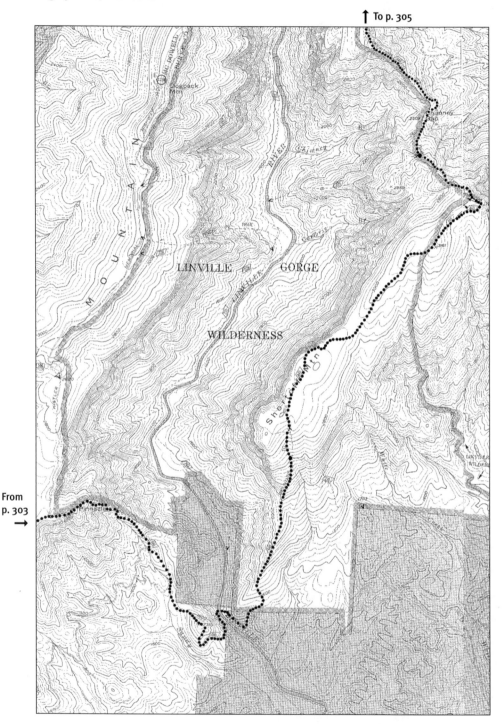

↑ To p. 305

From
p. 303
→

To p. 306 ↑

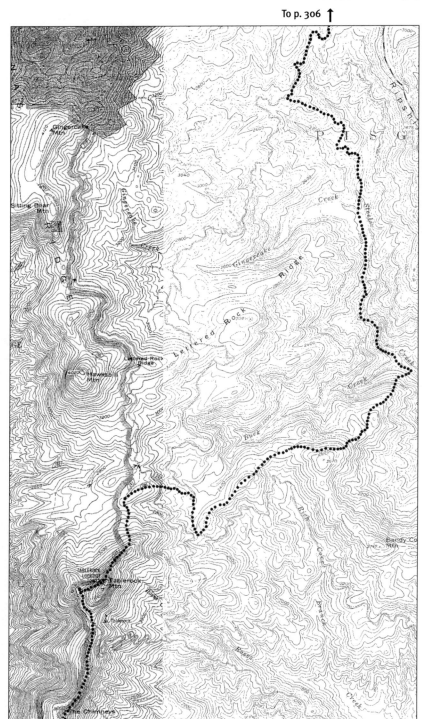

↑ From p. 304

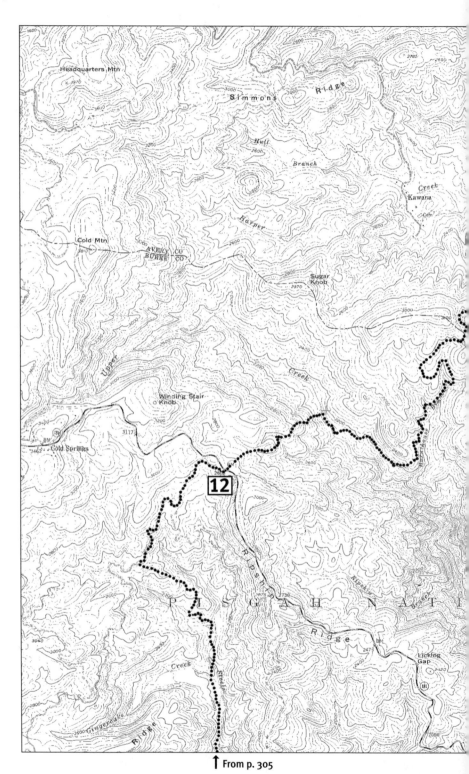

↑ From p. 305

↑ To p. 308

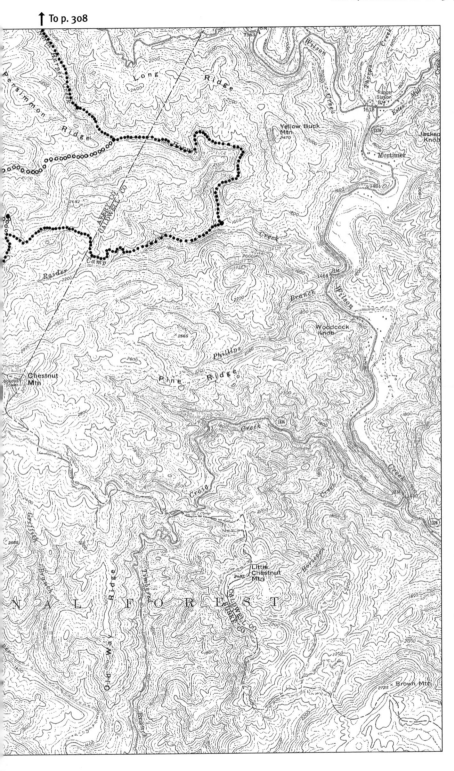

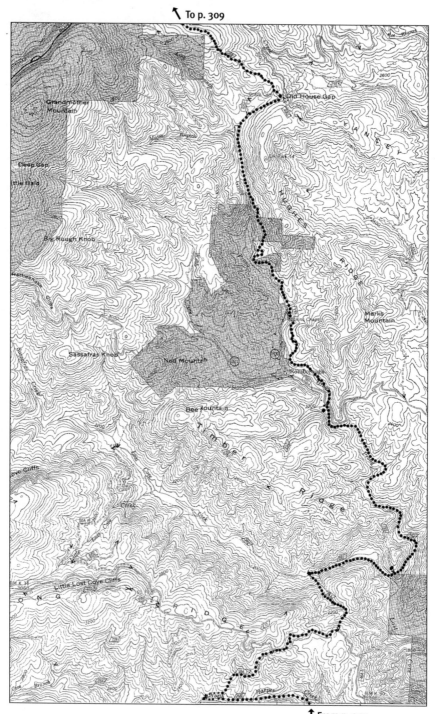

↑ To p. 309

↑ From p. 307

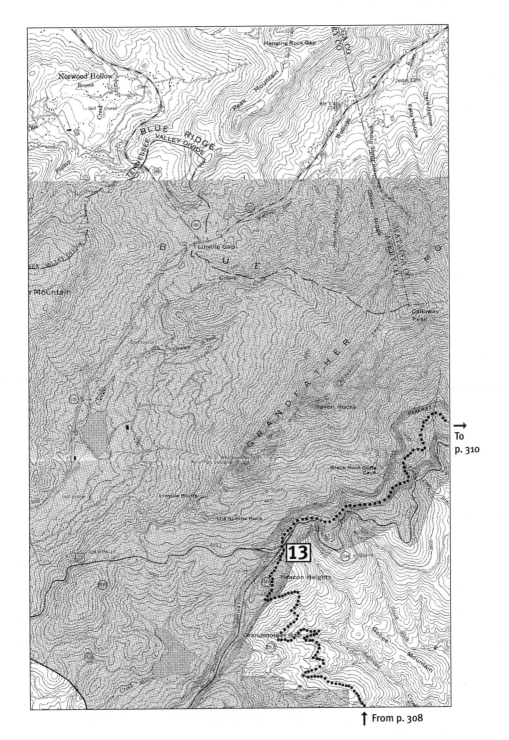

Hanging Rock Gap

Norwood Hollow

BLUE RIDGE
TENNESSEE VALLEY DIVIDE

Linville Gap

B L U E

Mountain

Calloway
Peak

G R A N D F A T H E R

Raven Rocks

Black Rock Cliffs
Cave

Linville Bluffs

The Stone Rock

13

Beacon Heights

Grandmother Gap

Mountain

→ To
p. 310

↑ From p. 308

To p. 311

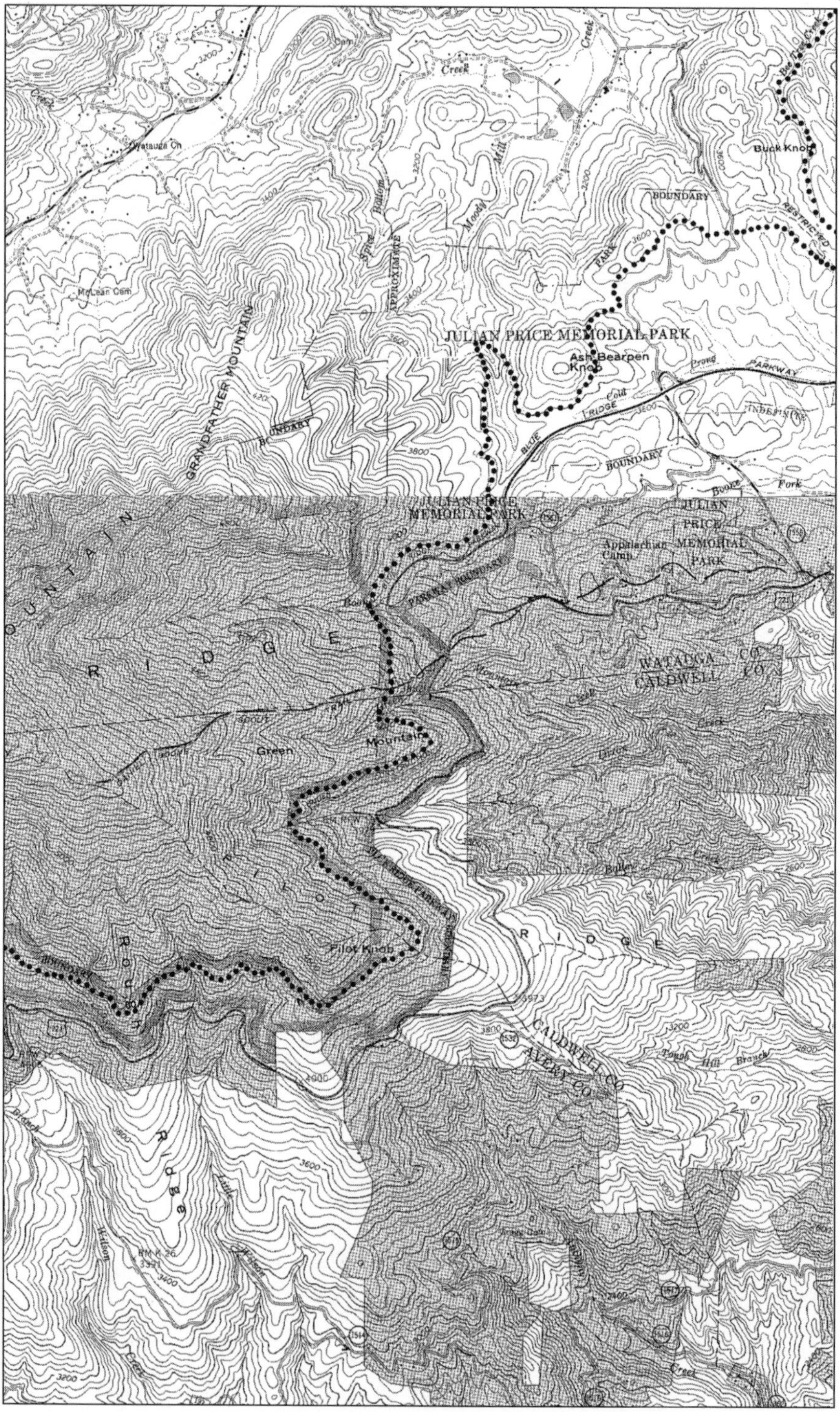

From
p. 309

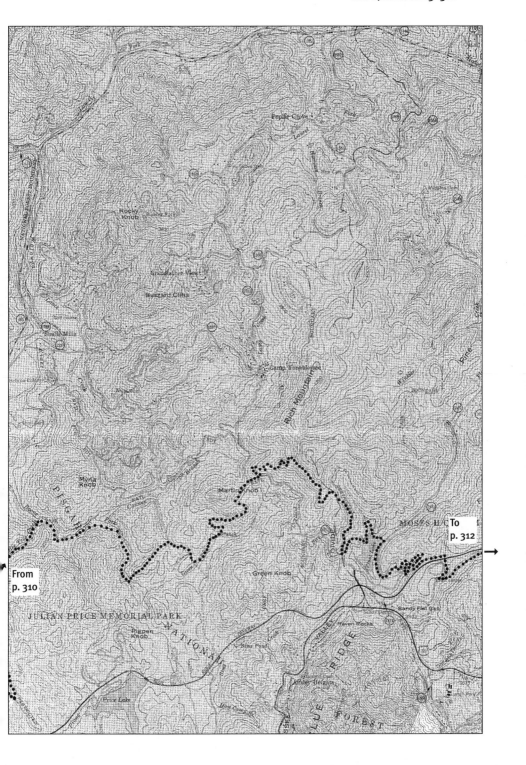

From
p. 310

To
p. 312

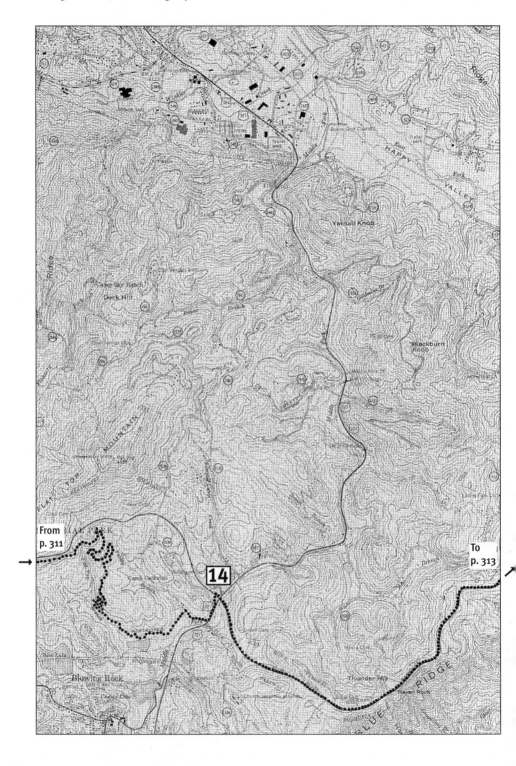

From
p. 311

To
p. 313

14

Blowing Rock

Thunder Hill

Camp Sky Ranch

Deck Hill

Yarnall Knob

'Blackburn
Knob

To p. 314

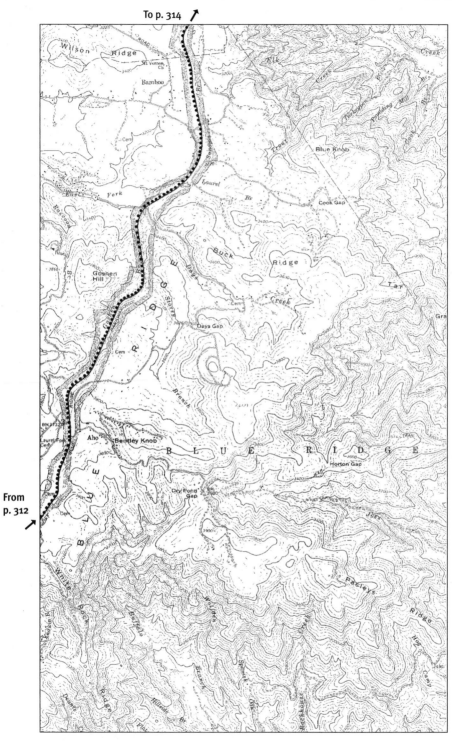

From
p. 312

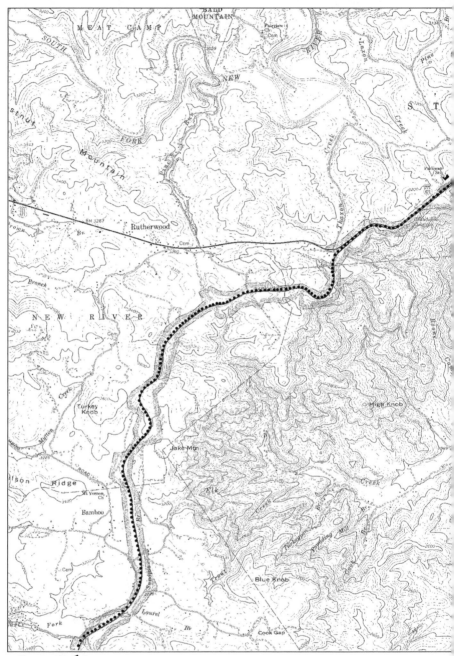

From p. 313 ↑

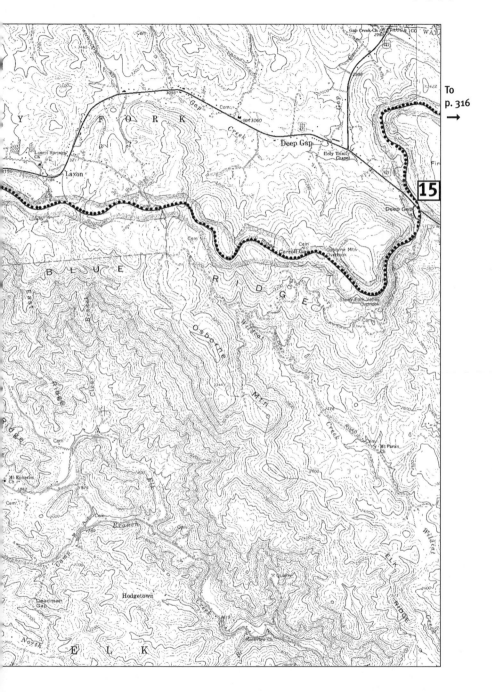

To
p. 316
→

15

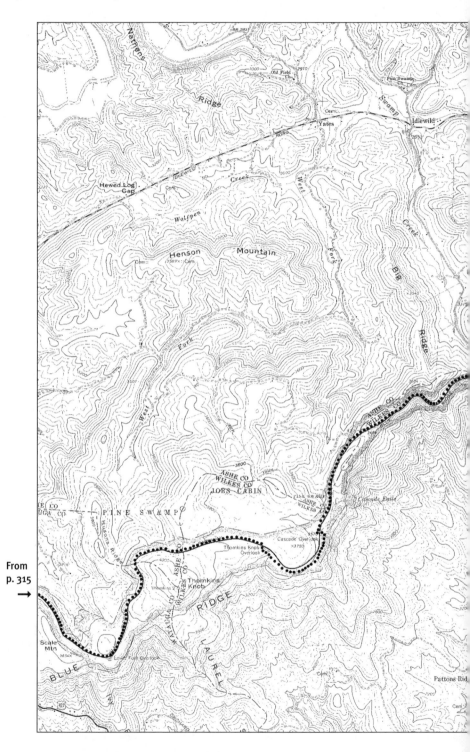

From
p. 315
→

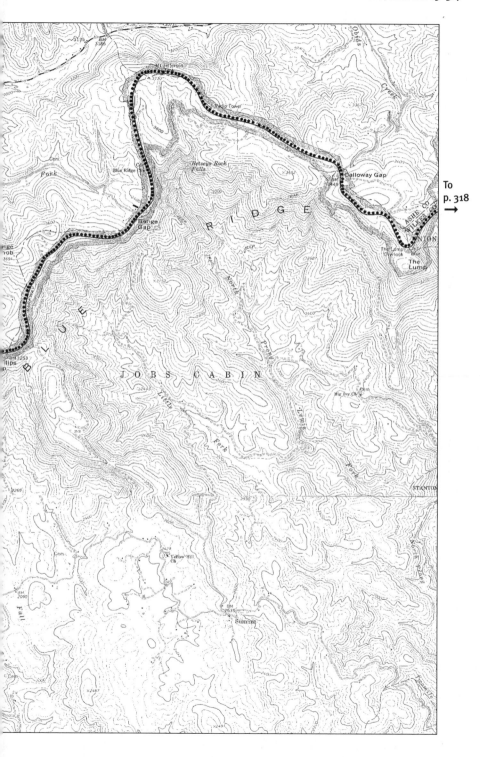

To
p. 318
→

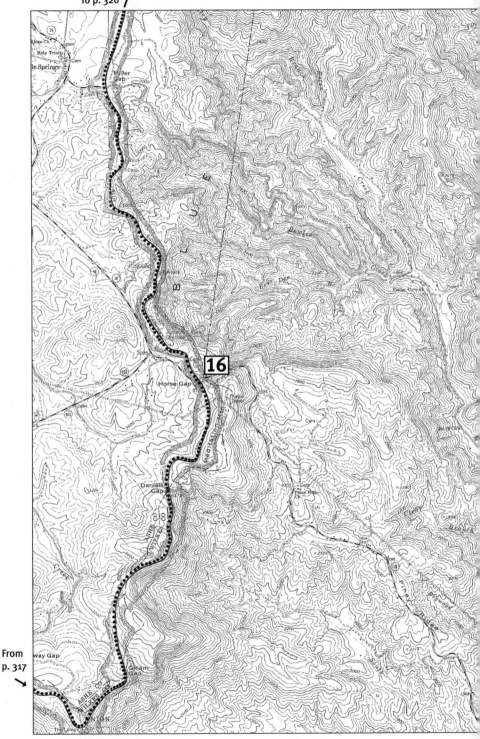

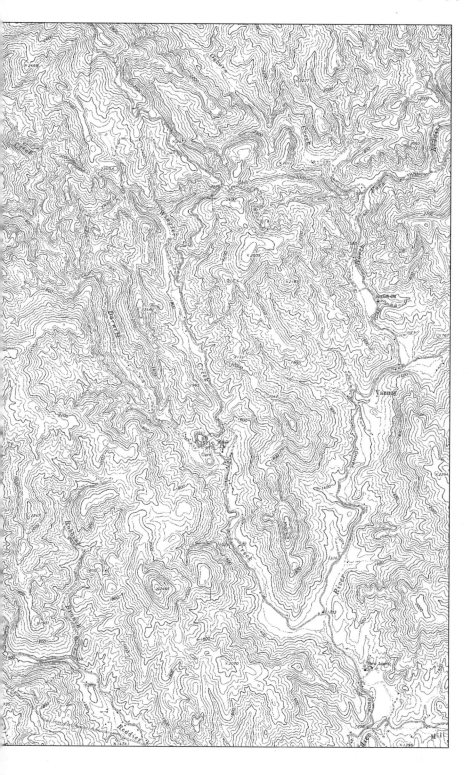

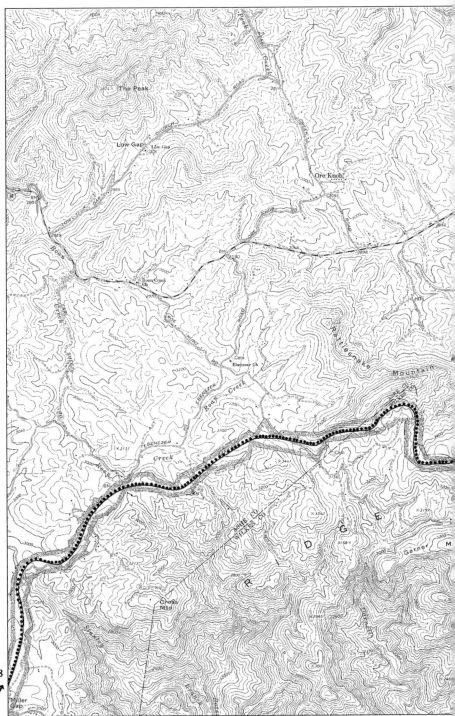

The Peak

Low Gap

Ore Knob

From
p. 318

Miller
Gap

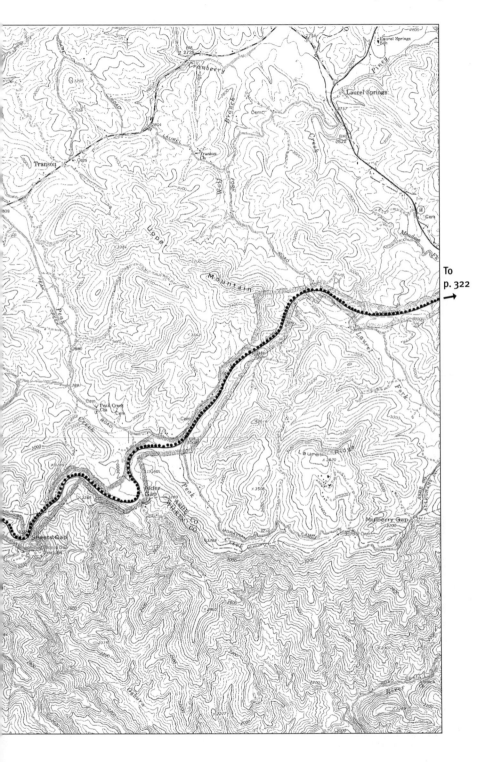

To
p. 322

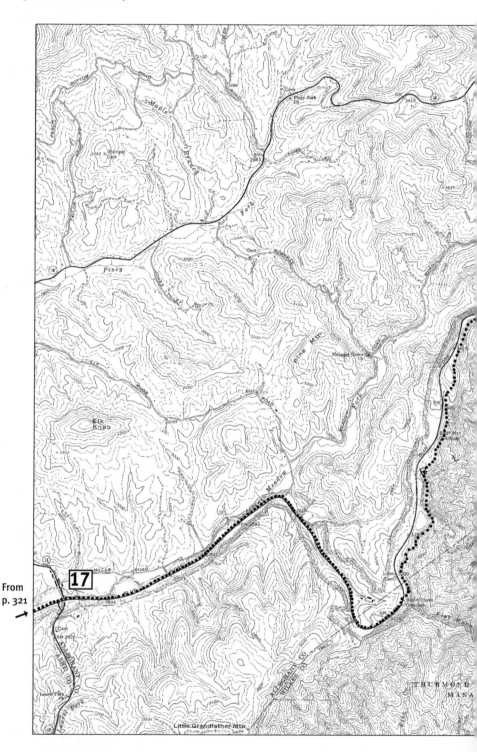

From
p. 321

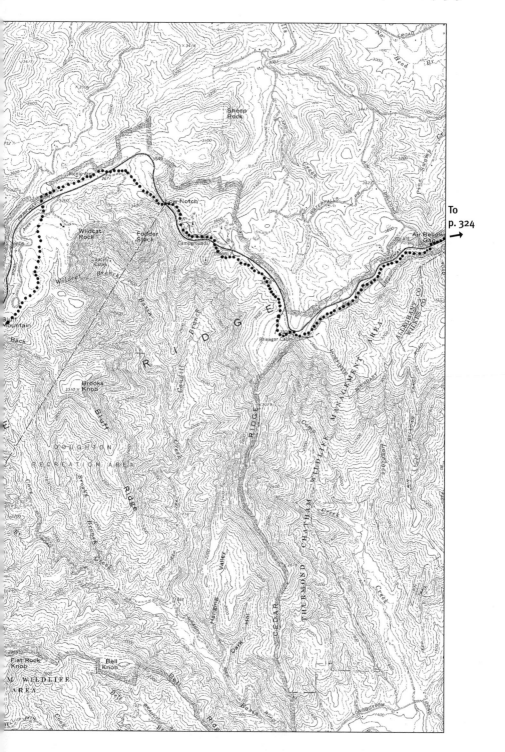

To
p. 324

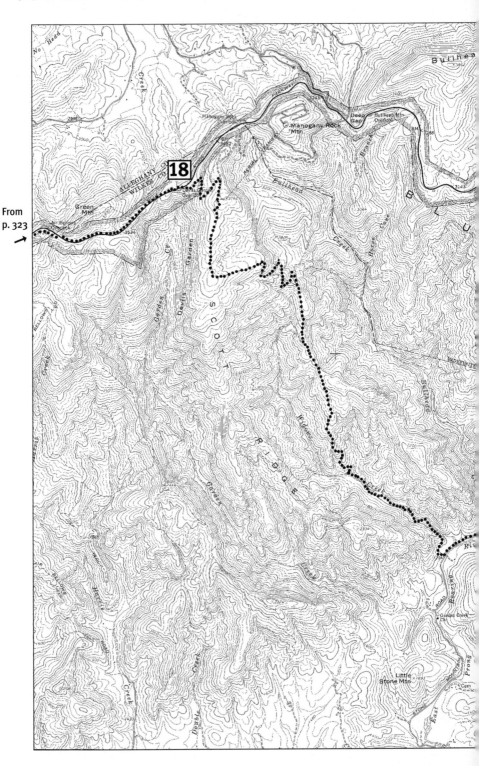

From
p. 323

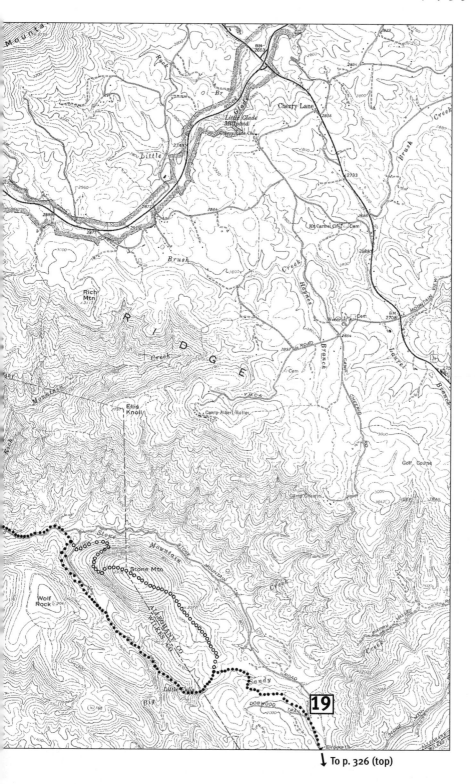

↓ To p. 326 (top)

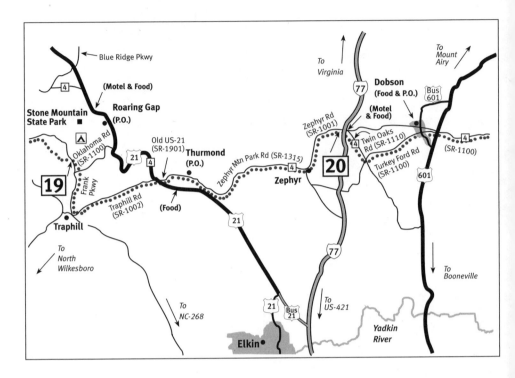

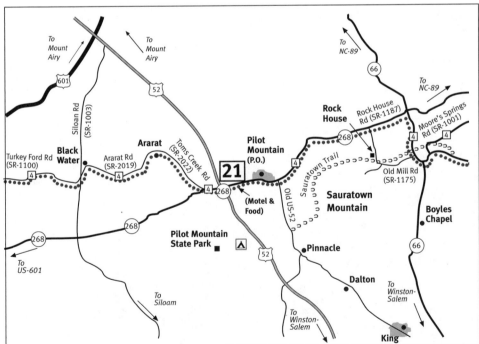

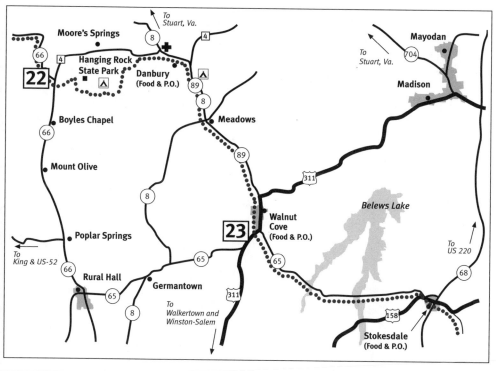

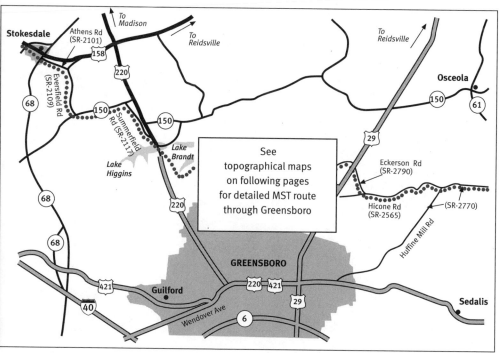

From
p. 327

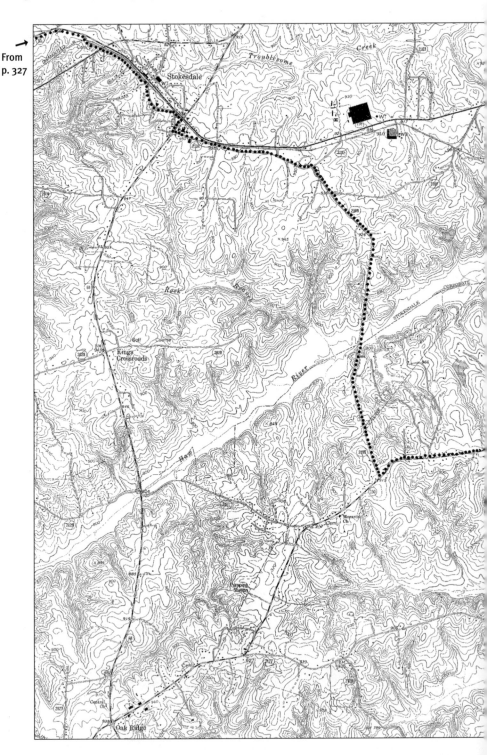

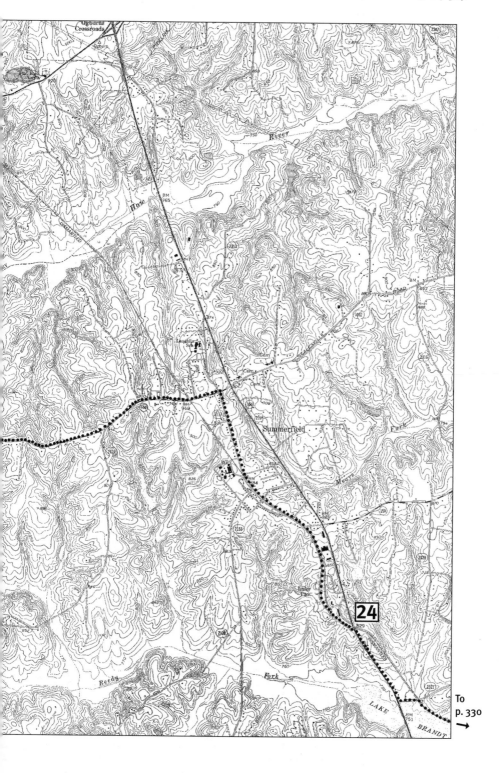

To
p. 330

From
p. 329

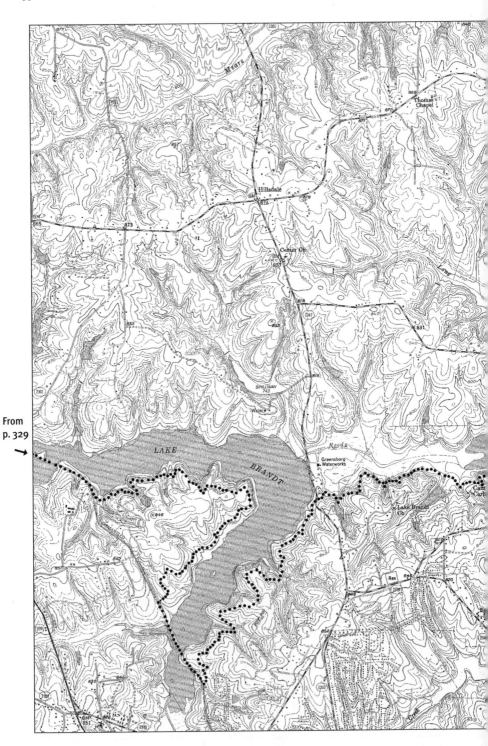

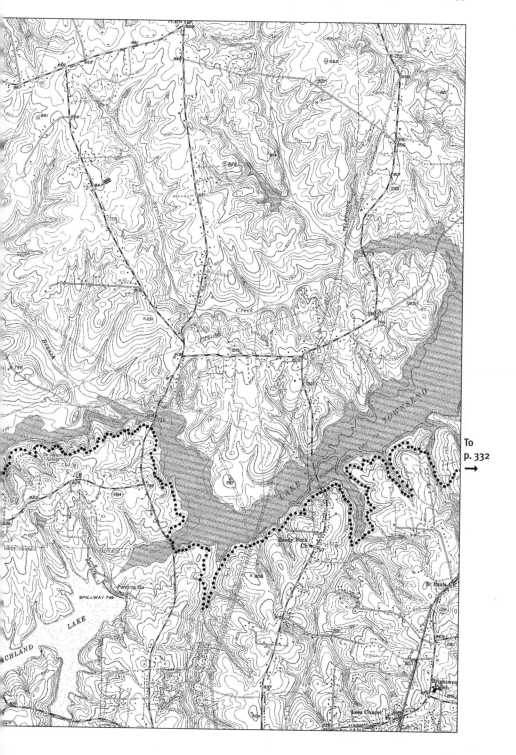

To
p. 332
→

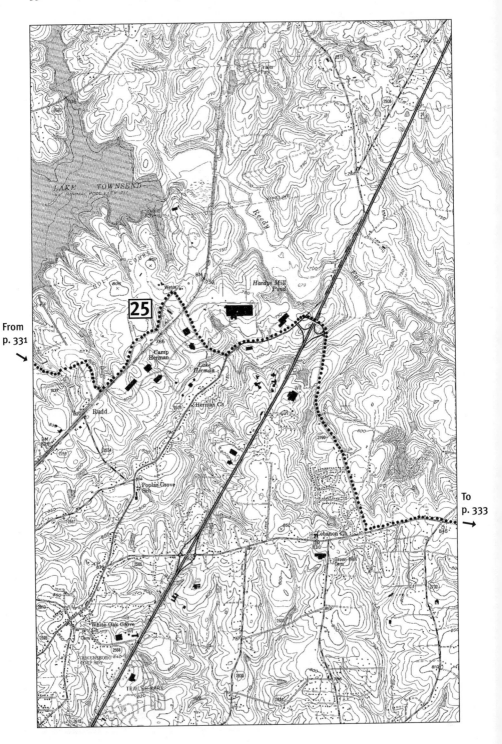

From
p. 331

To
p. 333

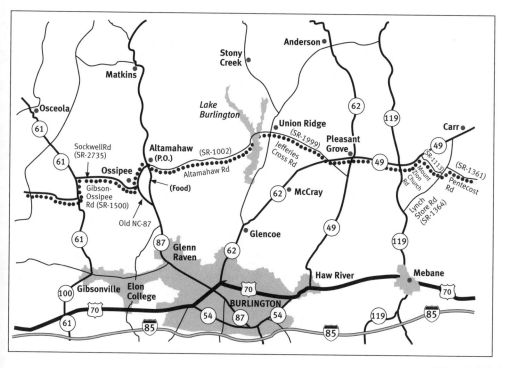

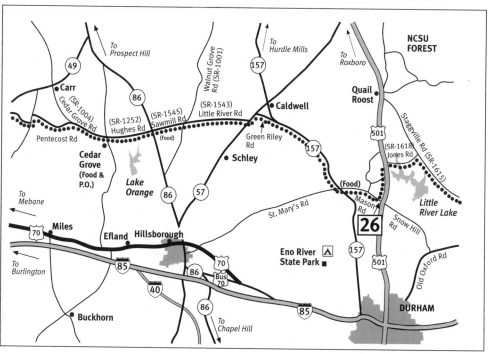

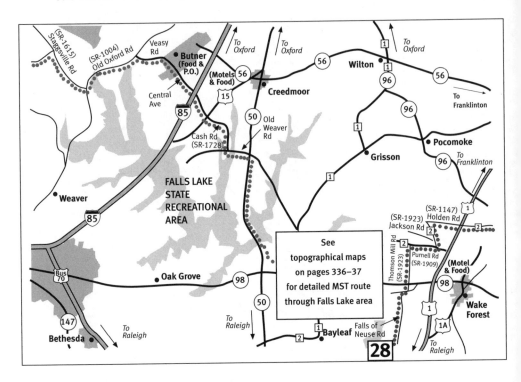

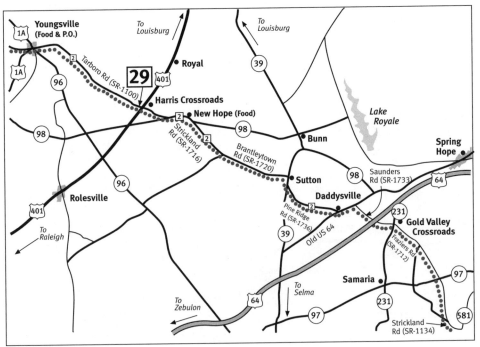

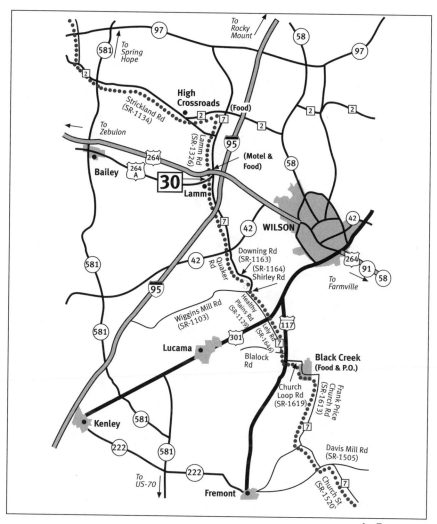

To
p. 338

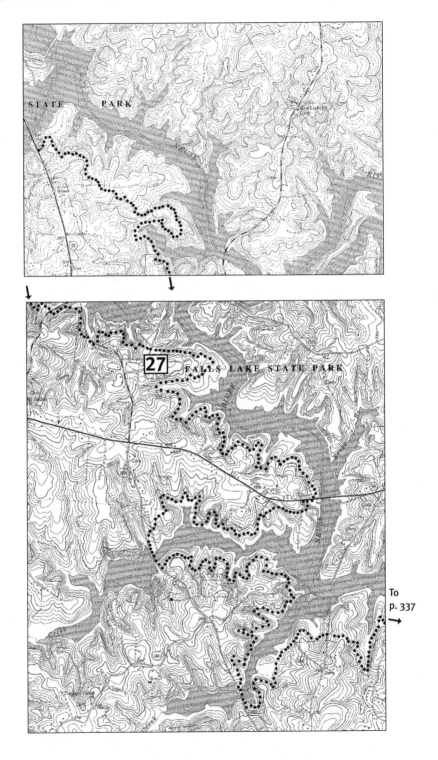

27

FALLS LAKE STATE PARK

STATE   PARK

To
p. 337

From
p. 336

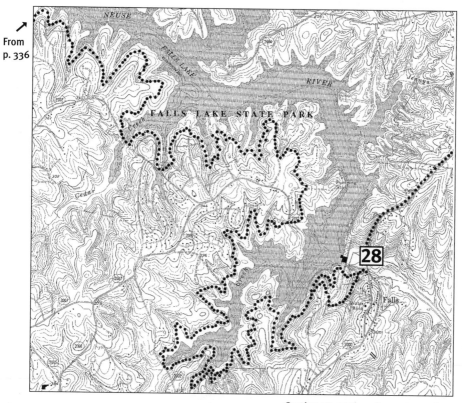

Section 28 continued on page 334 top.

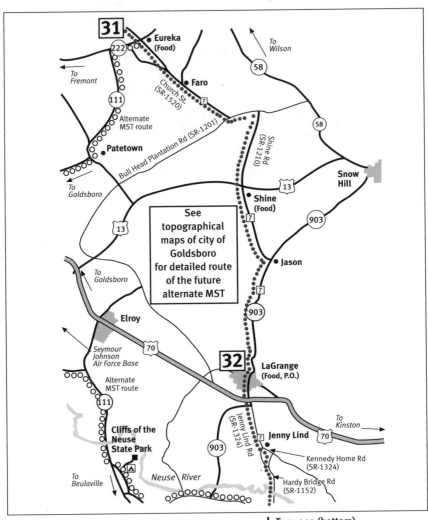

↓ To p. 340 (bottom)

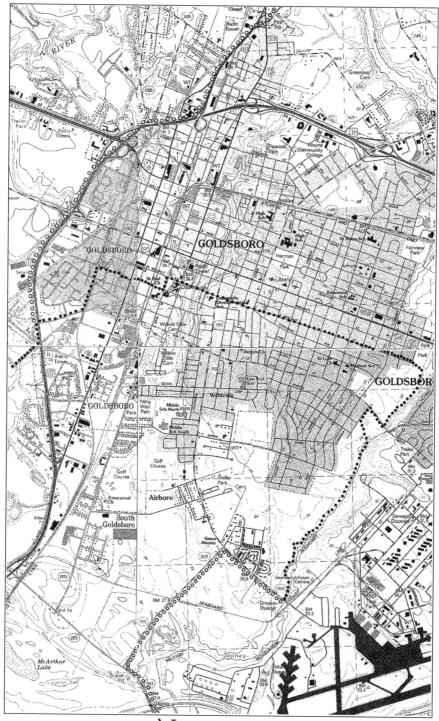

↘ To p. 340

From
p. 339

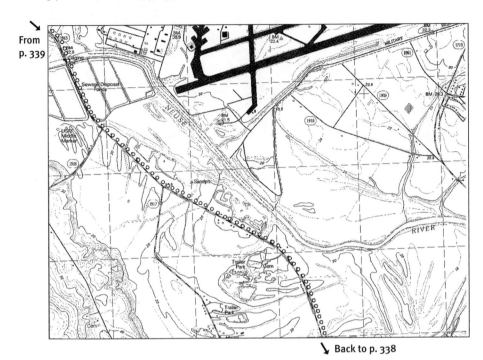

Back to p. 338

From p. 338

70 258

To
LaGrange

Byp
258

Byp
70

KINSTON

7

Neuse River

55

11

58

70

Dover
(Food & P.O.)

Davis-Hardy Rd
(SR-1300)

Sandy
Bottom

55

7

Wise Fork Rd
(SR-1002)

Burnett Rd
(SR-1313)

7

70

Albrittons
(Food)

258

Woodington
Rd (SR-1913)

Loftins
Crossing

Cobb Rd
(SR-1903)

To
New Bern

55

7

Green Hayes Rd
(SR-1161)

7

(Food)

7

To
Seven Springs

33

Loftins Rd
(SR-1913)

Silo Rd
(SR-1915)

Stroud
Rd (SR-1908)

Webb
Farm Rd
(SR-1306)

11

258

58

To
NC-41

To
Richlands

To
US-258

To
Trenton

Pink
Hill

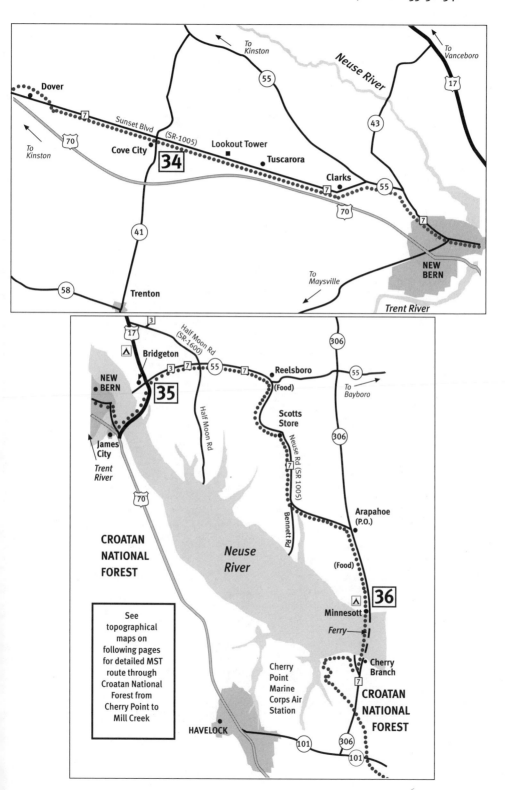

From p. 341 ↓

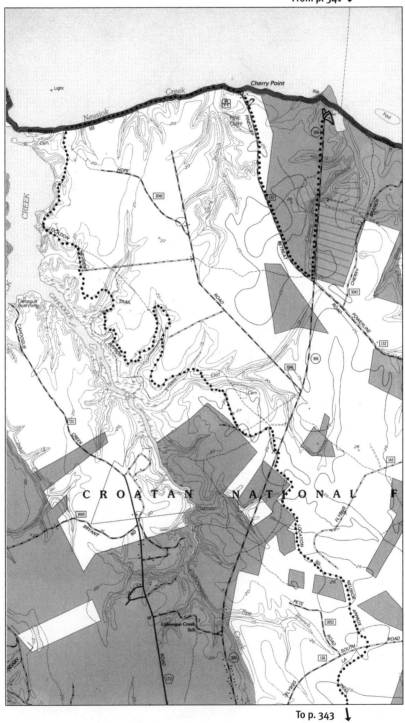

To p. 343 ↓

↓ From p. 342

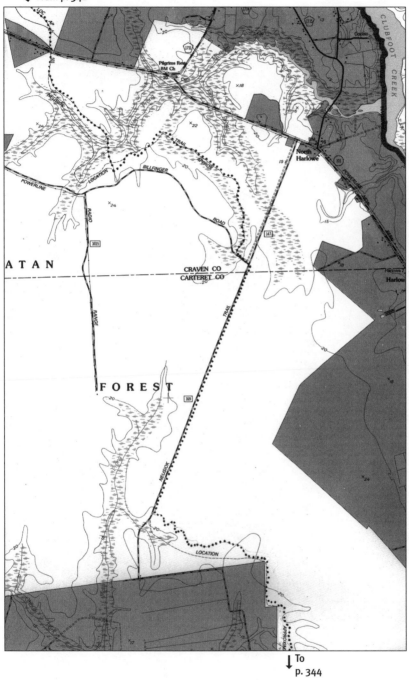

↓ To
p. 344

↓ From p. 343

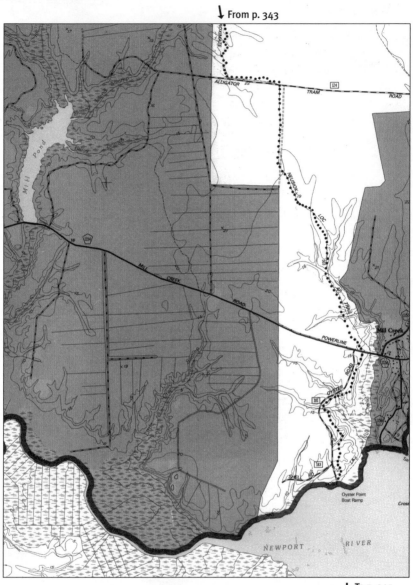

↓ To p. 345

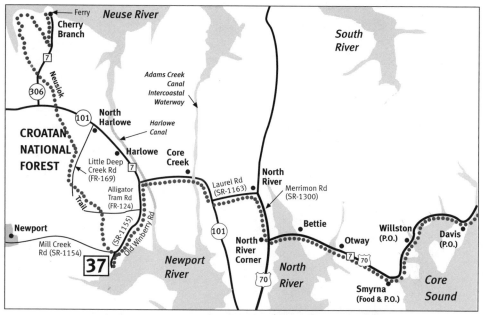

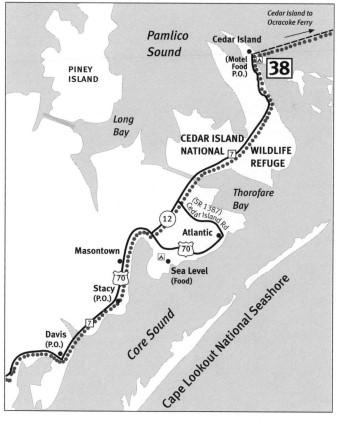

P

HOWARD   REEF

From
p. 345

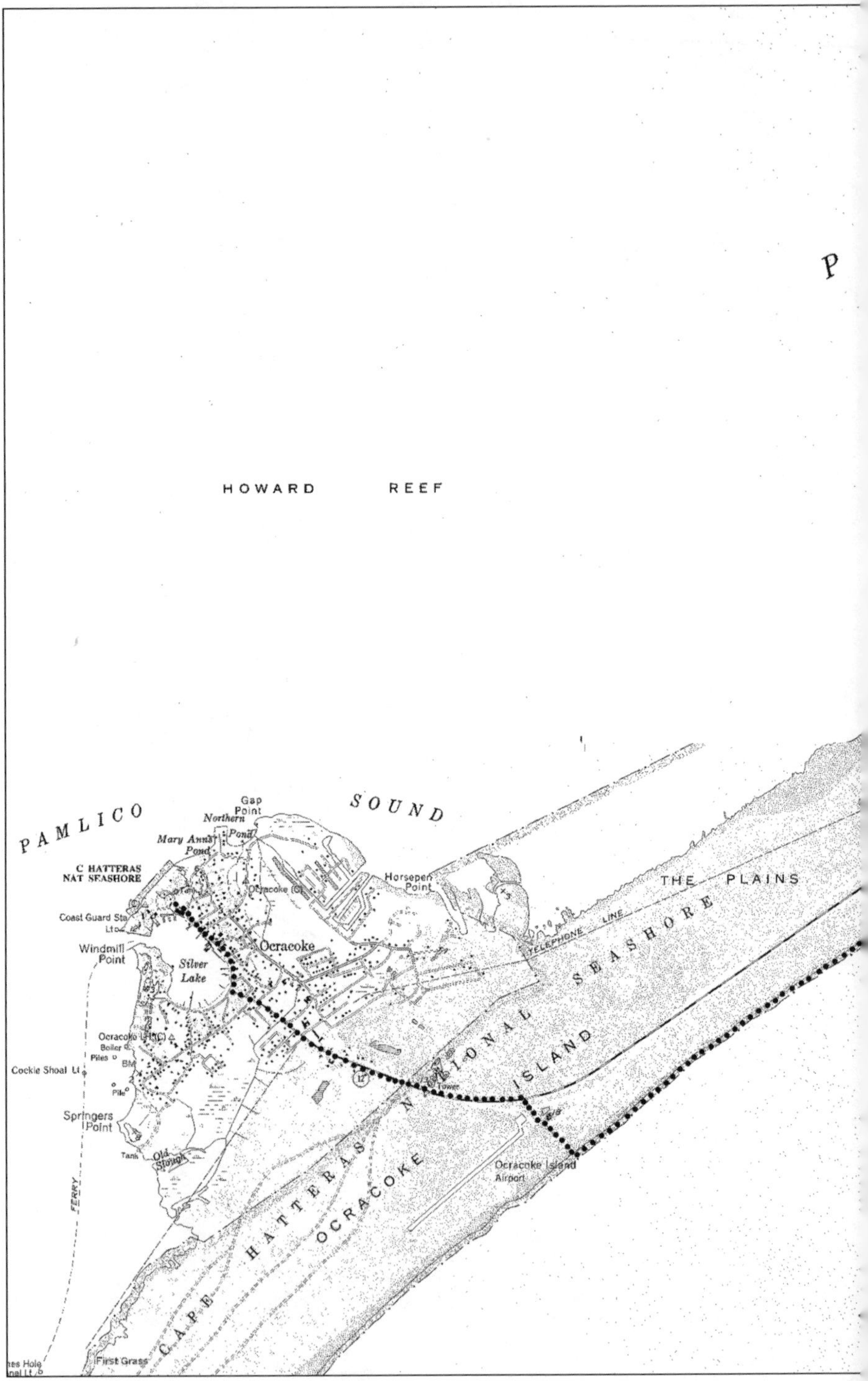

Gap
Point
Northern
Pond
Mary Ann's
Pond

S O U N D

P A M L I C O

Horsepen
Point

C HATTERAS
NAT SEASHORE

Ocracoke (C)

TELEPHONE LINE

THE   PLAINS

Coast Guard Sta
Lt bn

Windmill
Point

Silver
Lake

Ocracoke

O C R A C O K E   N A T I O N A L   S E A S H O R E

I S L A N D

Ocracoke
Boiler
Piles
BM

Cockle Shoal Lt

Pile

Springers
Point

Tank
Old
Stone

Ocracoke Island
Airport

C A P E   H A T T E R A S

O C R A C O K E

FERRY

tes Hole
nal Lt

First Grass

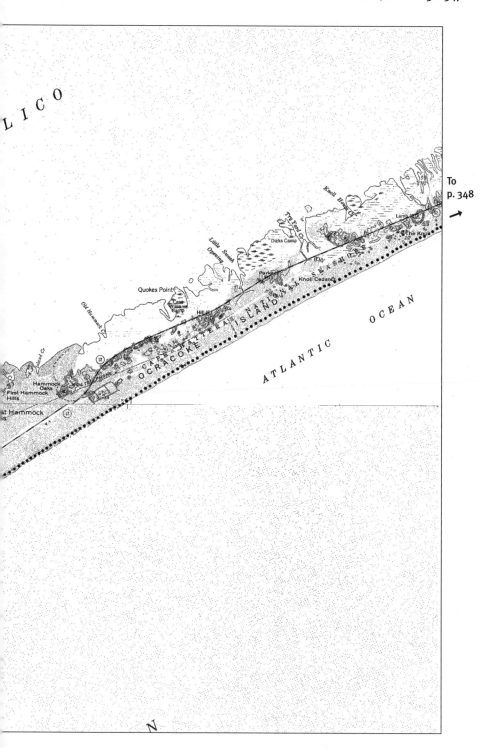

To
p. 348

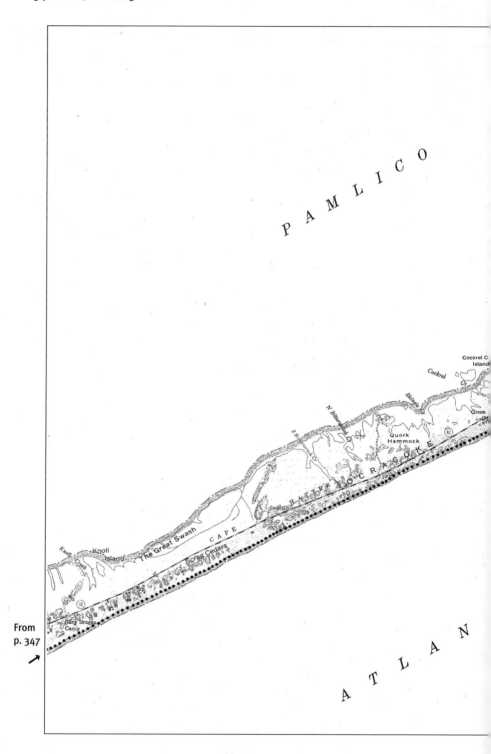

From
p. 347

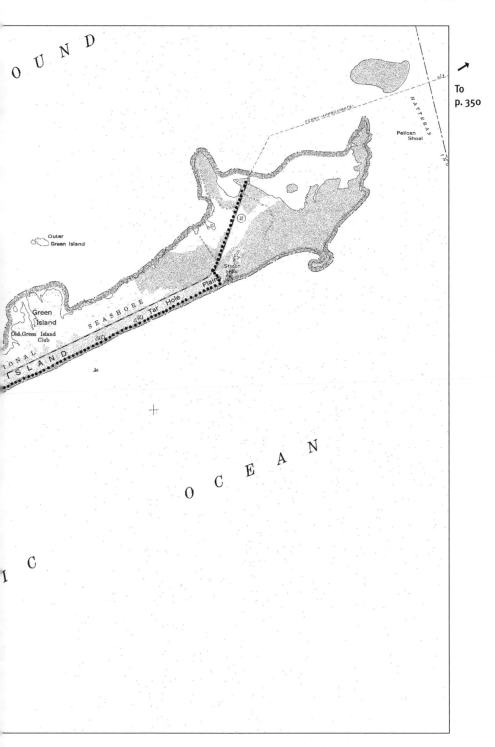

O U N D

To
p. 350

FERRY (APPROXIMATE)

HATTERAS IN

Pelican
Shoal

Outer
Green Island

12

Styron
Hole

Green
Island

Plains

SEASHORE Tar Hole

Old Green Island
Club

IONAL

ISLAND

O C E A N

I C

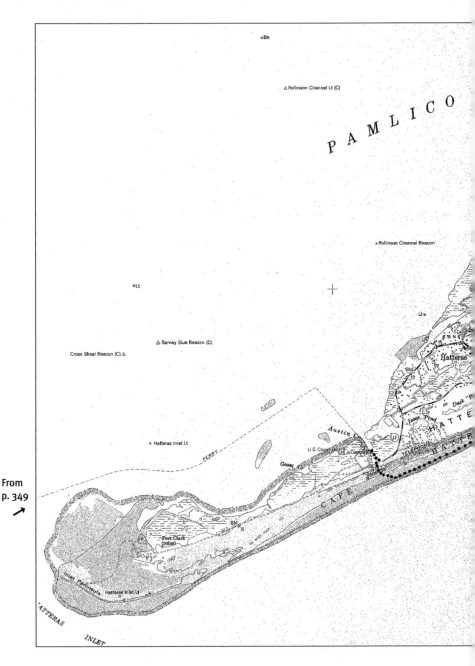

From
p. 349

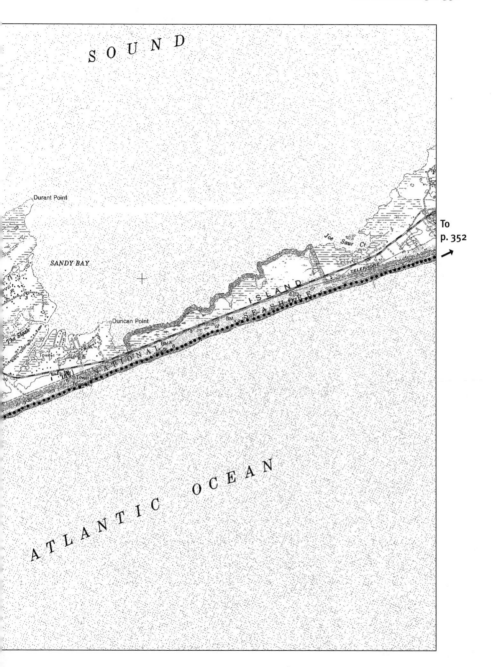

SOUND

Durant Point

SANDY BAY

Duncan Point

The Slash

Towne

ISLAND

NATIONAL SEASHORE

BM

Joe Saur Cr

TELEPHONE

To
p. 352

ATLANTIC OCEAN

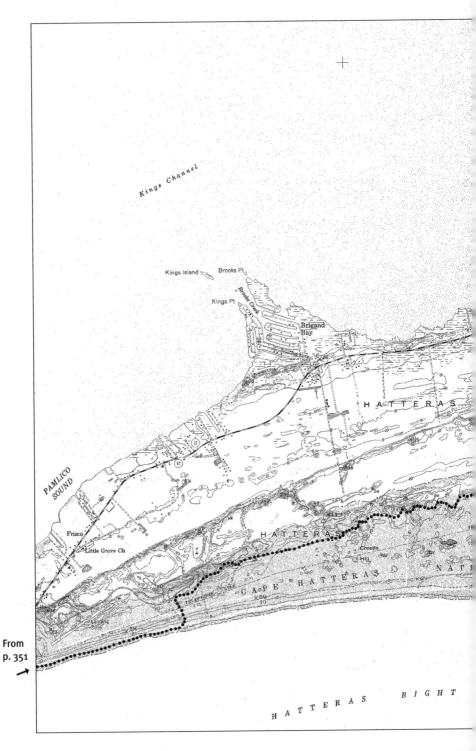

Kings Channel

Kings Island

Brooks Pt.

Kings Pt

Brooks Creek

Brigand
Bay

H A T T E R A S

PAMLICO
SOUND

12

12

Frisco

Little Grove Ch

H A T T E R A S

Creeds
Hill

C A P E   H A T T E R A S   N A T I

TELEPHONE

Landing Hill

From
p. 351

H A T T E R A S   B I G H T

To p. 354 (left) ↑

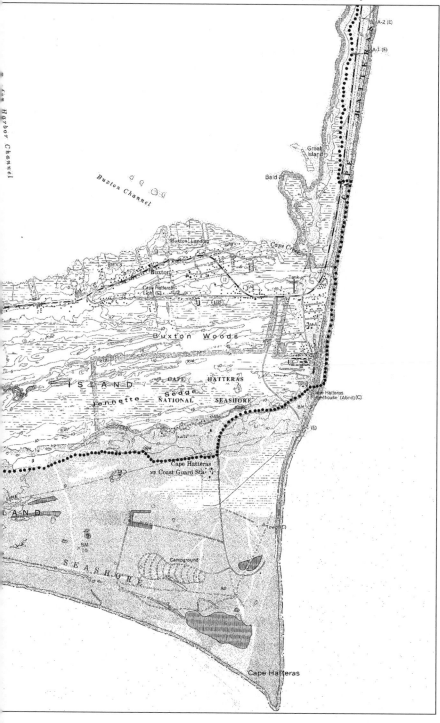

A-2 (E)

A-1 (E)

Great
Island

Bald I.

Buxton Channel

Buxton Landing

Cape Cre

Buxton

Tank
Tower

Cape Hatteras
Light (S)

1151

Buxton Woods

CAPE   HATTERAS

I S L A N D   Sedge

Pennette   NATIONAL   SEASHORE

BM

Cape Hatteras
Lighthouse (Abnd) (C)

BM

(E)

Cape Hatteras
x3 Coast Guard Sta.

L A N D

A Tower (C)

BM
10

S E A S H O R E   Campground

Cape Hatteras

Harbor Channel

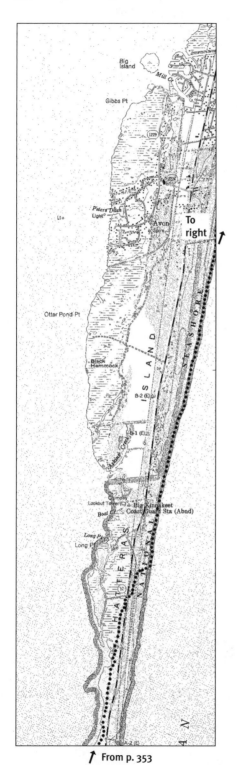

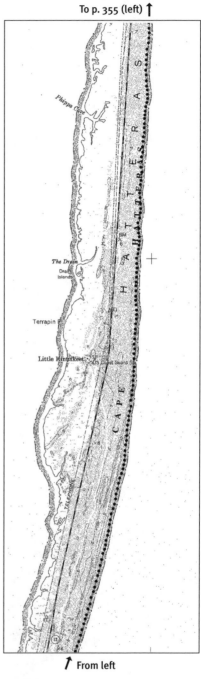

To p. 355 (left) ↑

To right ↑

↑ From left

↑ From p. 353

To right ↑

To p. 356 ↑

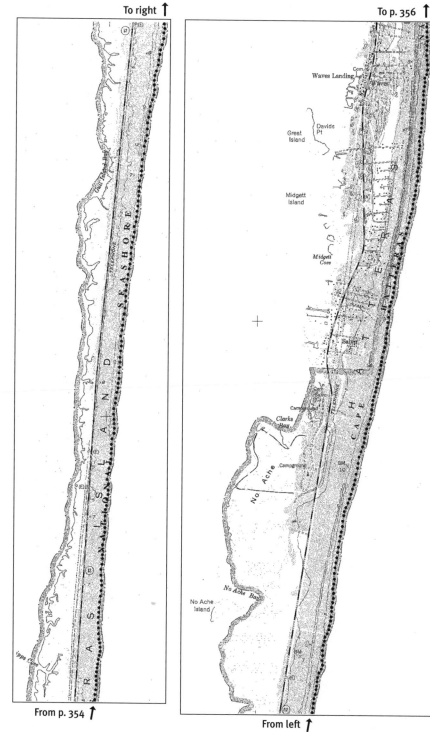

From p. 354 ↑

From left ↑

To p. 357 ↑

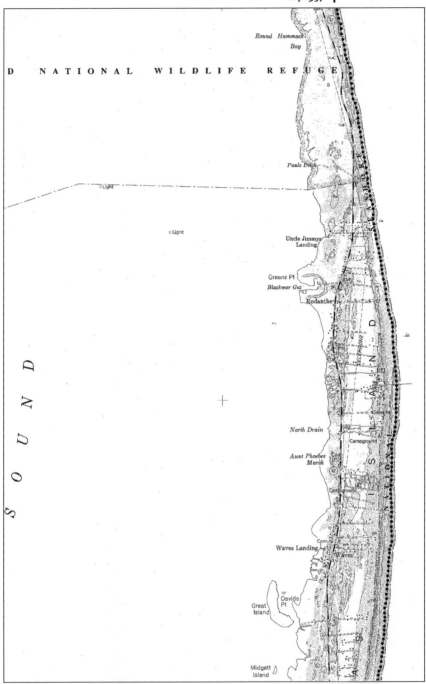

Round Hammock Bay

D NATIONAL WILDLIFE REFUGE

Pauls Ditch

○ Light

○ Light

Uncle Jimmys Landing

Greens Pt
Blackmar Gut
Rodanthe

S O U N D

North Drain

Campground

Aunt Phoebes Marsh

Campground

Cem

Waves Landing

Waves

Davids Pt

Great Island

Midgett Island

From p. 355 ↑

To p. 358 ↑

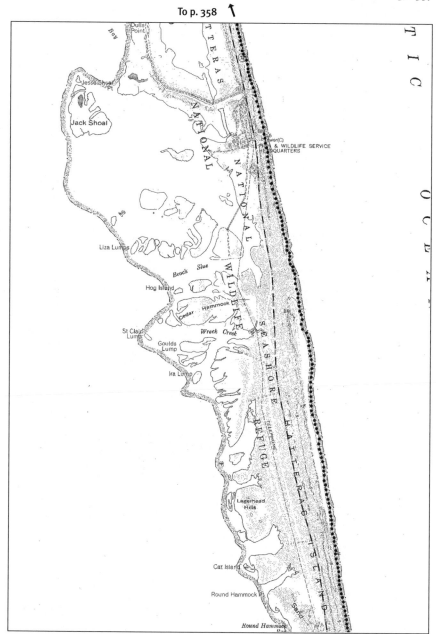

From p. 356 ↑

To p. 359

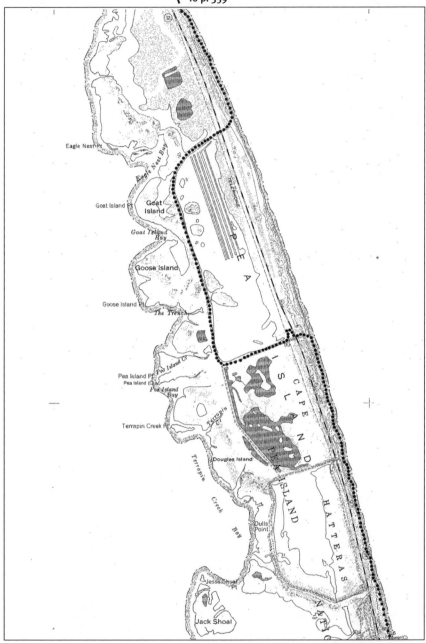

Eagle Nest Pt.

Eagle Nest Bay

Goat Island Pt.

Goat
Island

*Goat Island
Bay*

Goose Island

Goose Island Pt.

The Trench

P   E   A

TELEPHONE

Pea Island Ck.

Pea Island Pt.

Pea Island (Ch.)

*Pea Island
Bay*

Terrapin Creek Pt.

Terrapin

Douglas Island

Terrapin

Creek

Bay

Dulls
Point

Jesse Shoal
Pt.

Jack Shoal

I   S   L   A   N   D

C   A   P   E

P   E   A   I   S   L   A   N   D

H   A   T   T   E   R   A   S

N   A   T   L

From p. 357

To
p. 360

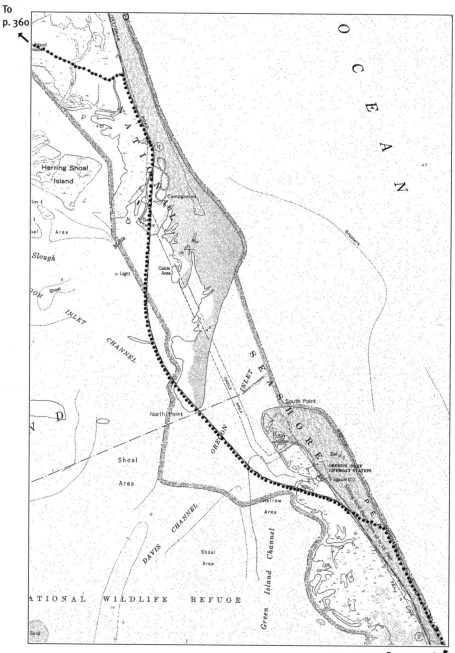

O
C
E
A
N

Breakers

Herring Shoal
Island

Slough

Campground

Cable
Area

Light

Cable
Area

S
E
A
S
H
O
R
E

North Point

South Point

Shoal

Area

BM

OREGON INLET
LIFEBOAT STATION
(lippole (O)

Shallow

Area

DAVIS CHANNEL

Shoal
Area

ATIONAL   WILDLIFE   REFUGE

Green Island Channel

Sand

From p. 358

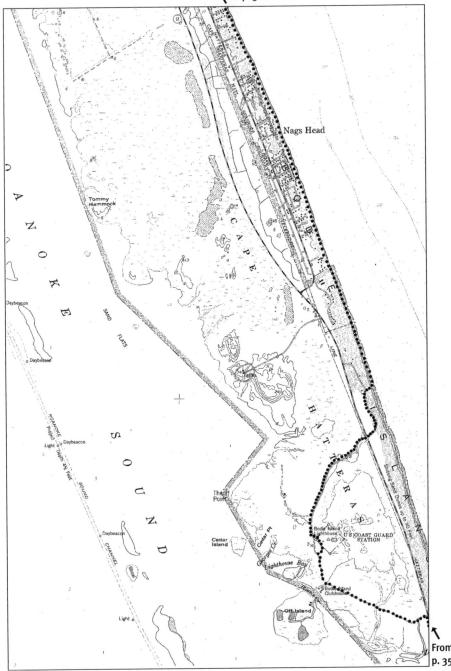

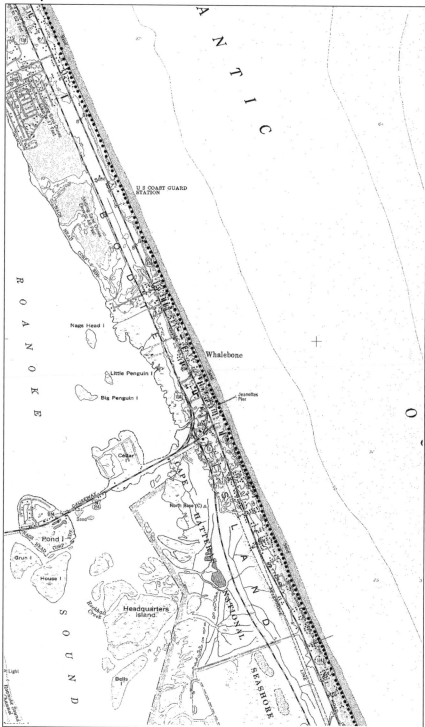

To p. 362

From p. 360

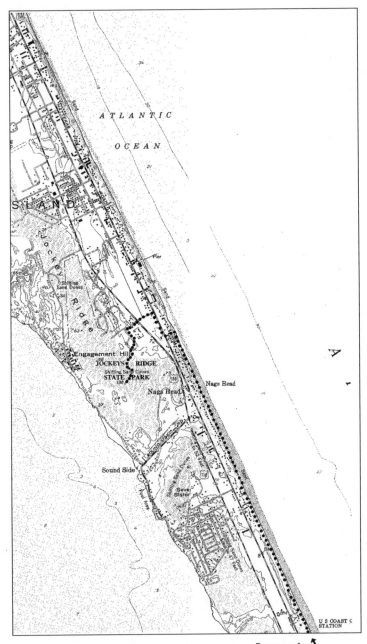

From p. 361 ↑

INDEX